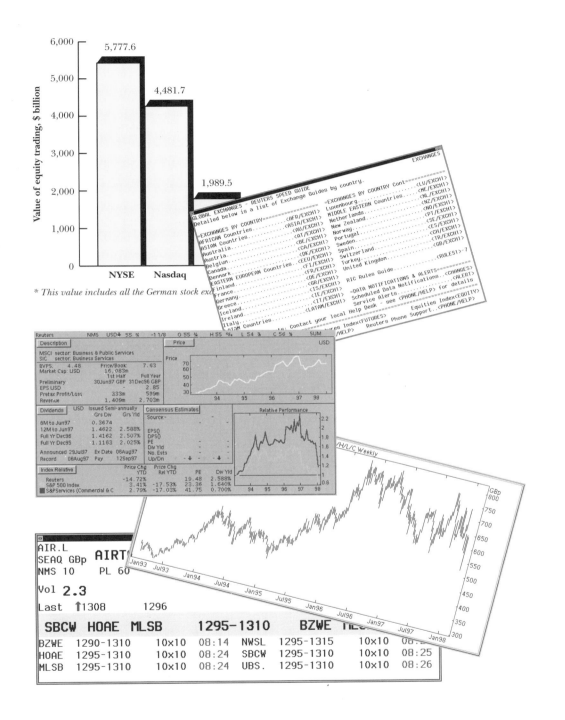

An Introduction to

Equity Markets

John Wiley & Sons (Asia) Pte Ltd
Singapore   New York   Chichester
Brisbane   Toronto   Weinheim

Other titles in the series

An Introduction to Technical Analysis *0-471-83127-1*
An Introduction to Derivatives *0-471-83176-X*
An Introduction to Foreign Exchange & Money Markets
0-471-83128-X
An Introduction to Bond Markets *0-471-83174-3*

You can get more information about the other titles in the series
from the Reuters Financial Training series companion web site at
http://www.wiley-rft.reuters.com.

Acknowledgments

The publishers and Reuters Limited would like to thank the
following people for their invaluable assistance in this book:

Colin Nicholson of the Australian Technical Analysts Association for
his thorough review of the book and constructive feedback.

Keith Rogers who wrote and produced the original version of the
book.

Professor Campbell Harvey of Duke University for use of his
hypertextual finance glossary at the back of this book.

Numa Financial Systems Ltd for use of their Directory of Futures &
Options Exchanges at the back of this book.

This publication is designed to provide accurate and authoritative information in
regard to the subject matter covered. It is sold with the understanding that the
publisher is not engaged in rendering professional services. If professional advice or
other expert assistance is required, the services of a competent professional person
should be sought.

Other Wiley Editorial Offices
John Wiley & Sons, Inc., 605 Third Avenue, New York, NY 10158-0012, USA
John Wiley & Sons Ltd, Baffins Lane, Chichester, West Sussex PO19
1UD, England
John Wiley & Sons (Canada) Ltd, 22 Worcester Road, Rexdale,
Ontario M9W 1L1, Canada
Jacaranda Wiley Ltd, 33 Park Road (PO Box 1226), Milton,
Queensland 4064, Australia
Wiley-VCH, Pappelallee 3, 69469 Weinheim, Germany

Library of Congress Cataloging-in-Publication Data
An introduction to equity markes.
        p.   cm. — (The Reuters financial training series)
    Includes bibliographical references.
    ISBN 0-471-83171-9
    1. Stock exchanges.   2. Securities.   I. Title: Equity markets.   II. Series.
HG4551.I57   1999   99-30667
332.64'2 — dc21   CIP

ISBN 0-471-83171-9

Typeset in 10/12 point New Baskerville
Printed in Singapore by Craft Print Pte Ltd
10 9 8 7 6 5 4 3 2 1

An Introduction to

Equity Markets

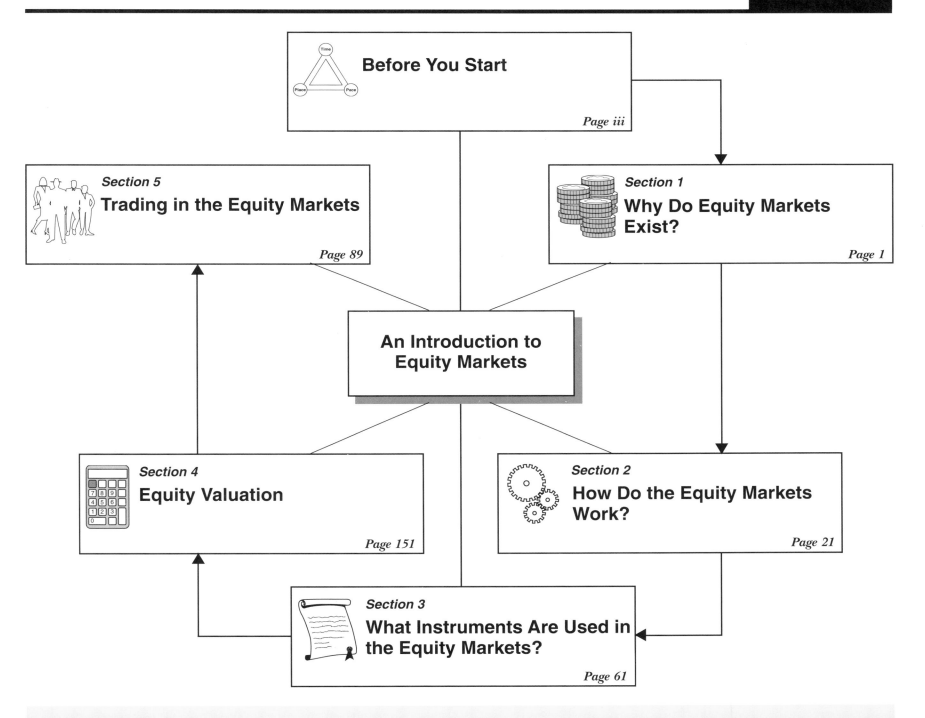

Before You Start

Page iii

Section 5
Trading in the Equity Markets

Page 89

Section 1
Why Do Equity Markets Exist?

Page 1

An Introduction to Equity Markets

Section 4
Equity Valuation

Page 151

Section 2
How Do the Equity Markets Work?

Page 21

Section 3
What Instruments Are Used in the Equity Markets?

Page 61

Contents

Who Should Use This Book?

 This book is designed to provide an overview of the equity markets for a variety of readers: salespeople, support and operations staff, trainers, managers or investors who want to learn more about the markets to refine their investing strategies. Also, anyone beginning an in-depth study of the markets will find this book to be a very useful primer.

Despite the complexity of the financial markets, more and more people need a working knowledge of what the basic instruments are and how the markets are structured, for for professional and personal pursuits. Such readers will find this book to be helpful as it provides not only the fundamental definitions, but also exercises and examples to make markets more accessible.

This book will take you through the basics of the equity market, from what the instruments are and why the market exists, to who the market players are, to how the markets are structured and regulated and how information is used. By the time you have completed this book, you should be able to participate in the equity markets in an informed fashion.

An Introduction to Equity Markets is one in the Reuters Financial Training series, designed to provide readers with an overall understanding of the financial markets. Other titles cover derivatives, technical analysis, foreign exchange and bond markets.

What Will You Find in This Book?

This book provides a new approach to gaining some basic familiarity with the essential concepts of the equity market. The book is written in a very accessible style with jargon kept to a minimum, but with market language clearly explained.

Most importantly, the book includes a range of materials to help you reinforce what you are learning. Each section offers a solid explanation of basic concepts, followed by actual examples for the reader to work through. Additional exercises and quick quizzes enable the reader to further enhance learning. Finally, each section concludes with a graphic overview – a visual outline – of what has been covered for quick yet thorough review, and ends with a listing of additional reference materials.

> In addition, the **RFT Web Site** has been created as this book series' companion web site, where additional quiz questions, updated screens and other information may be found. You can find this web site at:
> **http://www.wiley-rft.reuters.com**

This text focuses primarily on the UK and US stock markets for detailed descriptions of exchanges, issuing and trading procedures, and so forth. This is done to keep as much consistency as possible throughout the text and in recognition that these markets, given their size and standing, often set precedents for other markets. For the specifics of different markets throughout the world, the reader is advised to refer directly to the exchange in that market. Contact information for exchanges around the world is provided at the back of this book. Also refer to the **Further Resources** listings at the end of each section.

How is This Book Organised?

This book contains the following sections:

Before You Start

This section!

Why Do Equity Markets Exist?

This section covers the history and purpose of the market.

How Do Equity Markets Work?

This section explains operation or "mechanics" of the market and addresses market "jargon" and conventions.

What Instruments Are Used in the Equity Markets?

This section provides a brief overview of all the instruments used in the market. Each instrument is defined and accompanied by sample screens from Reuters' electronic information services to illustrate how information is provided to market players via data terminals.

Equity Valuation

This section explains how equity values – the most common ratios, for example – are determined by market players.

Trading in the Equity Markets

This section describes market players and their trading techniques. The section also provides examples of market player conversations so you can get a better idea of what they do in their jobs.

Throughout the book you will find that important terms or concepts are shown in **bold**, for example, **dividend**. You will also find that activities included to enhance your learning are indicated by the following icons:

 This indicates the definition of a term that you must know and understand to master the material.

 This means stop and think about the point being made. You may also want to jot a few words in the box provided.

 This indicates an activity for you to do. It is usually something written – for example, a definition, notes, or a calculation.

 This is the answer or response to an activity and it usually follows the activity or is close to it.

 This indicates the main points of the section.

 This indicates questions for you to answer to help you to review the material. The answers are also provided.

 This indicates the one-page summary that provides a quick overview of the entire section. This page serves as an excellent study tool.

Additional reference material is listed in **Further Resources** at the end of each section.

How to Use This Book

Before you start using this book, decide what you want from the material. If you are using it as part of your work, discuss with your manager how she will help by giving time for study and giving you feedback and support. Although your learning style is unique to you, you will find that your learning is much more effective if you allocate reasonable sized periods of time for study. The most effective learning period is about 30 minutes – so use this as a basis. If you try to fit your learning into odd moments in a busy schedule you will not get the best from the materials or yourself. You might like to schedule learning periods into your day just as you would business meetings.

Remember that the most effective learning is an interactive process and requires more than just reading the text. The exercises in this book make you think through the material you have just read and then apply your understanding through basic activities. Take time to do the exercises. This old Chinese saying sums up this concept:

> I hear and I forget
> I see and I remember
> I do and I understand

Try to make sure your study is uninterrupted. This probably means that your workplace is not a good environment! You will need to find both the time and place where you can study – you may have access to a quiet room at work, you may have a room at home, you may need to use a library.

Market Developments as This Book Was Published

The financial markets are constantly evolving and as this book was going to print in May 1999, changes of extraordinary significance were taking place. Individual sections of this book include some of these changes, but the below paragraphs highlight the key events the reader should bear in mind.

The Introduction of the Euro

Years in coming, the new European currency – the "euro" – was launched on January 1, 1999. At this time, the euro represents the coming together of eleven European countries' currencies into a single currency.

The impact of the single currency on the financial markets has been much anticipated, hotly debated, and extensively analysed, but will only be fully known as time passes. With respect to the equity markets, the euro has hastened the pace towards one pan-European equity market, which will affect how securities trade. The euro will affect how investors, especially institutional investors with large portfolios, evaluate risk and determine their holdings. The euro will cause the creation of indices and benchmarks to be modelled in new ways, for example, by industry sector, as the traditional criteria of country risk may become less significant. This in turn will affect what data information providers make available and how it is represented.

Changes at the Exchanges

1998 and 1999 have already been witness to the merging of some major exchanges, the announcement of collaborative agreements among others and an overall trend toward expanding services. These include:

- October 1998   The NASDAQ and AMEX exchanges merged
- January 1999   Paris and Swiss exchanges agree to allow cross membership to enable members to access both exchanges on the same screen
- February 1999   NYSE announces consideration of beginning trading earlier in the day and extending hours to midnight, to accommodate European and Asian investors and the individual investor
- March 1999   LSE and Frankfurt announce plans to consider creating a pan-European exchange; talks include Paris, Zurich, Milan, Madrid, Amsterdam and Brussels

These unions are occurring as the exchanges must address the same competitive and cost pressures as many other organisations do. The exchanges must find ways to collaborate to enable them to meet the demands of their clients, the market players, who want to reduce the cost of trading and have as broad access as possible to other exchanges. For example, the cost of developing and employing technology to keep up with a 24-hour marketplace are significant, and exchanges are finding that collaboration is a cost-effective way to address these issues. In addition, the exchanges must also address what the arrival of the euro means to their operations, as the characteristics of trading instruments and currencies alters and new instruments are created.

The Role of the Internet for the Individual Investor

Perhaps one of the greatest changes to take place in the investing world is the empowerment of the individual investor to trade on her own behalf through access to the Internet. Once the ability to trade around-the-clock was the sole privilege of institutional investors or very wealthy individuals with access to advisors around the globe.

Today, the average investor may place buy and sell orders 24 hours a day, obtain market research information around the clock, and track and calculate the ever-changing value of her portfolio throughout the day and night. Thus, the average investor demands more information about investments and wants assurances that the trades will be executed. The failure of one online trading service in early 1999 highlighted what happens when the system breaks down and investors – thousands of investors – are left hanging at their keyboards. These events will no doubt affect how these activities are regulated and the growth in how many of these services become available.

This section of the book should take about 30 minutes of study time. You may not take as long as this or you may take a little longer – remember your learning is individual to you.

There are few ways in which a man can be more innocently
employed than in getting money.

Samuel Johnson (1709–1784)

Introduction

What is "equity"? You may know the term to mean a share in the ownership of an organisation. You may have heard the term "negative equity" when an individual who has borrowed money for a home has debts which are greater than the value of the property. This section introduces the concept of equity and covers the following:

- The meaning of the term equity in the context of the capital markets

- The relationship among the money, debt and equity markets, their purposes and uses

- The relationship between risk and return and how debt and equity are positioned with respect to them

- An overview of the equity market players and the primary and secondary markets in which they operate

Before moving on, try the activity opposite to check your current understanding of the capital markets.

The capital markets have several distinguishing features. Can you describe two of them?

You can check your answer on the next page.

The capital markets have several distinguishing features. Can you describe two of them?

You may have mentioned the following or something similar:

- **Negotiability**
  Borrowing and investing is achieved using financial instruments that are negotiable. This means that the ownership can be transferred at any time.

- **Non-bank funding**
  An issuer in the capital markets does not borrow directly from a commercial bank but issues financial instruments for sale to investors.

- **Maturity period**
  In general the maturity period – the period over which money is lent or borrowed – is greater than one year.

- **Financial instruments**
  Within the capital markets, debt instruments such as bonds are issued which specify a maturity date, the interest to be paid and the payment periods. Within the equity market, shares are issued which represent part of the capital of the company.

The term **Capital Markets** refers to the financial markets in which money is raised and traded. The capital markets comprise three main types:

- **Money Markets**
  These are characterised by borrowing and lending large amounts of money for **short periods** – typically overnight up to, and including, 12 months.

- **Debt Markets**
  These are characterised by instruments that generally pay interest for a fixed period of time for loan periods over 12 months up to 30 years. For this reason the markets are also known as the **Fixed Income Markets**. The markets involve medium- to long-term borrowing.

- **Equity Markets**
  These markets also involve medium- to long-term borrowing, but in this case, interest is not paid to the lender. Instead the organisation borrowing the money issues **stocks** or **shares** to investors who become part-owners of the organisation – in other words, they become **shareholders** in the equity of the organisation. Investors may or may not be paid a dividend on their shares depending on how well the organisation performs.

The following diagram summarises the relationship among the money, debt and equity markets.

Money Markets	Debt Markets	Equity Markets
Short-term	Medium- to long-term Non-permanent funding	Long-term Permanent funding
0 1		
Years		

The capital markets can also be represented by the following diagram, which will be refined later in the book.

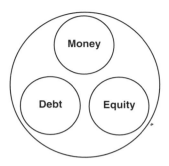

To understand the equity markets, it is important to understand the terms used. Financial instruments issued in the capital markets are collectively known as securities. Instruments issued in the **fixed income** debt markets are typically called **bonds** and **notes**. Instruments issued in the equity markets are commonly referred to as **stocks** or **shares**. These terms can vary in meaning depending on the geographical location of a particular market. The table below illustrates the differences in usage of the terms stock and share between the UK and US markets.

Term	in the UK =	in the US =
Stock	A fixed-interest security in many cases	Securities which are **not** bonds
A **share** in the equity capital of an organisation	An ordinary share	Common stock

Equity and Debt

There are fundamental differences between the equity and debt markets from both the issuers' and investors' perspectives. An organisation issuing equity is selling shares in the ownership and assets of itself. Investors holding these shares are not repaid, but instead expect a share of any profits. An organisation issuing debt is

raising a loan and will have to repay the loan in full, with interest, over a set period. Investors typically know how much interest they will receive and that their initial investment will be repaid.

Market Size

Within the global capital markets, the relative size of the equity versus the debt markets is difficult to determine precisely. Different markets around the world are subject to different reporting requirements and may report "size" differently – say, in terms of currency value, or number of trades. For example, equities are traded on exchange floors, such as on the **New York Stock Exchange (NYSE)** or **Over-The-Counter**, or "**OTC**" (a term that refers to the early days of the stock market when an investor literally handed shares over the bank counter) via computerised (called "automated") trading systems. At the same time, while debt market instruments are generally traded OTC, some government and corporate bonds, and Eurobonds, are listed and traded on stock exchanges, such as in New York, Tokyo and London. This makes differentiating the reporting more difficult.

Whatever the method of estimating market sizes, the debt markets far exceed the size of the equity markets in terms of money raised for organisations. For example, in 1997 the money raised on the LSE for new companies and further issues was less then a fifth of that raised for corporate and government bonds, as illustrated in the chart below.

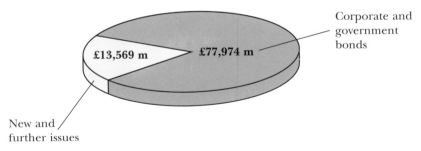

Source: LSE Fact File 1998

The value of equity trading on a number of stock exchanges across the world is shown in the chart below.

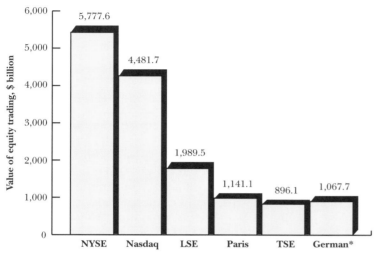

* This value includes all the German stock exchanges

Source: Nasdaq Fact Book 1998

As you can see, the distinction among the money, debt and equity markets is not clear cut. In addition, hybrid instruments such as equity-linked debt instruments make determining exact market size even more difficult. Another very significant component of the markets is foreign exchange volume, which at average daily levels of over US$ one, trillion must be considered for a full picture of market activity. (For additional information, refer to the *Introduction to Foreign Exchange and Money Markets*, ISBN 04-71-83128-X, in this series.) In reality, the capital markets diagram from earlier in this section looks more like this:

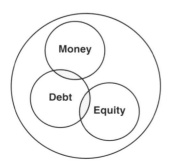

The following table summarises the main features of equity and debt instruments.

Equity	Debt
• Medium – long term • Shared ownership, assets and profits • Variable dividend • Normally voting rights • Negotiable	• Medium – long term • Defined lifetime • Maturity date • Normally pays a known rate of interest • Negotiable • Fixed coupon

Risk and Return

The investor encounters a direct relationship between risk and return when investing in equity and debt instruments. Generally, when people ask how "risky" an investment is they are referring to "market risk" or how much is the price (and therefore return on investment) likely to change. Market risk includes such elements as credit risk (how creditworthy is the issuer), country risk (the stability of the country's government and economy plays a role in the stability of its stock and bond markets) and industry risk (how volatile is that particular type of manufacturing or service, for example).

Equity investors are generally regarded as taking more risk than debt investors by putting their money into part ownership of an organisation that may or may not perform well. These investors subsequently expect a higher rate of return over the long-term, through a combination of growth in the value of their shares and through income from the dividend paid on the shares. However, sometimes dividends are not as expected or none are paid and share values can also fall. At worst, if the organisation fails, the investor may lose their original investment.

Debt market investors are looking for more security or more predictable payments. They will lend money to a government or large international company, reasonably secure in the knowledge that the organisation will exist for the term of the loan and will not default on its debt. Also, generally, if an organisation goes into liquidation, it must pay off debt before paying shareholders. In return for this security, investors accept a return on their investment that is lower than they might get from higher-risk investments such as equities. The very foundation of equities trading is risk. An investor may make a profit or even lose everything. How do you as an investor evaluate an organisation before investing money? You can find a great deal of information about organisations in the financial pages and stock market listings of the newspapers. You can also use financial information provided by services such as Reuters to examine current and historical data.

The Equity Markets

Clarify your ideas about what equity means in terms of the equity and capital markets by performing this activity.

Suppose a new member joins your team. How would you explain the following terms – stocks, shares and securities?

Why Do Organisations Issue Equity?

Organisations need to raise money for different purposes and for different lengths of time. The money can come from the organisation's profits, or from money raised using a range of financial instruments for short-, medium- and long-term periods.

- Short-term instruments (0–12 months) are traded in the money markets (see Reuters Financial Training Series title *An Introduction to Foreign Exchange and Money Markets*, ISBN 0-471-83176-X).

- Medium- and long-term financial instruments are issued in the debt and equity markets (see Reuters Financial Training Series title *An Introduction to Bond Markets*, ISBN 0-471-83174-3).

Organisations need to maintain a balance of funding between debt and equity to ensure that they neither over-borrow by issuing too much debt, nor dilute their shareholders' investment by issuing too much equity. If an organisation issues debt then it has to repay the loan on a prescribed schedule. One advantage of issuing equity is that the organisation can pay a variable dividend – the income generated by the share. The dividend is the share of profit paid to shareholders after provision has been made for all liabilities and the need for retained profits to fund the ongoing operations of the organisation. Likewise, dividends will be low when an organisation needs to apply a large part of profits to funding expansion or simply, when the organisation's performance is poor.

A disadvantage of issuing equity is that ownership and control of the organisation are split. In theory the shareholders own the organisation and they appoint a board of directors to manage it on their behalf.

Who Buys Shares?

Investors offer their money for capital requirements in the hope that they will get their money back together with some reward in exchange for its use. As you have already seen, the amount of reward is closely linked with the amount of risk taken in the capital markets.

Investors in the equities markets are of two main types:

- Individuals

- Institutions

Traditionally, shares were bought by individuals for long-term investment or savings. Investors will typically accept a low dividend one year if they can see a future capital gain as an organisation grows.

Today, however, institutions such as pension funds, insurance companies, unit trusts and investment trusts are the major owners of equity. These institutions have fund managers who look after large sums on behalf of individual investors, who are indirectly investing in shares through the purchase of, for example, unit trusts or pensions.

The trend towards increasing institutional ownership of equity is illustrated in the following charts taken from the US Federal Reserve Board – Flow of Funds quarterly reports. The graph below indicates the percentage holdings of US equity by households and non-profit organisations compared to those held by US financial institutions of all types since 1950. It is interesting to note the importance of holdings by pension funds – for the third quarter of 1996 it amounted to 22.4% of all equity holdings in the US.

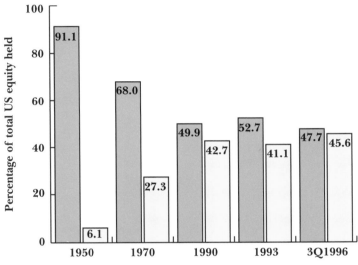

Householders and non-profit organisations

Financial institutions of all types

Source: US Federal Reserve Board – Flow of Funds 1996

But how do issuers, who are raising capital, meet the investors, who are looking for a safe and profitable return on their investment? In the equities markets **intermediaries** – broker dealers, market makers – match buyers and sellers to ensure transactions are beneficial to all parties, including themselves. The intermediaries are also responsible for managing the whole process of issuing equity and any subsequent trading in equity instruments.

What Types of Equity Markets Are There?

The **primary** or **new issue** market is where the original transfer of money from investors to organisations takes place with the issue of shares. As the shares are not repaid, the organisation in effect gets a perpetual loan. When a new organisation is **"floated"** on a stock exchange, the capital raised comes from the public marketplace. New issues such as these are sometimes referred to as **Initial Public Offerings (IPOs)**. If an organisation wishes to be floated it must meet certain financial criteria; the floatation process is described later in the Trading in the Equity Markets section. Once an organisation has been floated on an exchange, it is added to the official or main list and is thus 'listed'. The following chart indicates the amount of money raised for new companies by IPOs on Nasdaq since 1990.

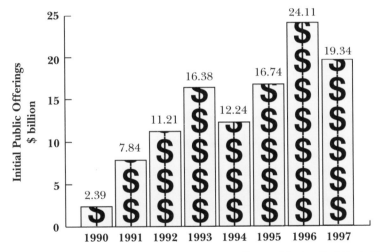

Source: Nasdaq Fact Book 1998

Some stock exchanges also operate markets for newer and smaller companies who wish to raise public capital but who do not fit all the listing requirements for the main list – **AIM** is such a market operated and regulated by the LSE . In 1997 AIM raised £691.5 million of new capital for smaller organisations. NASDAQ does the same in the US market and in 1997 raised over US$19 billion of new capital.

The majority of the world's stock markets' business is not in new issues but is concerned with the **secondary market** – the business of trading shares after original issuance. If everyone who bought shares kept them waiting to collect dividends there would be no secondary market. Compare the number of shares traded on the NYSE and LSE for the years 1992–1996 in the chart below.

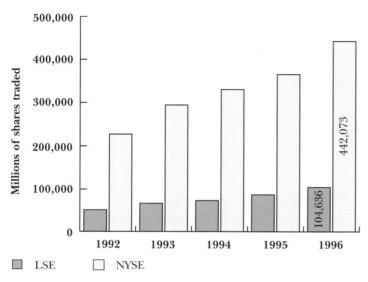

Source: LSE Fact File 1997 and NYSE Factbook 1997

Trading on stockmarkets depends on supply and demand and is affected by many factors. Trading in a particular company's equity is strongly influenced by financial performance and the expectations of its future financial performance. The general level of the stock market is affected by many international and domestic events, including inflation, interest rates and liquidity.

Where Are the Equity Markets?

There are stock exchanges in many world capitals and major cities. The six largest in terms of market value of listed and quoted securities and turnover are the:

- New York Stock Exchange (NYSE)
- Tokyo Stock Exchange (TSE)
- London Stock Exchange (LSE)
- Nasdaq
- Paris Bourse
- German Stock Exchanges – the largest is in Frankfurt

The chart below indicates the relative domestic market values of these exchanges.

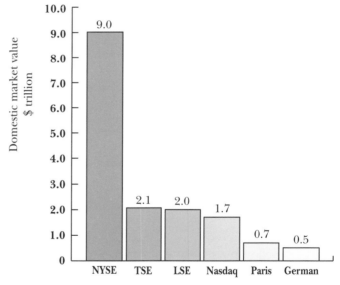

Source: LSE Fact File 1998

REUTERS

The original "trading floors" have largely been superseded by automated trading systems with which deals are done via telephone and computer screen, or even just by computer. For example, many large investors' trading systems trigger trades by price – when a security reaches a certain price, a buy/sell order occurs. In addition, as a result of Internet access, now even the average individual investor can execute trades from her own computer. The investor places the order through an intermediary, via the Internet, and the intermediary executes the trade. While all of these trading mechanisms exist off the actual trading floor, they are still governed by the same exchange regulations.

Emerging Markets

These are securities markets in developing economies with high economic growth rates instituted to attract investment. The markets are either formal exchanges or highly active OTC markets. The emerging markets offer investors the opportunities for relatively high returns on investments and diversification of their portfolios.

Organisations listed on emerging market exchanges are comparatively small by international standards, but the numbers of markets and organisations are growing. Financial institutions such as the International Financial Corporation (IFC) produce emerging market indices derived from stocks that can be bought by overseas investors in emerging markets.

Below is a table taken from a Reuters terminal that shows the IFC indices.

Index	Value	No.Stk	CHG(%)	WCH(%)	YTD(%)
Argentina	612650.18	32	4.35	-5.63	-10.49
Brazil	1843.19	75	1.81	-7.88	-8.53
Chile	1003.08	50	-1.39	-10.40	-11.17
China	39.55	43	4.99	-26.87	-31.56
Colombia	1810.88	16	0.04	0.17	-4.46
Czech Rep	60.33	6	0.20	-2.88	-4.36
Egypt	90.92	28	-0.35	-1.94	-2.55
Greece	603.02	54	1.56	-6.02	-3.14
Hungary	714.72	13	4.57	-7.57	-7.57
India	109.1	72	0.79	-7.74	-6.00
Indonesia	92.72	61	10.60	-8.29	-7.70
Israel	122.83	46	1.94	-7.50	-7.40
Jordan	311.14	6	-0.49	-0.18	-0.89
Korea	65.9	184	1.07	12.92	23.11
Malaysia	112.46	157	4.92	-4.97	-14.13
Mexico	2460.2	61	-0.40	-6.96	-10.18
Morocco	138.41	11	0.21	0.26	-0.13
Pakistan	431.25	24	1.91	-11.05	-13.43
Peru	341.28	24	0.47	-5.85	-7.51
Philippines	184.54	49	3.60	-15.02	-15.08
Poland	1224.93	29	2.97	-8.81	-7.49
Portugal	278.2	23	1.23	-1.23	4.30
Russia	135.22	30	3.06	-16.89	-14.76
Slovakia	100.57	5	-0.38	-5.80	-5.80
South Africa	163.81	77	2.15	-8.00	-9.32
Sri Lanka	160.62	5	-0.20	-1.94	2.48
Taiwan, China	157.18	98	1.75	-6.22	-9.14
Thailand	84.49	65	4.03	-6.12	-6.05
Turkey	29808.69	58	6.95	-6.58	-1.87
Venezuela	8943.78	12	1.90	-14.48	-15.71

You have now reviewed the relationships between the debt and equity markets. Before moving on try this activity.

Imagine you are a corporate treasurer looking to raise capital for a major expansion project for your stock exchange-listed organisation. List at least one advantage and disadvantage for issuing equity or debt.

	Advantage	Disadvantage
D E B T		
E Q U I T Y		

You can check your answer on the next page.

Imagine you are a corporate treasurer looking to raise capital for a major expansion project for your stock exchange-listed organisation. List at least one advantage and disadvantage for issuing equity or debt.

	Advantage	Disadvantage
D E B T	• Debt does not involve diluting the ownership of the company. The issue of debt does not confer any rights of ownership, such as voting, or a share in company profits. • It is faster to issue debt than equity. • The organisation can match the period of their debt to their funding requirements.	• Many issuers of debt do not have a choice to issue equity because the equity is not theirs to give away, for example, in the case of governments and nationalised industries. • The organisation must pay interest on the agreed payment dates and repay capital on the maturity of the debt, irrespective of the organisation's needs and circumstances.
E Q U I T Y	• Equity can be used to raise capital which does not need to be repaid – it is like raising a perpetual loan. • The dividend paid on shares can be varied depending on the organisation's needs and circumstances. • The organisation may not be of sufficient standing to be able to issue debt as it may be seen as an unacceptably high risk.	• Ownership and control of the organisation are split. The shareholders own the organisation and appoint the Board of Directors who can be voted out of office. • Share prices fluctuate constantly depending on supply and demand. • An organisation's performance and therefore share prices are affected by external factors such as international and domestic economic events, inflation and interest rates. • Rumours can affect share prices. • The initial cost of issuing shares is high.

Why Do Equity Markets Exist?

 Summary

You have now finished the first section of the book and you should have a clear understanding of:

- The meaning of the term equity in the context of the capital markets

- The relationship between money, debt and equity markets, their purposes and uses

- The relationship between risk and return and how debt and equity are positioned with respect to them

- An overview of the equity market players and the primary and secondary markets in which they operate

As a check on your understanding of this section, you should try the Quick Quiz Questions on the next page. You may also find the Overview section to be a helpful learning tool.

Your notes

REUTERS

Quick Quiz Questions

1. What is the main purpose of the capital markets?
   - ☐ a) To provide investment opportunities for individuals and institutions
   - ☐ b) To finance business, trade and commerce
   - ☐ c) To lend money for periods over one year

2. What are the generic names of the main types of financial instruments used in the:
   - ☐ a) Debt markets?
   - ☐ b) Equity markets?

3. Who are the owners of an organisation which has been floated on a stock exchange such as the LSE?
   - ☐ a) The stock exchange
   - ☐ b) The organisation's board of directors
   - ☐ c) The organisation's shareholders
   - ☐ d) The organisation's bankers

4. Who owns most of the equity of US organisations?

5. In general which is the lower risk investment, debt or equity?

6. A blue-chip organisation has a fixed-term, 10-year funding requirement for which it needs to raise funds quickly. If you were the company treasurer how would you raise the funds?

You can check your answers on page 23.

Overview

Market Overlap

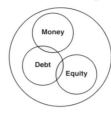

Equity and Debt

Equity	Debt
• Medium – long term	• Medium – long term
• Shared ownership, assets and profits	• Defined lifetime
• Variable dividend	• Maturity date
• Normally voting rights	• Normally pays a known rates of interest
• Negotiable	• Negotiable
	• Fixed coupon

Risk and Return

Why Do Equity Markets Exist?

Capital Markets

- Finance industry and commerce
- Secure investments
- Many of the instruments are traded OTC

Money Markets	Debt Markets	Equity Markets
Short-term	Medium- to long-term Non-permanent funding	Long-term Permanent funding

0   1
Years

Term	in the UK =	in the US =
Stock	A fixed-interest security in many cases	Securities which are **not** bonds
A **share** in the equity capital of an organisation	An ordinary share	Common stock

---

The Equity Markets

Why do organisations issue equity?
- To raise capital
- Dividend payments are variable

Who buys shares?
- Individuals
- Institutions

What types of equity markets are there?
- Primary markets
- Secondary markets

Where are the equity markets?
- New York Stock Exchange (NYSE)
- Tokyo Stock Exchange (TSE)
- London Stock Exchange (LSE)
- Nasdaq
- Paris Bourse
- German Stock Exchanges – the largest is in Frankfurt

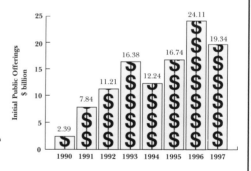

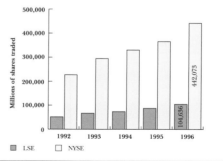

Quick Quiz Answers

✓ or ✗

1. b) ☐

2. a) Bonds ☐
   b) Shares ☐

3. c) ☐

4. Institutional investors ☐

5. Debt. If an organisation goes into liquidation, ☐
   then its debts are paid before shareholders.

6. Issue bonds – probably Eurobonds – in the ☐
   debt markets

How well did you score? You should have scored at least 5. If you didn't, you may need to review some of the materials.

Further Resources

Books

How the City of London works: An introduction to its financial markets
William M. Clarke, Waterlow Publishers, 3rd Edition 1991
ISBN   0 08 040867 2

Investor's Chronicle: Beginner's Guide to Investment
Bernard Gray, Business Books Ltd, 2nd Edition 1993
ISBN   0 7126 6026 7

A–Z of International Finance
Stephen Mahony, FT Pitman Pub., 1997
ISBN   0 273 62552 7

The Basics of Investing
Benton E. Gup (The Univ. of Alabama), John Wiley & Sons, 5th Edition 1992
ISBN   0 471 54853 7

The Bear Book: Survive and Profit in Ferocious Markets
John Rothchild, John Wiley & Sons, Inc., 1998
ISBN   0 471 19718 1

Common Stocks and Uncommon Profits
Philip A. Fisher, John Wiley & Sons, Inc., 1997
ISBN   0 471 24609 3

Getting Started in Stocks
Alvin D. Hall, John Wiley & Sons, Inc., 3rd Edition 1997
ISBN   0 471 17753 9

Further Resources (continued)

Your notes

Publications

London Stock Exchange
- Introduction to the London Stock Exchange
- Fact File 1998
- Order Book Trading – Stock Exchange Electronic Trading Service
- Share Ownership for All – All You Need to Know

New York Stock Exchange
- Fact Book 1998

Nasdaq
- Fact Book 1998

Internet

RFT Web Site
- **http://www.wiley.rft.reuters.com**

This is the series' companion web site where additional quiz questions, updated screens and other information may be found.

International Securities Market Association
- **http://www.isma.rdg.ac.uk**

United States Federal Reserve Board
- **http://www.bog.frb.us**

Exchanges

Refer to the back of this book for a listing of worldwide stock exchange contact information and websites.

This section of the book should take about one hour of study time. You may not take as long as this or you may take a little longer – remember your learning is individual to you.

October is one of the peculiarly dangerous months to speculate in stocks. The others are July, January, September, April, November, May, March, June, December, August and February.

Mark Twain (1835–1910)

Introduction

Established exchanges such as the LSE, NYSE and Philadelphia Stock Exchange (PHLX) have their origins dating back to the late 1700s when brokers and jobbers who had been trading various securities formalised their activities. Members of the Philadelphia Stock Exchange, the first US stock exchange, originally conducted their meetings in private; however, the LSE, whose origins lay in the coffee houses, had a colourful and noisy floor.

Most world capitals boast a stock exchange and you are probably familiar with many of these by now. Emerging market stock exchanges have also been mentioned. Globally, there are many stock exchanges that may or may not have a particular city location, for example, in the US there are stock exchanges in Boston, Chicago, Cincinnati, New York and Philadelphia. In addition, there is the Nasdaq AMEX, two separate exchanges that joined forces in October 1998. Prior to their merger, Nasdaq was recognized as the leading electronic stock market in the world. AMEX was the second-largest floor-based exchange in the US. In Europe, a stock exchange is sometimes referred to as a **bourse**, for example, the Paris Bourse.

This section is concerned with the following:

- How equity is issued in the primary markets

- Trading in the secondary markets

- The importance of stock indices

The screens below are an example of Reuters' electronic information services for global exchanges, from which you can obtain detailed information about any stock exchange in the world.

```
GLOBAL EXCHANGES - REUTERS SPEED GUIDE                    EXCHANGES
Detailed below is a list of Exchange Guides by country.

=EXCHANGES BY COUNTRY================   =EXCHANGES BY COUNTRY Cont============
AFRICAN Countries...........<AFR/EXCH1> Luxembourg..................<LU/EXCH1>
ASIAN Countries.............<ASIA/EXCH1> MIDDLE EASTERN Countries.....<ME/EXCH1>
Australia...................<AU/EXCH1>  Netherlands.................<NL/EXCH1>
Austria.....................<AT/EXCH1>  New Zealand.................<NZ/EXCH1>
Belgiun.....................<BE/EXCH1>  Norway......................<NO/EXCH1>
Canada
```

```
GERMAN EXCHANGE INFORMATION - REUTERS SPEED GUIDE          DE/EXCH1
Welcome to the German Exchanges Information Guide.  Detailed on the following
pages, is Information for all German Exchanges.

Berliner Börse..................................................<DE/EXCH2>
Frankfurter Wertpapierbörse.....................................<DE/EXCH3>
Hanseatische Wertpapierbörse....................................<DE/EXCH4>
Bayerische Börse                                               <DE/EXCH5>
```

```
US EXCHANGES INFORMATION - REUTERS SPEED GUIDE             US/EXCH1
Welcome to the US Exchanges Information Guide.  Detailed on the following
pages, is Information for all US Exchanges.

AMEX............................................................<US/EXCH2>
New York Stock Exchange (NYSE)..................................<US/EXCH3>
Boston Stock Exchange..........................................<US/EXCH4>
Chicago Stock Exchange.........................................<US/EXCH5>
Cincinatti Stock Exchange......................................<US/EXCH6>
Philadelphia Stock Exchange....................................<US/EXCH7>
Pacific Stock Exchange.........................................<US/EXCH8>
NASDAQ.........................................................<US/EXCH9>
Coffee, Sugar, Cocoa Exchange..................................<US/EXCH10>
Chicago Board of Trade (CBOT)..................................<US/EXCH11>
Chicago Mercantile Exchange (CME)..............................<US/EXCH12>
Chicago Options Exchange (CBOE)................................<US/EXCH13>
Kansas City Board of Trade.....................................<US/EXCH14>
MidAmerica Connodity Exchange..................................<US/EXCH15>
Minneapolis Grains Exchange....................................<US/EXCH16>
New York Merantile Exchange/Connodity Exchange Inc (NYMEX)......<US/EXCH17>
New York Futures/New York Cotton Exchange......................<US/EXCH18>
Philadelphia Board of Trade....................................<US/EXCH19>
================================================================
Global Exchanges<EXCHANGES>     U.S. Index<UNITEDSTATES>    Next page<US/EXCH2>
     Lost? Selective Access?..<USER/HELP>   Reuters Phone Support..<PHONE/HELP>
```

Exchange and OTC Trading

The primary role of a stock exchange is to provide a safe environment in which market players can trade. The exchanges have approved members, trading procedures and regulations governing the way trading takes place and disputes are resolved. In some cases trading still takes place on an exchange floor, for example, on the NYSE. In other cases, trading is carried out via exchange-based or remote electronic systems, for example, on the TSE and LSE respectively. In addition, exchanges carry out the following functions:

- Regulate the listing of securities, ensuring that a issuer meets exchange criteria (see more on regulation in the *Trading in the Equities Markets* section).

- Provides facilities for the settlement of trades – the transfer of cash for instruments. Some exchanges operate a **rolling settlement** system where transactions are normally settled a fixed number of days after the trade date. For example, a NYSE settlement usually takes place 3 business days after the trade date – this is written as T+3. Other exchanges operate a specified **account date** system.

- Exchanges monitor and report transaction data and other relevant information concerning the financial status of listed organisations.

The chart opposite indicates the number of new and total number of domestic and international organisations listed on a number of different exchanges for 1997.

Exchange	New		Total	
	Domestic	International	Domestic	International
LSE	242	41	2,465	526
NYSE	216	63	2,691	356
Nasdaq	581	75	5,033	454
TSE	50	1	1,805	60
Paris	82	5	744	193
German	35	–	700	–
Australian	78	9	1,159	60

Source: LSE Fact File 1998

If an organisation is not listed on an exchange because it has insufficient capitalisation or does not want to be listed in order to limit the shares to a few investors, then it is possible to trade the shares OTC. The OTC market is also suited to trading equity securities that are international in nature, for example, Global Depository Receipts, which are explained in the next section of the book.

Order-Driven and Quote-Driven Trading Systems

Exchanges worldwide developed according to the needs of their local markets and also to respond to the increasingly important role of international markets. A good example of this development is the LSE, which up until quite recently operated a quote-driven system. However, the exchange has now introduced an order-driven system to trade shares for the top 100 organisations listed – the organisations comprising the **FT Stock Exchange 100 Index** or **"Footsie 100"**.

Quote-Driven Systems

Quote-driven systems such as **SEAQ** – which is explained in detail later – operated by the LSE and Nasdaq in the US require **market makers** to quote continuous two-way bid and ask prices for listed securities. The market makers quote their prices on a screen-based system which brokers and investors can use to find the best prices. Below is an example of such a SEAQ screen, as taken from Reuters.

```
REX.L                                              11:28
SEAQ GBp  REXAM PLC            Cls   288-294        REUTER
NMS 50    PL 300                               GMT 11:28
                               Net -6      H 292    L 283
Vol 452.9                                          News  :
Last ↑283½    283      284      284      284        5/1

 HOAE  UBS.  DMG.      283-287      SBCW
AITK  281-288   50x50  09:10  MLSB  281-288   50x50  09:10
BZWE  283-290   50x50  09:48  NWSL  281-288   50x50  09:10
DMG.  283-293   50x50  08:29  RAML  283-290   25x25  08:21
GSCO  281-288   50x50  11:19  SBCW  280-287   50x50  09:10
HOAE  283-290   50x50  09:09  SGSL  281-288   50x50  09:13
HSBC  281-288   50x50  09:10  UBS.  283-290   50x50  09:00
KLWT  280-290   50x50  09:11
```

Quote-driven systems provide liquidity to the markets but are more expensive to trade on as the **difference between the bid and ask prices – the spread** – is relatively large. In return for acting as market makers, the relevant stock exchange grants these players privileges such as borrowing securities to cover positions and exemption from certain taxes.

Many large investment institutions prefer this type of system because it guarantees a minimum level of liquidity. There is the added advantage that these large investors, or their brokers, can negotiate large transactions with market makers at better terms than are quoted on-screen.

Order-Driven Systems

Order-driven systems such as **SETS** – which is also explained in detail later – operated by the LSE and those systems used on the NYSE and Paris Bourse, are based on a continuous **auction system**. In this case, investors, or their brokers, submit buy and sell orders to a centralised location which may be on the floor of an exchange as in the case of the NYSE or on a computerised system as in the case of SETS on the LSE. Once the orders are in the system they are matched, executed or deleted depending on the client instructions.

In order-driven systems, orders are submitted before prices are determined. There is no obligation on the part of market makers to make continuous two-way prices. Order-driven markets are cheaper to trade in because the bid/ask spread is narrower. This makes this type of market more attractive to many investors; however, the trading in some less popular securities may become illiquid if continuous prices are not quoted.

So far you have learned about trading systems used on various exchanges but these activities are concerned with the **secondary markets**. These are the markets where shares are traded **after** the shares have been issued and are discussed in more detail later.

How do shares reach the secondary markets? The next section describes the **primary markets**, the process by which organisations issue shares in the equity markets.

Before moving on, turn to the next page to look at a typical quotation for the shares of a LSE listed organisation traded using SETS, as shown on a Reuters screen.

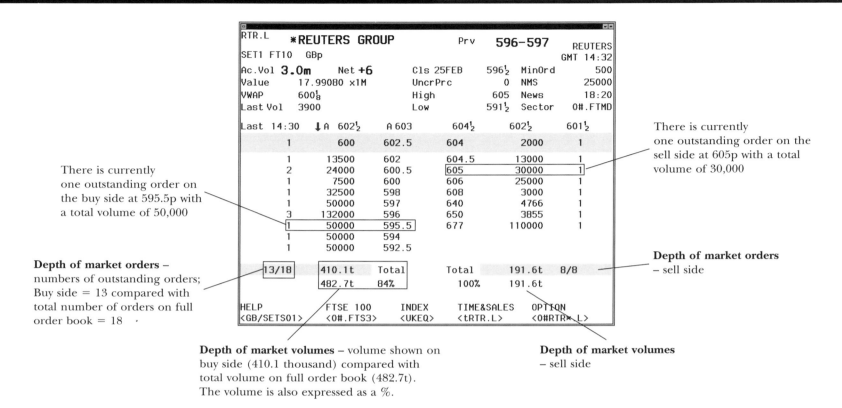

```
RTR.L        *REUTERS GROUP              Prv    596-597      REUTERS
SET1 FT10   GBp                                              GMT 14:32
Ac.Vol 3.0m        Net +6          Cls 25FEB   596½  MinOrd        500
Value      17.99080 x1M            UncrPrc        0  NMS         25000
VWAP       600⅛                    High         605  News        18:20
Last Vol   3900                    Low         591½  Sector   O#.FTMD

Last 14:30   ↓A 602½      A 603      604½      602½      601½
        1        600     602.5      604       2000        1
        1      13500     602        604.5    13000        1
        2      24000     600.5      605       30000       1
        1       7500     600        606      25000        1
        1      32500     598        608       3000        1
        1      50000     597        640       4766        1
        3     132000     596        650       3855        1
        1      50000     595.5      677      110000       1
        1      50000     594
        1      50000     592.5

    13/18     410.1t  Total      Total      191.6t   8/8
              482.7t    84%       100%      191.6t

HELP         FTSE 100      INDEX     TIME&SALES   OPTION
<GB/SETS01>  <O#.FTS3>    <UKEQ>    <tRTR.L>     <O#RTR*L>
```

There is currently one outstanding order on the sell side at 605p with a total volume of 30,000

There is currently one outstanding order on the buy side at 595.5p with a total volume of 50,000

Depth of market orders – numbers of outstanding orders; Buy side = 13 compared with total number of orders on full order book = 18

Depth of market orders – sell side

Depth of market volumes – volume shown on buy side (410.1 thousand) compared with total volume on full order book (482.7t). The volume is also expressed as a %.

Depth of market volumes – sell side

Primary Markets

The primary markets exist as a means by which organisations can raise capital in public markets. New issues can take place on a stock exchange or via the OTC markets. Different stock exchanges worldwide have different rules and procedures for **listing** and **floating** an organisation in the primary market; however, most exchanges follow the same broad principles and the rules and procedures differ only in detail. The LSE will be used as an example of the issuing process on a stock exchange – if you need to know the details for a different exchange these are usually freely available.

Do you want to know the issuing process for a different exchange? Refer to a stock exchange listed on the web (see listing at the end of this book) and review the information provided.

The LSE is the national stock exchange for the UK and it is also one of the world's leading market places for trading international equities. In 1995 it was estimated that 55% of the world's equities that are traded outside home markets passed through the LSE. In 1997 the LSE international equity turnover was £1,443.2 billion.

The central activities of the LSE are:

- Organising and regulating the UK central market in securities

- Organising and regulating the equity market in international securities on the LSE

- Providing the UK listing mechanism

- Providing a range of FTSE Stock Indices in a joint venture with the *Financial Times*

One of the principal economic roles of the LSE is to allow capital to be raised. Organisations wishing to raise capital apply to join the Official List and have to satisfy the existing listing requirements. But what are these requirements?

Listing Requirements

Each stock exchange has specific listing requirements. For example, the LSE requires that trading, financial and management information be disclosed, and that the following conditions are met for full listing:

- The market capitalisation of the prospective organisation must be at least £700,000

- The issued shares must be freely transferable

- At least 25% of the shares must be owned by shareholders other than directors of the organisation

- No individual shareholder must hold more than 30% of the voting power

The first time an organisation issues shares in the primary market it is called an **Initial Public Offering (IPO)**. It is also important to remember that even if an organisation is listed, if it wishes to issue new shares to raise capital – a **secondary issue** – then the

organisation still has to apply to the exchange to issue the new shares.

Before moving on, look at the examples below of IPOs taken from Reuters screens, to review the information made available.

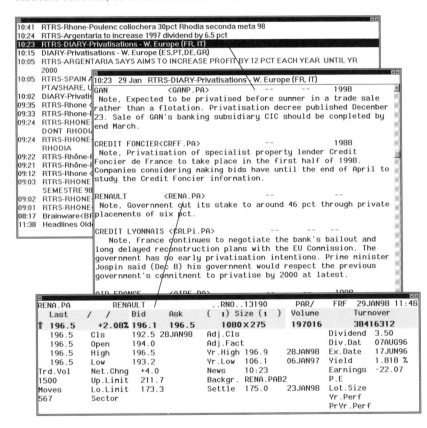

As with many other exchanges, for smaller organisations that cannot meet full listing requirements, the LSE has a second-tier market – **AIM**. Smaller organisations wishing to join AIM do not follow the complete flotation process which is described next, but use nominated advisers who are authorised by the LSE. You can view quotations on AIM securities on electronic information systems such as Reuters, as in the sample on the next page.

How Do the Equity Markets Work?

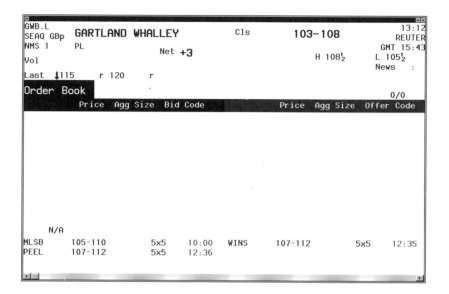

```
GWB.L                                              13:12
SEAQ GBp  GARTLAND WHALLEY    Cls    103-108        REUTER
NMS 1     PL                                     GMT 15:43
Vol                  Net +3           H 108½   L 105½
Last ↓115   r 120    r                  News  :
Order Book                                         0/0
         Price  Agg Size  Bid Code    Price  Agg Size  Offer Code




      N/A
MLSB    105-110     5x5    10:00  WINS   107-112     5x5    12:35
PEEL    107-112     5x5    12:36
```

Flotation

When a private organisation applies to a stock exchange to be listed and is accepted, then it is said to 'go public'. The organisation issues and sells shares to the public in an IPO. If the IPO raises totally new capital for the organisation, then the issue is termed a **primary offer**. If existing privately held shares are sold, thus raising no new capital, then the issue is termed a **secondary offer**. The following description of the process of floating and listing stock refers to the London market.

Once an organisation has made the decision that it wants to join an exchange such as the LSE, then the next major step is to decide what type of **offer** the issue will be. The main types of offer on the LSE are as follows:

- **Offer for Sale**
  In this case, shares are offered to the public by a sponsoring intermediary to buy new or existing shares. The sale is advertised and may be for a primary or secondary offer. The shares sold are sometimes those held by the organisation's founder or those being "on-sold" by a sponsor holding all of the primary issue.

- **Offer for Subscription**
  This type is also known as a **direct** offer and is a direct invitation by the issuer to the public to **subscribe** for new shares – hence the term offer for subscription. This type is typically a primary offer and does not involve a financial intermediary sponsoring the issue. For example, governments often issue by subscription for their privatisation schemes.

- **Placing**
  This involves the sale of new shares to institutions or individuals directly or using a financial intermediary. It does not involve an offer to the general public. This type of offer is common for smaller organisations because it involves less administration and expense than an offer for sale. Public companies need a **sponsor**, for example, an investment bank for this type of offer.

- **Intermediaries Offer**
  This is an offer of new shares which are placed with a syndicate of financial intermediaries who then market the shares to their clients.

- **An Introduction**
  In this case, an organisation may already be issuing equity but until the introduction has been effected, the organisation is not listed. For example, introductions can be used in the following cases:
  - Where the shares are already listed on a foreign stock exchange
  - Where existing shareholders wish to trade shares publicly
  - Where new shares are created by a listed organisation to replace shares of another listed organisation following an acquisition

In the first two examples, the introductions are secondary offers because the shares already exist.

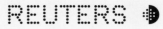

Once the type of offer has been decided, what needs to be done for the flotation? The following abbreviated planning sequence, process and timetable of events is taken from *The Going Public Handbook* produced by Price Waterhouse, Accountants.

Planning

Planning an issue includes such matters as the strategic timing affecting the launch date. For example, the LSE six month rule that the balance sheet included in the organisation's track record must fall within six months of the flotation date. The pricing of the shares must be considered and most importantly the flotation team must be chosen. The team members comprise:

- A **Sponsor** who is required by the LSE. This could be a stockbroker, merchant bank, securities house, firm of accountants etc.

- A **Broker Dealer** who will advise on pricing and establish market interest.

- A **Reporting Accountant** who will prepare a detailed, independent report on the organisation and its affairs – this is called the **Long Form Report**. A **Short Form Report**, which is an audited track record of the organisation's business, is also produced.

- A **Solicitor to the Company** who deals with the legal issues arising from the organisation's intended change in status. There is also a **Solicitor to the issue** who is appointed by the Sponsor to deal with the legal requirements of the flotation.

- A **Specialist PR Consultant** who manages the organisation's image and press matters.

Process

Once the organisation has assembled its team, there are four essential elements required for a successful flotation and share issue.

- The **Prospectus**. This is a fundamental document and requirement for the flotation and must cover a minimum of information including:
  - Organisation details dealing with capital structure, borrowings, number and price of shares in the offer, profits etc.
  - Underwriters to the issue who guarantee that the issuing organisation receives the funds required irrespective of any change in market conditions after the terms of the issue have been fixed.
  - Lead Managers and Co-Managers for a global issue.

- The **Placing/Underwriting Agreement.** This deals with the legal aspects of the flotation including the disclosure listing particulars, remedies for false and misleading particulars and any warranties or indemnities required by the Sponsor.

- The **Roadshow and Final Placing**. This element deals with the PR aspects of the flotation. Investors have to be persuaded to invest in the organisation. During this period the broker dealer 'firms-up' on the final flotation price. On **Impact Day** the issue price will have been finalised, the underwriting agreement signed and the LSE will list the Prospectus details.

- **Post Impact Day**. For a period of 1–2 weeks after Impact Day, share applications and cash are received by the Sponsor from investors. The applications list is then closed and the basis of share allocation is announced. The allocation is dependent on the number of investors and the volume of shares they are willing to buy. The listing becomes effective from this point and share dealing can commence.

Timetable

4–8 Months Before Flotation Detailed Planning	Organisation	Sponsor/Broker	Accountant	Solicitors	PR Consultancy
Appoints advisers	✓				
Overall timetable agreed, detailed instructions to team		✓			
Detailed timetable and list of documents prepared		✓			
Any problem areas reviewed	✓	✓	✓	✓	
Long Form Report started			✓		
2 – 3 Months Before Flotation **Drafting of Documentation**					
Draft prospectus/listing particulars	✓	✓		✓	
Draft Short Form Report			✓		
Draft other documents		✓			
Begin legal work				✓	
Submit draft documents to LSE		✓			
Begin PR/press meetings	✓	✓			✓

0–2 Months Before Flotation Submission of the Finalised Documents and Marketing	Organisation	Sponsor/Broker	Accountant	Solicitors	PR Consultancy
Issue terms finalised	✓	✓			
Verification of listing particulars	✓	✓	✓	✓	
Presentation to investors/PR	✓		✓		✓
Finalisation and submission of documents to LSE		✓			
Organisation re-registered as Plc				✓	
Flotation Week/Impact Day + 1 – 2 Weeks **Impact and Offer Period**					
Approval of documents by LSE	✓	✓	✓	✓	
Agree underwriting	✓	✓			
Listing particulars registered				✓	
Announce flotation/publish details	✓	✓			✓
Application lists open and close		✓			
Basis of allocation decided and announced	✓	✓			

Before moving on, look at examples of new issues, as shown on a Reuters screen.

```
NEW ISSUE DATA  Prev<UKEQ>  Next<ISSUE01>                    ISSUE
UK  Equities Speed guide  <GB/EQUITY>
                   <ISSUE01> - <ISSUE15>
                   ---------------------
The above page range gives details of new stock issues for listed companies.

Each entry is shown in the following order -

Stock name & type,  ISIN/SEDOL number,  issue type and details,
where ENT = entitlement (assignable open offer),  RTS = rights,
CAP = capitalisation and PRI = priority.

This is followed by the relevant date informaton,  where  RD = record date,
EX = ex date,  Ap = application date,  SDDCL = stock distribution daily
clains list date,  and LINKS = LINKS/CBTL date.

Any other information relating to the issue will then be given if available.

An entry beginning with a  #  indicates a line inserted for the first tine.
An entry beginning with a  *  indicates an anendnent has been nade.
```

```
NEW ISSUE DATA   prev<ISSUE04>  next<ISSUE06>               ISSUE05
    CORPORATION                    AT 13.5P
22/10/1997

    DOMESTIC & GEN      GB0002747193    4 NEW ORD FOR EACH ORD    12-Nov
17-Nov     N/A    17-Nov  1047/97/2
CAP
    GROUP                          HELD
15/10/1997

*  EURO SALES FIN      GB0003220380    5 NEW ORD 10P FOR 9 "A" ORD   27-Oct
03-Nov   25-Nov   28-Nov
1142/97/2     ENT
                                   HELD AT 150P
12/11/1997
                                   CO PROPOSES TO CONVERT "A" ORD INTO
ORD 10P SHARES SEE SSN FOR DETAILS

#  FAYREWOOD          GB0003324794    1 NEW ORD FOR 13 ORD HELD    30-Oct
10-Nov   01-Dec   09-Dec
1166/97/1     ENT
                                   AT 50P
11/11/1997
```

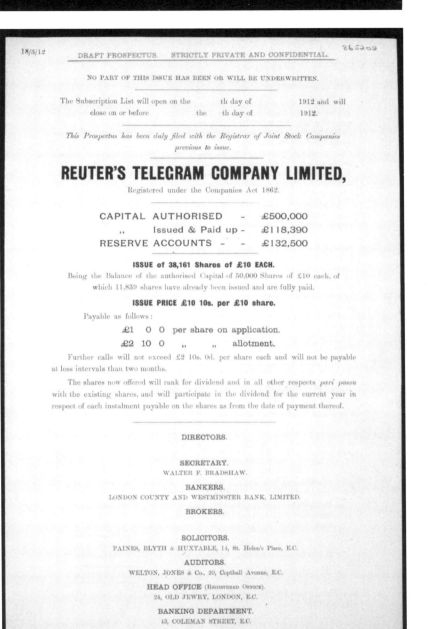

New Issue Procedures

Price Basis

New issues may be offered on a fixed price or tender basis which are described as follows:

Fixed Price Offer

Under this scheme the organisation pre-determines the price of the shares. Investors then apply for shares at this price. If the price is attractive, then the issue will be oversubscribed and the organisation will reduce the number of shares issued for each application as it sees fit.

An oversubscription means that when share trading begins in the secondary market, the opening price will move higher than the issue price. This has the effect of making the issue look a good investment. However, if the price moves too high, then the issue may have been underpriced initially. If a US investment bank acts as a sponsor, then the organisation may be asked for an over-allotment option – a **Green Shoe** – the term comes from the first time this option was used for the issue of the Green Shoe Manufacturing Company. This means that if the issue is oversubscribed, then the bank has the right to increase the number of shares by up to 15% without consulting the issuer.

Tender Offer

In this case the issuing organisation requires investors to state both the number of shares required and the price they are willing to pay for them. The issuer usually specifies a minimum price below which applications will be rejected.

Once all the applications have been received the issuer fixes a striking price at which all shares are allocated to investors who applied at that price or higher.

Sponsoring Organisations

A share issue for an organisation is typically sponsored by one or more member firms of a stock exchange on which the issue will be listed. Typically a Lead Manager – main sponsor – acts as adviser and represents the issuing organisation in its dealings with the exchange.

The Lead Manager usually appoints Co-Lead and Co-Managers as a syndicate to underwrite the issue and make a secondary market in the shares. The chart below shows a typical underwriting syndicate.

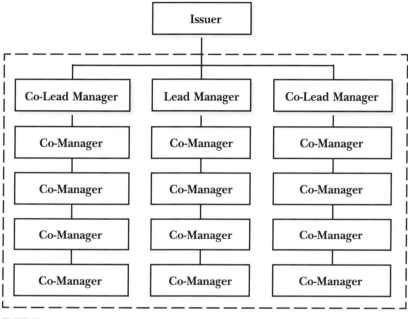

The underwriting syndicate

Underwriting is a form of insurance whereby the syndicate members agree to take up a specified number of shares of an issue, at the issue price, if there are not enough investors. In return, the syndicate members receive an underwriting fee for the risks involved.

The benefit to the issuer is that all the shares will be taken up at issue, thus guaranteeing the minimum amount of capital to be raised.

If the issue is successful, then the underwriting syndicate does not take up any shares. In the case of a partially successful issue, the syndicate members take up a pro-rata amount of shares depending on their proportion of the underwriting.

Book Building

This is the process whereby the sponsoring organisation or underwriting syndicate members determine the correct price for a new issue. The aim is to price the issue such that there is not a large discrepancy between the issue price and the price when the issue starts trading in the secondary markets.

In order to achieve this aim the sponsor organises **road shows** and carries out research to determine the likely demand from investors for a range of share prices.

The result of this research is that a demand curve can be constructed showing demand versus price. This curve is then used to determine the issue price. A typical demand curve is shown here.

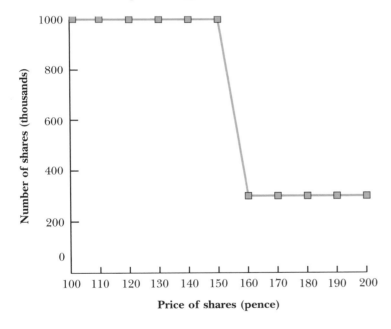

Book building minimises the risk of an undersubscribed issue and is an attractive activity for members of the underwriting syndicate. The more accurate the issue price the less chance they will have to buy shares and the higher the issue price the greater the fees involved.

Grey Markets

A **grey** or **when issued (w/i)** market is an informal market in which investors buy and sell shares that have not yet been issued. The grey market covers the period between the announcement of the issue and the actual allocation of the issued shares.

Grey market deals are settled after the issue date when the shares can be traded in the secondary market. These deals are risky because the contracts are verbal and issuers make no guarantees concerning the allotment of shares. If an issue is oversubscribed, then an investor could receive fewer shares than expected. This could be a costly mistake if the investor has sold more shares in the grey market than he or she actually received.

Secondary Markets

Worldwide stock exchanges exist to provide primary markets where new capital can be raised for organisations. These exchanges also provide secondary markets where securities can be bought and sold. Without the liquidity of the secondary markets it is unlikely that the primary markets could function so efficiently – if at all. Investors need secondary markets where they can buy and sell securities easily and with confidence.

Secondary markets can either operate quote- or order-driven systems as has been explained previously. Whichever system is used, secondary markets should possess the following characteristics:

- **Transparency**
  This means that timely and accurate information on transaction prices and volumes, supply and demand, etc is freely and easily available.

- **Liquidity**
  This covers the ability to buy and sell securities easily with little risk of capital loss. The narrower the bid/ask spread for shares, the greater the competition and the more efficient the market.

- **Efficiency**
  The quicker prices are adjusted, for whatever reason, the more efficiently the market will operate.

As has been mentioned previously, different worldwide stock exchanges have different ways of trading in the secondary markets. To help you understand these markets better, the following three stock exchanges are described in more detail to illustrate the 'mechanics' of the secondary markets.

The exchanges which are described are the:

- London Stock Exchange

- New York Stock Exchange

- Tokyo Stock Exchange

London Stock Exchange

To understand how much the equity markets have evolved in just the last decade, it is useful to look at how the LSE operated before the "Big Bang" of 1986. The Big Bang – so named because of its cataclysmic affect, not unlike the theory describing how our universe came to be – was implemented to make the equity markets more competitive and more accessible to a greater number of market players. Review how the exchange was run.

Prior to the Big Bang in October 1986 there were two mutually exclusive roles on the stock exchange:

- The **stockjobber or jobber**

- The **stockbroker or broker**

A member of the stock exchange could be either a broker or a jobber but never both. Jobbers stood on their pitches on the market floor, giving firm **bid (buying)** and **offer (selling)** prices for shares to enquiring brokers. **Offer** is a UK term, whereas in the US the term used is **ask**. (As most financial publications and Reuters screens use the term **ask** this will be used from now on.) Jobbers were also allowed to hold stock on their own books to trade but they were not allowed to deal directly with investors. All investors were obliged to trade through a broker who tried to find the best price for the investor. Brokers were not allowed to hold securities in a book – they could only trade on behalf of clients.

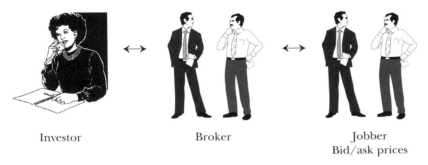

Investor   Broker   Jobber
Bid/ask prices

Jobbers and brokers never shook hands on a deal but merely noted the trade on their respective dealing pads. They operated on the principle of *Dictum meum pactum – My word is my bond*. You can see the Latin inscription on the LSE shield on the previous page. Big Bang did away with this method of operating and allowed firms to act as both brokers and jobbers – so-called dual capacity. The capital required to do this meant that commercial and investment banks formed the majority of such organisations.

The term 'jobber' was superseded by that of **market maker**. Immediately after Big Bang a **quote-driven** trading system was introduced.

Market makers were registered with the stock exchange to make a market in particular securities, being obliged to quote a two-way bid/ask price in a given size. Although market makers were allowed to deal directly with investors, in practice they did so only with the professional investing institutions such as pension funds, insurance companies and independent fund managers. Smaller investors used **broker dealers** or **agency brokers** as an agency service, paying them a commission, much as they used stockbrokers in the past.

Investor   Broker dealers or   Market markers
                  Agency brokers   Bid/ask prices

Agency brokers corresponded exactly to the pre-Big Bang stockbroker, charging a commission – now negotiable rather than fixed – but not taking positions in the shares themselves. Broker dealers now could take positions in securities should they wish and could act as principal in a deal with a client provided they met the various stock exchange requirements regarding the dealing price. However, acting as a principal, they were not obliged to make a two-way price in the same way that a market maker had to operate.

The market-dealing methodology became a screen-based system with participants communicating by telephone – the stock exchange ceased to be the physical market floor where equity dealings took place. The stock exchange still retained much of its regulatory authority over the market, detailing trade reporting requirements, procedures for bringing companies to the market, settlement of deals concluded etc; however, the stock exchange's regulatory role is now itself subject to the authority of the **Financial Services Authority (FSA)** which was formerly the **Securities Investment Board (SIB)**.

In conclusion, Big Bang brought about three major changes:

- The abolition of fixed commissions

- The abolition of single capacity roles, that is, jobbers and brokers

- Active trading no longer took place on the exchange floor but moved to a screen-based and telephone market

In addition, membership of the stock exchange was opened to outsiders including foreign firms.

The trading changes brought about by Big Bang in 1986 were successful and introduced the automated distribution of price information. However, the exchange did not move to an automated or quote-driven system of trading.

By late 1997, in order to trade more competitively with other global exchanges, the LSE launched an order-driven system called **SETS – Stock Exchange Electronic Trading System**. Initially SETS replaces the quote-driven system for the FTSE 100 Index listed organisations, but the intention is to move to include all the listed organisations in the FTSE 250 Index as soon as possible.

SETS is an electronic order-book system where buyers and sellers can indicate, via brokers, the prices and volumes at which they wish to trade – market makers no longer set the prices. An order-driven system tends to result in keener pricing – narrower spreads – for actively traded shares. This is why SETS is initially available for the FTSE 100 organisations as trading in these shares accounts for over a third of total trades.

The chart below indicates the relative proportions of total trades by type on the LSE for 1996.

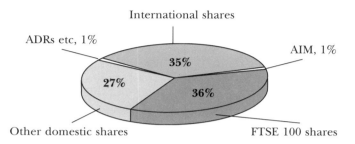

Source: LSE

As of 1998, the LSE operates both an order-driven system for FTSE 100 listed shares and a quote-driven system for all other domestic and international listed shares. The quote-driven system uses SEAQ and SEAQ International. SETS, SEAQ and SEAQ International are all explained in more detail later in this section.

New York Stock Exchange

The NYSE is an example of an order-driven marketplace which operates a **continuous auction** system on a trading floor using open outcry. Investors' buy and sell orders are submitted at a centralised location – a **trading post** – on the trading floor where the orders are matched. The NYSE trading floor is 36,000 square feet in area and houses 17 trading posts. The exchange does not control the prices of securities but exists to ensure that an orderly and fair marketplace exists for investors. As with other exchanges, in order to trade on the floor a market player must be a member of the exchange or requires a **seat**.

On the NYSE, each listed stock is assigned to a single trading post where buying and selling can take place. Each listed stock has a unique location at a trading post, above which is a computer monitor indicating financial data about the individual stocks.

Around the perimeter of the trading floor are about 1500 trading booths where client orders are received.

So who will you find on the NYSE trading floor? There are four important types of exchange members:

- **Specialists**
  These operate from a trading post and play a central role in the auction process. Specialists in effect act as market makers in one or more stocks listed at the trading post. Their main function is to maintain a fair and orderly market. They derive their income either from commissions for acting as a broker or from the bid/ask spread when acting as a dealer.

- **Commission brokers**
  These handle trades on the floor and are employed by brokerage houses to execute deals for their clients. Brokerage houses can also trade on their own account.

- **Floor brokers**
  These help other members handle orders and operate only for themselves – they are not allowed to deal directly with the public.

- **Registered traders**
  These trade on their own account and by being members of the exchange, save on brokerage commissions.

Although the NYSE floor uses open outcry, technology has not been overlooked. Member firms can send orders electronically from off-floor to specialists using the exchange SuperDot system. Orders received in this way are treated in the same way as if a broker or trader were physically present. On completion of a SuperDot order, the specialist reports the order execution using the same electronic system. Orders can be transmitted directly to floor trading booths using the electronic Broker Booth Support System (BBSS) and brokers on the floor can receive orders and relay market information using hand held devices – the NYSE Wireless Data System.

In early May 1996 a seat on the New York Stock Exchange was sold for a record $1.45 million. Other seats fetched $1.25 million in February and March 1996. The previous record of $1.15 million was paid for a seat in September 1987 – shortly before the stock market crashed.

Look at the screens below taken from Reuters, for examples of companies whose stock is traded on the NYSE.

```
GM.N          GENERAL MOTORS   370442105   NYS USD GM.NB2      07JAN98 15:58
Last        Last 1      Last 2      Status      Bid         Ask         Size
↓58\11      58\11       58¾         /R  /       58\11       58¾         200x200
Net.Chng    Cls:06JAN98 Open        High        Low         Volume      Blk.Vol
-0\12       59\07       59\01       59\05       58\11       842700      416900
P.E         Earnings    Yield       News                    DJ.News     L.Blocks
8.18        7.27        3.36 %      15:50                   15:36       16
Dividend    Div.Dat     Ex.Date     Yr.High     Yr.Low      Options     Headlines
2.00        18DEC97     19DEC97     72\07       52\04       W           XGM1
Exchange
```

Prices are in sixteenths – $59/07 = 59^7/_{16}$

```
KO.N          COCA COLA CO     191216100   NYS USD KO.NB2      28JAN98 21:00
Last        Last 1      Last 2      Status      Bid         Ask         Size
↑64\03      64\03       64⅛         /CQ /       64⅛         64\03       43x150
Net.Chng    Cls:27JAN98 Open        High        Low         Volume      Blk.Vol
+1          63\03       63¾         64\11       62⅜         4433200     2360000
P.E         Earnings    Yield       News                    DJ.News     L.Blocks
38.3        1.65        0.89 %      :                       18:37       98
Dividend    Div.Dat     Ex.Date     Yr.High     Yr.Low      Options     Headlines
0.56        15DEC97     26NOV97     72\10       52          W           XK01
Exchange
```

Tokyo Stock Exchange

On the TSE, the market is order-driven with a continuous two-way auction process taking place between buyers and sellers. All orders for stock are placed with TSE member broker/dealer firms who then pass their orders to **saitori** members. These members function as match-makers or middlemen who maintain a central order book for stocks allocated by the TSE. The saitori then match orders according to price, timing etc. The saitori are not allowed to trade on their own account nor are they allowed to trade with the public. The exchange operates a number of electronic systems for floor trading.

Floor Order Routing and Execution System (FORES)
This is used for the 150 most actively traded stocks. The system is designed to:

- Automate order routing for small orders

- Replace manual order books with electronic ones

- Computerise reporting and trade confirmation

Computer-assisted Order Routing and Execution System (CORES)
This is used for less actively traded stocks. The system is also used for various other securities as follows:

- CORES-F for futures on TOPIX and futures and options on Japanese Government Bonds

- CORES-O for options on TOPIX

Look below at the Reuters screens for information on Sony Corporation and Mitsubishi shares, both of which trade on the TSE.

```
6758.T    SONY CORP        TYO/    JPY 6758              29JAN98 06:00
Last↓C11800      06:00    Bid  11800    06:00  Section:   Trading: P Index :
      +700                Ask  11900    06:00
       11800                                   Toyo Keizai
       11900              V.W.A    11660.3     Background  6758.TK1
       11800                                   Sector Chn           /
       11900              EPS       193.90     Derivative           /
                          PER        60.86
Trd.Vol     16500         PBR         3.4      Margin
Tot.Vol   1196500   :     Yld         0.42     Buy       594     +20
                          Div        50.00     Sell     1904     +22
                          Ex Div  (26MAR98)    Ratio     0.31
Close  C11100   28JAN98   Ex.Right (      )
                                               News SNE1 08:52
                                               Home
               PM              AM
Open      11700 (03:30)    11500 (00:06)
High( )   11900 (04:50)    11800 (01:09)   Yr.High  12700 (19JAN98)
Low ( )   11700 (03:30)    11400 (00:07)   Yr.Low    7250 (13JAN97)
Cls                        11700 (02:00)   Lf.High  12700 (19JAN98)
Vol                       692100 (02:00)   Lf.Low     251 (  JUL65)
```

```
8058.T    MITSUBISHI CORP   TYO/    JPY 8058             29JAN98 06:00
Last↓C1100       06:00    Bid  1100     06:00  Section:   Trading: P Index :
      -20                 Ask  1110     06:00
       1100                                    Toyo Keizai
       1110               V.W.A    1103.6      Background  8058.TK1
       1100                                    Sector Chn           /
       1110               EPS       19.10      Derivative           /
                          PER       57.59
Trd.Vol     12000         PBR        2.9       Margin
Tot.Vol   2281000   :     Yld        0.73      Buy       515     -24
                          Div        8.00      Sell      625     -18
                          Ex Div  (26MAR98)    Ratio     0.82
Close  C1120    28JAN98   Ex.Right (      )
                                               News MUC1   :
                                               Home
               PM              AM
Open      1100 (03:30)     1110 (00:00)
High( )   1120 (05:45)     1120 (00:07)   Yr.High   1450 (17JUN97)
Low ( )   1090 (03:40)     1100 (00:43)   Yr.Low     820 (09JAN98)
Cls                        1100 (02:00)   Lf.High   2030 (20DEC89)
Vol                       994000 (02:00)  Lf.Low      64 (  NOV54)
```

Trading Systems – Some Examples

This section is concerned with some of the trading systems and their associated quote screens. The systems described here briefly are intended to illustrate some of those used worldwide, but they are by no means the only ones used. The systems that follow are those for:

- **LSE**
- **Nasdaq/EASDAQ**
- **Instinet**

Do you want to know about the trading system for a different exchange? Refer to a stock exchange listed on the web (see listings at the end of this book) and review the information provided.

London Stock Exchange

The LSE provides a number of systems for trading equities – some of which have been mentioned already. The following systems are described briefly:

- Stock Exchange Electronic Trading Service (SETS)
- Stock Exchange Automated Quotations (SEAQ)
- Stock Exchange Alternative Trading Service (SEATS PLUS)
- SEAQ International

Stock Exchange Electronic Trading Service (SETS)

On October 20, 1997, the LSE switched to SETS, an order book trading system – which partially replaces the quote-driven SEAQ system which was introduced after Big Bang. SETS initially replaces the quote-driven system for the top 100 organisations listed on the exchange – the FTSE 100 Index organisations.

Member firms can enter buy/sell orders into the order book on their own account or on behalf of clients. The entries are anonymous and once in the system the orders may be matched and executed, returned if they are not matched or held for future execution.

The process is automated as follows:

1. Orders for buy/sell are matched
2. Once matched orders are executed as a trade

As soon as a trade is executed, it is reported to the exchange, the market is informed of the trade and the counterparties to the trade are notified and their identities revealed.

The official best prices for shares on the order book are calculated **only** from orders input into the system.

Best **Bid** price = **highest**-priced **Buy** order on book

Best **Ask** price = **lowest**-priced **Sell** order on book

The best bid/ask prices are displayed on information screens and are used by brokers for trading. Closing prices are still published daily in the financial press. To see the Top 10 share moves on the LSE as they appear on a Reuters screen, look below.

```
.AT.L                    TOP 10 BY MOVES          LSE/                        09:49
RIC          Last     Net.Ch Open   High   Low    His.Cl   Volume   Moves Time
HFX.L       ×↓855     +20    842    865    842    845      1059379  314   09:49
LLOY.L      ×↓847     +1½    850    854    847    848½     1050634  287   09:49
BT.L        ×↓568     -4     570    570    568    573      2381348  242   09:49
MKS.L       ×↑562     +4     559    562    554    558      1138215  233   09:49
WWH.L       ↓355      -2     353¼   356    353¼   358      329368   212   09:49
BARC.L      ×↓1757    -3     1775   1775   1755   1763     378999   198   09:48
NU.L        ↓440      +3     440    443    439¾   440      514485   166   09:49
STAN.L      ×↑630     +20    609½   640    609½   610      832293   158   09:49
AL.L        ↓885      +9     882½   895    881    886      169571   152   09:49
GLXO.L      ×↑1630    +11    1623   1630   1620   1619     631184   149   09:48
```

The order book receives and executes orders between 8.30 am–4.30 pm daily, Monday to Friday. Between 8.00–8.30 am, member firms are allowed to enter/delete orders but no execution will take place. For 30 minutes after the order book closes member firms are allowed to delete orders from the book.

At 8.30 am the order book is temporarily frozen and the system calculates prices at which the maximum volume of shares for each security can be traded. All orders that can be executed at this price are then done so automatically. Once this **uncrossing** process is complete, new orders are received and attempted to be matched.

SETS is currently only available for the top 100 listed organisations. What happens if an organisation loses its rating? In practice, SETS is available for the top 100 organisations and those on the **reserve list**.

Before moving on, review this reserve list as it appears on a Reuters screen.

```
15:24 20DEC97   FTSE QUARTERLY CONSTITUENTS CHANGES   UK13B91      CONSTITUENTS1
RESERVE LIST

FTSE100 - TI GROUP (101), BLUE CIRCLE INDS (102), SOUTHERN ELECTRIC (104),
COMPASS GROUP (105), RMC GROUP (106)
FTSE250 & FTSE350 - COURTAULDS TEXTILES (335), MERCHANTS TRUSTS (342), CORPORATE
SERVICES GROUP (344), EXPRO (345), GALEN HOLDINGS (346), MICRO FOCUS GROUP
(347), MCBRIDE (349), SHIRE PHARMACEUTICALS (352), PSION (353), VENDOME LUXURY
GROUP (357), SCHRODER UK GROWTH FUND (358).
```

For shares of organisations that are not in the top 100 listed, the existing quote-driven SEAQ system is used. It is unlikely that the order book will be used for stocks below the top 350 in the future.

Stock Exchange Automated Quotations (SEAQ)

Shares outside the FTSE 100 are traded using the quote-driven trading structure introduced at Big Bang in October 1986. This structure is based on the competing market-maker system. Throughout the trading day, 31 registered market-makers are obliged to display to the market their bid (buying) and offer (selling) prices and the maximum bargain size to which these prices relate. These competing quotes are displayed on the exchange's SEAQ bulletin board.

Market-makers use their dealer terminals to enter two-way prices for the SEAQ stock in which they are registered and to report their trades. SEAQ takes in price information from SEAQ market-makers, from which competing bid-and-offer prices are collated. All equity prices displayed on SEAQ are firm.

SEAQ can be viewed via ICV TOPIC3 and Reuters – in the UK Telekurs TOPIC PLUS has now been acquired by ICV. The market makers bid and ask prices and sizes are used to create the SEAQ "Yellow Strip". This identifies the best bid and ask price for every SEAQ security from an investor's point of view and is known as the **touch**. The Yellow Strip also identifies up to three market makers quoting this price.

The screen shown here is for quotes for Airtours Plc shares.

```
AIR.L                                                          08:48
SEAQ GBp   AIRTOURS PLC              Cls   1295-1310          REUTER
NMS 10     PL 60                                        GMT 08:48
                                     Net 0      H 1308   L 1296
Vol 2.3                                                 News   :
Last ↑1308         1296                                      5/5

 SBCW  HOAE  MLSB        1295-1310        BZWE  MLSB  HOAE
BZWE   1290-1310    10x10   08:14   NWSL   1295-1315   10x10   08:27
HOAE   1295-1310    10x10   08:24   SBCW   1295-1310   10x10   08:25
MLSB   1295-1310    10x10   08:24   UBS.   1295-1310   10x10   08:26
```

Stock Exchange Alternative Trading Service (SEATS PLUS)

This service operates for shares that are traded infrequently and cannot support competing market makers. When more than one market maker registers on SEATS, the security is transferred to SEAQ.

SEATS PLUS

SEATS PLUS is an integrated and flexible trading system providing order-entry, order-hitting and competing quote facilities. It enables brokers to enter orders, report trades and input company information. SEATS PLUS supports two market segments: SEATS which comprises UK equities and equity warrants and AIM which comprises those securities admitted to the AIM market for small and growing companies. All trades in all segments in SEATS PLUS must be reported to the exchange within three minutes of dealing.

SEAQ – International

London is the largest market in the world for the trading of non-domestic equities. Its position within the European time zone enables its trading hours to bridge the working day between Japan and New York – making London the natural choice for trading in international equities. In 1985 SEAQ International, a screen-based price-information system, was initially introduced to provide a marketplace for the growing interest in European equities. SEAQ International now includes securities from 42 countries both in developed and emerging economies and displays real-time prices in over 1,100 securities. Over 50 market-makers enter prices directly onto the central exchange computer system and these are then distributed on over 12,000 screens across the world through commercial quote vendors including ADP, Bloomberg, Bridge, ICV, Quick, Reuters, Telekurs and Dow Jones Markets. Having found an attractive dealing price on an information screen, investors contact the appropriate market-maker by telephone to execute the trade. Settlement is determined by both parties at the time of transaction and is carried out in the country of origin of the share.

Quotes are displayed in US dollars or the home currency but market-makers are usually prepared to deal in other leading currencies. In addition to price information SEAQ International calculates and distributes a number of indices, based on SEAQ International prices and updated minute by minute. The TSE/Nikkei 50 is an index of the 50 leading Japanese stocks and closely tracks the Nikkei 225.

This is the international version of SEAQ for securities listed on an overseas stock exchange approved by the London Stock Exchange. The system allows a stock to trade outside the normal country of issue and operates in a similar way to SEAQ. It is divided into separate country sectors plus a developing market sector. The market makers representing major international securities houses quote continuous or indicative bid/ask prices. The share prices are usually quoted in the domestic currency of the country sector and any transactions are settled using local arrangements.

Trading can take place 24 hours a day but quotations can only be input between 7.00 am–8.00 pm UK time. The turnover for some of the foreign equities transactions in £billion on the stock exchange in 1997 is shown in the chart below.

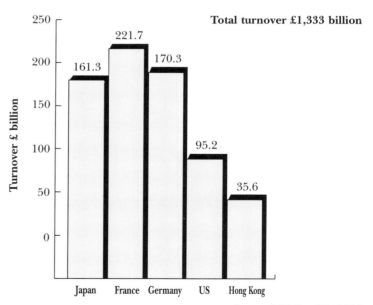

Total turnover £1,333 billion

Source: LSE Fact File 1998

The Reuters screens below show customer turnover.

```
MARKET TURNOVER STATISTICS INDEX     MAIN INDEX <UKEQ>              TURNOVER
DESCRIPTION                                      PAGE      UPDATED
UK EQUITIES-Customer Turnover×                  <TURNOVER01> Daily
UK EQUITIES-Intra Mkt Turnover× - (Market Makers) <TURNOVER02> Daily
UK EQUITIES-Intra Mkt Turnover× - (Other Principal) <TURNOVER03> Daily
OVERSEAS EQUITIES-Total Turnover×               <TURNOVER04> Daily
UK GILTS & COMPANY FXD INTEREST-Total Turnover  <TURNOVER05> Daily
CREST Daily Turnover                            <TURNOVER06> Daily
EQUITY TURNOVER-Week Ending (date)              <TOWEEK01>   Every Monday
UK GILTS-Customer Direct Turnover Week Ending (date) <TOWEEK02> Every Tue/Wed
UK GILTS-Customer Other  Turnover Week Ending (date) <TOWEEK02> Every Tue/Wed
UK GILTS-IDB            Turnover Week Ending (date) <TOWEEK03> Every Tue/Wed
UK GILTS-Other Principal Turnover Week Ending (date) <TOWEEK03> Every Tue/Wed
UK GILTS-Totals         Turnover Week Ending (date) <TOWEEK04> Every Tue/Wed
FIXED INT-Bdgs & Convs  Turnover Week Ending (date) <TOWEEK05> Every Tue/Wed
FIXED INT-Debs,C&C,Prefs Turnover Week Ending (date) <TOWEEK06> Every Tue/Wed
FIXED INT-UK&I,O/S Total Turnover Week Ending (date) <TOWEEK07> Every Tue/Wed

× PLEASE NOTE THESE TURNOVER FIGURES FROM 19 AUGUST 1996 DO NOT
  INCLUDE STOCKS SETTLED IN CREST.
```

```
MARKET TURNOVER STATISTICS  INDEX  <TURNOVER>                TURNOVER01
UK EQUITIES - CUSTOMER TURNOVER
DATE    BARGAINS VALUE (£M) SHARES (M)  DATE   BARGAINS VALUE (£M) SHARES (M)

27JAN98 55,818  2,573.2     692.2     02JAN98 16,411   427.6      147.8
26JAN98 50,752  2,236.7     732.2     31DEC97 N/A      N/A        N/A
-       -       -           -         30DEC97 27,459   776.3      286.8
23JAN98 57,208  3,081.9     856.4     29DEC97 24,767   918.7      380.8
22JAN98 44,601  2,532.6     720.1     -        -        -          -
21JAN98 51,131  2,341.3     756.8     24DEC97 15,912   1,664.4    359.7
20JAN98 57,605  2,239.5     702.6     23DEC97 32,491   1,441.3    451.8
19JAN98 58,012  2,647.8     1,000     22DEC97 36,642   2,302.2    678.0
-       -       -           -         -        -        -          -
16JAN98 56,774  2,570.6     768.5     19DEC97 34,788   1,785.3    640.5
15JAN98 48,994  2,502.3     725.3     18DEC97 36,837   2,530.9    727.3
14JAN98 42,932  2,147.7     627.8     17DEC97 41,049   2,623.5    709.1
13JAN98 54,216  2,387.5     708.7     16DEC97 44,217   2,396.9    691.7
12JAN98 45,804  2,208.7     715.6     15DEC97 42,057   1,761.8    522.0
-       -       -           -         -        -        -          -
09JAN98 51,773  2,315.4     684.0     12DEC97 32,609   1,603.1    481.7
08JAN98 49,582  2,090.5     641.8     11DEC97 40,056   2,931.5    823.4
07JAN98 48,417  1,699.0     507.3     10DEC97 40,127   2,673.0    732.3
06JAN98 49,764  1,712.8     523.7     09DEC97 45,905   2,971.6    868.7
05JAN97 43921   914.1       323.2
```

Normal Market Size (NMS)

On the LSE, transactions between member firms are known as **bargains**. The average number of daily bargains, in thousands, for the period 1986–1997 is shown in the chart below.

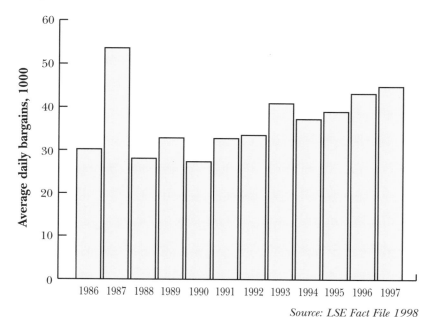

Source: LSE Fact File 1998

Although thousands of bargains are made daily on the LSE, are all the shares of equal standing? Up until 1991 the LSE used a SEAQ classification of shares based on the letters of the Greek alphabet. The most actively traded shares with the most market makers contributing bid and ask prices were designated **alpha** shares. The next most actively traded shares were **beta,** then **gamma** and finally **delta** shares which were the least traded and contributed to by market makers with bid and ask prices.

The Greek letter classification was replaced by an indicator of share liquidity called **Normal Market Size (NMS)**. The NMS for any share is calculated as follows:

1. The average daily customer turnover for a share, in the previous year, is multiplied by 2.5%. This figure gives an estimated average value of the normal LSE bargain.

2. The estimated average daily bargain value is then divided by the current share price to give a normal bargain size in terms of the number of shares.

3. The number of shares is then allocated to one of the 12 NMS bands according to the table below.

NMS Band	NMS Band Share Equivalent
500	0–667
1,000	668–1,333
2,000	1,334–2,400
3,000	2,401–3,750
5,000	3,751–6,667
10,000	6,668–12,000
15,000	12,001–18,000
25,000	18,001–33,000
50,000	33,001–60,000
75,000	60,001–93,000
100,000	93,001–160,000
200,000	more than 160,000

Example

XYZ plc shares' average daily turnover is found by dividing the annual turnover by the number of trading days in a year:

$$\frac{£2,500,000,000}{250} = £10,000,000$$

Value of the normal bargain = £10,000,000 × 2.5% = £250,000

XYZ plc shares are 450p, so the normal bargain in number of shares is

$$\frac{£250,000}{£4.50} = 55,556 \text{ shares}$$

The **Normal Market Size** is therefore **50,000** as the number of shares fits in the band 33,001–60,000.

All stocks with an NMS value greater than 2000 are liquid – all others are less liquid. All trades in liquid stocks, of which there are some 1000 listed, are subject to immediate publication on SEAQ screens if they are below three times NMS. Publication for larger trades is delayed for 90 minutes.

The following table may help to compare the old and new SEAQ share classifications.

Old	New
Alpha	FTSE 100
Beta	Liquid (excluding FTSE 100)
Gamma	Less liquid

Nasdaq

The **National Association of Securities Dealers Automated Quote (Nasdaq),** the world's first electronic stock market, was founded in 1971 and is now the second largest stock exchange in the US. (In October 1998, Nasdaq merged with the **American Stock Exchange**, the second largest floor-based exchange in the US, to form Nasdaq AMEX.) This stock market uses the Nasdaq computer system for automated screen-based trading in equities. The activities of this market are overseen and regulated by the self-regulatory organisation, the **National Association of Securities Dealers (NASD)**.

Nasdaq uses computers and telecommunications in place of a traditional trading floor. Some 535 dealers known as Market Makers, representing some of the world's largest securities firms, provide more than 60,000 competing bids to buy, and offers to sell, Nasdaq stocks through a vast computer network that displays the best of these quotations to investors in 52 countries.

Through the use of technology, Nasdaq has created one of the most efficient capital markets possible, able to handle trading volume in excess of one billion shares a day; comprehensive trading products and services via Nasdaq Workstation II^{TM} access to other markets operated by Nasdaq as well as a variety of technical support and training resources.

The Automated Confirmation Transaction (ACTS) service is an automated service that speeds the post-execution steps of price and volume reporting, comparison, and clearing of pre-negotiated trades completed in Nasdaq securities. As stated in NASD Rule 6120, ACT participation is mandatory for NASD member firms that meet at least one of the following criteria: member of a clearing corporation; clearing arrangement with a member of a clearing cooperation; or participant in any of Nasdaq's trading services.

ACT requires that market makers must enter trade details for all trade-reporting eligible and internalised transactions, within 90 seconds of execution, and must correct, decline, or cancel trades when necessary. ACT requires Order-Entry Firms to enter clearing eligible trade details within 20 minutes of a trade execution with a market maker; accept market maker trade entries within 20 minutes of the execution; decline incorrect Market Maker trade entries when necessary; and cancel trade entries when necessary.

ACT requires all trades other than those automatically processed by SOES, SelectNet, or Aces® Pass-Thru, to be input to Nasdaq electronically, for matching within 20 minutes of execution.

Nasdaq operates a quote-driven system where market makers enter bid/ask prices via computer terminals. The quotations are binding for a minimum size deal and are available simultaneously for all Nasdaq exchange members.

In 1992 Nasdaq introduced an international service designed to provide access to screen-based quotes across time zones. **Nasdaq International** allows brokers in London to trade in the US and the UK from the start of trading in London to the close of the US markets.

Securities that trade on Nasdaq International include:

- Equities listed on any US stock exchange
- Securities for US organisations listed on Nasdaq
- ADRs and foreign organisation equities listed on Nasdaq

Within the UK, Nasdaq is a Recognised Overseas Investment Exchange.

EASDAQ

The **European Association of Securities Dealers Automated Quote (EASDAQ)** is a stock market which has been created for the European equity markets and is based in Brussels. EASDAQ is a parallel organisation to Nasdaq and so organisations can be listed on both exchanges simultaneously.

EASDAQ allows investors to trade in the equities of foreign organisations without the disadvantages of cross-border share transactions on domestic markets.

Trading is quote-driven with a minimum of two (but typically five or six) market makers in each security. Trading is done by telephone with screen quotations managed and confirmed by TRAX, a global communications network which is operated by the **International Securities Market Association**. With one rule book and a single trading platform, EASDAQ is able to offer investors its members and its companies a single, transparent European stock market.

Settlement of EASDAQ transactions is carried out by Intersettle. A direct link between TRAX, the EASDAQ trading system, and Intersettle means there is no need for second input of trades by dealers' back office staff. The investors and their custodians can choose to hold securities in accounts with Intersettle, Euroclear or Cedel Bank, but the underlying security will be held within Intersettle. The settlement period for EASDAQ is normally T+3 (trade date plus three days).

Before moving on, look at Reuters ADRs as they appear on a Reuters screen.

RTRSY.0	REUTERS HLDGS	761324201	NMS USD			07JAN98 15:58
Last	Last 1	Last 2	St	Bid MMQ	Ask MMQ	Size
↓66¼	66¼	66¼	/ /	↓66¼	66\05	10x4
Net.Chng	Cls:06JAN98	Open	High	Low	Volume	Blk.Vol
-0\01	66\05	66⅛	66¾	66	132100	50000
P.E	Earnings	Yield	News		DJ.News	L.Blocks
22.87	2.90	2.21 %	:		:	3
Dividend	Div.Dat	Ex.Date	Yr.High	Yr.Low	Options	Headlines
1.46 12	23FEB98	18FEB98	75\12	56	A	RTR1

Below are examples of Reuters screens about Nasdaq.

```
US EQUITY STATISTICS - REUTERS SPEED GUIDE                    US/STATS1
Market statistics for US stock exchanges.

=EXCHANGE=====NET=======NET=======%=========%=======TOP 10====TOTAL=====MARKET=
              GAIN        LOSS      GAIN      LOSS    MOVES    VOLUME    DIGEST

American       <.NG.A>   <.NL.A>   <.PG.A>   <.PL.A>   <.AV.A>   <.TV.A>   <.AD.A>
AMEX Composite<.NG.AQ>  <.NL.AQ>  <.PG.AQ>  <.PL.AQ>  <.AV.AQ>  <.TV.AQ>  <.AD.AQ>
Boston         <.NG.B>   <.NL.B>   <.PG.B>   <.PL.B>   <.AV.B>   <.TV.B>   <.AD.B>
Chicago        <.NG.MW>  <.NL.MW>  <.PG.MW>  <.PL.MW>  <.AV.MW>  <.TV.MW>  <.AD.MW>
Cincinnati     <.NG.C>   <.NL.C>   <.PG.C>   <.PL.C>   <.AV.C>   <.TV.C>   <.AD.C>
Nasdaq         <.NG.O>   <.NL.O>   <.PG.O>   <.PL.O>   <.AV.O>   <.TV.O>   <.AD.O>
Nasdaq Int'l   <.NG.OI>  <.NL.OI>  <.PG.OI>  <.PL.OI>  <.AV.OI>  <.TV.OI>  <.AD.OI>
Nasdaq
Bulletin       <.NG.OB>  <.NL.OB>  <.PG.OB>  <.PL.OB>  <.AV.OB>  <.TV.OB>  <.AD.OB>
New York       <.NG.N>   <.NL.N>   <.PG.N>   <.PL.N>   <.AV.N>   <.TV.N>   <.AD.N>
NY Composite   <.NG.NQ>  <.NL.NQ>  <.PG.NQ>  <.PL.NQ>  <.AV.NQ>  <.TV.NQ>  <.AD.NQ>
Pacific        <.NG.P>   <.NL.P>   <.PG.P>   <.PL.P>   <.AV.P>   <.TV.P>   <.AD.P>
Philadelphia   <.NG.PH>  <.NL.PH>  <.PG.PH>  <.PL.PH>  <.AV.PH>  <.TV.PH>  <.AD.PH>
Third Mkts     <.NG.TH>  <.NL.TH>  <.PG.TH>  <.PL.TH>  <.AV.TH>  <.TV.TH>  <.AD.TH>
```

```
.AD.O            MARKET DIGEST            NAS/                      22:15


Issues Advanced           2564    Advancing Volume          545693050

Issues Declined           1819    Declining Volume          191866774

Issues Unchanged          1018    Unchanged Volume           47661429

Total Issues Traded       5401    Total Volume              785221253

New Highs                  113    New Lows                         79
```

Below are examples of Reuters screens about EASDAQ.

```
<BE/EXCH1>              EASDAQ INFORMATION PAGE                    EASDAQ

EASDAQ Security index                    <EAS01>
EASDAQ Information Page                   <EAS/INFO1>
EASDAQ Amendment pages                    <EAS/CHANGES01>-3
EASDAQ Constituents                       <O#.EASDAQ>
EASDAQ Company Announcements              [EAQ]
```

```
O#.EASDAQ            EASDAQ              LSE/                          :
Name           Last    Bid    Ask   Open   High   Low   His.Cl Volume  Time

ACTIVCARD              2.125  2.375                       2.25          15:38
ALGOL SPA              13100  13550                       13500         15:23
ARTWORK SYSTEMS        9.125  9.5                         9.125         15:23
CHEMUNEX S A           11     12                          12            15:35
CITY BIRD HLDGS        7.875  8.25                        8             15:30
DEBONAIR HLDGS         2.75   2.9                         2.9           15:11
EDAP TMS S.A.          6.25   6.75                        7             11:26
ESPACE PROD INTL       91.5   91.9                        91.9          08:36
ESAT TELECOM GRP       17.75  17.25                       18.25         09:23
ESPRIT TELECOM         11.75  12.25                       11.875        14:16
GRUPPO FORMULA         16800  17050                       17100         09:50
INNOGENETICS    ↓31.75 31.75  32.125 32.125 32.125 31.75  32.5  12080   08:33
LERNOUT & HAUSP        57.875 58.75                       57            15:50
MELEXIS N.V            0.5625 10.75                       10.5          15:49
MERCER INTL            8      8.375                       8.125         15:11
NTL INCORPORATED       31.75  32.25                       31.5          14:24
OPTION INTL NV  ↑18.875 18    18.875 18.875 18.875 18.875 18.75  500    08:32
PIXTECH INC            3.625  3.875                       4             10:22
INT SURGICAL SYS       9      9.9                         8.7           09:54
SCHOELLER-BLECK        1315   1355                        1355          14:50
DR SOLOMONS ADS        34.5   35.5                        35.625        10:04
TOPCALL INTL AG        6230   6375                        6350          09:56
TURBODYNE TECH  ↑2.85  2.8    3.05   2.85   2.85   2.85   2.8   900     08:31
```

Instinet

Instinet is an agency broker that provides trading services to fund managers, brokers and market makers located throughout Europe, Asia and the Americas. Instinet has been a subsidiary of Reuters since 1987 and the company's objective is to provide clients with best execution by combining advanced trading technology with traditional brokerage services.

Clients benefit from using Instinet's electronic trading services by reducing their total trading costs. Instinet gives clients the ability to:

- Execute trades in over 30 markets around the world

- Negotiate and trade without revealing their identity, strategy or location

- Maintain direct control of all aspects of trading

- Discuss trading strategies with Instinet's transaction desks around the clock

Instinet's trading services are supported by accurate and efficient clearing and settlement in all markets. Instinet is a member of many of the world's major stock exchanges and has offices in New York, Toronto, London, Frankfurt, Paris, Zurich, Hong Kong and Tokyo.

Other services provided by Instinet include electronically delivered research and analysis and independent services paid for through commission.

Typical Instinet screens displayed during trading.

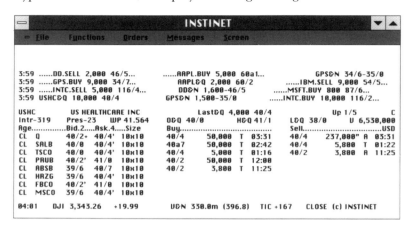

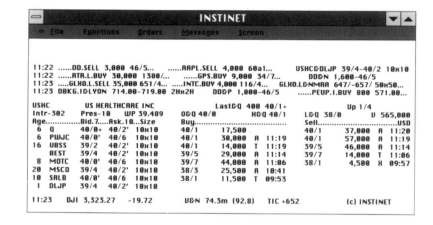

REUTERS

Publication Rules

The Investment Services Directive (ISD), which came into effect on January 2, 1996, requires the UK to have the same publication regime for UK and non-UK securities. All trades in European liquid securities up to and including a size of six times NMS are subject to immediate publication. Intermarket trades or other riskless principal trades are subject to immediate publication; this also applies to illiquid European securities. Trades greater than six times NMS and above are subject to a delay in publication of up to 60 minutes. Block trades of 75 times NMS and above will be published after five business days, when 90% is unwound, or when the firm is prepared to allow the exchange to release the trade for publication.

Broking – Placing An Order

Within most major equity markets the financial intermediaries responsible for buying and selling shares on behalf of investors are brokers. Depending on the type of transaction involved and the nature of the investor there are a number of types of broker who have slightly different roles and offer different services to their clients. In general brokers are one of the following types:

- Broker dealers

- Client or Agency brokers

- InterDealer brokers

The roles of each of these types is explained in more detail in the last section of this book. In the US and UK, staff qualified to deal with investors are also known as **registered representatives**. For the descriptions that follow, the term broker will be used rather than having to distinguish a specific type.

Brokers offer investors three basic types of broking services which are as follows:

- **Dealing or execution only**. In this case the broker simply carries out the client's instructions to buy or sell and arranges for settlement of the trade. In the US these brokers are also known as **discount brokers**.

- **Advisory**. The broker offers advice on the purchase and/or sale of shares in the investor's **portfolio** – the investor's holding of shares.

- **Discretionary**. This is a management service of buying and selling shares on behalf of the client, completely at the discretion of the broker.

Obviously the more complicated the services provided by the broker the greater the fee to the investor.

How Do the Equity Markets Work?

The process of buying/selling shares using brokers is quite straight forward and is illustrated in the chart below:

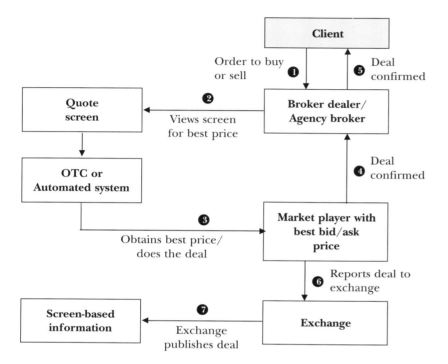

Placing an Order

An investor must supply the broker with the following information to place an order:

- Name of equity
- Nature of the order – buy or sell
- Order size – round amounts, for example, 100 or job lots
- Type of order

The information above needs little explanation except for the type of order involved.

Types of Orders

There are a number of different types of orders an investor can specify which vary in their complexity. There may be some variations in descriptions between countries and exchanges but the following cover most types of orders used worldwide:

- **'At best'** or **market order**
  This is simply an order to be executed immediately at the best possible price – no price limit is specified.

- **Limit order**
  This specifies the size, price and expiry time/date of order. The order can be executed in full or in part, immediately or it can be held 'on the books' until it can be executed, expires or is deleted at the request of the client.

- **Fill or Kill**
  This type of order is either executed or deleted immediately but it may include a limit price.

- **Execute and eliminate**
  This is a similar type of order to 'at best' but specifies a price limit. The order can be executed in full or part at a price no worse than that specified.

- **Stop-loss order**
  This protects a position by specifying a selling price **below** the current share price. If the share price of the shares falls, then they are sold automatically at, or as near as is possible, to the stop-loss order price.

- **Stop-limit order**
  This type combines a stop-loss order with a limit order. Once the stop price has been reached or passed, the limit order is created at the limit price.

- **Short-sell order**
  This type of order is used by investors who wish to sell shares that they do not actually own. This means that the shares will have to be borrowed, for which a charge is made. Investors use short-sell orders when they believe the share price is about to fall, which means that the shares can be bought back cheaper at a later date. The profit is the difference between the selling and buying prices less the interest charges.

- **Day order**
  This is good for one trading day only.

- **Open order**
  This is valid for a specific period of time, for example, one month, after which the order is either renewed or cancelled.

Security Identification

Every security traded has an identification or registration number, or code, which may be nationally or internationally issued.

Some of the more important national, local codes are indicated in the table below.

Country	National local code
US	CUSIP
UK	SEDOL
Switzerland	Valoren
Singapore	Singpaore Code
Germany	Wertpapierkennnummer
France	Sicovan

Internationally, the **International Security Identification Number (ISIN) Code** as devised by the International Standards Organisation (ISO) is used and is intended to replace other systems such as SEDOL and Valoren. The system is alpha numeric and follows these rules:

- Position 1–2: This is the two-character ISO alpha country code. For example, GB is used for the UK.

- Position 3–11: This is a nine digit code which contains the official country exchange code for the equity. The code is right justified and any leading space is filled with zeros.

- Position 12: This is a check digit.

Example: Royal Dutch, Netherlands

ISO country code	= NL
Amsterdam SE code	= 00945
Check digit	= 4
ISIN Code	= **NL0000009454**

Trading Settlement

For market makers and brokers, once a transaction or bargain has been confirmed the settlement process transfers ownership of the securities from the seller to the buyer and arranges for the corresponding payment of funds to the seller.

Methods of settlement vary from exchange to exchange. For example, on both the NYSE and Nasdaq, settlement takes place within three days of the trade date – T+3.

Some exchanges such as the LSE use a **rolling settlement** system under which settlement takes place a number of days after purchase – currently this is T+5.

Payment between brokers and their clients is arranged directly by the broker who also organises for the investor to receive a share certificate from the registrar of the organisation issuing the equity. Typically shares are computer print outs and are not very exciting to look at.

In order to reduce the need for handling share certificates the stock exchange introduced a computerised settlement system – **TAURUS – Transfer and Automated Registration of Uncertified Stock**. The system was designed to act as a clearing house by making book-entry changes in the ownership of shares and issuing confirmation notes to buyers and sellers. However, TAURUS was not a complete system as company registrars still needed to maintain their registers and issue share certificates. TAURUS was abandoned in 1993, but a new system, **CREST**, is now operational which uses **nominee accounts**. These are accounts recording shareholders' beneficial interests in shares legally owned by **nominee companies** set up by brokers. This system avoids the need for brokers to send share certificates and is the first step in 'paperless' settlement. This system is predominent in the UK and electronic settlement settlement systems around the world vary. With electronic settlement, shareholders retain the right not to use the system and to hold share certificates, but it may be expensive to do so.

Share Number 1 for £1 in The Eastern News Agency Ltd founded by Reuters in 1910

A share certificate for 50 shares in Reuter's Telegram Company issued in 1905

An example of a typical modern share certificate

Cash and Margin Accounts

Investors can settle their accounts in one of two basic ways:

- **Cash Account**
  This is the straight forward way – cash is paid as required for the purchase of securities.

- **Margin Account**
  This method uses a similar system to that when trading derivatives. In other words, the whole amount of the transaction is not paid in a lump sum. Instead investors have positions with an **initial margin** requirement which is set by the exchange or regulatory authority. Investors settle their margin accounts on a daily basis either in cash or using other securities as collateral using a system of **variation margin**. Margin trading can result in highly **leveraged** positions but the risks associated with such positions must be assessed carefully – losses as well as profits can be high!

Stock Market Indices

Most exchanges classify shares on their liquidity – how easy they are to buy and sell. In general, the larger the organisation the more investors trade and the greater the number of dealer brokers that are prepared to quote. Organisations in this category are sometimes known as **blue-chip** – the name coming from the highest value chip in poker. The table below shows the LSE 1997 data for some of the organisations in the top 20 blue-chip companies in the UK.

Company	Trading value (£m)	Shares traded (m)
HSBC	48,267.4	2,888.1
British Telecommunications	39,977.4	9,228.9
Shell Transport and Trading	25,879.0	4,242.8
British Petroleum	25,247.0	3,033.2
Glaxo Wellcome	24,313.1	1,961.6
Lloyds TSB	20,788.2	3,344.6
SmithKline Beecham	19,761.5	2,269.5
Barclays plc	19,462.1	1,555.8
B.A.T. Industries	14,764.4	2,700.2
Reuters	12,586.0	1,743.4
Imperial Chemical Industries	12,505.7	1,351.2
Unilever	12,076.8	1,087.4

Source: LSE Fact File 1998

But how can investors assess the performance of stock markets overall? The movement and therefore the performance of stock markets is charted by indices such as the Financial Times Stock Exchange 100 Index (FTSE 100) – "Footsie" (UK), the Nikkei 225 (Japan) and the Dow Jones Industrial Average Index (US).

How Do the Equity Markets Work?

The First Stock Index

Charles Henry Dow

The modern **Dow Jones Industrial Average (DJIA)** is the result of the first stock index to be devised. The origins of modern **technical analysis** or **charting** can be traced back to the work and theories of Charles Henry Dow (1851–1902). By studying the closing prices of shares, Dow concluded it was possible to produce a marker 'barometer' or stock index which could be used by investors to measure the overall performance of the stock market.

The first index calculated in 1884 was the average of 11 stocks. This index was called the Rail Road Index because nine of the stocks were rail road companies. By 1896 Dow had introduced the **Industrial Average** which was the simple arithmetic average price of 12 stocks. In 1928 the number of stocks used for the index had increased to 30 at which it remains today. The DJIA is updated and broadcast by the NYSE every thirty minutes of the trading day.

You can use a system such as Reuters to display the constituent shares of the DJIA and their current prices as shown below.

```
O#.DJI     DJ INDUSTRIAL    LT↓7915.47 +100.39    H7919.21    L7815.08              23:38
Up 19          Down 10           Unchanged 1

AA.N    72⅛   +2\03 EK.N   65\15     +2 JPM.N  101\07 -0\14 S.N    46⅞     +0¼
ALD.N   39\05  +2\08 GE.N   76¼          KO.N   64\03     +1 T.N    62\01  -1\06
AXP.N   82\15  -0\09 GM.N   59\07  +2\01 MCD.N  47⅝   +0\05 TRV.N  49\13  +0\07
BA.N    47\01  +2\06 GT.N   62         -0\03 MMM.N  84½  +3\15 UK.N   43\09  +1\09
CAT.N   48⅛   +1\13 HWP.N  63\05  -0\01 MO.N   ×41\05 -0\14 UTX.N  81\05  +2\06
CHV.N   75\13  -0\13 IBM.N  ×97        +0½ MRK.N  117⅞  +3\03 WMT.N  40⅝   +1\05
DD.N    ×57¾   +1⅝ IP.N   47½    +1\13 PG.N   79¼      -1¾ XON.N  59\03  -1\03
DIS.N   105⅛   +2\03 JNJ.N  66⅛   -0\09
```

If you need to know more about technical analysis, refer to *An Introduction to Technical Analysis*.

Calculating Stock Indices

A **stock market index** is a measure of return that would accrue to the holder of a particular set of equities. It is a numerical representation of the way the set of equities has performed relative to a base reference value for a start date in the past.

Stock market indices require the following characteristics if they are to be used successfully. Stock market indices should be:

- **Comprehensive** and include equities that are realistically available to market players under normal market conditions

- **Stable** such that the equities comprising the basket of prices should not change too often – when changes do take place investors should understand the reason for them

- **Reproducible** in that the market information about the composition of an index can be used by market players to reproduce the same index value

There are two basic ways in which these indices are compiled – both are based on the share prices of a **basket** of representative or chosen organisations. The baskets may represent an entire market – **broad-based** – or a market sector – **narrow-based**. The prices of the basket of equities comprising a given index are combined into a single number, usually by adding them together – **arithmetic index** – or multiplying them together – **geometric index**. The single number for an index then changes in value as the share prices of its components change, giving a convenient indicator for a given market or market sector.

REUTERS

In the case of arithmetic indices, the prices are added and an average value is calculated by dividing by the total number of stocks in the basket. The process is normally modified by weighting each organisation's share price by the number of shares in issue so that the organisations with larger market capital have a greater influence over the index movement. Thus, weighted indices are also known as market-weighted indices. The Dow Jones Industrial Average Index is an example of an unweighted arithmetic index and the FTSE 100 Index and Standard & Poor's 500 are weighted arithmetic indices.

Geometric indices are calculated by multiplying the prices together and then taking the nth root where n is the number of stocks in the basket. Geometric indices are unweighted and therefore need to be modified to take into account scrip and rights issues, for example. The FT 30 Share Index and Value Line Index in the US are examples of geometric indices.

If an arithmetic and geometric index were calculated for identical stocks having the same initial value, then the geometric index will rise more slowly and fall faster than the arithmetic index for the same price movements in the underlying stocks. These differences result from the way the indices are calculated and the following example illustrates this:

Example
Assume you have three stocks, all of which have the same share capitalisations and all with the price of 100 – this removes any weighting considerations. One stock now falls to 90 while the other two rise to 110. What are the arithmetic and geometric indices for the original stocks and after the changes?

Index	Original	After changes
Arithmetic	$\dfrac{100+100+00}{3} = 100$	$\dfrac{90+110+110}{3} = 103.33$
Geometric	$\sqrt[3]{100\times100\times100} = 100$	$\sqrt[3]{90\times110\times110} = 102.88$

Arithmetic indices are a better indication of the increase or decrease in the cash value of the underlying stocks. Most funds and their performance are rated against weighted indices.

Below are sample screens taken from Reuters, on which you can see the weightings and index movers pages.

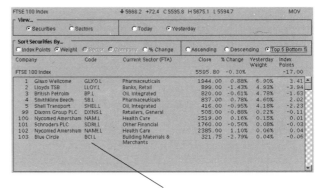

The FTSE 100 actually comprises 103 stocks in the index – stocks 101 to 103 are reserves

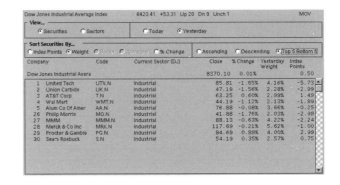

The weighted figure on the Reuters 3000 screens is calculated as follows:

$$\text{Price-weighted weight} = \frac{\text{Price of stock}}{\text{Total stock value}}$$

$$\text{Market-weighted weight} = \frac{\text{Price of stock} \times \text{No. of shares of stock}}{\text{Total stock value}}$$

You will therefore need to be careful when considering the term weight! **Market** or **capitalisation weighted** indices as they are also known are more common than unweighted indices.

Once the type of weighting for an index has been selected there is a choice as to the method of calculating the average or mean value – **arithmetic** or **geometric**.

For arithmetic averages the following equation can be used for the simplest form of index:

$$\text{Index} = \frac{V_1 + V_2 + V_3 + \dots + V_n}{n}$$

V_n = Share price for nth share weighted as required

n = Number of shares in index

For a geometric index in its simplest form the average is calculated from the nth root of the product of n values using this equation:

$$\text{Index} = \sqrt[n]{V_1 + V_2 + V_3 + \dots + V_n}$$

V_n = Share price for nth share weighted as required

n = Number of shares in index

Unless all values of V_1 to V_n are equal then the geometric index value is always smaller than that for the arithmetic index for the same share prices. It is much more common for the markets to use arithmetic indices although both methods of calculation are still used. For example, the FT 30 Share Index is a geometric average whereas the FTSE Actuaries Share Indices such as the FTSE 100 Index are arithmetic averages or means.

Most stock market indices are based on the price of the shares that comprise the index and ignore any dividend payments. However, some stock market indices such as the DAX 30 are **total return indices**. These indices are calculated gross of withholding tax and assume that dividends are received on the xd date which are then reinvested immediately.

Index Movers

What is the importance if the share price for a constituent organisation moves up or down? The impact on an index can be calculated simply using the following equation where the Index divisor is the base period market capitalisation:

$$\text{Impact on index} = \frac{\text{Shares issued} \times \text{Change in share price}}{\text{Index divisor}}$$

So for an index such as the FTSE 100 if all the constituent share prices change, then there are a 100 calculations to perform and the total change in index points is the sum of index point moves up and down. One method of simplifying this process is to use a chain linked index. In this case the index for the current period is related to the previous level as follows:

$$\text{Current index} = \text{Previous index} \times \text{Chaining factor}$$

The chaining factor is the ratio of the current market capitalisation of the index to the previous period's market capitalisation value. The advantage of chain linking is that calculations are carried out without having to return to the base period Index divisor. The Swiss Market Index (SMI) is an example of a chain linked index.

Worldwide Stock Market Indices

This table summarises details of some of the more important stock market indices used worldwide*.

Index	Composition	Weighting	Mean calculation	Initial value	Apr 1999 value	Derivatives
DJIA	30 blue-chip stocks on the NYSE	Price	Arithmetic	240	10,727.18	Futures – CBOT
TOPIX	Selection of stocks on the TSE	Market	Arithmetic	100	1,335.47	Futures – TSE
Value Line	1700 US stocks on the NYSE and AMEX	Price	Geometric	100	447.41	Futures – KCBT Options – PHLX
Hang Seng	30 stocks on the Hong Kong Stock Exchange	Market	Chain linked Arithmetic	100	12,933.54	Futures – HKFE
CAC 40	40 stocks	Market	Arithmetic	1000	4,291.85	Futures – MATIF Options – MONEP
DAX 30	30 selected blue-chip stocks	Market	Total return Arithmetic	1000	5,218.82	Futures – DTB Options – DTB
Major Market	20 Blue-chip industrial stocks on NYSE	Price	Arithmetic	226	1,150.66	Futures – CME Options – AMEX
Nikkei 225	225 stocks on the TSE	Price	Arithmetic	176	16,665.88	Futures – SIMEX, CME & Osaka Options – CME
S&P 500	500 stocks in 4 groups on the NYSE	Market	Arithmetic	10	1,358.83	Futures – CME Options – CME & CBOE
FTSE 100	100 stocks on the LSE	Market	Arithmetic	100	6,413.6	Futures – LIFFE Options – LIFFE

* Refer to the stock exchanges directly for more information about the calculation and composition of the indices. See the list of stock exchanges at the end of this book.

Investors

Stock market indices are widely used by investors to follow market trends and to assess the performance of fund managers. Stock market indices are also used as benchmarks against which individual fund performance is judged – has the fund out or underperformed its benchmark?

Although there are relatively few stock market indices which are used as benchmarks for the major equity markets, there are many indices which have been devised worldwide for specific market sectors, new markets, emerging markets etc. For example, you can use Reuters screens to find out about all the different FT and Dow Jones indices available as shown below.

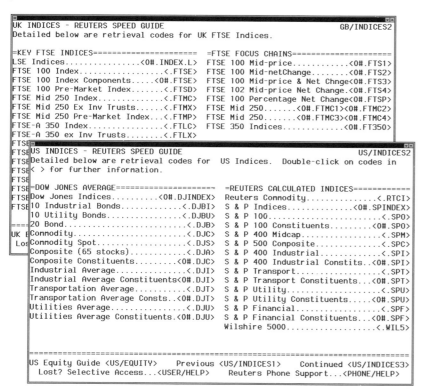

Depending on the type of investments being managed, fund managers and investors will base their activities on the following:

- The performance of their portfolio against a particular benchmark stock market index

- Their ability to **pick** stocks which are considered good investments and which will outperform the market

- Time their investment decisions on the market trends they perceive in stock market indices and the stocks in their portfolio

Fund managers and institutional managers will also use stock market indices to help determine their broad **asset allocation** decisions. In general investors have a choice of markets in which they can invest other than the equity markets. For example funds can be invested in the following:

- Money market cash instruments such as certificates of deposit

- Debt market instruments such as bonds

- Property

- Commodities such as gold

- Derivatives such as futures and options on a wide range of underlying instruments from all markets

On an institutional basis certain asset classes may not be available to fund managers. For example, a fund may not be allowed to trade in commodities or derivatives. Once such boundaries have been set the asset allocation policy is decided which determines the mix of assets, their geographical location and market sector split, which will maximise returns for the fund's investors.

There are two basic types of asset allocation policies commonly adopted which are:

1. **Top down policy**

   This determines the geographic or sector allocation of funds based on an evaluation of macro-economics. For example, decisions are made on hedging currency exposure of foreign investments and on the global allocation of investments in bonds, equities and cash instruments.

2. **Bottom up policy**

   This is based more on micro-economics. In other words the policy is based on identifying attractive investment opportunities based on the geographic or sector allocation. The emphasis is more on **stock picking** and an asset allocation which shows the greatest growth.

Below are Reuters screens illustrating news on mutual funds.

Stock Market Indices

- A **Stock market index** is a measure of return that would accrue to the holder of a particular set of equities

- An **unweighted** or **price-weighted** index in effect places **equal weightings** to the shares comprising the index

- **Market-weighted** indices take into account the influence of the organisations of which they are comprised using market capitalisation as the basis for the weighting

- There are two basic methods of calculating the average or mean value of an index – **arithmetic** or **geometric**

- A **total return index** takes into account dividend payments on the stocks comprising the index and their reinvestment

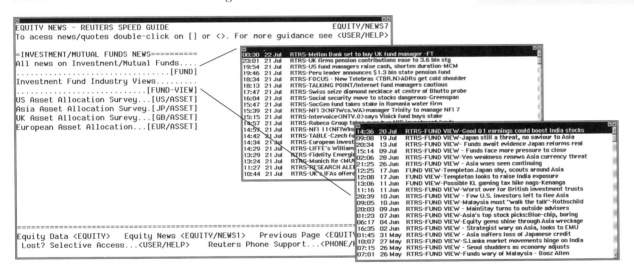

The following Reuters screens may help your understanding of stock market indices and how they are used. These pages display **Mid Price Net Change** which is the difference between the calculated Mid Close and current calculated Mid Price incorporating all trades to the LSE on and off the Order Book. **Net Change** is the difference between the previous day official Close and the last automatically executed Order Book trade.

.DJI ↑7902.27 -3.98 GBP=X 1.6225 GBPDEM=X 2.9687 10:59
209/ 209/ REUTER
.FTS1 FTSE 100 ↑ 5283.1 +59.0 at 10:59 H5296.4 L5222.9
Up 80 Down 18 Unchanged 2 SEAQ Vol 275.0m at 10:58

ABF	561½	BS	138½	GUS	782½×	ORA	253¼	SFW	352¼
AL	842½	BSCT	582½	HAS	846½	PO	713	SHEL	425¾×
ALLD	540	BSY	449½×	HFX	784½	PRU	804	SLP	498
ANL	1146	BT	502	HSBA	1468	PSON	807	SMIN	856½
ASSD	189½	BTR	186¼	ICI	988½	PWG	815½	SPW	540½
AVZ	523	CBRY	646	III	530	RBOS	815	STAN	631½
BA	1801	CCM	473½	KGF	876	RCOL	989½	SVT	1012
BAA	494½	CNA	92½×	LADB	285¾×	REED	624	TEG	687
BARC	1721	CUAC	908½	LAND	1004½	RIO	741½	TOMK	317½
BASS	921×	CW	517	LGEN	585×	RNK	344¾	TSCO	517¾
BATS	591	DGE	578×	LLOY	798½	RR	237¼×	TW	901½
BAY	594×	DXNS	586½	LSMR	265½	RSA	651	ULVR	521
BCI	333½	EMI	521¾	LVA	214¼	RTK	969	UNWS	739
BG	302½	ETP	568	MKS	603×	RTO	293×	UU	852½
BGY	420½	GAA	969	NAM	2212	RTR	688	VOD	446¾
BLND	689	GACC	1190	NGG	319	SB	657½	WLMS	343
BLT	153¾	GARD	369¾×	NPR	629½×	SBRY	506½	WLY	518
BOC	987	GEC	397¾×	NU	412	SCTN	749	WTB	904½
BOOT	923	GKN	1316	NWB	1072×	SDR	1993	WWH	337¾
BP	799×	GLXO	1554	NXT	720	SEBE	1192	ZEN	2236

Mid Price on FTSE 100 stocks

Number of stocks Up/Down/Unchanged on the day

Dow Jones Index value + direction tick

FTSE 100 Index + tick – up or down

Bid Spot prices – every 10 mins

Highest/Lowest values on the day

.DJI ↑7902.27 -3.98 GBP=X 1.6235 GBPDEM=X 2.9676 11:02
LSE/ 209/ REUTER
.FTS2 FTSE 100 ↑ 5280.8 +56.7 at 11:02H 5296.4 L5222.9
Up 78 Down 18 Unchanged 4 SEAQ Vol 278.7m at 11:01

ABF	+2	BS	+4¾	GUS	+8½×	ORA	+0¾	SFW	+6½×
AL	+12½	BSCT	+2½	HAS	+15	PO	+13½	SHEL	+6×
ALLD	+3	BSY	-0½×	HFX	+9	PRU	+4	SLP	+12
ANL	+36	BT	+12¼	HSBA	-28	PSON	-4	SMIN	0
ASSD	+3¼	BTR	+1¼	ICI	+8½	PWG	+10	SPW	+9½
AVZ	+10	CBRY	+13½	III	+4½	RBOS	-7½	STAN	-1½
BA	+32	CCM	+11	KGF	+9½	RCOL	+4	SVT	+15
BAA	-1	CNA	+1¼×	LADB	+4¾	REED	+7½	TEG	0
BARC	+15	CUAC	+7½	LAND	+6½	RIO	-6½	TOMK	+5
BASS	-16½	CW	-19	LGEN	+9½×	RNK	0	TSCO	+4¼
BATS	+5½	DGE	+5×	LLOY	+3	RR	+2½×	TW	+6
BAY	-10½×	DXNS	+11	LSMR	+0¾	RSA	-0½	ULVR	-1
BCI	-4¼	EMI	+8¼	LVA	+5	RTK	+22½	UNWS	+19½
BG	+11	ETP	-5	MKS	-0½×	RTO	+9×	UU	+20
BGY	+1	GAA	+1	NAM	-4	RTR	+7½	VOD	+3¾
BLND	+12	GACC	+29	NGG	+5¾	SB	+17	WLMS	+2½
BLT	-4½	GARD	+7	NPR	+11×	SBRY	+1	WLY	+19
BOC	+7½	GEC	+2¼×	NU	+6¾	SCTN	+2	WTB	+7
BOOT	+16	GKN	+3	NWB	+14½×	SDR	+14	WWH	-0½
BP	+20½×	GLXO	+22	NXT	+14½	SEBE	0	ZEN	+11

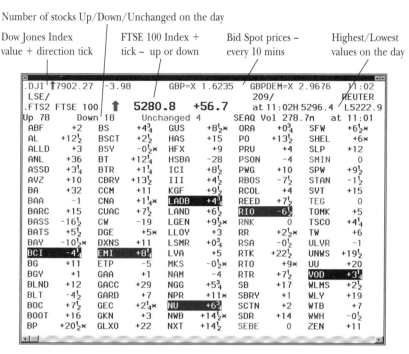

Mid Price Net Change on FTSE 100 stocks

.DJI ↑7902.27 -3.98 GBP=X 1.6235 GBPDEM=X 2.9676 11:05
LSE/ 209/ REUTER
.FTS3 FTSE 100 ↓ 5279.7 +55.6 at 11:05H 5296.4 L5222.9
Up 79 Down 19 Unchanged 2 SEAQ Vol 283.1m at 11:05

ABF	561½	+2	BS	138¼	+4½	GUS	782½	+8½×	ORA	253	+0½	SFW	352¼	+6½×
AL	841½	+12½	BSCT	582½	+2½	HAS	846½	+15	PO	713	+13½	SHEL	425¾	+6×
ALLD	539½	+2½	BSY	449½	-0½×	HFX	784½	+9	PRU	804	+4	SLP	498	+12
ANL	1146	+36	BT	502	+12¼	HSBA	1463	-26	PSON	807	-4	SMIN	857½	+2
ASSD	188¾	+3¼	BTR	186¼	+1¼	ICI	988	+8½	PWG	815½	+10	SPW	540	+9½
AVZ	522	+10	CBRY	646	+13½	III	528½	+3	RBOS	815½	-7½	STAN	630½	-1½
BA	1801	+32	CCM	473¾	+11¼	KGF	875½	+9	RCOL	986½	+3	SVT	1012	+15
BAA	493	-2½	CNA	92½	+1¼×	LADB	286¼	+4¾	REED	624	+7½	TEG	686½	0
BARC	1719	+13	CUAC	908	+7½	LAND	1004½	+6½	RIO	737	-6½	TOMK	317½	+5
BASS	921	-16½	CW	517	-19	LGEN	585	+9½×	RNK	344¾	0	TSCO	517¾	+4¼
BATS	590½	+5½	DGE	577	+4½×	LLOY	799	+3½	RR	237¼	+2½×	TW	901	+5
BAY	594	-10½×	DXNS	587	+11½	LSMR	265½	+0¾	RSA	651	-0½	ULVR	520½	-1½
BCI	332¾	-5½	EMI	517½	+6¼	LVA	213¾	+4½	RTK	969	+22½	UNWS	739	+19½
BG	302½	+11	ETP	568	-5	MKS	603	-0½×	RTO	292¾	+9×	UU	853	+20
BGY	420½	+1	GAA	969	+1	NAM	2212	-4	RTR	688	+7½	VOD	447¼	+3¼×
BLND	689	+12	GACC	1190	+29	NGG	318¼	+5¾	SB	657	+17	WLMS	343	+2½
BLT	153¾	-4½	GARD	369¾	+7	NPR	628½	+11½×	SBRY	506½	+1	WLY	518	+19
BOC	987	+7½	GEC	398	+2¼×	NU	411	+6	SCTN	749	+2	WTB	904½	+7
BOOT	922½	+15½	GKN	1316	+3	NWB	1072	+14½×	SDR	1987	+8	WWH	337½	-0½
BP	799	+20½×	GLXO	1554	+22	NXT	720½	+14½	SEBE	1191	-1	ZEN	2236	+12

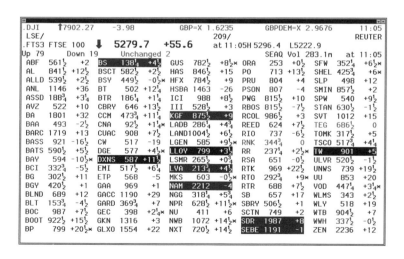

Mid Price and Mid Price Net Change

```
O#.FTS4   FTSE INDEX      209/    LT↑ 5278.3   +54.2   ×H5296.4   L5222.9  11:11
LSE/                Up 78        Down 21             Unchanged 1
ABF.L    +2½    BS.L      +4    HAS.L   +16   ORA.L    +1   SFW.L   +6½×
AL.L    +13½    BSCT.L   +5½    HFX.L    +6   PO.L    +16   SHEL.L  +6½×
ALLD.L   +3½    BSY.L   -0¾×    HSBA.L  -28   PRU.L   +2½   SLP.L    +22
ANL.L    +19    BT.L    +11½    HSBAx.L -25   PSON.L  +14   SMIN.L  +10½
ASSD.L    +3    BTR.L    +0¾    ICI.L    +8   PWG.L   +11   SPW.L   +10½
AVZ.L   +10¾    CBRY.L  +13½    III.L   +7½   RBOS.L   -8   STAN.L   -1½
BA.L     +37    CCM.L    +12    KGF.L   +10½  RCOL.L  +5½   SVT.L    +16
BAA.L     -3    CNA.L   +1½×    LADB.L  +5¾   REED.L  +10   TEG.L     +2
BARC.L   +15    CUAC.L    +9    LAND.L   +7   RIO.L    0×   TOMK.L   +4½
BASS.L  -13½    CW.L     -18    LGEN.L +10½×  RNK.L   +0¾   TSCO.L   +4¾
BATS.L   +5½    DGE.L   +3½×    LLOY.L  +5½   RR.L   +2¼×   TW.L     +8½
BAY.L   -11×    DXNS.L   +13    LSMR.L  +0½   RSA.L    -1   ULVR.L   +0¼
BCI.L    -5¼    EMI.L     +9    LVA.L   +5½   RTK.L   +23   UNWS.L   +16
BG.L    +11¼    ETP.L     -3    MKS.L   +1½   RTO.L  +7½×   UU.L     +19
BGY.L    +0½    GAA.L     +1    NAM.L    -6   RTR.L   +7½   VOD.L   +2½×
BLND.L   +13    GACC.L   +29    NAMt.L  -85   SB.L    +17   WLMS.L    +6
BLNDe.L          GARD.L   +8    NGG.L   +4¾   SBRY.L   +2   WLY.L  +17¼
BLT.L     -4    GEC.L   +3½×    NPR.L  +9½×   SCTN.L   +3   WTB.L    +5½
BOC.L   +19½    GKN.L    +11    NU.L    +7¾   SDR.L    +3   WWH.L    +0¼
BOOT.L  +12½    GLXO.L   +21    NWB.L   +16×  SDRt.L  +93   ZEN.L    +17
BP.L     +20    GUS.L   +10½    NXT.L   +16   SEBE.L    0
```

Net Change on FTSE 100 stocks

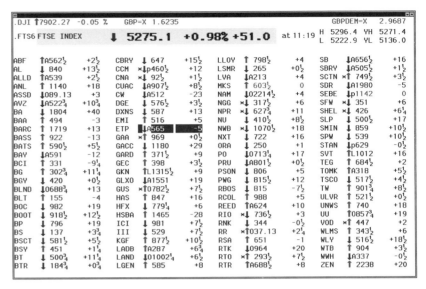

Last Trade Net Change on FTSE 100 stocks

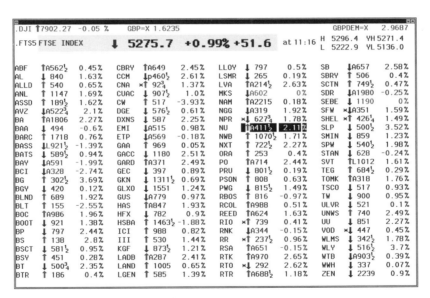

Last Trade and % Net Change on FTSE 100 stocks

These pages show information on weightings and futures, and an historical chart of the DJIA performance with respect to the S&P 500.

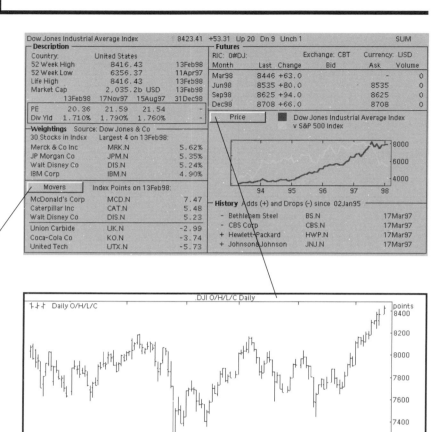

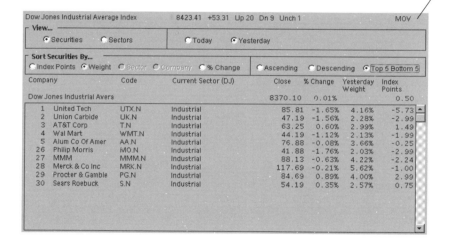

These screens display prices for organisations in a particular FTSE sector – the **Utilities Industry Sector** – where you can see specific information about **Water**:

```
O#.FTWA       WATER              LT            20:18  GBp IND      H
LSE                                            CL 3221.42 16FEB98  L
RIC     Stock Name     Last    NC    RIC    Stock Name      Last     NC
AW.L    ANGLIAN WATER  ↑ 845   +1    BTW.L  BRISTOL WATER HD↓p1435   +10
ESH.L   EAST SURREY HLDG↓p319  -1    HYR.L  HYDER PLC       ↓T960    -0½
MKH.L   MID KENT HLDGS     0         SVT.L  SEVERN TRENT WTR↓ 944    -4
SSW.L   STH.STAFFS WATER↑p3370  0    SWW.L  SOUTH WEST WATER↓↓894    -12½
TW.L    THAMES WATER   ↑A876   +16   UU.L   UNITED UTILITIES↑A825    -5
WXW.L   WESSEX WATER   ↓ 472    0    YW.L   YORKSHIRE WATER ↑ 484    -6
```

```
UK SHARE INDICES AND SECTORS   MAIN INDEX <UKEQ>                  FTAX

FTSE SHARE INDICES        <FTAY>
UK Equities Speed Guide   <GB/EQUITY>

SECTOR DISPLAYS                    ALTERNATIVE DISPLAYS FOR SECTOR INDICES
---------------                    -------------------------------------
FT-SE INDICES & SEAQ SECTORS       FTSE 350 INDEX    FT ALL SHARE INDEX
---------------------------        --------------    ------------------
Mineral Extraction    <FTAZ>        <FTBC>             <FTBF>
General Industrials   <FTAZ>        <FTBC>             <FTBF>
Consumer Goods        <FTBA>        <FTBD>             <FTBG>
Services              <FTBA>        <FTBD>             <FTBG>
Utilities             <FTBB>        <FTBE>             <FTBH>
Financials            <FTBB>        <FTBE>             <FTBH>
Investment Trusts     <FTBB>        <FTBE>             <FTBH>

OTHER INDICES
-------------
SEAQ International Sectors   <FTBI>
```

```
UK SHARE INDICES AND SECTORS       Next <FTBC> Prev <FTBA>            FTBB
INDUSTRY SECTOR        FTSE 350 INDEX     ALL SHARE INDEX    SEAQ SECTOR
CLASSIFICATION         RIC    CHAIN       RIC    CHAIN       CHAINS
--------------         ---------------    ---------------    -----------
UTILITIES                             <.FTUT>
Electricity            <.LCEY> <O#.LCEY>  <.FTEY> <O#.FTEY>  <O#.SSEYM>
Gas Distribution       <.LCGD> <O#.LCGD>  <.FTGD> <O#.FTGD>  <O#.SSGDM>
Telecommunications     <.LCTN> <O#.LCTN>  <.FTTN> <O#.FTTN>  <O#.SSTNM>
Water                  <.LCWA> <O#.LCWA>  <.FTWA> <O#.FTWA>  <O#.SSWAM>

FINANCIALS                            <.FTFN>
Banks Retail           <.LCBK> <O#.LCBK>  <.FTBK> <O#.FTBK>  <O#.SSBKM>
Insurance              <.LCIC> <O#.LCIC>  <.FTIC> <O#.FTIC>  <O#.SSICM>
Life Assurance         <.LCIL> <O#.LCIL>  <.FTIL> <O#.FTIL>  <O#.SSILM>
Other Financial        <.LCOF> <O#.LCOF>  <.FTOF> <O#.FTOF>  <O#.SSOFM>
Property               <.LCPY> <O#.LCPY>  <.FTPY> <O#.FTPY>  <O#.SSPYM>

INVESTMENT TRUST       <.LCTU> <O#.LCTU>  <.FTTU> <O#.FTTU>  <O#.SSTUM>
Offshore Inv Funds                                           <O#.SSSIM>
```

```
           UK  SECTOR   MID  PRICE   TRENDS  –  WATER
RIC        Stock Name      Mid.Cls  Mid4    Mid3    Mid2    Mid1    Mid
AW.L       ANGLIAN WATER   841      843½    844     843½    843½    843½
BHD.L      BROCKHAMPTON HLD 190                                     190
BHDa.L     BROCKHAMPTON A  104                              103     104
BTW.L      BRISTOL WATER HD 1452½                   1455    1452½   1462½
BTWt.L     BRIST.WTR HD NV 1137½                    1150    1142½   1137½
CWC.L      CAMBRIDGE WTR   307½                      310     307½
CWCt.L     CAMBRIDGE WTR NV 235                      237½    235
DVW.L      DEE VALLEY GROUP 472½                             472½
DVWt.L     DEE VALLEY N/V  430                               430
ESH.L      EAST SURREY HLDG 322½            322     322½    321½
ESHp.L     EAST SURRY CNV  124¼     124¼    124¼    124¼    124½    124¼
HWC.L      N/A
HYR.L      HYDER PLC       967½     968     967½    967     967½    967
MKH.L      MID KENT HLDGS  687½                     695     690     687½
SSW.L      STH.STAFFS WATER 3345                                    3345
SVT.L      SEVERN TRENT WTR 917      946    945     945     945     941
SVTb.L     SEVERN TRENT 'B' 34                                      34
SWW.L      SOUTH WEST WATER 909      899    898½    898     897½    896½
TW.L       THAMES WATER    865      875½    875     875½    874     875½
UU.L       UNITED UTILITIES 825     815     823½    815     822½    823
WXW.L      WESSEX WATER    473½     475     476     475     474½    473½
YKW.L      ×YORK WATERWORKS 320                             320     322½
YKWa.L     ×YORK WTRWKS 'A' 290                             290     292½
YW.L       YORKSHIRE WATER 487½     484½    484     483½    482     481½
YWb.L      YORKSHIRE WATR B 36½                                     36½
```

The FTSE 100 Index was launched in January 1984 with a value of 1000. The index grew steadily until October 1987 when the index stood at 2366. After the stock market crash the index dropped to 1579.9 by November 1987.

How much percentage value had been lost from the value of shares on the stock market as a result of the crash?

You can check your answer on the next page.

You can review the current values of indices around the world on systems such as Reuters. Below is an example.

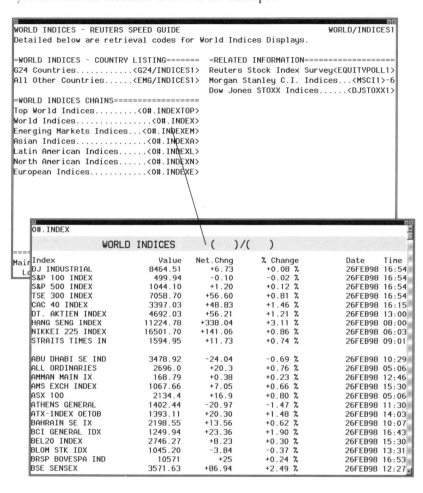

Review the summary pages for the FTSE 100, the DJIA and the Nikkei 225 Index on the Reuters screens below. These pages display information on weightings, stock movers, prices for futures contracts and historical price charts.

FTSE 100 Index — 5411.1 +38.5 C 5372.6 H 5411.2 L 5364.3 — SUM

Description

Country:	United Kingdom	
52 Week High	5415.30	28Jan98
52 Week Low	4197.20	29Jan97
Life High	5415.30	28Jan98
Market Cap	958.88b GBP	28Jan98

	28Jan98	29Oct97	29Jul97	31Dec98
PE	20.01	18.23	18.45	16.94
Div Yld	3.020%	3.350%	3.340%	2.860%

Futures — RIC: 0#FFI: Exchange: LIF Currency: GBP

Month	Last	Change	Bid	Ask	Volume
Mar98	5426.0	+23.0	5426.0	5428.0	2,993
Jun98	-	-	-	-	0
Sep98	-	-	-	-	0

Price ■ FTSE 100 Index v FTSE All Share Index

Weightings Source: FTSE Intl
103 Stocks in Index   Largest 4 on 28Jan98:

Glaxo Wellcome	GLXO.L	6.04%
British Petrolm	BP.L	4.75%
Lloyds TSB	LLOY.L	4.74%
Smithkline Beech	SB.L	4.47%

Movers   Index Points on 28Jan98:

HSBC	HSBAx.L	9.89
Barclays PLC	BARC.L	6.34
HSBC	HSBA.L	5.04
British Telecom	BT.L	-1.44
Reuters	RTR.L	-1.52
Marks & Spencer	MKS.L	-3.12

History Adds (+) and Drops (-) since 19Sep94

+ Blue Circle	BCI.L	24Dec97
- Mercury Asset	MAM.L	24Dec97
+ Amvescap	AVZ.L	22Dec97
- Blue Circle	BCI.L	22Dec97

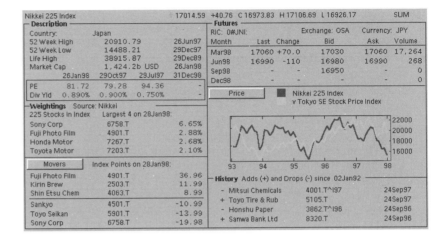

Nikkei 225 Index — 17014.59 +40.76 C 16973.83 H 17106.69 L 16926.17 — SUM

Description

Country:	Japan	
52 Week High	20910.79	26Jun97
52 Week Low	14488.21	29Dec97
Life High	38915.87	29Dec89
Market Cap	1,424.2b USD	26Jan98

	26Jan98	29Oct97	29Jul97	31Dec98
PE	81.72	79.28	94.36	-
Div Yld	0.890%	0.900%	0.750%	-

Futures — RIC: 0#JNI: Exchange: OSA Currency: JPY

Month	Last	Change	Bid	Ask	Volume
Mar98	17060	+70.0	17030	17060	17,264
Jun98	16990	-110	16980	16990	268
Sep98	-	-	16950	-	0
Dec98	-	-	-	-	0

Price ■ Nikkei 225 Index v Tokyo SE Stock Price Index

Weightings Source: Nikkei
225 Stocks in Index   Largest 4 on 28Jan98:

Sony Corp	6758.T	6.65%
Fuji Photo Film	4901.T	2.88%
Honda Motor	7267.T	2.68%
Toyota Motor	7203.T	2.10%

Movers   Index Points on 28Jan98:

Fuji Photo Film	4901.T	36.96
Kirin Brew	2503.T	11.99
Shin Etsu Chem	4063.T	8.99
Sankyo	4501.T	-10.99
Toyo Seikan	5901.T	-13.99
Sony Corp	6758.T	-19.98

History Adds (+) and Drops (-) since 02Jan92

- Mitsui Chemicals	4001.T^I97	24Sep97
+ Toyo Tire & Rub	5105.T	24Sep97
- Honshu Paper	3862.T^I96	24Sep96
+ Sanwa Bank Ltd	8320.T	24Sep96

Dow Jones Industrial Average Index — 7915.47 +100.39 Up 19 Dn 10 Unch 1 — SUM

Description

Country:	United States	
52 Week High	8299.49	07Aug97
52 Week Low	6356.37	14Apr97
Life High	8299.49	07Aug97
Market Cap	1,929.3b USD	27Jan98

	27Jan98	29Oct97	29Jul97	31Dec98
PE	19.70	21.06	23.01	-
Div Yld	1.810%	1.840%	1.660%	-

Futures — RIC: 0#DJ: Exchange: CBT Currency: USD

Month	Last	Change	Bid	Ask	Volume
Mar98	7942.00	93			0
Jun98	8018.00	94			0
Sep98	8094.00	95			0
Dec98	8172.00	96			0

Price ■ Dow Jones Industrial Average Index v S&P 500 Index

Weightings Source: Dow Jones & Co
30 Stocks in Index   Largest 4 on 28Jan98:

Merck & Co Inc	MRK.N	5.84%
Walt Disney Co	DIS.N	5.25%
JP Morgan Co	JPM.N	5.22%
IBM Corp	IBM.N	4.92%

Movers   Index Points on 28Jan98:

MMM	MMM.N	15.69
Merck & Co Inc	MRK.N	12.70
AlliedSignal Inc	ALD.N	9.96
Exxon Corp	XON.N	-4.73
AT&T Corp	T.N	-5.48
Procter & Gamble	PG.N	-6.98

History Adds (+) and Drops (-) since 02Jan95

- Bethlehem Steel	BS.N	17Mar97
- CBS Corp	CBS.N	17Mar97
+ Hewlett-Packard	HWP.N	17Mar97
+ Johnson&Johnson	JNJ.N	17Mar97

How much % value had been lost from the value of shares as a result of the crash?

The answer is about 33%.

After the crash the November shares were worth

$$\frac{1579.9}{2366.0} \times 100 = 66.77\%$$

of their October value.

Therefore the shares had lost $100 - 66.77 = 33.23\%$ of their value.

Summary

You have now finished the second section of the book and you should have a clear understanding of the following:

- How equity is issued in the primary markets

- Trading in the secondary markets

- The importance of stock indices

As a check on your understanding, try the Quick Quiz Questions on the next page. You may also find the Overview section to be a helpful learning tool.

Your notes

Quick Quiz Questions

1. On the LSE which market players replaced jobbers after Big Bang?
   - ☐ a) Broker dealers
   - ☐ b) Agency brokers
   - ☐ c) Market makers
   - ☐ d) Specialists

2. If a stock market is described as bullish, which way are share prices moving?
   - ☐ a) Up
   - ☐ b) Down

3. What is the best combination of highest bid/lowest ask prices called in the UK market?
   - ☐ a) Touch
   - ☐ b) Bargain
   - ☐ c) Yellow strip
   - ☐ d) Alpha

4. What is the most common way for private companies to raise capital through a new share issue on the LSE?
   - ☐ a) An introduction
   - ☐ b) Placing
   - ☐ c) Intermediaries offer
   - ☐ d) Offer for sale

5. Which of the following statements best describes an order-driven system?
   - ☐ a) Trades are filled as and when bid/offer prices can be matched
   - ☐ b) There are market makers willing to make two-way prices
   - ☐ c) Dealers quote prices and deal with each other using electronic trading systems
   - ☐ d) Market makers are required by an exchange to quote two-way prices in normal market size

6. Which combination of the following methods of constructing stock indices is most commonly used?
   - ☐ a) Arithmetic
   - ☐ b) Geometric
   - ☐ c) Unweighted
   - ☐ d) Weighted

You can check your answers on page 73.

Overview

Stock Exchanges

- **Exchange Floor and OTC Trading**
- **Quote-Driven Trading Systems**
  - Market makers
  - SEAQ on the LSE
  - Nasdaq
- **Order-Driven Trading Systems**
  - Auctions
  - SETS on the LSE
  - NYSE
  - Paris bourse

How Do the Equity Markets Work?

Primary Markets

- **Exchange Listing Requirements**
  - Primary and secondary issues
- **Initial Public Offerings (IPOs)**

- **Second-Tier Markets**
  - AIM on LSE
  - Nasdaq
- **Grey Markets**

Going Public

- **Flotation**
  - Offer for sale
  - Offer for subscription
  - Placing
  - Intermediaries offer
  - Introduction

- **Planning**
  - Sponsor
  - Broker dealer
  - Reporting accountant
  - Solicitor
  - PR consultant

- **Process**
  - Prospectus
  - Placing/Underwriting agreement
  - Roadshow
  - Post impact

Secondary Markets

- **London Stock Exchange**
  - Quote-driven and order-driven systems
- **New York Stock Exchange**
  - Order-driven system
  - Specialists
  - Commission brokers
  - Floor brokers
  - Registered traders
- **Tokyo Stock Exchange**
  - Order-driven system
  - Saitori
  - FORES

Investor — Broker dealers or Agency brokers

Quote-driven SEAQ system

Order-driven SETS system

Best **Bid** price = highest price **Buy** order on book
Best **Ask** price = lowest priced **Sell** order on book

Broking – Placing an Order

- **Types of broker**
  - Broker dealers
  - Client or Agency brokers
  - InterDealer Brokers (IDBs)
- **Types of service**
  - Dealing or execution only
  - Advisory
  - Discretionary
- **Types of order**
  - At best or market order
  - Limit
  - Fill or Kill
  - Execute and eliminate

Client
Order to buy or sell ❶
Deal confirmed ❺

Quote screen
Views screen for best price ❷
Broker dealer/ Agency broker

OTC or Automated system
Deal confirmed ❹

Obtains best price/ does the deal ❸
Market player with best bid/ask price

Reports deal to exchange ❻

Screen-based information
Exchange publishes deal ❼
Exchange

Stock Market Indices

- **Arithmetic**
- **Geometric**
- **Weighted**
- **Unweighted**

- **FTSE 100**
- **Value Line**
- **S&P 500**
- **Nikkei 225**

Quick Quiz Answers

	✓ or ✗
1. c)	☐
2. a)	☐
3. a)	☐
4. b)	☐
5. a)	☐
6. a) and d)	☐

How well did you score? You should have scored at least 5. If you didn't, review the material again.

Further Resources

Books

The Times Guide to International Finance
Margaret Allan, Times Books, 1991
ISBN   0 7230 0408 0

Investments
William F. Sharpe, Gordon J. Alexander & Jeffrey V. Bailey, Prentice Hall International, 5th Edition 1995
ISBN   0 13 18 3344 8

Getting Started in Stocks
Alvin D. Hall, John Wiley & Sons, Inc., 3rd Edition 1997
ISBN   0 471 17753 9

The Stock Market
Richard J. Teweles/Edward S. Bradley, John Wiley & Sons, Inc., 7th Edition 1998
ISBN   0 471 19134 5

Publications

London Stock Exchange
- How to Buy and Sell Shares
- A Glossary of Stock Market Terms
- A Guide to Going Public: On the Official List

Price Waterhouse
- The Going Public Handbook

Further Resources (continued)

Your notes

Internet

RFT Web Site
*   **http://www.wiley.rft.reuters.com**
This is the series' companion web site where additional quiz questions, updated screens and other information may be found.

ISMA Centre – The Business School for Financial Markets
*   **http://www.ISMAcentre.reading.ac.uk**

Value Line
*   **http://www.valueline.com**

Exchanges

Refer to the back of this book for a listing of worldwide stock exchange contact information and web sites.

This section of the book should take about two to three hours of study time. You may not take as long as this or you may take a little longer – remember your learning is individual to you.

A stag

A speculator who applies for a new share issue on the chance of selling the allotment at a profit when share dealings officially begin – in other words making a fast buck!

The term comes from the trading which used to take place on the pavement in Stag Lane, near the original Stock Exchange in London.

Introduction

You now recognise that the main instruments of the equity markets are shares, although there are a variety of different types of these you should know and understand.

This book does not attempt to cover every type of equity instrument available in detail, rather, the instrument types are classified to provide you with a broad overview of the instruments and their advantages and disadvantages to issuers and investors. In this section, expect to cover:

- The difference between ordinary and preference shares

- The reasons why rights and bonus shares are issued

- Some of the equity-linked securities that are available, including depository receipts, convertible bonds and bonds with warrants

- The derivatives used in the equity markets – futures, swaps and options

If you need to know more about derivatives in general, refer to the *Introduction to Derivatives* book in this series (ISBN 0-471-83176X).

Before moving on try the activity opposite.

How many different types of equity instruments do you know something about already? Write down a list here.

Equity Market Instruments

The following diagram places the instruments used in the equity markets into a simple classification based on the following:

- Shares and share issues

- Equity-linked securities

- Derivatives

Some equity-linked securities such as convertible bonds and bonds with warrants are also termed **hybrid** instruments, as they combine elements of both the debt and equity markets.

In addition, some derivatives are not based directly on an underlying equity instrument, rather, are based on stock indices, and are **cash settled**, since a stock index cannot be delivered.

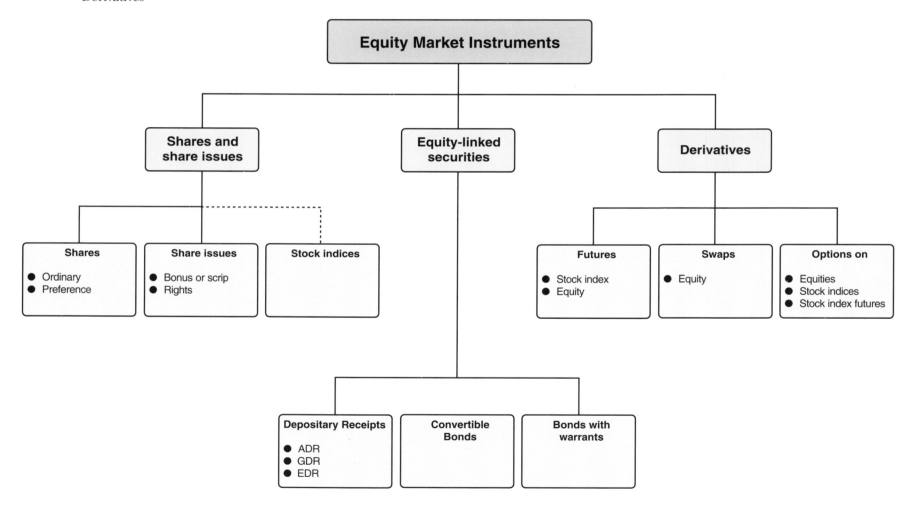

Shares and Share Issues

The following brief description of shares and share issues focuses on the process used in the UK equity market. The process in most other worldwide equity markets is similar with only minor differences in detail and terminology.

Most organisations are established on a **limited liability** basis which means that investors are only liable to the par or face value of the shares they own. If an organisation has not made a share issue to the public it is either a partnership or a **private company** with private shareholders. In the latter case the company name ends with **Ltd** or **Limited**. Once the organisation reaches a certain size and meets stock exchange criteria it can apply to become a **public company** with its name ending in **Plc***. This gives the organisation the right, but not obligation, to issue shares to the public. All organisations registered at the LSE must be of Plc status. As such they have to provide an **interim report** half way through the financial year together with an **annual report** at the year end. Before these reports are published, organisations usually produce preliminary announcements on how well, or not, they have performed.

Before moving on, review organisations who have released their interim or final reports. To the right are sample Reuters screens showing this data.

*Note: This terminology can vary not only around the world but even among other Commonwealth countries. For example, in Australia, a company with Ltd after its name is a public company; private companies are denoted by Pty Ltd.

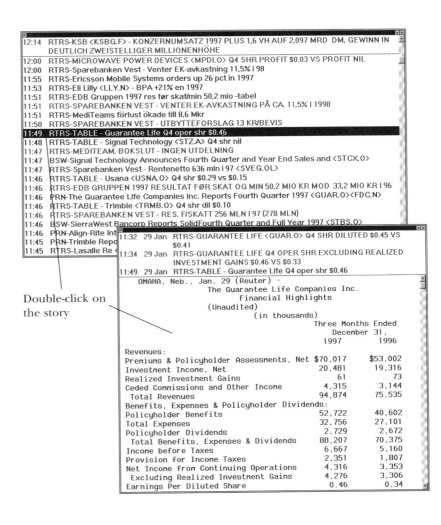

Double-click on the story

Ordinary and Preference Shares

The amount of equity share capital that can be issued by a public company is defined and divided into shares. Most shares are **registered** – the company's registrar keeps a register of shareholders details so that dividends can be paid. **Bearer** shares are rare now but these confer ownership on the person possessing the share certificate.

There are two basic types of shares that may be issued:

- Ordinary

- Preference

 An **Ordinary share** represents ownership in the net assets of a limited liability organisation and it gives the shareholder a claim or dividend on any profits generated by the organisation.

Example
As of 31.12.97 XYZ plc has a share capital of £100 million which consists of 100 million ordinary shares issued and fully paid of 100 pence each par value. The par value of shares is fixed at the time of issue.

The **market value** of an ordinary share fluctuates according to market conditions and is the price which investors are prepared to pay. There is no relationship between par and market values except that at issue, the issue price must equal or be greater than the par value.

It is important to remember the following when considering ordinary shares as an investment:

- There is no obligation on the part of an organisation to repurchase shares – in effect the investor makes a perpetual loan to the organisation

- The shareholder's liability is limited to the amount of money invested in equity

- Typically shareholders appoint directors to manage the organisation on their behalf

Issuers

Ordinary shares may be issued **fully** or **partially paid-up**. In the latter case the organisation does not need all the capital at once and therefore the price of the shares is paid in instalments with the dates and amount of future payments specified in the organisation's launch prospectus. These payments are a liability **not** an option. Partially paid-up share issues are quite common in privatisation issue as they are seen as attractive investments – the market price may be higher than the future installment price.

In some cases, for example, where a private company wants to raise capital without losing management control, **non-voting, A or B shares** are issued. These shares carry the same risks and rewards as ordinary shares but with no (or limited) voting rights. Non-voting issues are usually offered at a lower price than ordinary shares to take into account these reduced rights. Non-voting shares are not popular investments with the larger institutional investors – the lack of voting rights is seen as a disadvantage, particularly in the event of an organisational take-over.

Although ordinary shares represent the ownership of an organisation, some markets do not recognise the value of this ownership in the same way as in the US or UK. For example, in the Japanese market most organisations finance their activities through the debt market rather than by issuing equity. This means that dividends paid to Japanese shareholders are very low as the organisations do not feel that they have to keep investors happy.

A Preference or preferred share entitles the holder to a prior claim on any dividend paid by the organisation over ordinary shares, or to the organisation's assets in the event of liquidation.

The differences in share prices between ordinary and non-voting shares are illustrated in the prices in the quotes shown in the screens here.

Ordinary shares

```
YNGa.L      YOUNG BREWS A      000000988203 GBp NMS500      /   /      03FEB98 11:57
Last        Bid        Ask        Mid0        Mid Close   Volume     Sector
↓630        630        655        642½        642½                   OW.SSBR
 655        Open       High       Low         News        Headlines
            642½       642½       642½          :         ××××
            LT:02FEB98 Yr.High    Yr.Low       52WeekHigh  52WeekLow
            642½       702½       615
Div:10DEC97 Yield      Ex.Date    P.E          Earnings    Background
15.20       2.957 %    24NOV97    22.19        28.96       YNGa.LB1
Exchange
LSE/
```

Non-voting shares

```
YNGt.L      YOUNG & CO BREWS 000000988225 GBp NMS500      /   /      27JAN98 15:15
Last        Bid        Ask        Mid0        Mid Close   Volume     Sector
            540        565        552½        552½                   OW.SSBR
            Open       High       Low         News        Headlines
            552½       552½       552½          :         ××××
            LT:02FEB98 Yr.High    Yr.Low       52WeekHigh  52WeekLow
            552½       602½       520
Div:10DEC97 Yield      Ex.Date    P.E          Earnings    Background
15.20       3.439 %    24NOV97    20.93        26.40
Exchange
LSE/
```

Below is a Reuters screen that provides an illustration of codes indicating the various types of shares.

```
UK EQUITIES RETRIEVAL CODES - REUTERS SPEED GUIDE                    GB/CHAR1
Detailed below are retrieval codes for Equities information.

=UK EXCHANGES=========================    =BROKERAGE CHARACTERS ctd=============
London Stock Exchange          = .L       Zero Preference.......................o
London Traded Options          = ×.L      Convertible Preference................p
                                          Preference Shares.....................p
=TIME & SALES=========================     Partly Paid..........................pp
Time & Sales Flags...........<LSETAS01>   Partly Paid Convertible Preference..ppp
                                          Partly Paid ADR.....................ppy
=BROKERAGE CHARACTERS=================     SEAQ International.....................q
Class A...............................a   Ranking for Dividend..................r
Class B...............................b   Stepped Preference....................s
Class C...............................c   Non-Voting Share......................t
Class D ..............................d   Warrants............................._t
New Issues............................e   Traded in US Dollars..................u
Accumulation Stock....................f   Units................................_u
Fully Paid............................g   Bearer Share..........................w
Income Share..........................i   Different Nominal Value...............x
Restricted Transfer...................l   American Depository Receipts (ADRs)...y
Nil Paid..............................n
When issued...........................w   Finding conpany share prices.<DIR/USER>
=====================================================================
Main Guide <REUTERS>      Equities Guide <EQUITY>      UK Equity Guide <GB/EQUITY>
   Lost? Selective Access...<USER/HELP>        Reuters Phone Support..<PHONE/HELP>
```

Preference shares are another way in which equity can be issued but this type of issue is not as common as for ordinary shares. Although these shares are repaid before ordinary shares they usually have no voting rights except in what affects their class of shares. Because of their status these shares are usually sold at a **premium**, that is, at a price higher than stocks of a similar value. It is normal for preference shares to specify a fixed rate of dividend as a percentage of the share's par value, or rather, its offering price.

An ordinary share with a par value of 4 shillings

A 7.5% preference share in the same issue with a par value of £1

The chart below shows the nominal value of ordinary and preferred shares for domestic and foreign listed organisations on the LSE as of June 1997. As you can see, the majority of equity issued is for ordinary shares.

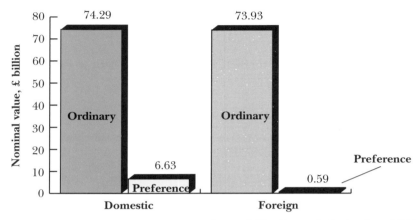

Source: LSE – Quarterly Review June 1997

Issuers

There are a variety of preference shares but the five main types are as follows:

Cumulative
This is the most common type. As the name implies, holders of these shares receive dividends which can be carried forward to a future time for payment if the dividend cannot be met in any particular year.

Non-cumulative
In this case any dividend arrears are **not** carried forward. If the issuing organisation can pay the dividend in full or in part then it will do so. If there are no profits then there is no dividend!

Redeemable
These usually have a fixed repayment date, similar to debt instruments, and redemption may be at par or at a premium.

Participating

This is not a common type of preference share. In effect it offers the possibility of higher dividends than the specified rate. Should the level of profits exceed a certain level specified in the conditions for the preference share, then the shareholder receives a greater dividend.

Convertible

This hybrid instrument is becoming increasingly more popular as it carries the right to switch to ordinary shares at specified dates and specified terms. They are profitable if the ordinary shares do well.

Most preference shares are non-participating, cumulative and irredeemable. As such these shares have similarities with both bonds – debt instruments – and shares – equity instruments.

Preference shares are similar to bonds in that:

- They pay a fixed annual dividend expressed as a percentage of the share's par value which does not vary with the profits made by the organisation.

- Holders receive their dividend before ordinary shareholders which means the income from preference shares is more reliable than for ordinary shares.

Preference shares are similar to ordinary shares in that:

- Failure to pay the dividend does not mean the organisation will face bankruptcy since most preference shares are cumulative.

- If the organisation does go into liquidation, then preference shareholders are usually entitled to be repaid only the par value of their holding, if anything.

It is important to remember the following when considering preference shares as an investment.

- A preference or preferred share entitles the holder to a **prior claim** on any dividend paid by an organisation over ordinary shares

- Preference shares may or may not have voting rights and usually specify a **fixed rate** of dividend as a **percentage** of the share's par value

- Preference shares may be a combination of any of the following:
  Cumulative/non-cumulative
  Redeemable/irredeemable
  Participating/non-participating
  Convertible

  Most preference shares are non-participating, cumulative and irredeemable

- Preference shares have similarities with both bonds and ordinary shares

Both ordinary and preferred shares are described in detail on the next page. You may encounter variations of these basic types which usually modify, to a greater or lesser extent, the voting rights of the shareholder.

Ordinary and Preference Shares

Ordinary Shares (UK) Common Stock (US)	Voting Rights	Dividends
These are irredeemable stocks that give the shareholders a part of the profit generated by an organisation. They are issued at **par** or **nominal value** although this value is of little practical significance, that is, not related to market value. If an organisation offers nominal shares at a higher price than par then the price difference is known as the **share premium**.	Most ordinary shares confer voting rights on shareholders. In theory the shareholders own the organisation and can vote at the annual general meeting. They also have the right to elect directors. The most common structure allows for one vote per share.	If the organisation makes sufficient profits a dividend may be paid. The size of the payment is discretionary and is determined by the board of directors. The dividend is usually in the form of cash but sometimes it is paid as extra shares. Ordinary shares represent the riskiest form of security of an organisation, as shareholders are the **last** to receive any profit from dividends. Interest on debts and preference share dividends is paid before dividends for ordinary shares.
Preference Shares (UK) Preferred Stock (US)	Voting Rights	Dividends
These rank above ordinary shares for certain specified rights in respect of their dividends and have priority in the event of the organisation's liquidation.	Preference shares may or may not have voting rights – it depends on the organisation issuing the shares.	Shareholders usually receive a fixed rate dividend expressed as a percentage of the nominal value of the share. This dividend is paid before that for any ordinary shares – hence the name. There are a number of different types of preference shares but most are cumulative. This means that if an organisation is not able to pay dividends in one year, then cumulative preference shareholders are entitled to all previous unpaid dividends when the organisation can afford to pay.

Bonus and Rights Issues

There are a number of types of ordinary shares which can be issued at the initial flotation – when the shares are offered to the public for the first time – or at some later date.

> A **Bonus issue.** In this case new shares are issued free to existing shareholders in a proportion to their existing holding. The new shares can be of a variety of types, for example, ordinary or preference shares. The share price will normally adjust to take account of the extra shares issued.

A **bonus** or **scrip** issue is a type of ordinary share which is issued as a device to bring an organisation's capital in line with the size of its business. No new capital is raised as the organisation simply recapitalises itself by transferring balance sheet reserves to share capital.

The number of shares issued to a shareholder increases but the overall holding of the shareholder's funds does not change. Therefore the price of each share must fall at the time of issue.

In some markets such as Japan and Spain, bonus issues are seen as evidence of how well an organisation is performing. Individual investors in these countries see these issues as a return on their investment – they erroneously believe that bonus shares increase the value of their investment.

In the US, a bonus issue is called a **stock dividend** or **stock split**. Both terms are probably a better description of the process involved.

Issuers

The issue is usually described in terms of the number of new shares received for every old share held, for example, 'two-for-one', 'three-for-four'. The conventions in the UK and US differ and it is important that you know the difference. If the issue is described as '**x**-for-**y**', then

- **In the UK**: x = Number of new shares received
  y = Number of original shares held

- **In the US**: x = Total number of shares held **after** the issue, that is, the original shares held plus the new shares
  y = Number of original shares held

In the UK, the new shares are just added to the previous holding whereas the convention used in the US effectively destroys the old shares and re-issues the shareholder with new shares. The following table may help to clarify the situation.

UK convention	US convention	Shares held orig.	Shares received	Total shares held after issue
One-for-one	Two-for-one	One	One	Two
Three-for-one	Four-for-one	One	Three	Four
One-for-three	Four-for-three	Three	One	Four
Two-for-three	Five-for-three	Three	Two	Five

What Instruments Are Used in the Equity Markets?

A **scrip issue** is simply an accounting transaction whereby an organisation capitalises part, or all, of its reserves – its assets in excess of its issued share capital – and issues these as shares to its current shareholders. The shareholders are not required to put up any extra investment which is why a scrip issue is also known as a **bonus issue**. If shareholders receive new or **'bonus'** shares for every old share held then their shareholding has increased. The term 'bonus' is rather misleading as the asset value and earnings of the organisation are just the same as before. Consider the following example of a UK company proposing a one-for-two scrip issue. This means the company will recapitalise* from its reserves on the basis of one new share for every two held. The company's assets remain the same as is shown in the table below:

	Before the scrip issue £	After the 1-fpr-2 scrip issue £
Issued ordinary capital	1,000,000	1,500,000
Reserves	1,000,000	500,000
Total assets	**2,000,000**	**2,000,000**

For a UK one-for-one scrip issue, the earnings per share are **half** their previous value. If the payout ratio is maintained then the dividend per share will also be half its previous value and the shareholders' income will not change. The shares will be expected to halve in price to reflect the fact that the organisation's value is the same as before. The capital value of the shareholding is therefore unchanged.

The same logic for determining share prices for a three-for-one, two-for-three etc issue would apply. The chief benefit of a bonus or scrip issue is that more shares are available at a more marketable price – two £5 shares are more liquid than one £10 share. For shares quoted on the London Stock Exchange there is a price differential between the old and new share prices. New shares are dealt for cash settlement and a lower rate of commission is frequently payable.

These factors make them slightly more attractive so the new shares are quoted at a slightly higher price. At a future, designated date the issues are merged.

It was a common misconception, when individuals formed the majority of shareholders, that scrip issues were a bonus and that shareholders were being given something by the organisation. The reason for this argument was that the dividend was often increased – for some one-for-one splits the dividend share was maintained thus doubling the shareholder's income. The same doubling of income could have been achieved by doubling the payout ratio and not splitting the shares.

So why does an organisation issue bonus or scrip shares? In effect the ordinary shares become more marketable as accumulated reserves are transferred to paid-up capital. As an organisation grows so too does its total assets which is reflected in its reserves – its capital is fixed. If this situation continues and the reserves become very large, then unless the organisation recapitalises* then its earnings per share and dividends will seem very large. A scrip issue is a way of balancing the organisation's capital with its reserves.

Stock Splits

An organisation may also issue "bonus" shares as a **stock split**. It is important to recognise that a stock split is **not** a recapitalisation of the organisation but a way of **reducing** the par value of its shares. After a stock split, shareholders own more shares than they held previously but their investment stake has not increased in value. For example, if a $2 par value stock is split two-for-one in the US, the holder of 100 old shares will receive 200 new $1 par value shares. With a stock split all, the old shares are destroyed and new ones issued. The main reason for a stock split is to make the price of an organisation's shares more desirable to investors.

Note: In some markets, for example – Australia – recapitalisation refers to the injection of additional capital into an ailing organisation.

REUTERS

But what makes a share more attractive or marketable to an investor?

This varies considerably between markets. In the UK, share prices are commonly less than 1000p (£10) and individual daily share price movements of over 60p are unusual. In the US, a stock is unlikely to be less than $20 and individual daily stock price moves of $1–2 are not uncommon. However, in some markets such as Japan and Switzerland, a **single share** in an organisation such as Nippon Telephone & Telegraph and Roche can be worth thousands of pounds sterling.

Example – a stock split
On April 18, 1994 Reuters effected a 4-for-1 stock split – 4 new shares of 2.5p par value were issued for every 1 old share of 10p par value held. At the close of market on Friday April 15th Reuters share price was £19.93 and was obviously starting to look very expensive to investors. By the close of business on Monday April 18th, after the share split, shares were trading at 483p. The result of the share split was to make shares in Reuters far more attractive and marketable to investors. You can see the details of share splits on the Reuters screen below:

Capital Changes

Announced	Ex Date	Dealing	Type	Shares in Issue	Adj Factor
04Dec97	18Feb98	18Feb98	13:15 Complex	1,417.3m	1.000
11Sep96	–	31Oct96	Rescinded	1,687.6m	1.000
08Feb94	18Apr94	18Apr94	4:1 Split	1,597.7m	0.250

The 1994 share split

Before moving on try the activity opposite.

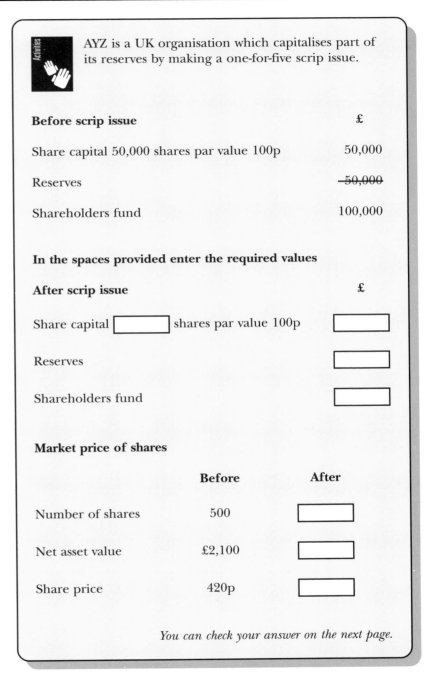

AYZ is a UK organisation which capitalises part of its reserves by making a one-for-five scrip issue.

Before scrip issue	£
Share capital 50,000 shares par value 100p	50,000
Reserves	~~50,000~~
Shareholders fund	100,000

In the spaces provided enter the required values

After scrip issue	£
Share capital [ ] shares par value 100p	[ ]
Reserves	[ ]
Shareholders fund	[ ]

Market price of shares

	Before	After
Number of shares	500	[ ]
Net asset value	£2,100	[ ]
Share price	420p	[ ]

You can check your answer on the next page.

In summary, here are the key points regarding a bonus or scrip issue:

- A bonus or scrip issue is a **recapitalisation** where new shares are issued free to existing shareholders in **proportion** to their existing holding

- The number of shares to be received compared with the number of shares held has **different conventions** in the UK and the US

- The shareholder's fund does not change but the number of shares issued does

---

R AYZ is a UK organisation which capitalises part of its reserves by making a one-for-five scrip issue.

Before scrip issue

	£
Share capital 50,000 shares par value 100p	50,000
Reserves	50,000
Shareholders fund	100,000

After scrip issue

	£
Share capital **60,000** shares par value 100p	**60,000**
Reserves	**40,000**
Shareholders fund	**100,000**

Market price of shares

	Before	After
Number of shares	500	**600**
Share price	420p	**350p**

You can use an electronic news service, such as Reuters, to view the latest news on active shares. Below are examples.

```
12:13  RTRS-Goldman Sachs dit de surpondérer la construction en Europe
12:09  RTRS-Filtronic<FCK.L>hits record on post-results buying
12:05  RTRS-RESEARCH ALERT-Goldman cuts Morris<MO.N>,RJR<RN.N>
12:04  RTRS-Alcatel poursuit son redressement, séduit la Bourse
11:50  RTRS-Granada<GAA.L> up on ITV hopes, BDB chief
11:47  RTRS-Whitbread<WTB.L> down as Panmure cuts to "hold"
11:46  RESEARCH ALERT-Cerj, Light still Paribas buys
11:44  RTRS-RESEARCH ALERT - GOLDMAN CUTS PHILIP MORRIS<MO.N>, RJR<RN.N> TO MARKET
       PERFORMERS
11:15  RTRS-UK's Rubicon<RBN.L> sees strategy shift pay off
10:35  RTRS-Smiths Inds <SMIN.L> climbs on Merrill upgrade
10:35  RTRS-InWear ventes ikke at falde yderligere - dealer
10:27  RTRS-Danone - Cheuvreux de Virieu passe à un achat prudent
10:26  RTRS-R-Poulenc - Etrangers détenaient 51,6% du capital fin 1997
10:24  RTRS-Air Liquide <AIRP.PA> up after turnover figures
10:24  RTRS-RESEARCH ALERT-Kleinwort Benson downgrades Novo
10:19  RTRS-DRESDNER KLEINWORT BENSON DOWNGRADES NOVO NORDISK<NVOb.CO> TO
       HOLD FROM BUY
09:56  RTRS-Rhone-Poulenc <RHON.PA> falls after '97 loss
09:52  RTRS-Bourse-Alcatel en hausse sur opérationnel meilleur que prévu
09:50  RTRS-Belgian CBR<CBRBt.BR>up three pct on cross trading
09:46  RTRS-StanChart
09:46  RTRS-Calwer De
09:45  RTRS-Railtrack<
```

```
11:50  29 Jan  RTRS-Granada<GAA.L> up on ITV hopes, BDB chief
   LONDON, Jan 29 (Reuters) - British hotels and media company Granada Group
Plc rose on Thursday on hopes for lower television licence payments and
optimism over the appointment of a chief executive for the British Digital
Broadcasting(BDB) group, dealers said.
   Stephen Grabiner, a board director of United News & Media<UNWS.L>, was
named as head of BDB, a 15-channel digital pay television service scheduled to be
launched late in 1998.
   "It is good news for Granada because he is seen as a strong candidate," a
trader said. BDB is a joint venture between Granada and fellow commercial TV
(ITV) broadcaster Carlton Communications Plc <CCM.L>.
   Granada traded 21p higher at 917p by 1140 GMT.
   Separately the Independent Television Commission said ITV companies may
benefit from lower licence fees when the licences come up for renewal from 1999
onwards.
   Analysts have said the payments, currently some 420 million pounds annually,
could fall by 100 million pounds to compensate for growing industry competition.
   United News & Media Plc, the third main ITV company along with Carlton and
Granada, added 6.5p to 723-1/2
   Broker Credit Lyonnais Laing highlighted United's potential for greater focus
and the scope for licence fee reduction in a research note issued on Thursday.
The brokerage rates the stocks as a "buy".
   Carlton shares slipped 1p to 429p. The company currently pays a very small
annual cash sum for its Central ITV franchise in the English Midlands and the
renewal process could prove to be a mixed blessing for the company.
   ((Patrick White, London Newsroom +44 171 542-8712, fax + 44 171 542-2120,
uk.stocks.news@reuters.com))
```

A **Rights issue.** In this case an organisation offers to sell to existing shareholders additional shares in a fixed proportion to the number of ordinary shares already held. The rights shares are usually sold at a slight discount to the current share price.

A rights issue is a type of ordinary share issue where the amount of shareholder's funds that can be utilised is changed. It is another way of recapitalisation involving a **transfer** of capital from shareholders to the organisation and the 'right' attached to the issue is to buy at a discount to the market value.

A one-for-two rights issue in the UK gives the right to buy one new share for every two shares held. After the new shares are issued but before the payment is due the shares trade in the market in **nil paid** form. If shareholders do not subscribe to the rights issue then their shareholding will be **diluted** – by a third in a one-for-two issue.

Issuers

A major advantage of a rights issue to an organisation is that it costs much less than a new issue. There is no requirement for a prospectus and underwriting fees are much lower. Investors are simply sent an offer and a deadline by which date they must reply if they wish to take up the offer. In many cases the rights issue alters the ownership pattern of the organisation little and therefore the shareholders' voting powers change little. Rights issues tend to be used by organisations with a high level of private shareholders who wish to maintain organisational control.

Example
Organisation XYZ offers its investors a 1-for-3 Rights issue – for every three shares held the investor can buy one new share at a cost of 80p. The current share price is 140p.

The investor takes up the offer of the rights issue and buys the share at 80p. How much are the investor's four shares now worth? The new price is calculated by adding the total current share price to the new share price and dividing by the number of shares:

3×140	– current share price	$= 420\text{p}$
1×80	– Rights issue price	$= 80\text{p}$
	Total	$= 500\text{p}$
	New share price	$= 500/4$
		$= 125\text{p}$

This new, theoretical share price is known as the **ex-rights** price and it is simply a weighted average of the old and rights issue prices. In the example, the original shares are now worth 15p less than before the rights issue. However, in most cases share prices rise after a rights issue and so the investor will probably gain in the long term.

In summary, here are the key points regarding a rights issue:

- A rights issue is a **recapitalisation** where **new shares** are sold to existing shareholders in a fixed proportion to their existing holding

- Rights shares are usually sold at a **discount** to the current market price in order to attract existing investors

The Reuters screen below illustrates news items concerning rights issues.

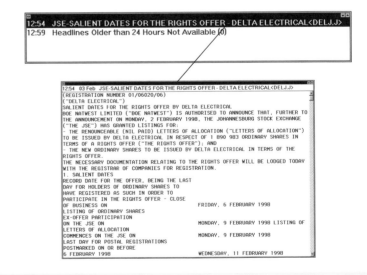

Equity-Linked Securities

This classification comprises **depositary receipts** which are based directly on equity shares, and **hybrid** instruments which have some features of the debt and equity markets. There are two important types of hybrid instruments discussed later where a debt market bond is either **convertible** or has **warrants** attached; but first is a review of depositary receipts.

Depositary Receipts

A **Depositary Receipt** is a negotiable certificate which usually represents equity instruments held by a custodian bank on deposit. Once deposited a certificate of receipt is issued for the instruments – hence the name.

Depositary receipts are instruments that allow investors in one country to become shareholders in a foreign organisation that enable buying/selling and receiving dividends in the investor's domestic currency.

For an organisation – particularly one in the emerging markets – issuing equity on a foreign exchange can be lengthy and expensive. The organisation may also encounter problems relating to foreign exchange and ownership of overseas investments, for itself and potential investors. Depositary receipts are one cost-effective solution.

A depositary receipt represents ownership in a specified number of underlying shares of the organisation. Once an organisation has placed its shares in a depositary in its own country, depositary receipts can be issued in a foreign country in the local currency. The depositary receipts are negotiable and once purchased the holder has all the rights attached to the underlying shares.

A depositary receipt can be issued as a **bearer** certificate but in most cases the certificate is **registered**.

The terms of a depositary receipt may vary from those of the underlying equity, for example, terms such as the currency of issue, denominated value and ownership rights. However, the holders of depositary receipts are entitled to all the dividends associated with the underlying shares but the dividend is paid in the **same** currency in which the depositary receipt is issued.

There are two types of depositary receipt* commonly encountered which are both very similar in structure and use.

- **American Depositary Receipts (ADRs)**
  These are denominated in US dollars and they are issued in the US by a depositary bank. An ADR represents ownership in the equity of non-US organisations. Any dividend due is paid to the holder in US Dollars. Once issued on a stock exchange ADRs trade in the same way as other shares.

- **Global Depositary Receipts (GDRs)**
  For many practical purposes there is little difference between these instruments and ADRs. However, GDRs are issued to access two or more international markets and are often launched to raise large amounts of capital which a single market may not be able to cope with. Although many GDRs are denominated in US Dollars, any currency can be used. GDRs are usually issued in registered form.

*Note: With the arrival of the euro in January 1999, the European Depositary Receipt (EDR) also arrived. At the time of publication, the London Stock Exchange was the first and only exchange to list euro-dominated EDRs.

REUTERS

American Depositary Receipts (ADRs)

An ADR is a negotiable instrument representing non-US – foreign – shares. The aim is to be able to trade foreign shares in the US markets without local listing. ADRs are traded in US dollars and dividends are paid in US dollars.

ADRs were first introduced in 1927 as a result of legislation in the UK that placed restrictions on UK organisations registering shares overseas and prohibited the share certificates from leaving the country.

Since the 1950s ADRs have become increasingly important as a way by which overseas investors can invest in the ordinary shares of foreign organisations in their own domestic markets. So how does the process of issuing an ADR work? In principle the system is quite simple and is outlined in the chart below.

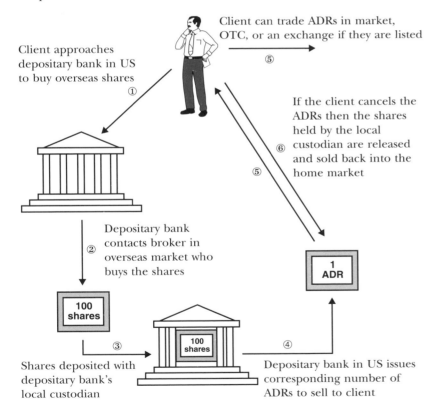

Client approaches depositary bank in US to buy overseas shares ①

Depositary bank contacts broker in overseas market who buys the shares ②

Shares deposited with depositary bank's local custodian ③

Depositary bank in US issues corresponding number of ADRs to sell to client ④

Client can trade ADRs in market, OTC, or an exchange if they are listed ⑤

If the client cancels the ADRs then the shares held by the local custodian are released and sold back into the home market ⑥

ADRs are important instruments in the US and they can be issued in a number of different ways which is somewhat dependent on whether they will be traded OTC or on an exchange. In the US, ADRs may be issued as follows:

- **Unsponsored ADRs**
  These programmes may be set up by a US bank on its own account without the involvement of the non-US issuing organisation.

- **Sponsored Level I ADRs**
  These are programmes set up by non-US organisations and maintained by a depositary bank. In this case there is a formal agreement between issuer and bank. Level I issues involve a minimum of regulatory and reporting requirements.

Both unsponsored and sponsored Level I ADRs trade **OTC**. The market trades are listed in the **Pink Sheets** published by the US National Quotation Bureau.

- **Sponsored Level II/III ADRs**
  Level II ADRs are listed on the NYSE, AMEX and Nasdaq and must meet the listing requirements of the relevant exchange. Level III ADRs are used by non-US organisations for both listing and capital raising purposes.

- **Rule 144A ADRs**
  In the US this rule allows for the resale of securities such as ADRs issued by private placement to qualified institutional investors where no reporting or registration is involved.

In 1996, some 400 ADR programmes were listed on the NYSE, AMEX and Nasdaq – the largest listing was on the NYSE with 247 ADRs. However, over 1300 ADRs were available for trading OTC and on these exchanges. The annual trading volume of exchange listed ADRs was approximately $380 billion in 1996.

What Instruments Are Used in the Equity Markets?

In the US, the top ten ADR trading volumes in $ billion for 1997 is indicated in the table below.

Organisation & Symbol	Volume (thousand)
LM Ericsson Telephone Company (ERICY)	332,495.1
Nokia Corporation (NOK)	269,605.0
Royal Dutch Petroleum Company (RD)	184,039.7
BP Amoco p.l.c. (BPA)	181,567.2
Telebras HOLDRS (TBH)	169,231.2
Telecommunicacces Brasileiras S.A. (TBR)	128,783.2
Telefonos de Mexico, S.A. de C.V. (TMX)	112,002.0
ASM Lithography Holding N.V. (ASML)	110,160.2
Saville Systems PLC (SAVLY)	106,565.6
YPF Sociedad Aronima (YPF)	91,394.4

Source: J.P. Morgan

Other equity markets issue ADRs on stock exchanges which have their own rules concerning listing. For example, in 1996, 24 depositary receipts were listed on the LSE raising some £2.4 billion.

Below are examples of Reuters screens showing information about Reuters ADRs.

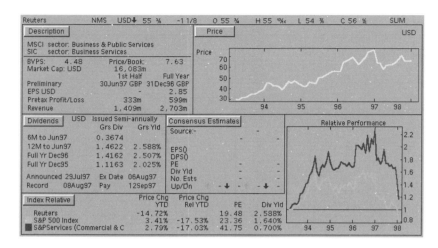

REUTERS

Global Depositary Receipts (GDRs)

GDRs are depositary receipts issued simultaneously in more than one country but in one specific currency. GDRs were first developed in the early 1990s and allow for relatively easy access to capital in different equity markets.

GDR transactions may be conducted OTC or on exchanges such as the NYSE. The transactions can be settled by computer entry through one of the international securities clearing houses such as CEDEL or Euroclear – this process is known as global book entry.

A typical example of a GDR issue is that of Lehman Brothers in 1996 who acted as a joint global co-ordinator for a $370 million offering for the State Bank of India. Lehman Brothers held meetings in 18 cities in Asia, Europe and the US to launch the issue, with the result that the offering was oversubscribed.

The benefits to investors trading these instruments include the following:

- Depositary receipts are a convenient way of holding shares in overseas organisations – many depositary receipts are denominated in US dollars and pay dividends in US dollars

- Depositary receipts simplify trading and settlement procedures in holding overseas shares compared with outright ownership, which involves custodial services, foreign exchange etc

- Depositary receipts are as liquid as the underlying shares in many cases

The benefits to issuers of depositary receipts include the following:

- A depositary receipt provides a simple way of accessing overseas markets to increase an organisation's shareholder base and to raise capital

- A depositary receipt issue can help to increase the liquidity of the underlying shares

- A depositary receipt issue can help to raise the profile of a non-US organisation in the US

- A GDR issue has the same benefits as an ADR but in addition it is used to access international markets to raise capital on a scale which may not be possible in a single market

- A GDR issue can help to raise the profile of a non-US organisation internationally

In summary, here are the key points regarding depositary receipts:

Depositary Receipts

- A **Depositary Receipt** is a negotiable certificate which usually represents equity instruments held by a custodian bank on deposit

- A depositary receipt can be issued as a **bearer** certificate but in most cases the certificate is **registered**

- **American Depositary Receipts (ADRs)** are denominated in US dollars and any dividend due is paid to the holder in US dollars

- **Global Depositary Receipts (GDRs)** are issued to access, two or more international markets and are often launched to raise large amounts of capital – many GDRs are denominated in US dollars although any currency can be used

- In the US ADRs may be issued as **Unsponsored ADRs, Sponsored Level I/II/III ADRs** and **Rule 144A ADRs**

- **European Depositary Receipts (EDR)** are euro-denominated and began trading in 1999.

Convertible Bond

A **convertible** bond is usually a fixed rate debt instrument giving the holder the right, but not obligation, to exchange the bond and all the remaining coupons for a pre-determined number of ordinary shares or other debt instruments of the issuer at a pre-stated price and pre-stated date/s.

A convertible bond is known as a **hybrid instrument** as it incorporates features of both the debt and equity markets for investors and issuers. A convertible bond may offer various options to both investors and issuers, including the option of what other instruments the bond may be converted into upon exercise. Convertible bonds have coupon rates that are lower than for conventional bonds because they offer a greater potential for profit.

Both governments and corporations issue convertible bonds, but most are issued are by corporations. Among the types of instruments into which a convertible bond can be exchanged include the following:

- **Conversion into further debt instruments**. Although convertible bonds typically involve shares, when an issuer – such as a government – has no shares to convert into, then the government can convert into further government debt. In effect, this is a way for a government to issue an interest rate option.

- **Conversion into shares of another organisation**. These bonds are known as **exchangeable bonds** and have been issued after take-overs or issued for shares in the parent organisation of the issuer.

- **Conversion into shares of a corporation**. Usually this type of convertible bond is a corporate bond with a call option held by the investor to buy ordinary shares in the organisation as agreed in the terms for conversion set out in the bond **indenture**. Many convertible bonds also have call features with respect to the issuer which limit the share appreciation limit. There are also convertible bonds which have put options for the issuer. These options give the issuer the right, but not obligation, to convert the bond into cash, shares or other debt instruments depending on the type of put specified. In practice, puts are exercised when the organisation is not performing well and share prices are low.

The right to exchange the bond into shares may extend over the whole lifetime of the bond or for only a portion of it – the indenture specifies the terms.

The pre-stated price is called the **conversion price** and is determined before issue – this price is higher than the organisation's current share trading price. Nearly all convertibles incorporate a call feature allowing the issuer to effectively force conversion after the share price reaches a certain level, for example, 130% of the conversion price. The actual number of shares that a bond can be converted into – the **bond conversion ratio** – is calculated using the following equation:

$$\text{Bond conversion ratio} = \frac{\text{Principal amount of bond}}{\text{Conversion price}}$$

The amount by which the market price of a convertible bond exceeds the market price of the ordinary shares is known as the **conversion premium**. This conversion premium can be used to determine whether or not conversion of a bond is profitable at some future date. The **initial conversion premium** is calculated from the following equation:

$$\textbf{Initial conversion premium} = \left(\frac{\textbf{Conversion price}}{\textbf{Current ordinary share price}} \right) \times \textbf{100}$$

Once the initial conversion premium has been exceeded the investor can profit by conversion and selling the shares in the markets. Review the following example to see how it works.

Example – A corporate convertible bond issue
A US corporation issues a convertible bond with the following details. What is the bond conversion ration and when can the bond be converted profitably?

Bond face value	:	$1,000 par
Coupon rate	:	6.00%; semi-annual
Maturity	:	10 years time
Conversion period	:	Until maturity
Conversion price	:	$20.00
Current share price	:	$16.50

The bond conversion ratio $= \dfrac{1000}{20} = 50$

This means that if an investor converts the bond, he or she would receive 50 shares.

The initial conversion ratio $= \left(\dfrac{20.00}{16.50} - 1 \right) \times 100 = 21.21\%$

This means that the issuer's ordinary shares have to appreciate by more than 21.21% before the bond can be converted by an investor profitably.

Once a convertible bond is exchanged for shares or other instruments it ceases to exist and is no longer a debt obligation of the issuer.

In the long term, the potential reward for investors is that the bond can be converted into shares which can be sold at a profit in the equity markets. This potential for profit is reflected in the coupon which is lower than for a straight bond. Usually the coupon gives the investor a slightly higher rate of return than the historic dividends on the ordinary share price.

Among the reasons organizations issue convertible bonds are the following:

- To avoid diluting Earnings Per Share (EPS) value – the greater the number of shares in an organisation, the lower the EPS value.

- To avoid approaching existing shareholders and to appeal to both equity and debt investors.

- The cost of issuing shares is much higher than issuing debt. New equity shares are sometimes discounted to attract new investors.

- Interest payments are a known, fixed cost, whereas dividend payments depend on company profits and can fluctuate greatly over time. In addition, making interest payments may have tax advantages.

- Up until conversion takes place, there is no dilution of dividends and there is no decrease in the control of the organisation, as there is no increase in the total number of shares.

- On conversion, the equity capital of the issuer increases and its long-term debt decreases. If conversion does not take place, then the result is a long-term, low-cost borrowing for the issuer.

Investors who buy convertible bonds are in effect buying an interest rate option on a future bond issue. Convertible bond investors have these advantages:

- Guaranteed fixed income versus dividend yields, until conversion

- In the case of conversion, the number of shares is known and there is no brokerage cost.

- The higher ranking of bonds over equity if the issuer goes into liquidation

Issuers – Convertible bonds

Advantages	Disadvantages
• Convertible bonds represent a cheaper way of issuing debt which is usually subordinated but unsecured • Equity is issued at a premium • There is no cost of carry associated with the deferred equity position – the cost of carry is the difference between interest generated and the cost to finance the position • Most convertible bonds incorporate a call feature for the issuer which effectively forces conversion after a specified share appreciation – often this is 130% of the conversion price	• This type of bond is not usually acceptable for swap transactions because the bond maturity date is uncertain – investors can convert within the specified conversion period • If the issuer has a high dividend yield, then the coupon rate may be too high for any significant cost savings

Investors – Convertible bonds

Advantages	Disadvantages
• A convertible bond provides a coupon payment until maturity or conversion • Geared exposure to equity of issuer	• If the bond incorporates a call feature for the issuer, forced conversion can result if the share price exceeds a specified conversion price • Lack of gearing on part of the issuer – gearing is the ratio of the issuer's debt to ordinary share capital

Below are Reuters screens, in increasing detail, showing information for new convertible bond issues.

```
            CONVERTIBLE BONDS - NEW ISSUES            CNVB
CODE          ISSUER         COUPON MAT DAT     RIC
Z5TD  NLG  BALLAST NEDAM     5.0000 09OCT02  NL008056587=  E
Z2YB  GBP  BAA PLC           4.8750 29SEP04  GB007928688=  E
Z7CB  USD  BANK PRZEMYSTOWO  3.0000 22MAY02  PL007526814=  E
```

```
    CNV            BAA PLC 4.8750 29SEP04              Z2YB
ISS DATE   06AUG97 LEAD        UBZ COMM  007928688 S&P   AA-
ISS PRICE  100.000 DENOM    1 5 50 GBP IS XS0079286885 MDY   A1
ISS AMT    200.0M PAY FREQ      SEMI VALOREN    -
AT CLOSE   28OCT97 LAST CNV  22SEP04 WERT      194387 CTRY  GBR
MAT YLD PA  -                     GUARANTOR    -
MAT YLD SA  -                     EQUITY       511.000
B/C     -/-      ACC INT     -    EQ RIC       <BAA.L>
CONVEXITY   -    YR HI     105.500
MID PRICE  99.375 YR LO      99.375 TERMS -CNV INTO SHARES OF
<GB007928688=>    <O#GB007928688=>   <GB007928688=RTR>
IF THE CHAIN IS DATA NOT AVAILABLE CLICK ON THE RIC FOR PRICES
```

```
BAA.L    BAA PLC      000000067340 GBp NMS50000  /  /  29OCT97 13:55
Last       Bid       Ask       Mid0      Mid Close   Volume     Sector
↓533       530       533       531½      531½        2879934    O#.FTTR
 533       Open      High      Low       News        Headlines
 533       562       562       530        :          BAA1
 533       LT:28OCT97 Yr.High  Yr.Low    52WeekHigh  52WeekLow
 533       533       615       470
Div:19AUG97 Yield    Ex.Date   P.E       Earnings    Background
12.40      2.908 %   16JUN97   18.77     28.40       BAA.LB1
Exchange
LSE/
```

In summary, here are the key points regarding a convertible bond:

- A **convertible bond** is usually a fixed rate debt instrument giving the holder the **option** to exchange the bond and its coupons into shares in the issuing organisation or that of another organisation or which can be exchanged for further debt instruments in the organisation

- The number of shares which can be received on exchange are specified in the bond **indentures** and is determined by the **conversion ratio** – the price of the shares is set at issuance and known as the **conversion price**

- The **initial conversion premium** is used to determine whether or not it is profitable to convert a bond

Below are the details of a corporate convertible bond issue.

Bond face value	: $1,000 par
Coupon rate	: 3.50%; semi-annual
Maturity	: 5 years time
Conversion period	: Until maturity
Conversion price	: $83.330
Current share price	: $74.125

Given the details of this US convertible bond what are the following?

a) What is the initial conversion premium?

b) What is the conversion ratio?

You can check your answer on page 100.

The Reuters screens on this page illustrate US convertible bonds and UK convertible bonds.

```
┌─────────────────────────────────────────────────────┐
│O#EUROUSDCAE=              CNV EUROS AE 1/2            │
│                                                       │
│  Issue/Issuer    Coupon Maturity      L a t e s t    │
│ACCOR               7.5 02JAN99         101.20         │
│ACER INC           1.25 27NOV06    B 125.000  A 130.000│
│AC INTL FINANCE       3 08JUN00    B 107.500  A 109.500│
│AC INTL FINANCE       0 08DEC00    B  75.000  A  76.500│
│AC INTL FINANCE     0.5 30JUL02    B  88.500  A  90.500│
│ADI CORP            1.5 08JUL03    B 107.000  A 109.000│
│ADVANCE AGRO PCL    3.5 14JUN01    B  88.500  A  90.500│
│AEGON NV           4.75 01NOV04    M 350.000           │
│AKER RGI ASA       5.25 23JUL02    B 107.500  A 109.000│
│ALCAN ALUMINIUM   4.000 30SEP03    B  84.000  A  88.000│
│ALCO HEALTH SVCS   6.25 01JUL01    B          A        │
│ALEX BROWN INC   5.7500 12JUN02    B 516.000  A 518.000│
│ALL AMER COMM       6.5 010CT03    B  80.00   A  84.50 │
│ALPHATEC              4 22JUN99    B 104.00   A 105.00 │
│ALUSUISSE-LONZA  2.0000 03APR01      116.25   A 117.25 │
│AMER               6.25 15JUN03    B  98.250  A 100.250│
│AMERICAN MEDICAL   5.25 01FEB01    B 105.000  A 106.000│
│AMOY PROPERTIES     5.5            B  70.000  A  71.000│
│ANAM IND           0.25 31DEC10    B  74.000  A  79.000│
│AOKAM PERDANA       3.5 13JUN04    B  42.000  A  44.125│
│APACHE CORP      6.0000 15JAN97    B↓ 106.00  A 107.00 │
│APP GLOBAL FIN        2 25JUL00    B  90.750  A  92.250│
└─────────────────────────────────────────────────────┘
```

```
┌──────────────────────────────────────────────────────────────────────┐
│CONVERTIBLE EUROBONDS - REUTERS SPEED GUIDE                   EUROBOND9  │
│Convertible Eurobond Issues (RIC-format only) listed by Currency.        │
│                                                                        │
│=CONVERTIBLES========================= =CONVERTIBLES CONT.============== │
│AUD Convertibles..........<O#EUROAUDC=> USD Convertibles F-L...<O#EUROUSDCFL1=>│
│CHF Convertibles..........<O#EUROCHFC=> USD Convertibles M-R....<O#EUROUSDCMR=>│
│CYP Convertibels..........<O#EUROCYPC=> USD Convertibles S-Z....<O#EUROUSDCSZ=>│
│DEM Convertibles..........<O#EURODEMC=> USD Convertibles S-Z...<O#EUROUSDCSZ1=>│
│ECU Convertibles..........<O#EUROXEUC=>                                  │
│FRF Convertibles..........<O#EUROFRFC=>                                  │
│GBP Convertibles..........<O#EUROGBPC=>                                  │
│ITL Convertibles..........<O#EUROITLC=>                                  │
│JPY Convertibles..........<O#EUROJPYC=>                                  │
│LUF Convertibles..........<O#EUROLUFC=>                                  │
│NLG Convertibles..........<O#EURONLGC=>                                  │
│USD Convertibles A-E...<O#EUROUSDCAE=>                                   │
│USD Convertibles A-E...<O#EUROUSDCAE1=>                                  │
│USD Convertibles F-L....<O#EUROUSDCFL=>                                  │
│                                                                        │
│Questions/Comments: Contact your local Help Desk - see <PHONE/HELP> for details.│
│========================================================================│
│Debt Guide<BONDS>       Eurobonds Guide<EUROBONDS>      Previous Page<EUROBOND8>│
│  Lost?Selective Access?...<USER/HELP>    Reuters Phone Support...<PHONE/HELP>│
└──────────────────────────────────────────────────────────────────────┘
```

```
┌──────────────────────────────────────────────────────┐
│O#EUROGBPC=                CNV EUROS                    │
│                                                        │
│  Issue/Issuer    Coupon Maturity      L a t e s t     │
│ADT LIMITED           8 31JUL05    B          A         │
│ALLIED DOMECQ      6.75 07JUL08    B 103.875  A 104.875 │
│ASEA BROWN BOVRI      3 03MAR99    B          A         │
│ASH CAPITAL FIN     9.5 15JUL06    B  95.500  A  99.000 │
│AVIS INC           5.25 12NOV02    M 123.000            │
│BAA PLC           4.875 29SEP04    B 100.500  A 101.000 │
│BAA PLC            5.75 29MAR06    B 109.000  A 110.000 │
│BLUE CIRCLE INDS  6.875 20MAY02    B 149.000  A 152.000 │
│BOND CORP             6 06JUL98    B          A         │
│BPB INDUSTRIES     7.25 25AUG08    B 122.000  A 123.000 │
│BR LAND CO          6.5 17JUN07    B 125.000  A 126.000 │
│BR LAND CO            6            B 151.750  A 152.750 │
│CAPITAL SHOPPING   6.25 31DEC06    B 128.500  A 129.500 │
│CARLTON COMMS       7.5 14AUG07    B 188.000  A 189.875 │
│COATS VIYELLA      6.25 09AUG03    B  92.500  A  93.500 │
│COMPASS GROUP      5.75 050CT07                         │
│COOKSON GRP PLC       7 02NOV04    B 100.000  A 101.000 │
│DAILY MAIL TRUST   5.75 26SEP03    B 126.250  A 126.750 │
│ECC GROUP           6.5 30SEP03    B  96.500  A  98.500 │
│FORTE              6.75 26MAY08    B 173.88   A 174.88  │
│GREENALLS GROUP       7 24SEP03    B 107.750  A 108.750 │
│HAMMERSON PROP      6.5 12JUN06    B 124.625  A 125.625 │
└──────────────────────────────────────────────────────┘
```

These Reuters screens illustrate convertible bonds on the Tokyo Stock Exchange.

```
JAPANESE CONVERTIBLES - REUTERS SPEED GUIDE                      JP/CNV1
CONVERTIBLE BONDS FROM TOKYO SE.

=CONVERTIBLES BY MARKET SECTOR=========  =CONVERTIBLES BY MARKET SECTOR=========
Air Transport...............<O#CAIR.T>  Other Manufacturers.........<O#CMIS.T>
Banks.......................<O#CBNK.T>  Pharmaceuticals.............<O#CPHA.T>
Chenicals...................<O#CCHE.T>  Precision Machinery.........<O#CPRC.T>
Connunications..............<O#CCOM.T>  Pulp/Paper..................<O#CPAP.T>
Construction................<O#CCON.T>  Real Estate.................<O#CREA.T>
Electrical Mac..............<O#CELC.T>  Retailers...................<O#CRET.T>
Foods.......................<O#CFOD.T>  Rubber Products.............<O#CRUB.T>
Glass/Ceranics..............<O#CGLS.T>  Sea Transport...............<O#CSHP.T>
Insurance...................<O#CINS.T>  Securities..................<O#CSEC.T>
Land Transport..............<O#CRRL.T>  Services....................<O#CSVC.T>
Machinery...................<O#CMAC.T>  Steel/Iron..................<O#CSTL.T>
Metals......................<O#CMET.T>  Textiles....................<O#CTXT.T>
Mining......................<O#CMNG.T>  Transport Equipment.........<O#CTEQ.T>
Non-Ferrous Metals..........<O#CNFR.T>  Utilities...................<O#CELG.T>
Oil/Coal....................<O#COIL.T>  Warehouses..................<O#CWHS.T>
Other Finance...............<O#CFIN.T>  Wholesales..................<O#CWHO.T>
```

```
O#CBNK.T          CB BANKS          TYO/   JPY
RIC         Coupon Maturity Last   Cls    Kassa   High   Low    Yield %  Time
8315C62.T   6.20 31MAR98           140.00                       4.43   :
8326C2.T    1.10 28SEP07 ↑94.20    94.00          94.20  93.20  1.17 06:00
8334C4.T    0.45 28SEP01           105.00                       0.43   :
8341C2.T    1.50 31MAR99           99.40                        1.51   :
8341C3.T    0.45 29MAR02 ↓106.00   108.50         106.00 106.00 0.42 04:33
8353C1.T    1.90 31MAR03           88.10                        2.18   :
8361C1.T    2.50 31MAR98           99.20                        2.52   :
8362C1.T    2.20 31MAR98           99.70                        2.21   :
8379C1.T    1.80 30SEP02 ↓92.20    92.10          92.30  92.20  1.95 03:38
8396C1.T    2.00 31MAR03           101.00                       1.98   :
8396C2.T    1.70 31MAR99           98.20                        1.73   :
8401C4.T    1.40 30SEP98 ↓99.00    99.10          99.10  99.00  1.41 03:30
8522C1.T    2.00 31MAR98           98.00                        2.04   :
```

```
O#CNV.XSEC                                                        JPY
             CONVERTIBLE
Issue        Coupon Maturity Price    Net.Ch  Sinple Net.Ch Conp   JBRI
HIGASHI N HS 1  1.30 27APR01 ↓ 86.000 -0.900 ↑6.568 +0.394         BBB
SHINNIH COR 1   1.90 29SEP00                                       BBB-
SHIRAISHI 1     2.30 31MAR99                                       BB+
TOHOKU MISAWA 1 2.30 29MAR02                                       BBB-
TECHNO RYOWA 1  1.30 31MAR99                                       BBB
TAKAHASHI C 1   1.90 29DEC00   79.000        ↑11.584 +0.009
TOKATSU FOOD 1  1.20 30MAR01 ↓ 80.000 -0.500 ↑9.455  +0.263        BBB-
MORISHITA CO. 1 0.90 31MAR98   98.500        ↑11.401 +0.195
ASAHI PRIN&PAC 1 0.80 31MAR03 ↑ 80.300 +0.300 ↓5.764 -0.092        BBB
MIKASA SEIYA 2  1.30 30MAR01                                       BBB-
SEIKAGAKU 2     2.70 31MAR00 ↓ 99.500 -0.200 ↑2.947 +0.099         ·
NOEVIR 1        0.45 20SEP04 ↓ 79.900 -0.200 ↑4.362 +0.050         BBB+
MANDOM CO 1     2.20 31MAR00 ↑ 96.500 +1.500 ↓3.968 -0.794         BBB
NITTA CROP 1    1.10 30MAR01
SUIDO KIKO 1    1.10 31MAR04   78.200        ↑5.941 +0.002
RISO KAGAKU 1   4.50 31MAR99 ↓107.400 -0.500 ↑1.826 +0.381
RISO KAGAKU 2   1.50 31MAR09   82.000         3.798
FUKUSIMA INDS 1 2.30 29MAR02                                       BBB
THK CO LTD 2    4.20 31MAR99  100.000         4.200               BBB+
THK CO LTD 3    0.30 30SEP03 ↑ 82.700 +0.500 ↓4.067 -0.131        BBB+
SANKO 1         1.00 30MAR01   88.000        ↑5.475 +0.004        BBB-
```

Given the details of the US convertible bond:

a) *What is the initial conversion premium?*

Initial conversion premium

$$= \left(\frac{\text{Conversion price}}{\text{Current price}} - 1 \right) \times 100$$

$$= \left(\frac{83.330}{74.125} - 1 \right) \times 100 = 12.42\%$$

b) *What is the conversion ratio?*

Conversion ratio for shares

$$= \left(\frac{\text{Bond par value}}{\text{Conversion price}} \right)$$

$$= \left(\frac{1000}{83.33} \right) = 12 \text{ shares}$$

Bond with Warrants

> A **bond with warrants** is a standard bond with coupons but has a pre-determined number of warrants attached. Each warrant gives the holder the right, but not obligation, to buy an agreed number of shares of the issuer at a specified price – the **warrant exercise price** – and at a specified future date/s. If the warrant is exercised, then **additional** payment is required to purchase the shares.

A bond with warrants is also a **hybrid instrument**. As with convertible bonds, these instruments may have options for issuers and investors and have coupon rates which are lower than for conventional bonds because they offer a greater potential for profit.

Bonds with warrants are similar to convertible bonds for corporate shares in that they provide the investor with an option to obtain shares in the issuing organisation at a specified price and thus could be considered to be a long-term call option on shares that is sold with the bond. A bond with warrants is a standard corporate bond with coupons to which a specified number of warrants have been attached. However, as for convertible bonds, not all warrants are for shares. Warrants have been issued for other debt instruments and commodities such as gold. The following description covers the case of warrants for ordinary shares.

A warrant confers on the holder the right, but not obligation, to buy a specified number of ordinary shares at a specified price – the warrant exercise price. If the warrant is exercised, then additional funds are paid to the issuer for the shares over and above the price of the original bond.

Bonds with warrants attached can be retained as an entity and traded as **cum-warrants**; they carry a higher price which reflects the bond's greater profit potential. However, an investor also has the opportunity to detach the warrants and trade both the **ex-warrant** or **stripped** bond and the warrants separately. The remaining underlying bond and stripped warrant are bought by different types of investors with differing requirements. Bonds with warrants are unlike convertible bonds in that there are no call features for issuers which allow the exercise of warrants to be forced if the price of the ordinary shares exceeds a specified limit.

Equity warrants are exercised for shares at a pre-determined price that is paid on exercise. Warrants are primarily aimed at investors seeking long-term options for shares at pre-determined prices. Equity warrants are speculative and volatile instruments and investors have to be aware constantly of the relationship between the exercise price and the current market price of the shares.

Below is an example of Reuters screens for Asian warrants, together with a pertinent news story.

```
08:36 13NOV97    INTERNATIONAL INSIDER -ASIA SERVICE-  HK27349          IIJL
---- ASIAN WARRANTS - THURSDAY - HK TEL (852) 2525-5863  -----
<IIJM> SOC GEN LAUNCHES PUTS ON THE S&P 500
<IIJN> MERRILL LYNCH LAUNCHES CALLS ON HSBC
<IIJO> MORGAN STANLEY LAUNCHES FURTHER PUTS ON S&P 500
<IIJP> × SOC GEN LAUNCHES PUTS ON HANG SENG INDEX ×
<IIJQ> BEAR STEARNS CALLS ON CHINATRUST COMM BANK
<IIJR> BEAR STEARNS LAUNCHES CALLS ON SHIHLIN ELEC & ENG
××× FOR DETAILS OF THE PREVIOUS 21 ISSUES SEE PAGE <IIJK> ×××
```

```
16:26 07OCT97    INTERNATIONAL INSIDER -ASIA SERVICE-  HK27349          IIJQ

   - THE BEAR STEARNS COMPANIES INC IS ISSUING 10 MILLION AMERICAN
STYLE CALL WARRANTS ON SHARES OF CHINATRUST COMMERCIAL BANK
<2815.TW>. PRICED AT TWD$3.8586 EACH, ONE WARRANT CONTROLS ONE
SHARE AT A STRIKE PRICE OF TWD43.758 (REFERENCE PRICE TWD39.78).
EXPIRY DATE IS APRIL 2, 1998. EXERCISE SETTLEMENT IN US$ CASH.
PAYMENT DATE IS OCTOBER 9. MINIMUM TRADING SIZE IS 50,000
WARRANTS.
```

Below is a sample Reuters screen showing warrant prices for Dartmoor Investment Trust PLC.

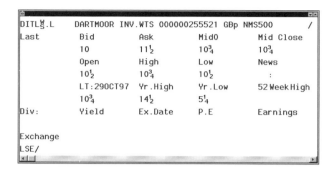

```
DITLₓ.L   DARTMOOR INV.WTS 000000255521 GBp NMS500        /
Last      Bid       Ask       Mid0      Mid Close
          10        11½       10¾       10¾
          Open      High      Low       News
          10½       10¾       10½         :
          LT:29OCT97 Yr.High  Yr.Low    52 Week High
          10¾       14½       5¼
Div:      Yield     Ex.Date   P.E       Earnings

Exchange
LSE/
```

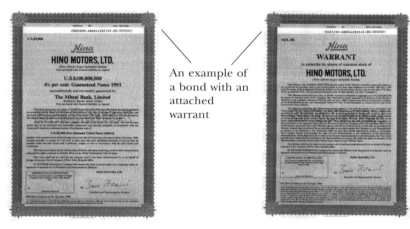

An example of a bond with an attached warrant

One of the major features of equity related instruments in general is their **gearing effect**. This is the change in price of a warrant or quality premium for a convertible compared with that of the market price of the share for which it can be exchanged. For example, the purchase price of a warrant is less than the purchase price of the underlying shares. This means that the price change in a warrant compared to that for the shares represents proportionally greater percentage profits or losses relative to the amount invested. A look at the following example to see how gearing works.

Example – The gearing effect of a warrant
A warrant for XYZ shares can be bought for \$7.00 and the current ordinary share price is \$28.00. Suppose XYZ shares appreciate to \$30.00. This rise represents an increase of 7.14% ($30 - 28 \div 28$) in price. An increase in the underlying share price also produces an increase in the warrant price – the price rises to \$9.00. The rise in warrant price represents an increase of 28.57% ($9 - 7 \div 7$).

So the share price has increased by 7.14% producing a warrant price increase of 28.57%. In other words, the share price change has produced a gearing effect of 4 times in the warrant price.

Issuers in some high growth business sectors do not necessarily have a track record in issuing debt and therefore have to offer a "sweetener" such as warrants in order to attract investors. For issuers of these bonds, providing that the shares in the organisation appreciate, on exercise of the warrants, the equity capital of the organisation will increase.

Investors are attracted to warrants because they have the flexibility of retaining or selling the bond, with or without the warrants. In the event of liquidation of the organisation, the investor holding the bond is ranked senior to equity holders.

Issuers – Bonds with Warrants

Advantages	Disadvantages
• Reduced coupon payments because the warrant has a value • Cost of issuing a bond is less than issuing shares • As with convertible bonds, until the warrants are exercised, there are no changes in the number of shares or the capital of the organisation • The debt element of the bond can be used for swap transactions	• Warrants can only be exercised at specific dates by the investor, so if share prices increase dramatically the investor can profit – the issuer cannot force exercise of the warrant • The debt element of the bond is senior if the issuer goes in liquidation

Investors – Bonds with Warrants

Advantages	Disadvantages
• Advantages of gearing • Bond coupon provides a cash flow similar to a fixed coupon bond • The issuer cannot impose any call features on warrant exercise	• There is an element of risk associated with warrants – share prices can rise and fall • The warrant element of the bond generates no income – it is a speculative instrument

In summary, here are the key points regarding a bond with warrants:

- A **bond with warrants** is a conventional bond with coupons which has a number of warrants attached which give the holder the option of buying shares or further debt instruments in the issuing organisation or commodities

- The holder can retain and/or sell the bond with its attached warrants – **cum-warrant** – or the holder can detach the warrants and retain and/or sell the **stripped** bond – **ex-warrant** – and warrants separately

- One of the major features of warrants is their **gearing effect** – small changes in share prices can have dramatic effects on warrant prices

To test your understanding of these bonds try the following exercise...

Exercise – A bond with warrants
Total issue amount $150,000,000

Bond face value	:	$1,000 par
Coupon rate	:	3.50%; semi-annual
Maturity	:	5 years time
Conversion period	:	Until maturity
Warrants	:	2 warrants per bond for 5 shares each @ $93.00 per share
Current share price	:	$77.00

Given the details of this bond with warrant what are the following?

a) How much additional cash will the issuer receive if all the warrants are exercised?

b) What is the initial warrant exercise premium?

You can check your answer on the next page.

Given the details of the bond with warrants:

a) *How much additional cash will the issuer receive if all the warrants are exercised?*

No. of bonds in issue = 150,000,000 ÷ 1000 = 150,000

On exercise additional capital raised
= No. of bonds × No. of shares × Price of shares
= 150,000 × (2 × 5) × $93.00
= $139,500,000

b) *What is the initial warrant exercise premium?*

Initial warrant exercise premium

$$= \left(\frac{\text{Conversion price}}{\text{Current price}} \right) \times 100$$

$$= \left(\frac{93.00}{77.00} - 1 \right) \times 100 = 20.78\%$$

The Reuters screens below show the exchange-traded warrants traded on LSE listed equities. Compare the warrant prices with the share prices.

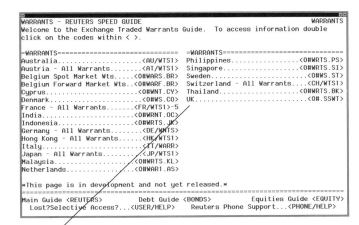

What Instruments Are Used in the Equity Markets?

The Reuters screen below shows the top 20 warrants by volume on the TSE.

```
JAPANESE RANKINGS/STATISTICS - REUTERS SPEED GUIDE              JP/STATS1
Ranking Statistics from all Japanese Exchanges
=EXCHANGE========VOLUME=====NET GAIN===NET LOSS====% GAIN=====% LOSS===TOTAL VOL
Tokyo   1st      <.AV.T>    <.NG.T>    <.NL.T>    <.PG.T>    <.PL.T>    <.TV.T>
        2nd      <.AV2.T>   <.NG2.T>   <.NL2.T>   <.PG2.T>   <.PL2.T>
        Foreign  <.AVF.T>   <.NGF.T>   <.NLF.T>   <.PGF.T>   <.PLF.T>
        CB       <.AVCB.T>  <.NGCB.T>  <.NLCB.T>  <.PGCB.T>  <.PLCB.T>
        Warrant  <.AVWS.T>  <.NGWS.T>  <.NLWS.T>  <.PGWS.T>  <.PLWS.T>
Osaka   1st      <.AV.OS>   <.NG.OS>   <.NL.OS>   <.PG.OS>   <.PL.OS>   <.TV.OS>
        2nd      <.AV2.OS>  <.NG2.OS>  <.NL2.OS>  <.PG2.OS>  <.PL2.OS>
        Foreign  <.AVF.OS>  <.NGF.OS>  <.NLF.OS>  <.PGF.OS>  <.PLF.OS>
        CB       <.AVCB.OS> <.NGCB.OS> <.NLCB.OS> <.PGCB.OS> <.PLCB.OS>
        Warrant  <.AVWS.OS> <.NGWS.OS> <.NLWS.OS> <.PGWS.OS> <.PLWS.OS>
Nagoya           <.AV.NG>   <.NG.NG>   <.NL.NG>   <.PG.NG>   <.PL.NG>   <.TV.NG>
Sapporo          <.AV.SP>   <.NG.SP>   <.NL.SP>   <.PG.SP>   <.PL.SP>
Niigata          <.AV.NI>   <.NG.NI>   <.NL.NI>   <.PG.NI>   <.PL.NI>
Kyoto            <.AV.KY>   <.NG.KY>   <.NL.KY>   <.PG.KY>   <.PL.KY>
Hiroshima        <.AV.HI>   <.NG.HI>   <.NL.HI>   <.PG.HI>   <.PL.HI>
Fukuoka          <.AV.FU>   <.NG.FU>   <.NL.FU>   <.PG.FU>   <.PL.FU>
JASDAQ  Stock    <.AV.Q>    <.NG.Q>    <.NL.Q>    <.PG.Q>    <.PL.Q>    <.TV.Q>
        CB       <.AVCB.Q>  <.NGCB.Q>  <.NLCB.Q>  <.PGCB.Q>  <.PLCB.Q>
JBT Warrants     <.AV.BW>  <O#.NGWS.BW><O#.NLWS.BW>
================================================================================
Japanese Debt<JP/DEBT> Japanese Equity Guide<JP/EQUITY>Exchange Stats<JP/STATS2>
  Lost? Selective Access...<USER/HELP>   Reuters Phone Support...<PHONE/HELP>
```

```
.AVWS.T            TOP 20 BY VOLUME       TYO/   JPY            01:11
Name               Last   Net.Ch Open  High  Low   His.Cl Volume    Time
OJI PAPER 14       ↑×0.80  +0.20 0.80  0.80  0.75  0.60        144 03:59
FUJITSU 2          ↑×27.80 -1.25 27.85 27.90 26.80 29.05        80 05:59
MITSUB MTRS 1      ↑×1.45  +0.15 1.30  1.45  1.30  1.30         66 05:59
SUMITOMO ELEC 1    ↑×37.00       37.30 37.30 35.10 37.00        12 05:59
SAPPORO BREW 1     ×0.45         0.45  0.45  0.45  0.45          1 01:10
```

Derivatives

Following are brief descriptions of the derivatives used in the equity markets. If you need to know more about derivatives in general, their trading conventions and techniques used in the markets, then you may find it useful to refer to the *Introduction to Derivatives* book in this series.

As has been mentioned the underlying instruments are not always 'instruments' as such but involve a variety of different stock market indices. Within the equity markets, the following derivatives involving equities and stock indices are traded on exchanges and OTC.

- Futures contracts
  - Stock index
  - Equities

- Swaps
  - Equity swaps

- Options
  - Options on equities
  - Options on stock indices
  - Options on stock index futures

If you need an overview of futures derivatives or you need to remind yourself about derivatives in general, refer to the *Introduction to Derivatives* book in this series.

Futures Contracts

Stock index futures contracts are forward transactions with standard contract sizes and maturity dates which are traded on a formal exchange. The contracts are cash settled based on an Exchange Delivery Settlement Price (EDSP). Depending on the exchange and the contract the EDSP is an average, opening or closing value of the index for the last trading day.

Equity futures contracts are available on a few exchanges and in this case settlement can take place with the physical delivery of the shares.

Stock Index Futures

Within the equity markets the most important financial futures contracts are based on stock indices – not on the equities themselves (see below). One of the first such contracts was the Chicago Mercantile Exchange futures contract offered in 1982 on the Standard & Poor's 500 Index. In the UK, LIFFE offers a futures contract based on the FTSE 100 Index. Why do investors use these contracts? Investors use this type of contract to either hedge against or profit from increases or decreases in the overall level of equity prices. The futures track a portfolio or **basket** of stock prices represented by the market's index. It is important to note that on settlement only cash changes hands – there is no delivery of the basket of stocks. Therefore, on the agreed contract date buyers and sellers settle losses and gains, in cash, with the clearing house.

Financial futures are in essence bets on the future price of a financial instrument between two counterparties. These derivatives are often termed off-balance sheet transactions because there is no movement in assets or liabilities of an organisation until settlement takes place at a future date.

For example, if an investor buys shares, then at purchase his or her cash reserves will go down but at the same time his or her investment assets will increase by the same amount. Until settlement a futures contract does not generate the same balance sheet movement of cash or assets. However it is important to recognise that the risks involved with futures contracts are just as great as in the cash markets – in some cases the risks are considerably greater as illustrated by some of the more spectacular losses in derivatives trading.

An exchange-traded futures contract has the following characteristics:

- A **standardised specification** in terms of unit of trading, trading cycle of contract months, delivery days, quotation, minimum price movement etc.

- The **opportunity to trade** the instrument and offset the original contract with an equal and opposite trade. Very few contracts, less than 2%, reach maturity.

- A **public market,** in that prices for contracts are freely available. Trading takes place open outcry on an exchange floor and prices are published on exchange indicator boards, in the financial press and by providers such as Reuters.

- Once a trade has been made a **clearing house** acts as the counterparty to both sides of the trade. The contract is not directly between buyer and seller. The clearing house takes on the credit risk should a counterparty default. This is important because it means anyone can have access to the markets provided they have the creditworthiness required by the clearing house – in this way large organisations have no advantage over smaller organisations or investors.

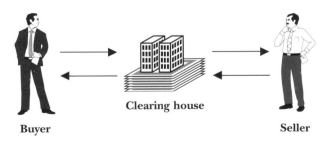

Buyer   Clearing house   Seller

Exchange Contracts

By far the most important futures contracts in the equity markets are those for stock indices and the following descriptions in this section concentrate on these instruments. Futures contracts on stock indices are traded on exchanges worldwide. The Reuters screens here show various exchange traded indices.

```
EXCHANGE TRADED INDEX FUTURES - REUTERS SPEED GUIDE            EQUITY/FUT1
To access information, double-click on the code in < > or [ ].  For more
guidance see <USER/HELP>.

=FUTURES STATISTICS====================    =NEWS and ANALYSIS====================
Garantifonden (Denmark).........<FUTOP>    Equity Derivatives News.........[E-DRV]
                                           Equity News Directory.............[E/]
                                           Company Results..................[RES]
                                           Stock Market Reports.............[STX]
=EXCHANGE TRADED INDEX FUTURES=========    All Other Reports................[E/R]
Americas Based Exchanges...<EQUITY/FUT2>
Europe/African Exchanges...<EQUITY/FUT3>
Asian Exchanges............<EQUITY/FUT4>




===============================================================================
Main Guide<REUTERS>  Equities Guide<EQUITY>   Equities Deriv Guide<EQUITY/DERIV>
    Lost?Selective Access?..<USER/HELP>    Reuters Phone Support..<PHONE/HELP>
```

```
EXCHANGE TRADED INDEX FUTURES - REUTERS SPEED GUIDE            EQUITY/FUT2
To access information, double-click on the code in < > or [ ].  For more
guidance see <USER/HELP>.

=AMERICAS BASED EXCHANGES==============    =AMERICAS BASED EXCHANGES Cont=========
CBOT Dow Jones Index............<O#DJ:>    NYFE Commod Research Bureau Ind.<O#CR:>
CME Dow Jones Taiwan Index......<O#TA:>    NYFE NYSE Composite Index.......<O#YX:>
CME Goldman Sachs CI Index......<O#GI:>    NYFE PSE Technology Index.......<O#TK:>
CME IPC Stock Index.............<O#MX:>    Sao Paulo BMF BOVESPA Index....<O#IND:>
CME Major Market Index..........<O#BC:>    Toronto FE TSE 35 Index.......<O#TXF:>
CME Nasdaq 100 Index............<O#ND:>    Toronto FE TSE 100 Comp Index..<O#TOF:>
CME Nikkei Stock Average........<O#NK:>    Toronto FE TSE 300 Spot Index..<O#TSE:>
CME Russell 2000 Index..........<O#RL:>
CME S&P 500 Index...............<O#SP:>    =NEWS and ANALYSIS====================
CME Mini S&P 500 Index..........<O#ES:>    Equity News Directory.............[E/]
CME S&P Growth Index............<O#SG:>    Equity Derivatives.............[E-DRV]
CME S&P MidCap 400 Index........<O#MD:>    Company Results..................[RES]
CME S&P Value Index.............<O#SU:>    Stock Market Reports.............[STX]
COMEX Eurotop Index.............<O#ER:>    All Other Reports................[E/R]
KCBT Mini Value Line Index......<O#MV:>
KCBT Value Line Index...........<O#KV:>
```

```
EXCHANGE TRADED INDEX FUTURES - REUTERS SPEED GUIDE            EQUITY/FUT3
To access information, double-click on the code in < > or [ ].  For more
guidance see <USER/HELP>.

=EXCHANGES=============================    =EXCHANGES=============================
Austrian ATX Index.............<O#ATX:>    SOFFEX Swiss Market Index......<O#SMI:>
Belgian FOX 20 Stock Index.....<O#BFX:>    SOFFEX Index Page.............<SOFFEXA>
Danish KFX Index...............<O#KFX:>    SAFEX - All Share.............<O#ALS:>
Deutsche Terminboerse DAX......<O#FDX:>    SAFEX - JSE Industrial........<O#INI:>
AEX Eurotop 100................<O#EUR:>    SAFEX - Top 30 Fin Instit.....<O#FIN:>
AEX Dutch Top 5 Index..........<O#TOP:>
AEX Stock Index................<O#AEX:>    =NEWS and ANALYSIS====================
FIB 30 Index...................<O#IFX:>    Equity Derivatives News.........[E-DRV]
LIFFE FTSE 100 Index...........<O#FFI:>    Equity News Directory.............[E/]
MATIF CAC 40 Index.............<O#FCH:>    Company Results..................[RES]
MDAX Index.....................<O#MDX:>    Stock Market Reports.............[STX]
MRV IBEX 35 Index..............<O#MFXI:>   All Other Reports................[E/R]
MRV IBEX 35 Timespread.......<O#MFXI-:>
Norwegian OBX Index............<O#OBX:>
Stockholm OM Block OMX Idx.....<O#OMX:>
Suomen Optoneklarit FOX.......<O#FOXO:>
```

```
EXCHANGE TRADED INDEX FUTURES - REUTERS SPEED GUIDE            EQUITY/FUT4
To access information, double-click on the code in < > or [ ].  For more
guidance see <USER/HELP>.

=ASIAN EXCHANGES======================     =ASIAN EXCHANGES======================
Hong Kong FE Index Page.........<HKFD>     Tokyo FE TOPIX Index..........<O#JTI:>
Hong Kong MSCI Index Futures...<O#SHI:>
HKFE Hang Seng Comm & Indus....<O#HSC:>
HKFE Hang Seng Finance Index...<O#HSF:>
HKFE Hang Seng Index...........<O#HSI:>
HKFE Property Index............<O#HSP:>
HKFE Hang Seng Utilities.......<O#HUT:>
KLF Composite Index............<O#KLI:>
KOSPI 200 Index................<O#KS:>
MSCI Taiwan Index..............<O#STW:>
New Zealand 10 Share Index.....<O#NTP:>    =NEWS and ANALYSIS====================
Osaka Nikkei 225 Index.........<O#JNI:>    Equity Derivatives News.........[E-DRV]
Osaka Nikkei 300 Index.........<O#JNW:>    Equity News Directory.............[E/]
SIMEX Nikkei Stock Average.....<O#SSI:>    Company Results..................[RES]
SIMEX Nikkei 300 Index.........<O#SNW:>    Stock Market Reports.............[STX]
Sydney FE All Ords Index.......<O#YIX:>    All Other Reports................[E/R]

===============================================================================
Equity Deriv <EQUITY/DERIV>   Equity Guide<EQUITY>    Previous Page <EQUITY/FUT3>
    Lost?Selective Access?...<USER/HELP>    Reuters Phone Support...<PHONE/HELP>
```

The table below indicates some of the annual volumes of stock index futures traded in 1996.

Index	Exchange	Volume
S&P 500	CME	19,700,597
CAC40	MATIF	5,853,172
Nikkei 225	SIMEX	4,887,912
FTSE 100	LIFFE	3,627,044
Nikkei 225	CME	531,097
Value Line	KCBT	34,624

Typical Contract Specifications

Futures contracts specifications vary depending on the underlying stock index and from exchange to exchange. Exchanges publish details of their contracts in printed form, on the Internet and via information providers such as Reuters. Look at a typical bond futures contract taken from LIFFE contract specifications shown opposite.

LIFE
FT-SE 100 Index Future

Unit of Trading	Valued at £25 per index point
Delivery Months	Mar, Jun, Sept, Dec
Delivery Day	First business day after the last trading day
Last Trading Day	10.30 Third Friday of delivery month
Quotation	Index points
Minimum price movement (Tick size and value)	0.5 (£12.50)
Trading hours	08.35–16.10 London time
APT Trading hours	16.32–17.30

This is the standard contract size – for contracts June 1998 on the value is £10

This is the trading cycle of contract months

This is the day contracts are settled

This is the last day and time on which trading can take place

The futures price is quoted on the number of index points

This is the smallest amount a contract can change value and the 'tick' size – for contracts June 1998 on the tick value is £5

Exchange trading hours – open out-cry

Automatic Pit Trading – the computer-based trading system hours

What Instruments Are Used in the Equity Markets?

The Reuters screens below show contract specifications for the LIFFE FTSE 100 and the CME S&P 500 Index contracts.

```
LIFFE FTSE 100 INDEX CONTRACT DETAILS                              LIF/FFI
Contract Details, Trading Hours, for the LIFFE FTSE 100 INDEX FUTURE.


FUTURES CHAIN       -    <O#FFI:>
OPTIONS             -    N/A
UNIT OF TRADING     -    Valued at GBP 25 per Index point ×GBP 10
DELIVERY MONTHS     -    March(H) June(M) September(U) December(Z)
TRADING MONTHS      -    3 Forward months
LAST TRADING DAY    -    The third Friday in the delivery month
QUOTATION           -    Index Points
MIN. PRICE MOVE     -    0.5
TICK SIZE & VALUE   -    GBP 12.50 ×GBP 5

TRADING HOURS       -    08.35 - 16.10
APT TRADING         -    16.32 - 17.30

×=The June 1998 FTSE 100 Index future contract



===============================================================================
Futures/Opts Guide<FUTURES> UKI Futures Guide<GB/FUTEX1> LIFFE Guide<LIF/FUTEX1>
   Lost? Selective Access...<USER/HELP>   Reuters Phone Support...<PHONE/HELP>
```

```
STANDARD & POORS STOCK PRICE INDEX FUTURE                           CME/SP
Contract Details, Trading Hours for CME S&P Stock Price Index Future

CHAIN RIC           -    <O#SP:>
OPTIONS RIC         -    SP (see <RULES1>-7 on how to construct an Option)
UNIT OF TRADING     -    USD250 times the S&P500 Stock Price Index
CONTRACT MONTHS     -    Mar(H) Jun(M) Sep(U) Dec(Z)
MINIMUM PRICE LIMIT -    0.05 index points or USD25 per contract
POSITION LIMITS     -    5000 contracts net long or net short in all
                         contract months combined.
TERMINATION OF TRADING - Futures trading will terminate on the business day
                         immediately preceding the day of determination of
                         the final settlement price.
DELIVERY            -    Cash settlement to the final settlement price.
                         Final settlement is usually on the 3rd Friday of
                         the contract month.

TRADING HOURS       -    Monday to Friday:    8:30am to 3:15pm
GLOBEX              -    Monday to Thursday: 3:45pm to 08:15am
                         Sundays & Holdiays: 17:30pm to 08:15am


===============================================================================
Global Futures<FUTURES>      US Futures<US/FUTEX1>      CME Futures<CME/FUTEX1>
   Lost? Selective Access...<USER/HELP>      Reuters Phone Support<PHONE/HELP>
```

But what does all this information mean?

Typically for financial futures there are four delivery months per year – March, June, September and December. It is also possible to have maturity dates out to several years but 'far month' contracts are much less liquid than the 'near months'. This means that it is not always possible to get prices for 'far months'.

The price movement of a futures contract is measured in **ticks**. The **minimum price movement** for a contract is determined by the exchange. Depending on the contract, it varies from a fraction of an index point to a whole point.

Example

You use an electronic information service such as Reuters to display the LIFFE FTSE 100 Index futures price for Mar 98. As indicated opposite the contracts are valued at £25 per index point for delivery in March, after this delivery date the value will be £10.

```
O#FFI:           FTSE INDEX       LIF/   GBP
Mth   Last Net.Ch Bid    Ask   Settle Open  High   Low    Volume Op.Int Time
MAR8 ↑5619.0  -2.0 5618.0 5619.0      5640.0 5679.0 5612.0   2928  61192 12:46
JUN8                                                         2449 15:34
SEP8                                                              :
```

The purchase of a contract with a current index of 5619.0 for delivery in March implies a payment of 5619.0 × £25 = £140,475 on delivery.

Profit and Loss on a Futures Contract

This is easy to calculate using the following method:

1. Determine the number of points the index has moved up or down. From this determine the number of ticks that the index has moved.

$$\text{Number of ticks} = \frac{\text{Number of index}}{\text{Minimum index movement in points}}$$

2. Multiply the number of ticks by the tick value and the number of contracts.

$$\text{Profit/loss} = \text{Number of ticks} \times \text{Tick value} \times \text{Number of contracts}$$

Example

25 March CME S&P 500 futures contracts are bought with an index value of 1021.20 on 9th February. On 13th February the contracts are sold with a settlement price of 1024.50. The tick size for the contract is 0.05 index points and the tick value is $25.

$$\begin{aligned}
\text{Profit or loss} &= \frac{(1024.50 - 1021.20)}{0.05} \times 25 \times 25 \\
&= 66 \text{ ticks} \times 25 \times 25 \\
&= \$41,250 \text{ profit}
\end{aligned}$$

Typical Contract Quotations

Stock index futures quotations are available from the financial press such as the *Financial Times* and *The Wall Street Journal* and from electronic information products such as Reuters 3000 Equities. The information appears in formats similar to those following.

Financial press

FTSE 100 Index Futures (LIFFE) £25 per full index point					
	Open	Settle	High	Low	Open Int
Mar	5430.0	5457.0	5480.0	5410.0	64000
Jun	5485.0	5520.0	5524.0	5482.0	450

These screen illustrate contracts on the FTSE 100, CAC 40 and Nikkei 225.

FTSE 100

Futures
RIC: 0#FFI: Exchange: LIF   Currency: GBP

Month	Last	Change	Bid	Ask	Volume
Mar98	5621.0	-1.00	5620.0	5621.0	3,437
Jun98	-	-	-	-	0
Sep98	-	-	-	-	0

CAC 40

Futures
RIC: 0#FCH: Exchange: MAT   Currency: FRF

Month	Last	Change	Bid	Ask	Volume
Feb98	3247.0	+19.0	3247.0	3248.0	7,096
Mar98	3255.0	+18.5	-	3257.0	374
Apr98	3261.5	+21.0	-	-	1
Jun98	-	-	-	-	0

Nikkei 225

Futures
RIC: 0#JNI: Exchange: OSA   Currency: JPY

Month	Last	Change	Bid	Ask	Volume
Mar98	17190	+60.0	17160	17190	14,238
Jun98	17090	+40.0	17090	17150	2,795
Sep98	-	-	-	-	0
Dec98	-	-	-	-	0

What Instruments Are Used in the Equity Markets?

Hedgers and Speculators

Originally futures contracts were devised so that holders of an asset could hedge or insure its price today for sometime in the future. Hedgers seek to transfer the risk of future price fluctuations by selling future contracts which guarantee them a future price for their asset. If the future cash price of their asset falls then they have protected themselves. However, if the future cash price rises then they have lost the opportunity to profit. Hedging offers some degree of certainty for future prices and therefore allows market players to fix prices, interest rate payments or receipts etc.

Hedgers are typically market makers and institutional investors whereas speculators are typically traders who take on the risk of a futures contract for an appropriate price and the potential rewards.

The transfer of risk sought by hedgers is possible in the markets because different market players have different strategies and include:

- Hedgers with opposite risks

- Hedgers already holding positions who need to offset their positions

- Speculators with market views on likely price changes who provide the futures markets with extra liquidity

As in any futures market place for commodities, hedgers can hold **long** or **short** positions and in order to hedge their positions market players need to take an **opposite** position to the ones they hold.

It is important to understand that the principle of hedging is to maintain a neutral position. As prices in the cash market for the asset move one way, the move is compensated by an equal and opposite move in the futures' price. You can imagine the situation similar to the movement of the pans on a pair of scales.

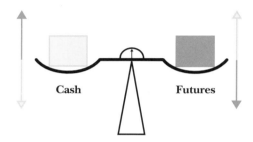

Going short futures
If a market player **holds**, or intends to hold, an asset in the cash market, then he has a **long** position. The opposite position in the futures markets means he must **go short** or **sell futures**. A **short hedge** will therefore lock in a selling price.

Going long futures
If a market player is short, or intends to go short, in the cash market, then the opposite position in the futures markets means he must **go long** or **buy futures**. A **long hedge** will therefore lock in a buying price.

Another way of considering market players using stock index futures contracts is to look at whether they are **buyers** or **sellers** of the contracts.

Buyers of Stock Index Futures

- Wish to buy equities in the future and therefore **go long**.

- Expect the value of the Stock index to **rise**. If the index does rise, then any losses in buying the underlying equities in the future are offset by gains from the cash settlement of the futures contract on delivery.

The diagrams below show how the losses in the underlying instrument are offset by gains in the futures market.

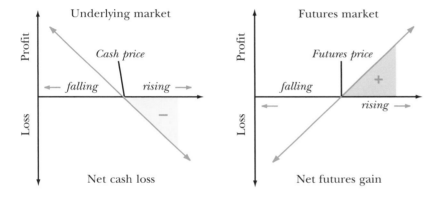

As stock index	So futures prices
Rises	Fall
Falls	Rise

Sellers of Stock Index Futures

- Wish to sell equities in the future and therefore **go short**.

- Expect the value of the stock index to **fall**. If the index does fall, then any losses in buying the underlying equities in the future are offset by gains from the cash settlement of the futures contract on delivery.

The diagrams below show how the losses in the underlying instrument are offset by gains in the futures market.

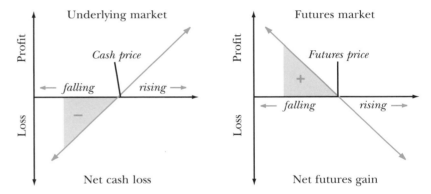

Short hedge	Long hedge
• Sell futures	• Buy futures
• **Protects against** fall in stock index value	• **Protects against** rise in stock index value
• Locks in selling price	• Locks in buying price

What Instruments Are Used in the Equity Markets?

Hedging with Index Futures

Stock index futures allow hedgers to buy or sell equities in the future such that their position is protected, at least partially, from changes in market conditions. Suppose a fund manager has taken a decision to buy or sell shares in a portfolio in the future. She decides to hedge her position with stock index futures but how many contracts should she buy/sell?

The number of contracts is simply calculated from the following equation which relies on the beta value, ß, for the shares in the portfolio being known.

$$\text{No. of contracts} = \frac{\text{Value of portfolio} \times \text{Average ß}}{\text{Index level} \times \text{Contract value per index point}}$$

ß values obtained from Reuters 3000 Equities

Current stock index value

Given in contract specification

Example

A fund manager has 25 million French francs value in a portfolio divided between five shares. The value of the CAC 40 is 3221.45 and the contract value for the MATIF CAC 40 futures contract is 200 FRF. The manager uses Reuters 3000 Equities to find the ß values of the shares...

Share	Market value, FRF	Shares as %	Share ß
Rhone Poulenc SA	5,000,000	20	0.92
Renault SA	2,500,000	10	1.39
SGS Thomson Micr	12,500,000	50	0.94
BNP	2,500,000	10	1.05
Eridania Beguin	2,500,000	10	0.86
Total	25,000,000	100	

To calculate the number of contracts required:

1. Calculate the average ß value of the portfolio. This is a weighted average of the ß values of the 5 shares in the portfolio. The weighting is taken from the % share of the total market value of the portfolio.

$$\begin{aligned} \text{Average ß} &= (0.92 \times 0.20) + (1.39 \times 0.10) + (0.94 \times 0.50) \\ &\quad + (1.05 \times 0.10) + (0.86 \times 0.10) \\ &= 0.184 + 0.139 + 0.47 + 0.105 + 0.086 \\ &= 0.984 \end{aligned}$$

2. Calculate the number of contracts.

$$\begin{aligned} \text{No. of contracts} &= \frac{25,000,000 \times 0.984}{3221.45 \times 200} \\ &= 38.2 \text{ or } \textbf{38 contracts} \end{aligned}$$

As the ß value is less than 1 this means that the portfolio is likely to underperform the market. The fund manager needs to buy/sell 38 contracts to hedge her position.

REUTERS

Stock Index Futures in the Market Place

This section deals with a number of important matters concerning stock index futures which you will need to understand.

How a Stock Index Futures Contract Works

When a futures contract is agreed upon, no payment is made. Instead both parties are required to deposit a **margin** with the clearing house which acts as the counterparty to both sides. The **initial margin** is only a small percentage of the contract price and it is used to cover daily price movements of the futures' price in relation to the agreed price. Each day the futures' position is **marked-to-market** which means it is revalued at the current market price. Any profits and losses are paid over daily. By marking-to-market and settling all positions daily the clearing house effectively rewrites all futures contracts at the prevailing market price.

If the initial margin is depleted then extra margin – **variation margin** – is required. If a profit is made the account will receive it and it may be withdrawn. The system of maintaining the correct margin ensures that the loser can bear any losses and the winner is credited with gains.

Example
25 June LIFFE FTSE 100 Index futures contracts are bought on 2nd February at 5622. On 9th February the contracts are sold at 5607. The tick size is 0.5 and the tick value is £12.50. The table below shows the actual course of events – there is a loss in this case.

Date	Settlement price	Previous price	Ticks	Variation margin, £
2.2	5625	5622	16	75
3.2	5627	5625	14	50
4.2	5617	5627	220	2250
5.2	5595	5617	244	2550
6.2	5604	5595	118	225
9.2	5607	5604	236	2450
Total	**5607**	**5622**	**272**	**2900**

Dealing on margin is an example of **gearing** or **leverage**. Gearing allows investors to make a larger investment than could otherwise be afforded. Small investments are used to generate large profits, however, losses can be correspondingly large! For example, a £1000 investment in a futures contract is equivalent to buying a basic investment of £10,000–20,000.

As the expiry date of the contract approaches the futures price will equal the current instrument price and so the differential is not very large. This is why the vast majority, over 98%, of futures contracts are closed out before the contract reaches the agreed expiry date.

The process is illustrated as here:

On the contract date
The Seller sells a contract to the Buyer and both deposit initial margin with the clearing house.

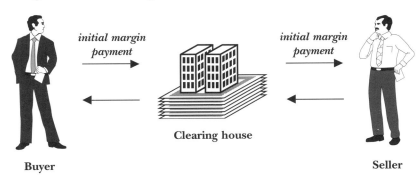

initial margin payment

Clearing house

Buyer   **Seller**

During the contract

The Seller's and the Buyer's profit and loss accounts are adjusted daily.

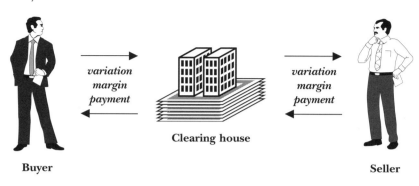

Buyer   **Clearing house**   **Seller**

On the delivery date or contract closure

The Seller's and the Buyer's profit and loss accounts are settled for the last time.

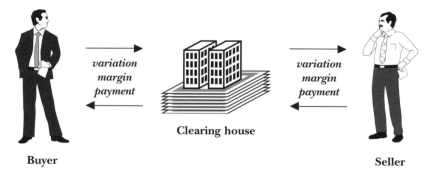

Buyer   **Clearing house**   **Seller**

Synthetic Equity Market Exposure

About 90% of equity funds underperform their benchmark stock market index – the number of funds outperforming the market consistently are few in number. One method of overcoming this problem is to use an **index portfolio** which comprises the shares of the relevant index, for example, S&P 500 or FTSE 100, weighted in the same way as the index itself. If you invest in an index portfolio you should never underperform the index significantly but you will never outperform it.

Investors can simulate an index portfolio using a combination of stock index futures and money market instruments. In other words they do not actually own the shares – they invest in a **synthetic** portfolio.

Suppose the FTSE 100 Index stands at 5406. The initial margin requirement for a futures contract is, for example, £2,500. Every point move represents a change in value of £25 – up or down.

To obtain the same market exposure in equities, an investor would have to invest 5406 x £25 = £135,150. In other words, point for point a £2,500 initial margin payment in a futures contract results in the same profit potential as a £135,150 investment in equities.

The synthetic fund is simulated by investing £2,500 in the futures contract and placing the balance of £132,650 in money market instruments. So the synthetic fund does not actually own any shares, has ready access to its funds, and trading costs are kept to a minimum.

In summary, here are the key points regarding stock index futures.

- A stock index future is an **exchange-traded forward transaction** with a standard contract size, and maturity dates

- Stock index futures are **cash settled** against an **Exchange Delivery Settlement Price**

- Market players **buy futures** or **go long**, to protect against any **rise** in stock index values

- Market players **sell futures** or **go short**, to protect against any **fall** in stock index values

- A **clearing house** acts as **counterparty** to both buyers and sellers of a futures contract which is marked-to-market daily

The Reuters screens below and opposite compare the Nikkei 225 futures contracts prices and contract specifications on the Osaka Stock Exchange with those on SIMEX.

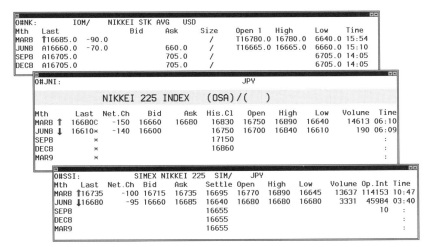

```
NIKKEI STOCK INDEX AVERAGE FUTURES                                    CME/NK
Contract Details, Trading Hours for CME Nikkei Stock Index Average futures

CHAIN RIC              -    <O#NK:>
OPTIONS RIC            -    NK (see <RULES1>-7 on how to construct an Option)
UNIT OF TRADING        -    USD5 times the Nikkei Stock Average
CONTRACT MONTHS        -    Mar(H) Jun(M) Sep(U) Dec(Z)
MINIMUM PRICE LIMIT    -    5 points or $25 per contract
POSITION LIMITS        -    5000 contracts net long or net short in all
                           contracts combined
TERMINATION OF TRADING -    The 1st business day preceding the day of
                           determination of the final settlement price
DELIVERY               -    Cash settlement to the final settlement price,
                           determined by a special open quote of the Nikkei
                           Stock Average rounded to the nearest 1/10 of an
```

```
NIKKEI 225 INDEX CONTRACT DETAILS                                    OSE/JNI
Contract Details, Trading Hours etc for the NIKKEI 225 INDEX FUTURE.

CHAIN RIC             -    <O#JNI:>
OPTIONS RIC           -    <O#JNI*.OS>
UNDERLYING INDEX      -    <.N225> NIKKEI 225
CONTRACT SIZE         -    JPY 1000 times NIKKEI 225
DELIVERY MONTHS       -    5 Quarterly month cycle
DAILY PRICE LIMIT     -    Around 3% of the previous day's last price
LAST TRADING DAY      -    The business day before the second Friday of each
                          contract month
LAST SETTLEMENT DAY   -    The fourth business day following the last day of
                          each contract month
SETTLEMENT METHOD     -    Cash settled
```

```
             SIMEX Nikkei 225 Futures Contract Details              SIM/SSI
Contract Details, Trading Hours etc for the Nikkei 225 Futures.

CHAIN RIC...<O#SSI:>,<O#1SSI:>,<O#2SSI:>    OPTIONS <SSISUM> OR SSI<MTH><YR>+ F3
SPOT & FUTURES...............<O#SSI1:> OR <SMXNI>
UNIT OF TRADING..............INDEX POINTS
DELIVERY MONTHS..............5 QUARTERLY MONTH CYCLE
LAST TRADING DAY.............THE DAY BEFORE 2ND FRIDAY OF CONTRACT MONTH
MINIMUM FLUCTUATION..........5.0 POINTS OF NIKKEI 225 INDEX = YEN 2500
MAXIMUM FLUCTUATION..........WHEN THE PRICE MOVES 7.5% IN EITHER DIRECTION FROM
                            PREVIOUS DAY'S SETTLE, TRADING WITHIN THE PRICE
                            LIMIT OF 7.5% IS ALLOWED FOR THE NEXT 15 MINITUES
                            AFTERWHICH THE PRICE LIMIT IS EXPANDED TO 12.5%.
                            IF PRICE MOVES 12.5% FROM PREVIOUS SETTLE, TRADING
                            WITHIN 12.5% PRICE LIMIT IS ALLOWED FOR THE NEXT
                            15 MIN AFTERWHICH THERE IS NO MORE LIMIT THAT DAY.
                            NO LIMITS DURING LAST 30 MIN OF ANY DAY.
                            NO LIMITS ON LAST TRADING DAY.
QUOTATION SIZE...............YEN 500 X NIKKEI 225 STOCK AVERAGE FUTURES PRICE
TRADING HOURS................07:55-10:15 11:15-14:25  1500-1900(ATS) (SST)
                             23:55-02:15 03:15-06:25  0700-1100      (GMT)

==============================================================================
Futures/Options Guide<FUTURES> S'PORE Futures<SG/FUTEX1> SIMEX Guide<SIM/FUTEX1>
Lost? Selective Access...<USER/HELP>   Reuter Phone Support...<PHONE/HELP>
```

The Reuters screens on this page display information about the debt and equity market indices for the emerging markets in Latin America. The International Finance Corporation on the left is a member of the World Bank and provides loans and equity financing for projects in developing economies. On the right is the Reuters Survey of Forecasts for World Stock Indices.

```
INDICES                        (Page 1 of 3)                    INDICES

COUNTRY OR REGION    INDICE NAME                  MARKET       PAGE/RIC
All Latin America...Baring Securities...............Equity.........<BEMI>
All Latin America...International Finance Corp......Equity.........<IFCINDEX>
All Latin America...J.P. Morgan (Brady Bonds).......Debt..........<EMBI> \
All Latin America...J.P. Morgan (Eurobonds).........Debt..........<EMBK>
All Latin America...Lehman Brothers.................Debt.(Monthly)..<LEH/EMERA>
All Latin America...Lehman Brothers.................Debt.(Weekly)...<LEH/EMERN>
All Latin America...Morgan Stanley Emerging Mkts.....Equity........<.LTX>
All Latin America...Salomon Bros. (Brady Bonds)......Debt..........<BRDY>
Argentina..........Merval.........................Equity.........<.MERV>
Argentina..........Burcap.........................Equity.........<.BURC>
Argentina..........General........................Equity.........<.IGB>
Brazil (Sao P.)....Bovespa........................Equity.........<.BVSP>
Braz
Braz
Braz
Braz
Chil
Chil
Chil
×Thi
```

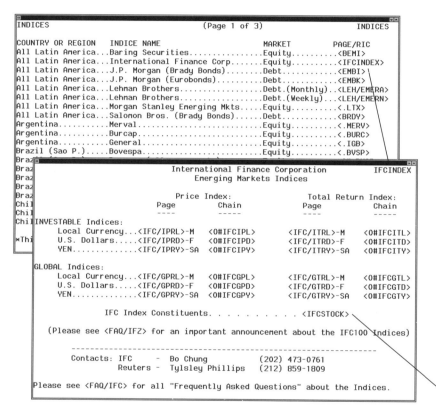

```
               International Finance Corporation        IFCINDEX
                      Emerging Markets Indices

                  Price Index:              Total Return Index:
                Page       Chain            Page        Chain
                ----       -----            ----        -----
INVESTABLE Indices:
    Local Currency...<IFC/IPRL>-M  <O#IFCIPL>   <IFC/ITRL>-M  <O#IFCITL>
    U.S. Dollars.....<IFC/IPRD>-F  <O#IFCIPD>   <IFC/ITRD>-F  <O#IFCITD>
    YEN..............<IFC/IPRY>-SA <O#IFCIPY>   <IFC/ITRY>-SA <O#IFCITY>

GLOBAL Indices:
    Local Currency...<IFC/GPRL>-M  <O#IFCGPL>   <IFC/GTRL>-M  <O#IFCGTL>
    U.S. Dollars.....<IFC/GPRD>-F  <O#IFCGPD>   <IFC/GTRD>-F  <O#IFCGTD>
    YEN..............<IFC/GPRY>-SA <O#IFCGPY>   <IFC/GTRY>-SA <O#IFCGTY>

         IFC Index Constituents. . . . . . . . . .<IFCSTOCK>

    (Please see <FAQ/IFZ> for an important announcement about the IFC100 Indices)

    ------------------------------------------------------------
    Contacts: IFC    - Bo Chung          (202) 473-0761
              Reuters - Tylsley Phillips   (212) 859-1809

Please see <FAQ/IFC> for all "Frequently Asked Questions" about the Indices.
```

```
12:05 16DEC97        WORLD STOCK INDEX FORECASTS    UK30507     EQUITYPOLL22
                           SUMMARY OF FINDINGS
Index <EQUITYPOLL1>
    LONDON, Dec 12 - Following is a summary of the average predicted percentage
increases/decreases in each bourse index by end-1998 and end 1999 compared with
the closing level on December 12.

                                        END-98      END-99

Australia All Ordinaries                 9.9         16.2
Belgium Bel 20                           7.3         10.0
Britain FTSE-100                        12.1         22.1
Canada TSE300                           17.6         32.5
France CAC40                            15.4         30.7
Germany DAX30                            7.2         14.2
Hong Kong Hang Seng                     31.7         58.2
Italy BCI Conit                         10.1         16.9
Nikkei 225                              24.6         34.5
Korea KOSPI                             33.2         89.4
```

```
12:08 16DEC97        WORLD STOCK INDEX FORECASTS    UK30507     EQUITYPOLL23
                           SUMMARY OF FINDINGS
Index <EQUITYPOLL1>
Continued from <EQUITYPOLL22>

                                        END-98      END-99

Netherlands AEX                         11.1         24.9
Singapore STII                           5.0         27.8
South africa All share                  22.3         40.8
Spain IBEX35                            14.0          -
Sweden OMX                              19.6         30.5
Switzerland - SMI                        7.2          -
Switzerland - SPI                        7.2          -
Taiwan TAIEX                             7.8         41.7
United States Dow Jones                 12.0         14.5
United States NASDAQ                    14.5         25.5
Unites States - AMEX                    11.6         12.2
```

```
IFCGPD          Global Price              USD
 Index        Value    No.Stk  CHG(%)  WCH(%)  YTD(%)Net.ChngLoc  Time
Argentina    1767.01      35   -0.09   -1.24   -2.76      WAS  18:00
Asia          252.64    1078   -0.08    3.30   11.79      WAS  18:00
Brazil        386.61      87    0.65   -0.71   -2.53      WAS  18:00
Chile        2475.98      53   -0.20    4.60   -8.90      WAS  18:00
China         129.46     195   -0.77   -1.37    0.05      WAS  18:00
Colombia     1425.27      28    0.65    2.16  -20.92      WAS  18:00
Composite     328.88    1984    0.01    1.47    0.23      WAS  18:00
Czech Rep      50.58      41    0.72   -0.63   -4.02      WAS  18:00
Egypt         152.53      54   -0.12    0.17   -6.86      WAS  18:00
Greece        445.96      56   -1.38   -4.39   -3.73      WAS  18:00
Hungary       203.53      15    0.40   -0.05   -6.28      WAS  18:00
India         268.91     133   -0.62    1.43   -5.53      WAS  18:00
Indonesia      23.82      62   -7.53   12.31  -25.72      WAS  18:00
Israel        109.73      49   -0.06    2.36   -9.97      WAS  18:00
Jordan        162.06      44    0.07   -0.19   -1.39      WAS  18:00
Korea         148.39     195    3.21    2.15   45.05      WAS  18:00
Latin America  733.7     333   -0.01   -0.41   -9.60      WAS  18:00
Malaysia      131.09     157   -1.19    6.60   30.84      WAS  18:00
Mexico       1656.78      74   -0.77   -1.96  -16.54      WAS  18:00
Morocco       198.71      17    0.11    1.11    4.19      WAS  18:00
Nigeria        72.73      31   -0.55   -0.67  -11.09      WAS  18:00
Pakistan      237.12      55    1.55   -0.86   -2.41      WAS  18:00
Peru          223.73      37    0.13   -3.90  -13.06      WAS  18:00
Philippines  1594.86      59    0.10    2.39   12.04      WAS  18:00
Poland        719.22      29    0.56    6.98   21.04      WAS  18:00
Portugal     1360.58      23    0.38    3.87   18.97      WAS  18:00
Russia        475.78      37    0.40   -0.93  -23.41      WAS  18:00
```

Equity Futures

Although uncommon, some of the Scandinavian exchanges such as the Swedish electronic market for derivatives – OM Stockholm and its real-time linked London Securities and Derivatives Exchange (OMLX) – offer both futures contracts on stock indices and a number of leading Swedish stocks, for example, Nokia, Scania and Volvo. Futures contracts on a few Danish stocks are available on the Copenhagen Stock Exchange. For futures on equities, settlement can take place with the physical delivery of the shares – most of the contracts are for an underlying 100 shares.

These Reuters screens show the Copenhagen and Stockholm contract details.

```
COPENHAGEN STOCK EXCHANGE - REUTERS SPEED GUIDE            CPH/FUTEX1
To access information double click in the <> brackets.

COPENHAGEN STOCK EXCHANGE:          THE FUTOP CLEARING CENTRE:
Address :  6 - Nikolaj Plads        Address :  5 - Nytorv
           P.O. Box 1040 DK-1007               P.O. Box 2017 DK-1012
           Copenhagen K, Denmark              Copenhagen K, Denmark
Tel No  :  45-33 933366             Tel No  :  45-33 933311


=LISTED CONTRACTS=====================NEAREST MONTH======CONTRACT DETAILS=
3-month CIBOR...................<O#RDK:>  <RDKc1>...................<CPH/RDK>
MTG Realkredit Mtg 6% 2026.......<O#RKE:>  <RKEc1>...................<CPH/RKE>
DSL Danish Govt 8% 2001........<O#DK01T:>  <DK01Tc1>................<CPH/DK01T>
DSL Danish Govt 8% 2003........<O#DK03T:>  <DK03Tc1>................<CPH/DK03T>
DSL Danish Govt 7% 2007........<O#DK07T:>  <DK07Tc1>................<CPH/DK07T>
KFX Index Futures...............<O#KFX:>  <KFXc1>...................<CPH/KFX>
Danisco Futures................<O#DEMC:>  <DEMCc1>..................<CPH/EQFUT>
Novo Futures....................<O#NVO:>  <NVOc1>...................<CPH/EQFUT>
Teledanmark Futures.............<O#TLD:>  <TLDc1>...................<CPH/EQFUT>




====================================================================
Main Futures Index<FUTURES>   Country Index<DENMARK>   Danish Futures<DK/FUTEX1>
  Lost? Selective Access?..<USER/HELP>    Reuters Phone Support..<PHONE/HELP>
```

```
STOCKHOLMS OPTIONS MARKNAD FK AB (OM)    INDEX SEE <OM/MENU>        OM/MENW
COMPANY/SHARE       OPTIONS     FORWARDS   LENDINGS      UNDERLYING SHARE
NETCOM SYSTEMS B... <O#NCOM*.o>  <O#NCOM:>  <NCOMbl.o>    <NCOMb.ST>
NOKIA A.(SEK).......<O#NOKI*.o>  <O#NOKI:>  <NOKIal.o>    <NOKIa.ST>
NOKIA A.(FIM).......<O#NOKA*.o>  <O#NOKA:>                <NOKSa.HE>
NORDBANKEN HLDG.....<O#NBHD*.o>  <O#NBHD:>                <NBH.ST>
NORDSTRÖM THULIN B. <O#NDRS*.o>  <O#NDRS:>  <NDRSbl.o>    <NTb.ST>
PHARMACIA & UPJOHN. <O#PHU*.o>   <O#PHU:>                 <PHU.ST>
SANDVIK A.........      -           -       <SVIKal.o>    <SANDa.ST>
SANDVIK B......... <O#SVIK*.o>    <O#SVIK:>  <SVIKbl.o>    <SANDb.ST>
SCA B.............. <O#SCAS*.o>   <O#SCAS:>  <SCASbl.o>    <SCAb.ST>
SCANIA B...........<O#SCV*.o>     <O#SCV:>                 <SCVb.ST>
SE BANKEN A........<O#SEBS*.o>    <O#SEBS:>  <SEBSal.o>    <SEBa.ST>
SHB A..............<O#SHBS*.o>    <O#SHBS:>  <SHBSal.o>    <SHBa.ST>
SKANDIA ...........<O#SKDS*.o>    <O#SKDS:>  <SKDSl.o>     <SDIA.ST>
SKF B..............<O#SKFR*.o>    <O#SKFR:>  <SKFRbl.o>    <SKFb.ST>
SKANSKA B..........<O#SKKS*.o>    <O#SKKS:>  <SKKSbl.o>    <SKAb.ST>
SPARBANKEN A.......<O#SPAR*.o>    <O#SPAR:>  <SPARal.o>    <SPARa.ST>
SSAB A.............<O#SSAB*.o>    <O#SSAB:>  <SSABal.o>    <SSABa.ST>
STORA A............<O#STOR*.o>    <O#STOR:>  <STORal.o>    <STORa.ST>
STORA B............     -            -       <STORbl.o>    <STORb.ST>
SWEDISH MATCH......<O#SWMA*.o>    <O#SWMA:>  <SWMAl:o>     <SWMA.ST>
SYDKRAFT C.........     -                    <SYDScl.o>    <SYDc.ST>
TRELLEBORG B.......<O#TLBS*.o>    <O#TLBS:>  <TLBSbl.o>    <TRELb.ST>
VOLVO B............<O#VOLV*.o>    <O#VOLV:>  <VOLVbl.o>    <VOLVb.ST>
```

```
O#VOLV:              VOLVO b FUTURES   SOM/      SEK
Mth    Last  Net.Ch  Bid     Ask   Settle Open   High   Low    Volume Op.Int Time
MAR8                 219.25  225.25                                     110   :
MAYB  ↑224.50        216.00  222.00        224.00 224.50 224.00    20          11:47
JULB                                                                       :
JAN9                 230.00                                             10   :
JANO                                                                       :
```

Swaps

An **Equity swap** is an agreement between counterparties in which at least one party agrees to pay the other a rate of return based on a stock index, according to a schedule of future dates for the maturity period of the agreement. The other party makes payments based on a fixed or floating rate, or another stock index. The payments are based on an agreed percentage of an underlying notional principal amount.

If you need an overview of swaps derivatives or you need to remind yourself about derivatives in general, then you may find it useful to refer to the *Introduction to Derivatives* book in this series.

Equity swaps provide fund managers, portfolio managers and institutional investors with a method of transferring assets, particularly cross-border, without incurring the high fees involved in buying and selling transactions. The swap also provides a means of avoiding the complexities of foreign regulations, taxes, dividend payments, etc relating to overseas equity markets.

It is important to remember that the notional amount of the swap is **not** exchanged. In principle an equity swap is simple and straightforward.

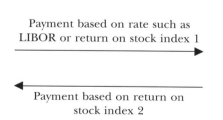

Payment based on rate such as LIBOR or return on stock index 1

Payment based on return on stock index 2

Party A

Party B

An equity swap is a convenient, cost-effective method by which these market players can swap assets for cash, using notional amounts and contracts with maturities from months up to 10 years. Equity swaps are becoming increasingly more important as they allow the following:

- The rapid switching and diversification of international equity portfolios

- Access to emerging markets without the risk of holding an equity portfolio in these markets

- Access to international equity markets which an investor may not normally have due to legal or regulatory reasons

Most equity swaps are **plain vanilla** instruments and involve two basic types of swap:

- **Asset allocation**
  This is where the swap is based on a cash market interest payment such as LIBOR and a cash payment based on the return of a stock index. In this case the currencies for both payments are usually the same but may be different.

- **International equity swaps**
  In this case the swap may be between an interest payment and the return on a stock index or where returns on two different stock indices are swapped. In this case the currencies involved for payments may be the same or different.

There are other variations of equity swaps such as **call swaps** where the equity payment is paid only if the stock index rises and **currency-hedged swaps** where currency risk is eliminated if the swap transaction involves foreign exchange for payments.

Review the following examples to see how an equity swap works.

Example – A plain vanilla asset allocation equity swap

A US fund manager expects short-term interest rates to remain low over the next year but the indications are that US equities will have a higher return. The manager has a portfolio of money market instruments which could be sold to buy a US equity portfolio; however, this process involves costly transactions and administration.

The manager decides to use an equity swap for one year. In this case he swaps floating USD LIBOR payments on a quarterly basis and receives the total return on the S&P 500 Index from a **swap bank**, AYZ. A swap bank is simply a commercial or investment bank specialising in swap deals.

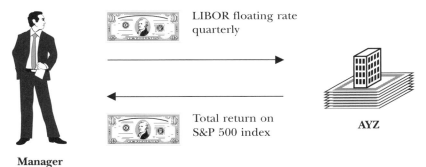

LIBOR floating rate
quarterly

Total return on
S&P 500 index

AYZ

Manager

It is usually the case that the LIBOR payer also pays an amount equal to any decreases in the stock index unless otherwise agreed. In such a case the payer of the stock index return has effectively negotiated a **floor** to protect the bank against adverse changes in the index.

If the fund manager had wished to gain access to an overseas equity market such as that in Japan, then he could have swapped floating USD LIBOR payments for the total returns on the Nikkei 225 Index; however, the payments associated with the Nikkei 225 Index could have been made in USD or Yen.

In this type of equity swap the fund manager only has one transaction to set up, no cash instruments have to be sold and he achieves the returns he requires without the concern of dividends, taxes etc.

Example – A plain vanilla international equity swap

A US portfolio manager at XYZ Inc has a fund which currently exists entirely of US stocks. The manager believes she should diversify into the German market and buy German blue-chip company stocks. She is prepared to allocate 15% of her portfolio to German stocks. What can she do?

She could sell 15% of her US stock holdings and use the funds to buy German stocks. However, this would incur high transaction costs in both buying and selling together with the added complications of holding foreign instruments

This is how the equity swap works...

❶ The manager enters into a swap with a bank
The manager agrees the notional principal amount is equivalent to 15% of the market value of her portfolio and that payments will be made on a quarterly basis.

❷ Counterparties exchange payments
The portfolio manager pays the S&P 500 Stock Index rate of return based on the notional principal to AYZ every quarter. In return AYZ pay the manager the DAX Stock Index rate of return for the same notional principal every quarter.

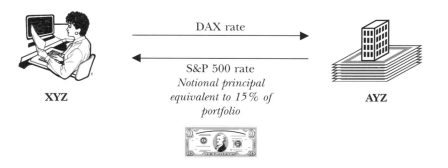

XYZ — DAX rate → **AYZ**

← S&P 500 rate
*Notional principal
equivalent to 15% of
portfolio*

There are a number of ways equity swaps can be structured to cater for different needs.

- **Fixed and Variable Notional Principal Amounts**
  A fixed notional principal means that the portfolio is rebalanced periodically to maintain the same percentage allocation as agreed originally.

  A variable notional principal amount means that the portfolio is not rebalanced and grows or declines from the original according to the markets.

- **Currency Risk**
  If a currency risk is unacceptable then the portfolio manager will require the payments to be based on the DAX return applied to a USD notional principal.

  However, if a currency risk is acceptable then payments are based on a DEM notional principal. If the final payments are to be in USD, then the DEM would need to be exchanged in the spot FX market.

- **Specialised Basis for Payments**
  It is possible to structure an equity swap so that payments are made on specific stock market sectors or even on individual stocks, although the latter case is unusual.

The overall result of the swap is that the portfolio manager has in effect sold US stock and bought German stock for a notional value of 15% of her portfolio.

One difference between equity swaps and other types of swaps is that one party can be responsible for both payments. How can this be? In the example, suppose there is a simultaneous fall in the S&P 500 and a rise in the DAX. If the S&P 500 falls, then the portfolio has effectively been devalued, for example, to 14% of the notional principal. This means the portfolio manager will have to compensate AYZ for this loss. On the other side AYZ has to pay an amount on a revalued portfolio, for example, to 16% of the notional principal because the DAX has gone up. This means that AYZ is paying on a portfolio size which is greater than agreed. So the portfolio manager also has to compensate the bank for the difference in DAX payments.

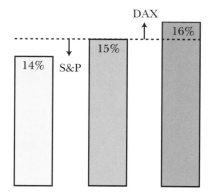

In summary, here are the key points regarding an equity swap.

- At least **one payment** is based on the **rate of return** of a **stock index** for an agreed percentage of a notional principal amount

- An equity swap is in effect a transfer of assets **without** involving the physical buying and selling of equities or other financial instruments

- An equity swap provides an effective method of entering into **overseas equity markets** without the restraints and complications of actually trading abroad

The Reuters screens on this page show the Equity News Speed Guide, using detail on the US Asset Allocation Survey to show the Globel Equity Fund allocations for major US funds.

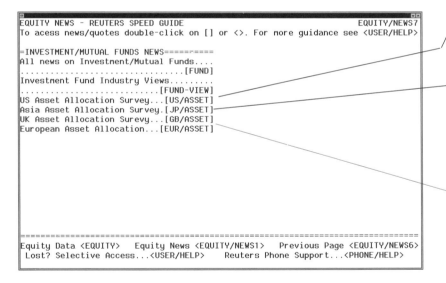

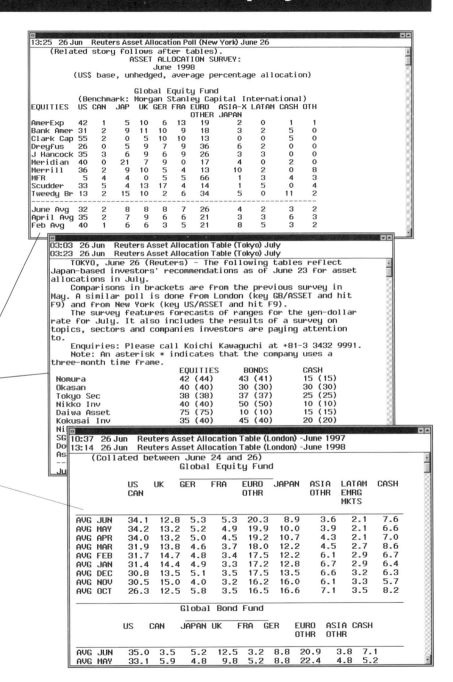

Options

In general an options contract may be defined as follows:

 An **options** contract is an agreement giving the holder the right, but not the obligation, to buy or sell financial instruments at a price and at a time in the future for an agreed upon **premium** (price).

There are two basic types of options contract available and there are two important styles for trading options:

Call option	This is the right, but not obligation, to **buy** an underlying instrument in the future.
Put option	This is the right, but not obligation, to **sell** an underlying instrument in the future.

American style	This may be exercised any time **prior** to expiry.
European style	This may be exercised **only** on the expiry date.

There are three types of instruments, reviewed in this section, on which options are traded both OTC and on exchanges. These are:

- Options on equities
- Options on stock indices
- Options on stock index futures contracts

If you need an overview of options or you need to remind yourself about derivatives in general, then you may find it useful to refer to the *Introduction to Derivatives, ISBN 0-471-83176-X* book in this series.

The relationship between the rights and obligations for the different types of options is summarised in the following diagram – you may find it useful to refer to when considering some of the examples which follow.

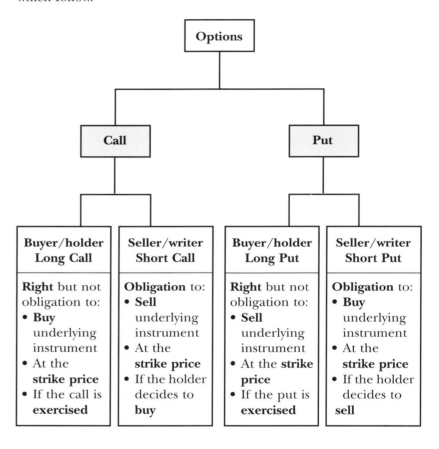

Options on equities are both OTC and exchange traded and if exercised, are settled by physical delivery of the underlying shares. OTC options on equities are also known as **traditional options** whereas options on equities traded on exchanges such as the LSE, CBOE, AMEX or PHLX are termed **traded options**.

Options on stock indices are traded on LIFFE and options on stock index futures are available on CME.

The diagram below indicates the availability of options on equity instruments.

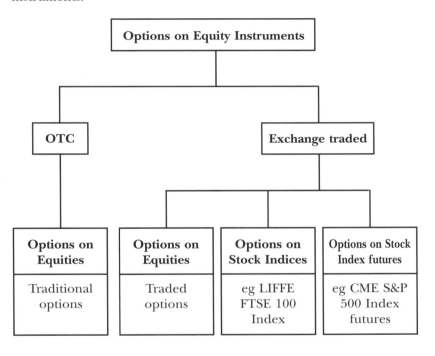

Options on Equities

For exchange-traded equity options, in the case of a put option, if the contract is exercised then an option seller is obliged to deliver the underlying shares at the agreed price. In the case of a Put option, the seller has to buy the underlying shares at the agreed price if the option is exercised.

Traded options or equity options are available through exchanges such as LIFFE and the **Chicago Board Options Exchange (CBOE)**. These instruments are traded and cleared in a similar way as futures contracts. In other words, the exchange clearing house becomes counter-party to each side of the options contract and margin payments are made as in the case for futures contracts.

In general, traded options have a limited life-span of nine months and involve a contract for 1000 of the underlying shares in the UK and 100 shares in the US. Equity options are often available for a particular market's most actively traded shares, for example, traded options are available on some 70 of the FTSE 100 Index organisations on LIFFE. Typically, premium prices for traded options are reported in the financial press such as the *Financial Times* and appear as calls and puts for the current expiry cycle of months in a similar way to that shown here.

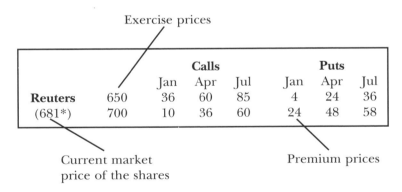

In the US, CBOE is one of the most important option exchanges, accounting for nearly half of the total trading in equities options. CBOE began trading call options in 16 stocks in 1973, introduced put options in 1977 and by 1998, options were available on more than 680 domestic and foreign stocks and ADRs.

What Instruments Are Used in the Equity Markets?

You can use electronic information systems, such as Reuters, to review information about traded options. Below are sample screens. Note that as the call price goes down, the put price goes up.

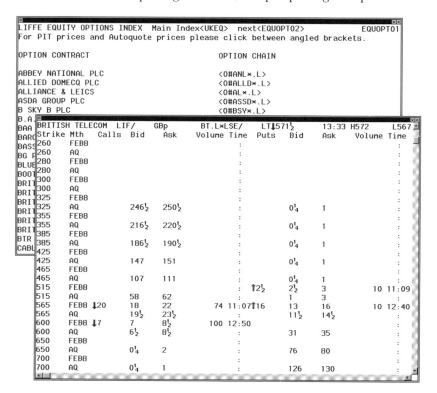

LIFFE EQUITY OPTIONS INDEX Main Index<UKEQ> next<EQUOPT02> EQUOPT01
For PIT prices and Autoquote prices please click between angled brackets.

OPTION CONTRACT	OPTION CHAIN
ABBEY NATIONAL PLC	<0#ANL*.L>
ALLIED DOMECQ PLC	<0#ALLD*.L>
ALLIANCE & LEICS	<0#AL*.L>
ASDA GROUP PLC	<0#ASSD*.L>
B SKY B PLC	<0#BSY*.L>
B.A.	
BAA	
BARC	
BASS	
BG P	
BLUE	
BOOT	
BRIT	
BRIT	
BRIT	
BRIT	
BRIT	
BRIT	
BTR	
CABL	

BRITISH TELECOM LIF/ GBp BT.L*LSE/ LT↓571½ 13:33 H572 L567

Strike	Mth	Calls	Bid	Ask	Volume	Time	Puts	Bid	Ask	Volume	Time
260	FEB8					:					:
260	AQ					:					:
280	FEB8					:					:
280	AQ					:					:
300	FEB8					:					:
300	AQ					:					:
325	FEB8					:					:
325	AQ		246½	250½		:		0¼	1		:
355	FEB8					:					:
355	AQ		216½	220½		:		0¼	1		:
385	FEB8					:					:
385	AQ		186½	190½		:		0¼	1		:
425	FEB8					:					:
425	AQ		147	151		:		0¼	1		:
465	FEB8					:					:
465	AQ		107	111		:		0¼	1		:
515	FEB8					:	↑2½	2½	3	10	11:09
515	AQ		58	62		:		1	3		:
565	FEB8	↓20	18	22	74	11:07	↑16	13	16	10	12:40
565	AQ		19½	23½		:		11½	14½		:
600	FEB8	↓7	7	8½	100	12:50					:
600	AQ		6½	8½		:		31	35		:
650	FEB8					:					:
650	AQ		0¼	2		:		76	80		:
700	FEB8					:					:
700	AQ		0¼	1		:		126	130		:

Below is an example of a screen showing the options for Apple Computers Inc.

APPLE COMP INC AOE/ USD AAPL.O NMS/ LT↓18⅞ 14:39 H19 L18⅞

Strike	Mth	Calls	Bid	Ask	Volume	Time	Puts	Bid	Ask	Volume	Time
12.5	FEB8		6⅜	6⅝		19:53			0\01		20:27
15	FEB8		3⅞	4⅛		17:00		0\01	0⅛		18:20
17.5	FEB8		1¾	1\15		21:00		0¼	0\05		17:48
20	FEB8		0½	0⅝		21:00		1½	1\11		20:52
22.5	FEB8		0⅛	0¼		19:06		3½	3¾		19:43
17.5	MAR8		2\03	2⅜		16:14		0\09	0¾		15:00
20	MAR8	↓0\15	0\15	1⅛	2	14:30		1\13	2		20:43
12.5	APR8		6⅝	6⅞		16:43		0⅛	0\03		14:31
15	APR8		4⅜	4⅝		15:23		0⅜	0½		20:35
17.5	APR8		2\11	2\15		20:13		1	1\03		19:23
20	APR8		1½	1\11		19:55		2¼	2\07		18:25
22.5	APR8		0¾	0\15		20:11		4	4¼		20:44
25	APR8		0\05	0½		20:27		6⅛	6⅜		17:00
27.5	APR8		0⅛	0¼		17:27		8½	8¾		14:57
12.5	JUL8		7⅛	7⅜		19:57		0¼	0\07		19:02
15	JUL8		5⅛	5⅜		17:12		0\13	1		14:48
17.5	JUL8		3¾	4		15:06		1¾	1\15		20:04
20	JUL8		2½	2\11		19:47		3	3¼		19:58
22.5	JUL8		1⅝	1\13		19:34		4⅝	4⅞		18:22

As has been mentioned, exchange-traded options are relatively short-term instruments with expiry dates of up to nine months in advance. However, long-term options on equities with expiry dates up to three years in advance are available on exchanges such as the American Stock Exchange (AMEX), CBOE, Pacific Stock Exchange and PHLX. These options usually involve contracts for 100 shares of the underlying stock and are known as **Long-term Equity Anticipation Securities (LEAPS)**. The contracts are traded and cleared by the exchange clearing house, as for other option contracts and if exercised, delivery involves the physical stocks. Another long-term contract is the FLEX, an option that allows the investor to specify the exercise price and expiry date of an option, making the instrument very flexible – having some of the advantages of an OTC instrument while retaining the security of trading on an exchange.

COCA COLA CO		WCB/	USD		KO NYQ/		LT↑69\05		15:34 H69¾		L69\01
Strike	Mth	Calls	Bid	Ask	Volume	Time	Puts	Bid	Ask	Volume	Time
35	JAN9		34¾	35¾		20:44		0\01	0\05		17:29
40	JAN9		30	31		15:46		0⅛	0\05		20:46
45	JAN9		25⅜	26⅜		14:32		0⅜	0½		20:40
50	JAN9		21	22		19:11		0½	0¾		20:59
55	JAN9	↓17⅛	17	17¾	2	15:26		1⅛	1⅜		20:12
60	JAN9	↓13¼	13¼	14	10	15:15		2	2⅜		20:58
65	JAN9		10	10⅜		20:52	↓3⅜	3½	3⅞	3	14:58
70	JAN9		7¼	7¾		21:00		5½	6		21:04
75	JAN9		4⅞	5¼		20:24		8	8½		:
80	JAN9	↓3⅛	3⅛	3½	7	15:16		11½	12¼		19:33
90	JAN9	↓1	0\15	1\03	40	14:39		20⅜	21⅛		15:56

Exchange-traded equity options are not the only way in which options on equities can be traded.

Traditional options on shares have been available for some time and are private and confidential OTC agreements between a single seller and a single buyer, distinct from traded options that have standard published contract conditions. Traditional options on shares are for the right to buy (call) or sell (put) the shares within a stipulated time period, for example, three months at a price fixed when the option is bought. **Double** options give the right to buy or sell.

The major difference between traded and traditional options is that the former can be freely bought and sold whereas the latter is 'locked-in' until exercise and are not negotiable in the secondary market. Traditional options on shares can be American or European style. Any cash profits must be raised by buying or selling shows that are received/declined.

Traditional options are available on many equities listed on stock exchanges such as the LSE. On the LSE certain member firms are officially registered dealers for options on equities and quote prices provided that a ready market already exists in the underlying shares. Traditional option transactions by these member firms are settled using the CREST system on the LSE – the same system for trading ordinary shares.

Thus, trading traditional call options is a complicated process of buying and selling options and equities. However, traditional options are still traded, so how do they work? You will see information on traditional options in the financial press such as the *Financial Times* which appears something like this.

Traditional options			
First dealings	Feb 2	Expiry	Apr 30
Last dealings	Feb 13	Settlement	May 8
Calls: Anglo Pacific, GEC			
Puts: MSB Int			
Calls and Puts: Applied Holo, Premier Asset			

What does this information convey to interested market players?

- **First and Last dealing dates**
  These are the beginning and end dates of the latest trading period for 3-month option contracts. For **Calls** the strike price is usually set at the current **offer** or **ask** price for the share; **Puts** have strike prices set at the current **bid** price. Calls and Puts are **double** options where the option gives the right to **buy or sell**.

- **Expiry and settlement dates**

  On the expiry date or **declaration date** as it is also known, the holder of an option must state whether or not the right to buy or sell the underlying shares will be exercised. For a Call option the holder has to buy shares on exercise; a Put option holder has to sell shares. After expiry the settlement date for an exercised contract is 5 days.

- **Options available**

  This is a list of the options available on shares in the specified trading period. These options may be Calls, Puts or Calls and Puts. However, not all option types are necessarily available for all trading periods.

Example

An investor approaches a broker for a traditional call option on 10,000 ICI shares. The broker trades an OTC contract with a market maker for the required shares with an exercise price of £10, a fixed expiry date of 27th February and settlement date of 6th March. The option price is 25p per share.

The investor therefore has to pay a premium of:

$$10,000 \times 0.25 = £2,500$$

On the expiry day the market price of the shares has risen to £11 and the investor declares his right to buy the shares. The market maker therefore has to deliver 10,000 ICI shares at a price of £10.

This means that the total cost of the shares + premium for the investor = £102,500. To realise the profits the investor has to sell the shares in the market at £11. The total investor profits are:

$$110,000 - 102,500 = £7,500$$

Exchange-Traded Options on Stock Indices and Stock Index Futures Contracts

The underlying instruments for stock index options is a basket of stocks represented by an index such as the FTSE 100. If the market conditions are favourable to the holder of an option, on exercise of a stock index option the buyer receives a cash payment equal to the difference between the settlement and exercise prices multiplied by a factor specified in the contract – the holder does not receive the basket of stocks.

Options on Stock Indices

Options on the FTSE 100 Index are available on LIFFE both as American and European style. As with options on equities these instruments are relatively short-term, but as before, long-term instruments are also available. These instruments are called **Index LEAPS** and are traded on the same exchanges trading Equity LEAPS. Index LEAPS are options based either on one-tenth or the full value of the underlying stock index – it depends on the particular stock index. LEAPS are also cash-settled and are available American or European style. For example, Index LEAPS are available on PHL on the Value Line Composite Index and CBOE trades Index LEAPS on the Major Market Index, S&P 500 and the Value Line Composite Index.

For options on stock index futures contracts, if the market conditions are favourable to the holder of an option, on exercise the underlying futures contract is delivered in theory. In practice, as these options expire on the same day as the underlying futures contract, expiry is cash settled just as if the futures position had been closed. Also for most of these option contracts the multiplier factor used is the same for both futures and options contracts. This simplifies calculations for cash payments, break-even prices etc.

Exchange traded options on stock indices and stock index futures are standardised in terms of:

- Underlying instrument and a multiplier if necessary

- Strike prices – in general exchanges try to have a range of In-The-Money, At-The-Money and Out-of-The-Money strike prices

- Expiry dates

- Style – most exchange options are American although European style are available on some contracts

- Premium quotations – these are expressed as a stipulated amount of US Dollars or UK Pounds per index point

- Margin payments are required to be paid to the Clearing house

Exchange Contracts

Options on stock indices and stock index futures are available on a number of exchanges worldwide. The chart below indicates a selection of these contracts.

Exchange	Style	Unit of trading/ Underlying futures contract
LIFFE		
FTSE 100 Index	American	£10 per Index point
FTSE 100 Index	European	£10 per Index point
CBOE		
S&P 500 Index	European	Index points/fractions × $100
Nasdaq 100 Index	European	Index points/fractions × $100
PHLX		
Value Line Index	European	Index points/fractions 3 $100
CME		
Major Market Index	American	1 × MMI futures contract
S&P 500 Index	American	1 × S&P 500 futures contract
Nikkei Stock Average	American	1 × Nikkei 225 futures contract
KCBT		
Value Line Index	American	1 × Value Line Index futures con.

Look at the sample Reuters screen below showing prices for calls and puts on the CBOE S&P 500 Index 98 LEAPS contract.

The Reuters screens below illustrate a chain of options prices for the CME S&P 500 Index contract.

What Instruments Are Used in the Equity Markets?

Typical Contract Specifications

Options contracts details vary from type to type and from exchange to exchange but the following examples taken from a LIFFE contract and a CME contract are typical specifications.

Option on equity – LIFFE	
Underlying contract	100 shares
Premium quotations	Pence per share
Minimum Price Fluctuation (Tick)	0.5 pence per share (£5.00)
Contract expiry	3 nearest expiry months from: January cycle – Jan, Apr, Jul, Oct February cycle – Feb, May, Aug, Nov March cycle – Mar, Jun, Sep, Dec The nearest 3 expiry months of each cycle are available for trading = 9 months in total.
Exercise procedure	American Settlement date is relevant LSE account day following exercise day

This is the standard contract size.

Quotes as either price per share or per index point

This is the smallest amount a contract can change value and the 'tick' size.

Option contracts are referred to by the these trading cycles

This means that contract can be exercised on or before expiry date – American

Options on S&P 500 futures contract – CME	
Underlying contract	One S&P 500 futures contract
Premium quotations	US Dollars per index point
Minimum Price Fluctuation (Tick)	0.05 Index point ($25.00)
Contract expiry	All 12 Calendar months. At any point you can choose from options that expire in the next 3 calendar months + 2 quarter-end expirations for futures contracts.
Exercise procedure	American

REUTERS

Buyers/Sellers of Options on Equity Instruments

There are a number of reasons that market players use options on equity instruments. These include the following:

- **Hedging**
  Investors can buy call or put options on equities to protect the value of individual shares against price rises or falls depending on whether the investor is buying or selling the shares. If an investor holds the underlying shares then the investor can still take advantage of any share dividends while holding an option position. In a similar way options on stock index and stock index futures can be used to protect the value of a portfolio against stock index rises and falls.

- **Earning Extra Revenue**
  If an investor believes that share prices will remain flat in the future, then extra revenue can be earned by writing – selling – options without changing the structure of the underlying portfolio.

- **Speculating**
  Market players with particular views on individual shares or the market as a whole can use options on equity instruments to profit from predicted falls/rises in share prices/index values.

As with options in general the risk to the buyer is limited to the premium cost whereas the risk to the seller can be unlimited. The examples of trading strategies given later may help to clarify buying and selling puts and calls.

OTC Contracts

Traditional options are a relatively small market and the process of realising profits involves more transactions than required for traded options.

Exchange-Traded Contracts

The chart below indicates the buyers and sellers of options on equities and stock index futures and the rights to the respective underlying instruments if the options are exercised.

Options on futures contract	Buyer/holder has right to:	On exercise Seller/ writer has obligation to:
Call	**Buy** underlying shares/ Stock index futures **Go long**	**Sell** underlying shares/ Stock index futures **Go short**
Put	**Sell** underlying shares/ Stock index futures **Go short**	**Buy** underlying shares/ Stock index futures **Go long**

The following chart describes the same information as given above but in a slightly different way and describes the way market players might use the different types of options.

Option type:	On exercise:	Use:
Long put	**Right** to **sell** underlying shares/Stock Index futures contract	Protect share holding from price/Stock Index value **fall**
Short put	**Obligation** to **buy** underlying shares/Stock Index futures contract	To earn extra revenue in a neutral or bearish market
Long call	**Right** to **buy** underlying shares/Stock Index futures contract	Profit from share price/ Stock Index value **rise**
Short call	**Obligation** to **sell** underlying shares/Stock Index futures contract	To earn extra revenue in a neutral or bearish market

What Instruments Are Used in the Equity Markets?

It is important to remember that options are traded independently and separately from the underlying instruments. Long puts and long calls are often used as hedges whereas short puts and short calls are more speculative in their use.

It is also important to remember that when selling calls or puts the writer may take a **covered** or **uncovered – naked –** position. A covered position is when the writer possesses the underlying instrument, for example, shares, or has sufficient funds or other instruments available to cover his or her position if the option is exercised. A naked position is when the writer does **not** have the resources to cover the position and is therefore taking a considerable risk.

Options on Equity Instruments in the Market Place

This section deals with typical contract quotations, how options are traded and how premiums are calculated for the exchange traded options on equities, stock indices and stock index futures contracts.

Typical Exchange-traded Option on Equity Quotations

Equity option quotations are available from the financial press such as the *Financial Times* and *The Wall Street Journal* and from electronic information services such as Reuters. The information appears in a similar style to those in the following examples.

Financial press – Option on an equity

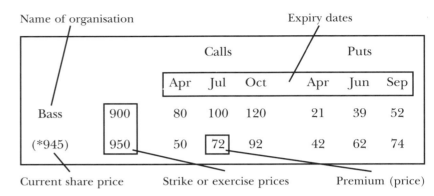

How can this information be used? For example, how much will the premium be for a Jul950 call? In other words how much does it cost for the right to buy 1000 Bass shares on or before the July expiry date at an exercise price of 950p per share?

From the information the premium is 72p per share. Therefore the premium for one option contract is $1000 \times 0.72 = £720$. If an investor decided to buy this contract, then the premium would be paid, in full, the day following the purchase.

In practice, for each quoted price there is always a bid and an offer/ask side. For example, the Jul950 Call price will be probably be 70–74. This means that the investor would pay a premium of 74p per share to buy the option and receive 70p per share if he or she was selling the option.

There are also dealing fees and commissions to take into account which further affect calculations of costs.

Below are Reuters screens showing the LIFFE Equity Options Index, and a more detailed display of call and put bid and ask prices for a selected contract.

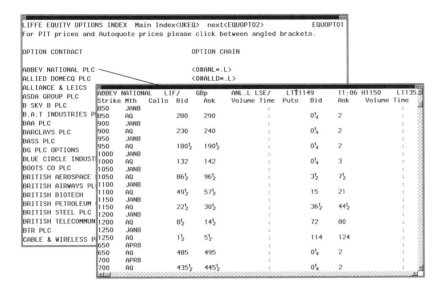

LIFFE EQUITY OPTIONS INDEX Main Index<UKEQ> next<EQUOPT02> EQUOPT01
For PIT prices and Autoquote prices please click between angled brackets.

OPTION CONTRACT	OPTION CHAIN
ABBEY NATIONAL PLC	<0#ANL*.L>
ALLIED DOMECQ PLC	<0#ALLD*.L>
ALLIANCE & LEICS	
ASDA GROUP PLC	
B SKY B PLC	
B.A.T INDUSTRIES P	
BAA PLC	
BARCLAYS PLC	
BASS PLC	
BG PLC OPTIONS	
BLUE CIRCLE INDUST	
BOOTS CO PLC	
BRITISH AEROSPACE	
BRITISH AIRWAYS PL	
BRITISH BIOTECH	
BRITISH PETROLEUM	
BRITISH STEEL PLC	
BRITISH TELECOMMUN	
BTR PLC	
CABLE & WIRELESS P	

ABBEY NATIONAL LIF/ GBp ANL.L LSE/ LT↑1149 11:06 H1150 L1135

Strike	Mth	Calls	Bid	Ask	Volume	Time	Puts	Bid	Ask	Volume	Time
850	JAN8					:					:
850	AQ		280	290		:		0¼	2		:
900	JAN8					:					:
900	AQ		230	240		:		0¼	2		:
950	JAN8					:					:
950	AQ		180½	190½		:		0¼	2		:
1000	JAN8					:					:
1000	AQ		132	142		:		0¼	3		:
1050	JAN8					:					:
1050	AQ		86½	96½		:		3½	7½		:
1100	JAN8					:					:
1100	AQ		49½	57½		:		15	21		:
1150	JAN8					:					:
1150	AQ		22½	30½		:		36½	44½		:
1200	JAN8					:					:
1200	AQ		8½	14½		:		72	80		:
1250	JAN8					:					:
1250	AQ		1½	5½		:		114	124		:
650	APR8					:					:
650	AQ		485	495		:		0¼	2		:
700	APR8					:					:
700	AQ		435½	445½		:		0¼	2		:

Exchange-traded Options on Stock Indices

The examples below are for the LIFFE contracts on the FTSE 100 Index. There are two contracts available, one American style and the other European style. Option premium prices for different strike prices are available on services such as Reuters, as shown below.

American style contract

FTSE 100 INDEX LIF/ GBp .FTSE*209/ LT↑5239.5 09:24 H5246.5 L5229.0

Strike	Mth	Calls	Bid	Ask	Volume	Time	Puts	Bid	Ask	Volume	Time
4900	AQ		354	364		:		10	18		:
4950	JAN8					:					:
4950	AQ		308	318		:		10	19		:
5000	JAN8	↓258	250	260	6	08:58	↑28	23	28	14	08:53
5000	AQ		265	276		:		17	25		:
5050	JAN8	↓208	200	215	1	08:46					:
5050	AQ		219	229		:		19	29		:
5100	JAN8	↑170	170	180	12	08:47		35	45		:
5100	AQ		182	192		:		29	40		:
5150	JAN8					:	↑60	50	60	2	08:44
5150	AQ		138	148		:		45	55		:
5200	JAN8	↓95	90	100	2	08:43	↓70	60	70	4	08:38
5200	AQ		100	110		:		52	62		:
5250	JAN8	↑71	70	71	120	08:45	↓88	80	90	82	09:12
5250	AQ		74	85		:		75	86		:
5300	JAN8		40	50		:	↓118	120	125	4	08:43
5300	AQ		48	58		:		107	118		:
5350	JAN8	↑28	25	35	93	08:46	↑155	150	160	1	09:05
5350	AQ		29	40		:		136	147		:
5400	JAN8		15	20		:		195	205		:
5400	AQ		14	24		:		175	185		:
5450	JAN8					:					:
5450	AQ		4½	13		:		228	239		:

Note the different pricing structure

European style contract

FTSE 100 INDEX LIF/ GBp .FTSE*209/ LT↑5243.7 09:31 H5246.5 L5229.0

Strike	Mth	Calls	Bid	Ask	Volume	Time	Puts	Bid	Ask	Volume	Time
5025	AQ		242	252		:		22	31		:
5075	JAN8					:		35	45		:
5075	AQ		195	205		:		24	35		:
5125	JAN8					:					:
5125	AQ		153	164		:		32	43		:
5175	JAN8					:					:
5175	AQ		116	126		:		45	55		:
5225	JAN8					:					:
5225	AQ		83	93		:		62	72		:
5275	JAN8					:					:
5275	AQ		55	65		:		84	94		:
5325	JAN8					:					:
5325	AQ		33	43		:		111	122		:
5375	JAN8	↓20	15	25	20	08:56					:
5375	AQ		18	28		:		146	157		:
5425	JAN8		5	15		:					:
5425	AQ		8½	17		:		186	196		:
5475	JAN8					:					:
5475	AQ		1	9		:		228	239		:
5525	JAN8					:					:
5525	AQ		0¼	6		:		275	286		:
5575	JAN8					:					:
5575	AQ		0¼	4½		:		324	334		:

What Instruments Are Used in the Equity Markets?

The premium for an option can be calculated simply, as the quotation is in index points and each point is priced at £10.

From the Reuters screen below, you can see that the premium a market player would pay to buy an American style Jan 98 5000 call is 250 × £10 = £2500.

Strike	Mth	Calls	Bid	Ask	Volume	Time	Puts	Bid	Ask	Volume	Time
4900	AQ		354	364		:		10	18		:
4950	JAN8					:					:
4950	AQ		308	318		:		10	19		:
5000	JAN8	↓258	250	260	6	08:58	↑28	23	28	14	08:53
5000	AQ		265	276		:		17	25		:

AQ means the price is an Automated Quote

You can also use a service such as Reuters to display quotes for the CBOE S&P 500 Stock Index options and for the S&P 500 Stock Index LEAPS – long-term – contracts, as shown below.

S&P 500 INDEX WCB/ USD .SPX WCB/ LT↑1020.01 22:01 H1020.71 L1016

Strike	Mth	Calls	Bid	Ask	Volume	Time	Puts	Bid	Ask	Volume	Time
960	FEB8	↑59	60 1/4	62 1/4	49	20:20	↑1	0 3/8	0 7/8	279	19:02
965	FEB8	↓56	55 1/2	57 1/2	2	15:52	↓0\15	0\09	1\01	65	21:03
970	FEB8	↓50 1/4	50 3/4	52 3/4	201	19:10	↑1 1/4	1	1 1/4	300	20:36
975	FEB8	↑47	46	48	300	21:07	↓1 3/8	1 1/8	1 5/8	640	21:14
980	FEB8	↓40 3/4	41 3/8	43 3/8	1	20:30	↓1 5/8	1\09	1\15	243	20:56
985	FEB8		36 3/4	38 3/4		20:48	↑2 1/4	1\13	2 1/8	110	18:27
990	FEB8	↑32 1/8	32 1/4	34 1/4	493	21:03	↓2\13	2 1/4	3	2053	21:02
995	FEB8	↑29	28	30	331	21:20	↓3	3	3 3/8	1308	21:04
1005	FEB8	↓19 3/4	19 5/8	21	1688	21:06	↓4 3/4	4 1/2	5 1/8	2301	21:07
1010	FEB8	↑16 1/2	16 1/2	17 5/8	766	21:05	↓6	6	6 3/4	2052	21:20
1015	F										
1020	F										
1025	F										
1030	F										
1035	F										
1040	F										
1050	F										
1055	F										
1060	F										
1075	F										
400	M										
500	M										
525	M										
550	M										
575	M										

S&P 500 LT INDEX WCB/ USD .SPL WCB/ LT↑1020.01 22:01 H1020.71 L1016

Strike	Mth	Calls	Bid	Ask	Volume	Time	Puts	Bid	Ask	Volume	Time
550	JUN9					:					:
675	JUN9		379 5/8	382 5/8		:		9 5/8	11 1/8		18:11
700	JUN9		358 1/2	361 1/2		19:39		11 1/8	13 3/8		18:11
725	JUN9		337 5/8	340 5/8		15:41		13 3/8	15 5/8		19:15
750	JUN9		317 1/8	320 1/8		15:26	↓16	16	18 1/4	1	14:49
800	JUN9		276 3/4	279 3/4		20:23		21 3/8	24 3/8		19:01
825	JUN9		257 1/8	260 1/8		:	↑26	24 7/8	27 7/8	15	14:46
850	JUN9		237 7/8	240 7/8		21:10		28 3/4	31 3/4		21:14
875	JUN9		219 1/2	222 1/2		:		33 3/8	36 3/8		17:05
900	JUN9		201 1/8	204 1/8		16:37		38 1/4	41 1/4		17:16
925	JUN9		183 3/4	186 3/4		19:17		43 7/8	46 7/8		21:12
950	JUN9		167	170		19:11		50 1/8	53 1/8		15:04
975	JUN9	↑151	150 3/8	153 3/8	2	16:23		56 3/4	59 3/4		18:23
995	JUN9		138	141		19:12		62 3/4	65 3/4		18:43
1025	JUN9		120 1/4	122 1/4		17:24		72 5/8	74 5/8		16:15
1050	JUN9		106 1/4	108 1/4		18:51		81 3/4	83 3/4		18:47
1075	JUN9		93	95		16:59		91 5/8	93 5/8		18:16
1100	JUN9		81	83		14:36		102 3/4	104 3/4		17:36
1125	JUN9		69 5/8	71 5/8		:		114 3/8	116 3/8		20:30
1150	JUN9		59 3/8	61 3/8		20:43		127 1/4	129 1/4		:
1175	JUN9		50 1/4	52 1/4		21:14		141 1/8	143 1/8		21:13
1200	JUN9		41 7/8	43 7/8		15:43		155 7/8	157 7/8		20:09
1250	JUN9		28 1/4	30 1/4		20:46	↓190	188 1/2	190 1/2	25	21:14
700	DEC9		373	375		:		16	17 1/2		15:58
750	DEC9		333 3/4	335 3/4		:		21 3/8	23 3/8		16:44

Exchange-traded Options on Stock Index Futures

The CME has options on stock index futures for a number of indices including the S&P 500, Major Market Index and Nikkei Stock Average.

On exercise these contracts, in theory, deliver the underlying futures contract. However, in practice, as these options expire on the same day as the underlying futures contract, exercise at expiry is cash settled – just as for closing the futures position. If the option is American style and is exercised before expiry, then it is cash settled against the exchange settlement price for the underlying futures contract.

The contract premium price in this case is calculated using the following simple equation.

$$\textbf{Premium} = \frac{\textbf{Number of index points}}{\textbf{tick size}} \times \textbf{tick value}$$

$$= \textbf{Number of ticks} \times \textbf{tick value}$$

Prices for CME options on stock index futures are shown on the Reuters screen below. In this case the screen is for the March 1998 contract on the S&P 500 futures.

S+P 500 OPTION IOM/ USD SPH8 IOM/ LT ↑1012.30 -11.40 H1024.00

Strike		Last			Bid	Ask	Size	Open 1	High	Low	Time
970	P	PS8.20	-0.30	BBO	10.20	11.20	/				18:02
975	C	PS57.40	-0.80				/				17:42
975	P	↑11.50	+2.50	BBO	11.20	11.50	/	10.50	11.50	10.50	16:11
980	C	PS53.30	-0.80				/				17:38
980	P	B12.20	-0.30	BBO	12.20	12.70	/		12.20		16:07
985	C	PS49.30	-0.90				/				19:46
985	P	PS10.80	-0.40	BBO	13.60	14.60	/				16:02
990	C	↓37.80	-7.60	BBO			/	37.80	37.80	37.80	16:08
990	P	↑15.80	+3.90	BBO	15.20	16.00	/	13.40	15.80	13.20	16:13
995	C	PS41.60	-0.90				/				20:27
995	P	PS13.10	-0.40	BBO	16.50	17.50	/				20:16
1000	C	↓34.80	-3.40	BBO			/	34.80	34.80	34.80	15:38
1000	P	↑18.20	+3.60	BBO	18.20	19.20	/	16.20	18.20	16.00	16:04
1005	C	PS34.70	-0.90				/				18:55
1005	P	↑21.00	+4.90	BBO	20.00	21.00	/	17.80	21.00	17.50	16:12
1010	C	PS31.30	-1.00				/				17:08
1010	P	↑22.00	+4.30	BBO	21.80	22.00	/	20.00	22.00	20.00	16:08

From the screen you see that the price for a March 1000 Call is 34.80. The tick size for this contract is 0.05 and the tick value is $25. This means a market player would have to pay a premium of:

$$\frac{34.80}{0.05} \times 25 = 696 \times 25 = \$17,400$$

In effect this is the same as the number of index points times the contract multiplier of $500 ($34.80 \times 500 = \$17,400$) which is the same multiplier used for the futures contract.

How an Exchange-traded Option Contract Works

Exchange traded options on equity instruments are traded in a similar way to exchange-traded futures contracts in that margin payments are required by the clearing house. Initial margin is payable by the appropriate party at the time of the trade.

The price of an option is marked-to-market every day that the option is open and the resulting profits/losses are credited/debited to both counterparty margin accounts.

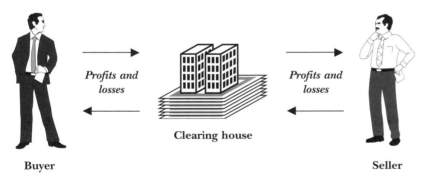

Buyer　　　*Profits and losses*　　**Clearing house**　　*Profits and losses*　　**Seller**

If an option on an equity is exercised, then the **underlying shares** are delivered or received. For options on Stock Indices and Stock Index futures contracts if the contract is exercised then they are **cash settled**.

A simple way of calculating the profit/loss on an option is to use the following equation.

$$\text{Profit/loss} = (\text{Premium}_{Exercise} - \text{Premium}_{Start}) \times \text{Unit of trading/multiplier} \times \text{No. of contracts}$$

Example – Buying an index call

It is early March and the FTSE 100 Index stands at 3040. An investment manager thinks the market is improving and expects the index to rise by April. The price of a May3100 Call is 59. If the manager bought an index option contract and the index rises in April, then the outcome is as follows...

Time	FT SE 100 Index	Action
Early March	3040	Buys May3100 Call at 59 Premium = 59 x £10 = £590
End April	3102	Sells May3100 Call which is now quoted at 110 = 110 x £10 = £1100
Outcome		• £510 profit • 86% increase on investment

Trading Strategies for Options

There are many strategies available in the options markets – some are quite complex and have colourful names.

The various strategies are usually represented diagrammatically as **break-even graphs** which show the potential for making a profit. The diagrams use the break-even point as the basis for the diagram where:

> **Break-even point = Strike price ± premium**

The most basic buy/sell strategies for puts and calls are illustrated using profit/loss charts in the following examples. You may find it useful to refer to option strategies in general described in the *Introduction to Derivatives* in this series.

The following examples apply to options on equities. The case for options on stock indices and stock index futures contacts is much simpler. **Calls** are used when investors believe a stock index will **rise** in value. **Puts** are used if the value of a stock index is expected to **fall**.

Buying a Call Option – Long Call

There are a number of reasons why a market player would buy the right to buy underlying shares including these three:

- **To profit from an expected rise in the price of the underlying shares**
  A Call option allows an investor to make high percentage profits on premium costs and on shares if the contract is exercised. However, in the latter case the shares will need to be sold in the market to realise any profits.

- **To establish a maximum cost at which to purchase shares in the future**
  In this case the market player does not have the necessary funds to buy shares in the current market but anticipates having funds in the future. So the market player buys an option which is a cheaper solution. If share prices do increase, then the option can be sold and the profits used to offset the higher share price. If exercised, then the shares are acquired at an exercise price which is less than the current market price.

- **To hedge against a fall in share prices**
  A market player can hedge against a fall in share prices by buying a call option at the same time as selling the shareholding. The market player has any profits from the sale of shares and at the same time can benefit from any increase in the price of the underlying shares as described above. If share prices fall then the option is allowed to expire worthless. In other words the market player has locked in profits from the shares while retaining the possibility of profiting more if share prices increase.

Example – Buying a call option

In this case investors think that the price of shares will rise and so on exercise they will recover their premium and make a profit. To show the differences in using the equities and options markets, compare the following hypothetical cases based on the XYZ share option information as follows. In this case an investor thinks the shares will rise to 420p by March.

Option		Calls			Puts		
		Apr	Jul	Oct	Apr	Jul	Oct
XYZ	360	29	37	39	4	10	12
(*381)	390	12	19	23	16	24	26

Action	Equities Markets	Options Markets
On 1st Jan	XYZ shares @ 381p Buy 100 shares = £3810	Oct390 Call @ 23p Buy 1 contract for 1000 shares = £230
On 1st Mar	XYZ shares @ 420p Sell shares = £4200	Oct390 Call is now @ 34p (This is the intrinsic value plus a small amount, 420 − 390 + 4) Sell contract for £340

Outcome	• Large outlay
	• £390 profit
	• 10% increase on
	  investment
		• Small outlay
		• £110 profit
		• 48% increase on
		  investment

This example shows that the potential percentage increase on investment is large – the share price could have gone the other way and losses incurred.

At expiry the profit/loss chart for the long call looks like this:

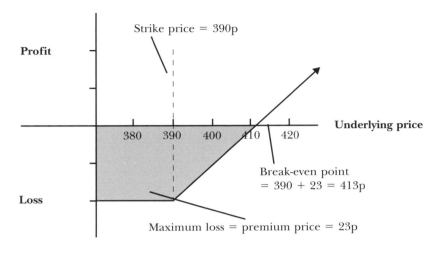

Market price	Outcome
> 413p	Profit increases as underlying share price rises and is unlimited
413p	Break-even point
390–413p	Loss which increases as underlying share price price falls
< 390	Loss is limited to a maximum of the premium price

Buying a Put Option – Long Put

Puts are used by market players who expect share prices to fall in the future. The option gives the holder the right to sell the underlying shares to the writer. There are a number of reasons that long puts are used including the following:

- **To profit from an expected fall in the price of the underlying shares**
  The holder of a long put does not have to own the underlying shares as the option can be sold before expiry. As share prices fall, the option premium increases. This means that the market player can profit from the difference in premiums in buying and selling the option.

- **To protect the value of a share portfolio against falling prices**
  If share prices fall, then the holder of a long put will see premiums rise. As before if the option is sold before expiry, then any profits can be used to offset losses in the value of the portfolio.

- **To protect a future share sale**
  By buying a long put a market player can protect a future share sale against falling prices. If the share price falls, then profits from the sale of the option contract before expiry can be used to offset the losses when the shares are sold in the market.

Example – Buying a Put Option

In this case, investors think that the price of shares will fall and so on exercise they will recover their premium and make a profit. Using the information as before this time the investor thinks the share price of XYZ will fall to 340p by March.

Action	Equities Markets	Options Markets
On 1st Jan	XYZ shares @ 381p Investor holds 1000 shares. Value = £3810	Oct 360 Put @ 12p Buy 1 contract for 1000 shares = £120
On 1st Mar	XYZ shares @ 340p	Oct 360 Put is now @ 24p (This is the intrinsic value plus a small amount, $360 - 340 + 4$) Sell contract for £240
Outcome	• Theoretical loss £410 • 10.8% decrease on investment	• Small outlay • £140 profit • 100% increase on investment

This example highlights why large institutional investors will hedge on shares using the options markets.

At expiry the profit/loss chart for the long put looks like this:

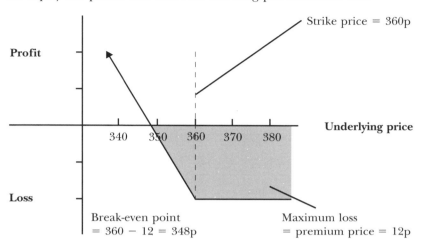

Strike price = 360p

Break-even point
= 360 − 12 = 348p

Maximum loss
= premium price = 12p

Market price	Outcome
> 360p	Maximum loss is equal to the premium
360 − 348p	Loss decreases as underlying share price falls
348p	Break-even point
< 348p	Profit increases as underlying share price falls and is unlimited

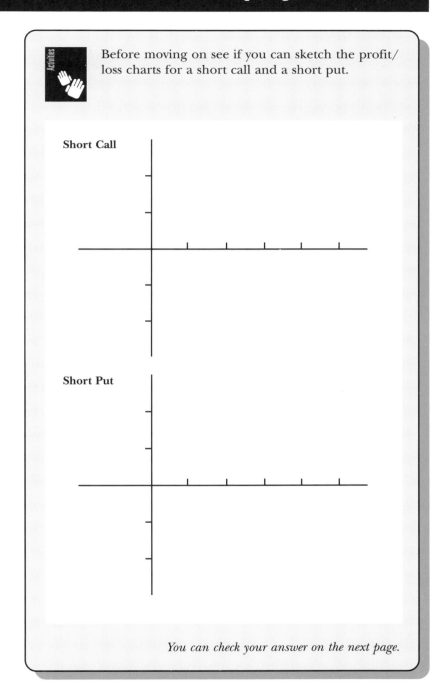

Before moving on see if you can sketch the profit/loss charts for a short call and a short put.

Short Call

Short Put

You can check your answer on the next page.

Selling a Call Option – Short Call

Market players who have a neutral or bearish view of the equity markets sell or write call options. The options can be **covered** if the writer holds the underlying shares or **naked** if the writer does not hold the shares. If a covered option is exercised, then the writer can deliver the underlying shares. However, if a naked option is exercised, then the writer has to buy the shares for delivery which has the potential for unlimited losses. There are two basic reasons why market players might sell a call option:

- **To earn additional revenue for a share portfolio**
  In this case the market player takes the risk that the share price at or before expiry does not rise above the exercise price. In such circumstances the option will expire worthless and the market player retains the premium as extra income.

- **To purchase shares simultaneously as selling a Call option**
  As long as share prices do not exceed the exercise price, then the premium profit can be used to reduce the overall cost of the share purchase.

At expiry the profit/loss chart for the short call looks like this:

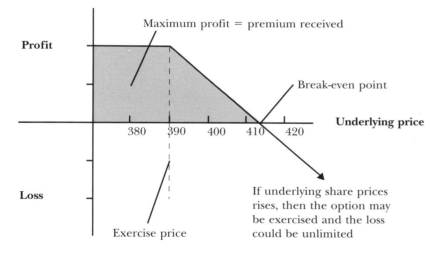

Selling a Put option – Short Put

This is more or less the same scenario as for a short call but in this case the writer is obliged to buy shares if the option is exercised. In this case a covered position means that the writer has sufficient funds available for the purchase whereas a naked position writer does not have the required funds. There are a number of reasons short puts are written, including the following:

- **To earn additional revenue for a share portfolios for a Short Call**

- **The simultaneous purchase of shares and sale of a Put option**
  As in the case of a Short Put this combination is used to reduce the overall purchase cost of the shares.

- **Speculation**
  In this case a speculator has seen prices fall but thinks that the market will flatten or possibly rise in the future.

At expiry the profit/loss chart for the short put looks like this:

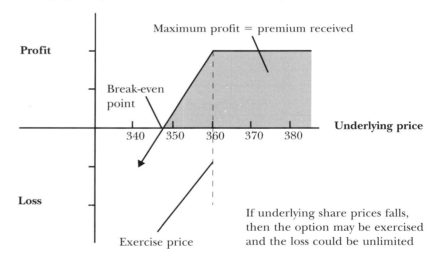

In summary, here are the key points regarding options of equity instruments.

Options on Equity Instruments

- Options on equities are traded both OTC and on exchanges and if exercised they are settled by **physical delivery** of the underlying shares

- OTC options on equities are known as **traditional options** whereas exchange traded equity options are termed **traded options**

- Options on Stock Indices and Stock Index futures contracts are exchange traded and **cash settled** if exercised

- For options on equities and Stock Index futures the **buyer** or **holder** of a **Call/Put** has the **right** to **sell/buy** the **underlying instrument** if the option is exercised

- For options on equities and Stock Index futures the **seller** or **writer** of a **Call/Put** has the **obligation** to **sell/buy** the **underlying instrument** if the option is exercised

- Most options on equities traded on exchanges are **American style** whereas exchange traded options on Stock Indices and Stock Index futures can be either **American** or **European style**

- Premium quotations on equity options are expressed as a value per share whereas options on Stock Indices and Stock Index futures are expressed as a value per index point or fraction of index point

Your notes

The Reuters screens below display information about options contracts traded on the DTB. Provided are the prices on the DAX Index and the call and put prices for Deutsche Telecom options and futures traded on the DTB.

```
            DEUTSCHE BOERSE AG FRANKFURT                      DAX09
**DTB -Deutsche Ternin Börse (German futures and options statistics page 2/2 )**
Options        RIC        RIC        Contract Volume      Volume ratios
              Options____Exchange____Call_____Put____Put/Call__Call/Put_
DAX            <O#GDAX*.d><.GDAXI>    74.741    61.357    0.821    1.21B
DAX  Future    <DE/DTB2>  <.GDAX>      0          0       0.000    0.000
Bund Future    <DE/DTB2>  <O#BDL:>     1.105     681      0.616    1.623
Bobl Future    <DE/DTB2>  <O#BDM:>     450      1.030     2.289    0.437
Bund+Bond F.   <DE/DTB2>  <    >       1.555    1.711
USD/DEM Options<DE/DTB4>  <O#OUSD*.d>  331       10       0.030   33.100
```

```
Futu XETRA DAX INDEX DTB/    DEM    .GDAXI IBS/   LT↑4596.67   11:36 H4601.68 L4580.02
    Strike Mth  Calls Bid   Ask    Volume Time Puts  Bid    Ask    Volume Time
DAX 3650   FEB8 ↑936.00              5  08:30              0.10           :
MDAX 3700  FEB8 ↑887.00              3  08:56              0.10           :
Bund 3750  FEB8 ↑846.00             10  10:22              0.10           :
Bobl 3800  FEB8 ↑787.00 790.00      25  09:09              0.10           :
Libo 3850  FEB8                          :                 0.10           :
Libo 3900  FEB8                          :                 0.10           :
     3950  FEB8         589.90            :                 0.10           :
     4000  FEB8                          :                 0.10           :
     4050  FEB8 ↑539.00             51  09:53              0.10           :
Equi 4100  FEB8 ↓488.00 489.90      97  10:55              0.10           :
     4150  FEB8 ↑436.00             16  08:57              0.10           :
     4200  FEB8 ↓389.00 389.90     165  10:52↓0.10         0.10        30  09:13
Inde 4250  FEB8                          :                 0.10           :
     4300  FEB8 ↑292.00 291.00 295.00 676 11:29↓0.20       0.10        50  07:40
     4350  FEB8 ↓240.00             11  10:48              0.10           :
     4400  FEB8 ↑190.00 192.00 198.00 998 11:19↓0.10       0.10       752  08:18
     4450  FEB8 ↑145.00 140.00 145.00  93 11:34↓0.10       0.10       720  08:33
     4500  FEB8 ↑95.00  92.50  95.00 2297 11:35↓0.10       0.10       862  10:15
     4550  FEB8 ↓44.50  41.50  44.50 1484 11:36↓0.10 0.10  0.20      5109  11:32
     4600  FEB8 ↓1.70   1.50   1.80 10170 11:35↓8.00 7.00  8.00      3964  11:34
     4650  FEB8 ↑0.30          0.10 2835 08:36↓57.00       73.00       24  11:22
     4700  FEB8 ↓0.10          0.10   50 07:44↓110.00     115.00      242  11:17
     4750  FEB8               0.10         : ↓157.20                   10  11:16
     4800  FEB8 ↓0.10          0.10  350 08:29            210.00          :
     4850  FEB8               0.10         :
```

```
             DEUTSCHE BOERSE AG FRANKFURT                      DAX06
**DTB -Deutsche Ternin Börse (German futures and options statistics  page 1/2)**
Stock options RIC        RIC        Contract Volume    Open Interest
             Options____Exchange____CALL_____PUT_____Call_____Put_
ADIDAS        <O#ADSG*.d> <ADSG.F>      0         0       0          0
Allianz Hldg  <O#ALVG*.d> <ALVG.F>    3.024     464       0          0
BASF          <O#BASF*.d> <BASF.F>    2.280     73B       0          0
BAYER         <O#BAYG*.d> <BAYG.F>    1.146     546       0          0
BAY.HYPOB.    <O#BHWG*.d> <BHWG.F>     387      134       0          0
BMW           <O#BMWG*.d> <BMWG.F>      20      120       0          0
BAY.VEREINSB. <O#BVMG*.d> <BVMG.F>     546      584       0          0
COMMERZBANK   <O#CBKG*.d> <CBKG.F>     967      394       0          0
CONTINENTAL   <O#CONG*.d> <CONG.F>      56        0       0          0
DAIMLER BENZ  <O#DAIG*.d> <DAIG.F>     914      296       0          0
DEUTSCHE BANK <O#DBKG*.d> <DBKG.F>    3.355     810       0          0
DEGUSSA       <O#DGSG*.d> <DGSG.F>       8        0       0          0
DOUGLAS       <O#DOHG*.d> <DOHG.F>       0        0       0          0
DRESDNER BANK <O#DRSD*.d> <DRSD.F>     712      130       0          0
D.TELECOM     <O#DTKG*.d> <DTEG.F>    3.343    1.985      0          0
FRESENIUS     <O#FREG_p*.d><FREG_p.F>   0         0       0          0
BILFINGER+BERG<O#GBFG*.d> <GBFG.F>      0         0       0          0
HENKEL        <O#HNKG_p*.d><HNKG_p.F>   0         0       0          0
HOECHST       <O#HOEG*.d> <HOEG.F>    1.656     890       0          0
PHIL.HOLZMANN <O#HOZG*.d> <HOZG.F>      0         0       0          0
```

```
DEUTSCHE TELEKOM DTB/     DEM     DTEG.DE*IBS/    LT↑33.95     16:02 H34.15  L33.40
Strike Mth  Calls Bid   Ask    Volume Time Puts  Bid    Ask    Volume Time
28    FEB8                          :                 0.01  0.05
30    FEB8                          : ↓0.02   0.01    0.40        102  16:01
32    FEB8 ↓2.00         2.50  452 16:01↓0.18  0.12   0.22        365  16:01
34    FEB8 ↓0.70  0.32  0.75  480 16:01↑0.75   0.52               50  16:01
36    FEB8 ↑0.13  0.02  0.20   40 16:01↓2.01                       1  16:01
38    FEB8 ↑0.03        0.25   75 16:01                             :
40    FEB8               0.10        : ↓6.18                      10  16:01
28    MAR8                          :                 0.01  0.14
30    MAR8 ↑4.20               13 16:01↓0.20   0.10   0.27        849  16:01
32    MAR8 ↑2.55         3.00  100 16:01↓0.55          0.60       61  16:01
34    MAR8 ↓1.25  1.17  1.30  310 16:01↑1.32          4.50        20  16:01
36    MAR8 ↑0.50  0.50  0.55  212 16:01↓2.50   1.40                6  16:01
38    MAR8 ↓0.16  0.14  0.30   21 16:01                             :
40    MAR8 ↓0.12  0.04  0.10    3 16:01                7.25          :
42    MAR8        0.02  0.07         :
44    MAR8        0.01  0.05         :
46    MAR8        0.01  0.04         :
48    MAR8        0.01  0.05         :
```

Below is the screen showing the Reuters FLEX Option Service Index in which you can see the latest CBOE S&P 500 Index FLEX option reports.

```
REUTERS FLEX OPTION SERVICE INDEX                                    FLEXOPT

   OPRA FLEX Options

   <OEX/FLXA>              CBOE S&P 100 - Most Recent Activity
   <OEX/FLXB>-OEX/FLXZ     CBOE S&P 100 - Today's History
   <SPX/FLXA>              CBOE S&P 500 - Most Recent Activity
   <SPX/FLXB>-SPX/FLXZ     CBOE S&P 500 - Today's History
   <RUT/FLXA>              CBOE Russell 2000 - Most Recent Activity
   <RUT/FLXB>-RUT/FLXZ     CBOE Russell 2000 - Today's History
   <XMI/FLXA>              AMEX Major Market Index - Most Recent Activity
   <XMI/FLXB>-XMI/FLXZ     AMEX Major Market Index - Today's History
   <XII/FLXA>              AMEX Institutional Index - Most Recent Activity
   <XII/FLXB>-XII/FLXZ     AMEX Institutional Index - Today's History
   <JPN/FLXA>              AMEX Japan Index - Most Recent Activity
   <JPN/FLXB>-JPN/FLXZ     AMEX Japan Index - Today's History
   <MID/FLXA>              AMEX S&P Midcap 400 - Most Recent Activity
   <MID/FLXB>-MID/FLXZ     AMEX S&P Midcap 400 - Today's History
   <TST/FLXA>              General Flex Messages - Most Recent Activity
   <TST/FLXB>-TST/FLXZ     General Flex Messages - Today's History

See <FLEXOPU> for CBOT FLEX Options Index
See <FLEXOPV> for Philadelphia UCOM FLEX Options Index
See <FLEXOPW> for OPRA FLEX Options Abbreviations
See <FLEXOPZ> for CME FLEX Options Index
```

```
LATEST CBOE S&P 500 INDEX FLEX OPTION REPORTS                        SPX/FLXA
      12-FEB-98
10:20 FLEX I SPX ADM SPX01 268 TO BUY @ 747.17 CXLD
10:19 FLEX I SPX ADM SPX01 268 TO BUY @ 747.14 RESTING
10:14 FLEX I SPX ADM SPX04 268 TO SELL @ 713.20 RESTING
10:13 FLEX I SPX ADM SPX04 268 TO BUY @ 709.50 RESTING
10:13 FLEX I SPX ADM SPX03 268 TO SELL @ 736.32 RESTING
10:13 FLEX I SPX ADM SPX03 268 TO BUY @ 735.58 RESTING
10:13 FLEX I SPX ADM SPX02 268 TO SELL @ 746.30 RESTING
10:13 FLEX I SPX ADM SPX02 268 TO BUY @ 746.11 RESTING
10:12 FLEX I SPX SDM SPX01 268 TO SELL @ 747.30 RESTING
10:12 FLEX I SPX ADM SPX01 268 TO BUY @ 747.17 RESTING
10:12 FLEX I SPX QTE SPX04 709.50-713.20  268 X 268
10:12 FLEX I SPX QTE SPX03 735.58-736.32  268 X 268
10:12 FLEX I SPX QTE SPX02 746.11-746.30  268 X 268
10:12 FLEX I SPX QTE SPX01 747.14-747.30  268 X 268
10:02 FLEX I SPX QTE SPX05 0.50-1.00    200X 200
09:48 FLEX I SPX RFQ SPX05 QTE IN $ BY 0900CST
09:48 FLEX I SPX RFQ SPX05 $100M 1030C PM EUR 2.13.98
09:48 FLEX I SPX RFQ SPX01-04 QTE IN $ BY 0900CST
09:48 FLEX I SPX RFQ SPX04 750PT BOX AM EUR1.26.99
09:48 FLEX I SPX RFQ SPX03 750PT BOX AM EUR6.16.98
09:48 FLEX I SPX RFQ SPX02 750PT BOX AM EUR3.17.98
09:47 FLEX I SPX RFQ SPX01 750PT BOX AM EUR3.6.98
                 Most recent history available on page <SPX/FLXB >
```

Below are Reuters screens showing share and options data for Coca Cola.

Bid and ask prices for Coca Cola shares traded on NYSE.

KO.N	COCA COLA CO		191216100	NYS USD KO.NB2		23FEB98 16:01
Last	Last 1	Last 2	Status	Bid	Ask	Size
↓68¾	68\13	68\13	/R /	68¾	68\13	15x20
Net.Chng	Cls:20FEB98	Open	High	Low	Volume	Blk.Vol
-0\13	69\09	69\11	69\11	68⅝	634900	246300
P.E	Earnings	Yield	News		DJ.News	L.Blocks
42.42	1.64	0.86 %	:		:	12
Dividend	Div.Dat	Ex.Date	Yr.High	Yr.Low	Options	Headlines
0.60	01APR98	11MAR98	72\10	52	W	XK01
Exchange						

Bid and ask prices for call and put options on Coca Cola shares traded on CBOE with 1998 expiry dates.

COCA COLA CO		WCB/		USD		KO NYQ/	LT↓69\05		15:32 H69¾		L69\01
Strike	Mth	Calls	Bid	Ask	Volume	Time	Puts	Bid	Ask	Volume	Time
60	MAR8		9¼	9¾		19:48		0\01	0¼		19:26
65	MAR8		4¾	5⅛		21:03	↓0⅜	0\05	0\09	10	15:09
70	MAR8	↑1⅜	1¼	1⅜	125	15:30	↑2\03	1\15	2\03	110	15:00
75	MAR8	↓0\03	0⅛	0¼	50	15:16	↓5½	5½	6	3	15:07
60	APR8		9¾	10¼		:		0\03	0\07		:
65	APR8		5⅜	5⅞		:		0⅞	1		:
70	APR8	2	2	2⅜	10	15:23		2½	2⅞		:
75	APR8	0\09	0½	0\11	4	15:30		5¾	6¼		:
50	MAY8		19½	20⅛		19:34		0\01	0¼		18:14
55	MAY8		14¾	15⅜		15:05		0⅛	0⅜		20:20
60	MAY8		10⅛	10¾		19:44		0⅜	0\09		20:55
65	MAY8	↑6½	6	6½	12	14:41	↓1⅛	1¼	1½	30	14:59
70	MAY8	↓2⅞	2¾	3⅛	55	15:28	↓3¼	3	3⅜	2	14:47
75	MAY8	↓0\15	0⅞	1⅛	305	15:24		6⅛	6⅝		20:23
60	AUG8		11⅝	12⅜		20:57	↑1⅜	1\03	1\07	54	15:23
65	AUG8		8	8½		20:14	↓2½	2\07	2\13	6	15:08
70	AUG8	↓5¼	4¾	5⅛	10	14:40		4⅜	4¾		15:19
75	AUG8	↓2⅝	2⅝	3	31	15:28	↓7¼	7⅛	7⅝	80	14:49

Bid and ask prices for call and put options on Coca Cola LEAPS shares traded on CBOE with 1999 expiry dates

COCA COLA CO		WCB/		USD		KO NYQ/	LT↑69\05		15:34 H69¾		L69\01
Strike	Mth	Calls	Bid	Ask	Volume	Time	Puts	Bid	Ask	Volume	Time
35	JAN9		34¾	35¾		20:44		0\01	0\05		17:29
40	JAN9		30	31		15:46		0⅛	0\05		20:46
45	JAN9		25⅜	26⅜		14:32		0⅜	0½		20:40
50	JAN9		21	22		19:11		0½	0¾		20:59
55	JAN9	↓17⅛	17	17¾	2	15:26		1⅛	1⅜		20:12
60	JAN9	↓13¼	13¼	14	10	15:15		2	2⅜		20:58
65	JAN9		10	10⅜		20:52	↓3⅜	3½	3⅞	3	14:58
70	JAN9		7¼	7¾		21:00		5½	6		21:04
75	JAN9		4⅞	5¼		20:24		8	8½		:
80	JAN9	↓3⅛	3⅛	3½	7	15:16		11½	12¼		19:33
90	JAN9	↓1	0\15	1\03	40	14:39		20⅜	21⅛		15:56

Summary

You have now finished the third section of the book and you should have a clear understanding of the following:

- The difference between ordinary and preference shares

- The reasons why rights and bonus shares are issued

- Some of the equity-linked securities that are available, including depositary receipts, convertible bonds and bonds with warrants.

- The derivatives used in the equity markets

As you've seen, innovative ways of raising capital and generating revenue are constantly being developed in the equity markets. While most of the important types of equity instruments have been covered, you may encounter variations not reviewed here. You will find more details about shares, their valuation, derivatives and other equity-linked instruments in the remaining sections of this book.

As a check on your understanding, try the Quick Quiz Questions on the next page. You may also find the Overview section to be a helpful learning tool.

Your notes

Quick Quiz Questions

1. Which of the following types of share pays a dividend before ordinary shares?
   - ☐ a) Rights
   - ☐ b) Scrip
   - ☐ c) Preference
   - ☐ d) Bonus

2. What is a share called which is given "free" to existing shareholders?
   - ☐ a) Rights
   - ☐ b) Scrip
   - ☐ c) Preference
   - ☐ d) Bonus

3. In what currency are dividends on ADRs paid?
   - ☐ a) Sterling
   - ☐ b) US Dollars
   - ☐ c) Sterling or US Dollars at the discretion of the holder
   - ☐ d) Sterling or US Dollars at the discretion of the issuer

4. Does the issuer of a warrant have the right or obligation to sell the number of shares at the price specified on exercise?
   - ☐ a) Right
   - ☐ b) Obligation

5. If a futures contract on a LIFFE FTSE 100 Index is allowed to expire then how is the contract settled?
   - ☐ a) Delivery of 100 shares comprising the index
   - ☐ b) Cash based on the top 10 shares in the index
   - ☐ c) Cash based on the EDSP
   - ☐ d) Delivery of 100 shares selected by buyer

6. What is the difference between traded and traditional options on equities?

7. What is the difference between American and European style options?

8. Which of the following conditions does a futures contract specify?
   - ☐ a) Contract asset
   - ☐ b) Delivery date
   - ☐ c) Delivery price
   - ☐ d) Standard specification

9. If you place an order for a futures contract, when will you be required to pay initial margin?
   - ☐ a) At expiry of the contract
   - ☐ b) Only if you buy a contract
   - ☐ c) At the time of trading the contract
   - ☐ d) Only if you sell a contract

10. A FTSE 100 Index futures contract has a tick size of 0.50 index points and a tick value of £12.50. If a contract is sold at 5300 and bought back at 5240. What is the profit or loss made?
    - ☐ a) £750 loss
    - ☐ b) £750 profit
    - ☐ c) £1500 loss
    - ☐ d) £1500 profit

11. A market player buys 3 CME S&P 500 Index futures when the S&P 500 stands at 1010. The contract multiplier is $500. What is the market player's exposure to the US Equity market?
    - ☐ a) $515,000
    - ☐ b) $1,500,000
    - ☐ c) $1,515,000
    - ☐ d) None of the above

12. Which of the following descriptions best describes a synthetic index fund?
    - ☐ a) Buy the underlying shares and hedge by buying index futures
    - ☐ b) Buy index futures and invest cash in Money Market instruments
    - ☐ c) Buy index futures with all the funds available
    - ☐ d) Buy index futures and options on index futures with all the funds available

13. What is the variation margin payable on a FTSE 100 Index contract sold at 5302 and with an EDSP of 5318.5 on the trade day. The tick size is 0.50 index points and the tick value is £12.50.
    - ☐ a) £412.50
    - ☐ b) £330
    - ☐ c) £206.25
    - ☐ d) £165

14. If a market player is hedging his or her position, then the market player:
    - ☐ a) Holds only a futures position
    - ☐ b) Holds only a cash position
    - ☐ c) Holds a futures position the same as the cash position
    - ☐ d) Holds a futures position opposite to the cash position

15. Which contracts do the OM Stockholm Exchange and the London Securities and Derivatives Exchange (OMLX) trade?
    - ☐ a) Swedish equity stocks
    - ☐ b) UK equity stocks
    - ☐ c) OMLX index options
    - ☐ d) OMLX index futures

16. Which of the following statements describes a call option?
    - ☐ a) The other side of a put option transaction
    - ☐ b) The right to buy an underlying security in the future
    - ☐ c) The right to sell an underlying security in the future
    - ☐ d) The obligation to buy an underlying security in the future

17. Which of the following statements is/are true? An in-the-money call option has a –
    - ☐ a) Future price greater than its strike price
    - ☐ b) Future price less than its strike price
    - ☐ c) Intrinsic value
    - ☐ d) Time value only

18. Which of the following statements are true for an equity option traded on an exchange?
    - ☐ a) The buyer has the right, but not the obligation, to buy shares
    - ☐ b) The premium is payable when the trade is made
    - ☐ c) The option can be exercised at any price set by the buyer
    - ☐ d) The contract is the same for an OTC traditional option

19. Which of the following statements are true for an American style option? The holder can exercise the option
    - ☐ a) Only if the strike price is above the exercise price
    - ☐ b) An option with premiums paid in US Dollars
    - ☐ c) Only on the expiry date
    - ☐ d) At any time up to and including the expiry date

20. Which of the following terms describes the buyer of a traded equity option?
    - ☐ a) Grantor
    - ☐ b) Holder
    - ☐ c) Taker
    - ☐ d) Payer

21. Which of the following strategies could a market player adopt if he thought that share prices were likely to fall considerably in the future.
    - ☐ a) Short Put
    - ☐ b) Long Put
    - ☐ c) Short Call
    - ☐ d) Long Call

22. What is the breakeven point for a Call option on XYZ shares with an exercise price of 496p and a premium of 27p. The current market price of the shares is 500p.
    - ☐ a) 469p
    - ☐ b) 496p
    - ☐ c) 523p
    - ☐ d) 527p

23. What cash sum would be delivered following the exercise of a LIFFE European style FTSE 100 Index Call option with an exercise price of 5325 and a settlement price of 5413. The tick size is one index point and the tick value is £10.
    - ☐ a) £880
    - ☐ b) £1000
    - ☐ c) £1500
    - ☐ d) £1760

You can check your answers on page 149.

Overview

What Instruments Are Used in the Equity Markets?

Ordinary and Preference Shares

Ordinary Shares (UK) Common Stock (US)	Voting Rights	Dividends
These are irredeemable stocks that give the shareholders a part of the profit generated by an organisation. They are issued at **par** or **nominal value** although this value is of little practical significance, that is, not related to market value. If an organisation offers nominal shares at a higher price than par then the price difference is known as the **share premium**.	Most ordinary shares confer voting rights on shareholders. In theory the shareholders own the organisation and can vote at the annual general meeting. They also have the right to elect directors. The most common structure allows for one vote per share.	If the organisation makes sufficient profits a dividend may be paid. The size of the payment is discretionary and is determined by the board of directors. The dividend is usually in the form of cash but sometimes it is paid as extra shares. Ordinary shares represent the riskiest form of security of an organisation, shareholders are the **last** to receive any profit from dividends. Any interest on debts and preference share dividends is paid before dividends for ordinary shares.
Preference Shares (UK) Preferred Stock (US)	**Voting Rights**	**Dividends**
These rank above ordinary shares for certain specified rights in respect of their dividends and have priority in the event of the organisation's liquidation.	Preference shares may or may not have voting rights – it depends on the organisation issuing the shares.	Shareholders usually receive a fixed rate dividend expressed as a percentage of the nominal value of the share. This dividend is paid before that for any ordinary shares – hence the name. There are a number of different types of preference shares but most are cumulative. This means that if an organisation is not able to pay dividends in one year, then cumulative preference shareholders are entitled to all previous unpaid dividends when the organisation can afford to pay.

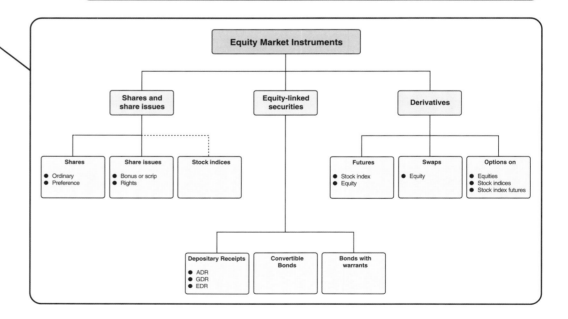

Quick Quiz Answers

✓ or ✗

1. c) ☐

2. b) and d) – a trick question! ☐

3. b) ☐

4. b) ☐

5. c ☐

6. A traded option is traded on an exchange, has standard contract conditions and the contract is with the Clearing house ☐

    A traditional option is an OTC contract ☐

7. An American style option can be exercised up until its expiry date ☐

    A European style option can be exercised only on its expiry date ☐

8. a), b) and d) ☐

9. c) ☐

10. d) ☐

11. c) ☐

12. b) ☐

13. a) ☐

14. d) ☐

15. a), c) and d) ☐

16. b) ☐

17. a) and c) ☐

18. a) and b) ☐

19. d) ☐

20. b) ☐

21. b) ☐

22. c) ☐

23. a) ☐

How well did you score? You should have scored at least 22. If you didn't, review the materials again.

Further Resources

Books

The Financial Times Guide to Using the Financial Pages
Romesh Vaitilingam, FT Pitman Pub., 3rd Edition 1996
ISBN   0 273 6220 13

How to Read the Financial Pages
Michael Brett, Century Business, 3rd Edition 1991
ISBN   0 09 174889 5

The Penguin International Dictionary of Finance
Graham Bannock & William Manser, Penguin, 2nd Edition 1995
ISBN   0 14 051279 9

The Basics of Investing
Benton E. Gup, John Wiley & Sons, Inc., 5th Edition 1992
ISBN   0 471 54853 7

Getting Started in Bonds
Sharon Saltzgiver Wright, John Wiley & Sons, Inc., 1999
ISBN   0 471 32377 2

Getting Started in Stocks
Alvin D. Hall, John Wiley & Sons, Inc., 1997
ISBN   0 471 17753 9

The Stock Market
Richard J. Teweles and Edward S. Bradley, John Wiley & Sons, Inc., 7th Edition 1998
ISBN   047 19134 5

Publications

London International Financial Futures and Options Exchange
• LIFFE: An introduction

Chicago Mercantile Exchange
• Equity Index Futures & Options Information Guide

New York Stock Exchange
• ADRs

Internet

RTF Web Site
• **http://www.wiley.rft.reuters.com**
This is the series' companion web site where additional quiz questions, updated screens and other information may be found.

JP Morgan — ADRs
• **http://www.adr.com**

Exchanges

Refer to the back of this book for a listing of worldwide stock exchange contact infromation and web sites.

This section of the book should take about 60 minutes of study time. You may not take as long as this or you may take a little longer – remember your learning is individual to you.

There are two times in a man's life when he should not speculate: when he can't afford it, and when he can.

Mark Twain

Introduction

All investors, whether institutions or private individuals, must determine upon what criteria they will invest money. What characteristics of a stock make it an attractive investment? As importantly, when is that investment no longer attractive? The various methods of analysing a stock's value is collectively called **equity valuation**. Many analysts and researchers are employed in this part of the market and investors rely heavily on the information they provide. This section provides an overview of the more common methods for determining a stock's value. It is important to note that different methods of stock valuation go in and out of vogue periodically, so that some methods will be more popular at any one time. In this section you will review:

- how to calculate important ratios to evaluate a stock

- sources of financial and technical information

- how to determine rate of return and present and future value

Dividends

The return on equities may result from two sources:

1. The **capital gain** or **loss** resulting from any rise or fall in the market price if the share is sold

2. The **dividend payment** made periodically by the organisation if profits are to be distributed

Organisations normally declare or propose a dividend when profits are announced. Most publicly quoted organisations listed on stock exchanges pay dividends in stages.

- **Interim dividends**, on account, are declared quarterly for most US organisations and half-yearly for UK organisations

- The **final dividend** is announced when the financial results for the full year are published

The board of directors may have the power to declare and pay interim dividends but in most cases the final dividend has to be agreed by the shareholders at the organisation's annual general meeting (AGM).

Trading in shares is taking place all the time but who is entitled to any dividend due? A simple system of codes or status indicators is used in both the financial press and on electronic financial information services such as Reuters to inform investors of what they will or will not receive if they decide to invest in a particular stock.

These status indicators are based on the following:

cum (c) = with
ex (x) = without or excluding

The following table of the more common indicators may help.

cum/ex	Buyer is/is not entitled to
cd/xd cr/xr ca/xa	Receive the next dividend A rights issue All benefits

Example

In the *Financial Times* you see that the price of Bass Plc shares are quoted at 970xd which means that if you buy the shares you are not entitled to receive any dividends due. On the Reuters screen below the full quote looks like this:

Status indicator

```
BASS.L      BASS PLC              000000083205 GBp NMS25000   XD /
Last        Bid          Ask          Mid+27½       Mid Close
↑970        967          979          973           945½
```

It is also important to know a little more about **cd** and **xd**.

cd   This is indicated for shares on the date the organisation announces its dividend. Shares traded on that day, after the announcement, are quoted and traded including the dividend per share – **cum dividend**.

xd   This date is fixed by the stock exchange and is the date when shares start being quoted and traded without the dividend. This means the price quoted **excludes** the value of the dividend per share

In order to receive any dividend an investor has to register shares purchased **cd** by the deadline date known as the **record date**. There is usually a period of about one week between the **xd** date and the record date. The payment date is when the dividend is paid to all shareholders, including the cd shareholders who have been registered by the record date.

But how can investors judge whether or not a particular share is a good investment? How can they judge how well their existing share portfolio is performing compared with other shares and the market as a whole? Investing in equities is a risk business and share market prices fluctuate constantly, even on a daily basis. The following ratios and techniques are used to help investors and each has a specific use.

- Price/Book value and Book Value per Share (BVPS)

- Dividend yield

- Earnings Per Share (EPS)

- Price Earnings Ratio (P/E or PER)

- Dividend cover

- Payout ratio

- Financial and technical information

- Total return techniques

- Stock market indices

All of these ratios and techniques require accurate information on organisations. Electronic information services such as Reuters provide such data. Before moving on, look at the Reuters screens opposite for Reuters share comparisons and the annual report pages. You can also display technical analysis charts very easily.

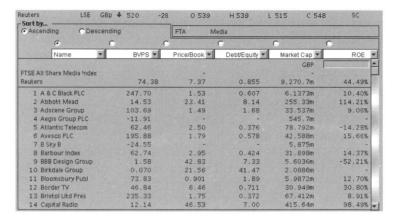

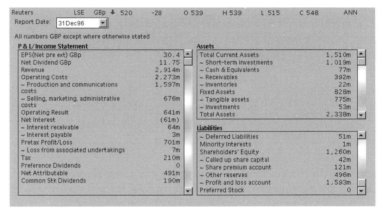

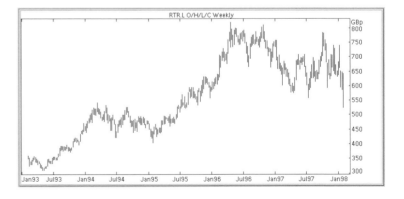

Price/Book Value and Book Value Per Share (BVPS)

There is generally little relationship between the net asset value of an organisation and its market capitalisation. The net asset value usually refers to the book value of an organisation's assets as stated in its year-end balance sheet and represents the organisation's "cash value" or close to it. The net asset value can be used as an indication of the wealth of an organisation should it be subject to a take-over bid. A high net asset value is seen by investors as a support to the market share price. As an organisation performs better the gap between net assets and market capitalisation widens and is seen as a measure of the organisation's ability to "grow the profits".

Over a period of time, a successful organisation's value becomes greater then its net asset value. The **Price/Book ratio** compares the market's valuation of an organisation with its book value.

$$\text{Price/Book ratio} = \frac{\text{Market capitalisation}}{\text{Shareholder's fund}}$$

The size of the Price/Book is important when valuing an organisation if a take-over bid is likely. If the shares in an organisation are near to the net asset value, then the cash balance is not large which reduces the likelihood of a take-over, particularly in a bear market.

The **Book Value per Share (BVPS)** is the ratio of shareholders' funds to the number of shares issued.

$$\text{Book Value Per Share} = \frac{\text{Shareholders' fund}}{\text{Number of shares issued}}$$

So the Price/Book ratio on a share basis is:

$$\text{Price/Book ratio} = \frac{\text{Market share price}}{\text{BVPS}}$$

Most organisation's shares trade at a premium to book value.

Below is a Reuters screen showing both the Price/Book ratio and the BVPS for Reuters shares.

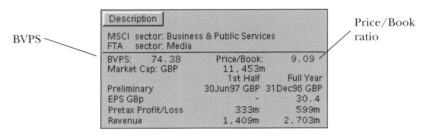

The Reuters screen below provides a sector comparison to compare the performance of other organisations in the same market sector.

Use the drop-down menus to select BVPS, Price/Book ratio ratio

Reuters	LSE	GBp ↓ 512	-36	O 539	H 539	L 512	C 548	SC

Sort by...
◉ Ascending   ○ Descending   FTA   Media

Name	BVPS	Price/Book	Market Cap	Debt/Equity	ROE
			GBP		
FTSE All Share Media Index		-			
Reuters	74.38	7.37	9,256.9m	0.855	44.49%
1 A & C Black PLC	247.70	1.53	6.1281m	0.607	10.40%
2 Abbott Mead	14.53	23.41	254.95m	8.14	114.21%
3 Adscene Group	103.69	1.49	33.487m	1.68	9.06%
4 Aegis Group PLC	-11.91	-	544.89m	-	-
5 Atlantic Telecom	62.46	2.50	78.674m	0.376	-14.28%
6 Avesco PLC	195.88	1.79	42.525m	0.578	15.66%
7 B Sky B	-24.55	-	5,866.3m	-	-
8 Barbour Index	62.74	2.95	31.85m	0.424	14.37%
9 BBB Design Group	1.58	42.83	5.5952m	7.33	-52.21%
10 Birkdale Group	0.070	21.56	2.0855m	41.47	-
11 Bloomsbury Publ	73.83	0.901	5.9783m	1.89	12.70%
12 Border TV	46.84	6.46	30.902m	0.711	30.80%
13 Bristol Utd Pres	235.33	1.75	67.312m	0.372	8.91%
14 Capital Radio	12.14	46.53	415.02m	7.00	98.49%

Dividend Yield

This is a measure of the income-generating value of an investment and is simply the **current dividend** as a percentage of the market price of a share.

$$\text{Dividend yield} = \frac{\text{Gross dividend per share} \times 100}{\text{Share price}}$$

The dividends paid are only for **ordinary shares** and in some markets the amount is paid net of tax. However, dividend yield percentages are gross values.

Based on the most recently paid dividend it shows the percentage return that can be expected if a share is bought at today's market price. Investors use the yield figures to compare the income from shares in the same or different market sectors. They also compare the yields with investment returns from other types of financial instruments and interest rates. In general, dividend yields are significantly lower than yields on comparable fixed-income securities. It is important to remember that the dividend yield is based on historic data and is not necessarily a real indicator of company performance – growth organisations purposely pay low dividends.

So how are dividend yields used by investors?

 Use the following information to calculate the dividend yields for Tesco and Sainsbury shares.

Year to July 1997	Tesco	Sainsbury
Historic dividend	13.3	15.7
Share price	535	504
Dividend yield		

You should have calculated that the dividend yield for Tesco was 2.48%, whereas that for Sainsbury was 3.11%. Using these results it would seem that Sainsbury looks the better investment as it returns £3.11 for every £100 invested.

However, if Tesco had retained some of its profits for future expansion and growth which was recognised by the market as representing good future prospects, then the more highly valued the shares and the **lower** the dividend yield. Many high growth organisations adopt this policy of retaining large amounts of earnings for reinvestment in **growth** and purposely pay low dividends.

At the opposite end of the dividend spectrum, some organisations pay high dividend yields and are termed **high income** shares. In this case if the organisation decides to cut the dividend then it may adversely affect its market share price.

In the UK unit trusts fund managers divide their investments between these **growth** and **high income** shares.

As has been mentioned, dividend yields are based on historic data and what many investors are looking for is a way of predicting future share prices based on historic dividend growth and current share prices. Some of the models used are discussed briefly later in the section.

Earnings Per Share (EPS)

The EPS will normally be higher than the dividend per share because some earnings are retained in the organisation as reserves and not distributed as dividends.

$$EPS = \frac{\text{Total profits after taxes and interest have been paid}}{\text{Number of shares issued}}$$

It is important that the ratio captures the true level of earnings per share. Profits in an organisation can be inflated by factors such as:

- Decreasing the rate of depreciation of an organisation's assets

- Selling off assets such as property

- Selling off profitable parts of the organisation

In most markets investors are looking for repeatable and sustainable earnings. Many organisations publish the EPS figure in their annual report and the information is also available on electronic information services. Below is a Reuters screen showing an organisation's summary data.

Price Earnings Ratio (P/E or PER)

This is the ratio used by many investors to describe whether a share is **cheap** or **expensive**. The ratio is a measure of the confidence in an organisation – the higher the P/E value the greater the investor's expectations of profits. P/E values should only be used to compare organisations in like businesses.

Another way of viewing P/E is that it is the number of years earnings required to equal the organisation's market value. P/E is the quoted price of an ordinary share divided by the most recent EPS value.

$$P/E = \frac{\text{Market price per share}}{\text{Earnings per share}}$$

Using the following information calculate the EPS and P/E ratios for Tesco and Safeway.

Year to July 1997	Tesco	Safeway
Net attributable profits	£520m	£294.4
Issued ordinary shares	2,162m	1,100m
EPS		
Share price	532p	73p
P/E ratio		

You can check your answers on the next page.

You should see from these simple calculations that the P/E ratio for Tesco is about 22 and that for Safeway about 14. This means that the market is prepared to pay 22 times for Tesco's earnings but only 14 times for Safeway's. It would therefore appear that Tesco's shares are overpriced in their sector. But are they overpriced? Why does the market place a higher value on Tesco shares than those of Safeway's?

To help make these important investment decisions, market players rely on information about the company, including shares in issue, market capitalisation, BVPS, Price/Book ratio, historic EPS etc.

The Reuters screens below show the type of information available. Here is a typical company description.

Reuters	LSE GBp	685 +4 1/2	O 676	H 690	L 676	C 676	DES
85 Fleet Street		Tel: 44 171 250 1122		Officers/Directors:	Sir Christopher Hogg		
London		Fax: 44 171 542 3002			Peter Job		
EC4P 4AJ		Investor Rel: 44 171 542 7703			Rob Rowley		
UK		Telex:					

Background Last Updated: 21Feb97

Supplies the global business community and news media with a range of products including real-time financial data, transaction systems, information management systems, access to numeric and textual databases, news and news pictures and certain brokerage services. During the year the Group acquired The Micro Solutions group plc, Distal S.A., the

Share Capital

Shares in Issue: 1,694.1m Market Cap: GBP 11,447m
(as of 30Nov97)
Average Shares: 1,616m No. of Employees: 14917
(Year to 31Dec96)
BVPS: 74.38 Price/Book: 9.09
18Feb98 13:15 Complex
– Rescinded

Revenue Breakdown

Europe, Middle East and Africa	1,564m	53.67%
Asia/Pacific	504m	17.30%

Industry

MSCI Business & Public Services
FTA Media

P&L/Income Statement
Consolidated/Preliminary

	1st Half 30Jun97 GBP	Full Year 31Dec96 GBP	Full Year 31Dec95 GBP	Full Year 31Dec94 GBP	Full Year 31Dec93 GBP
EPS(Net pre ext)(GBp)	–	30.4	25.8	21.7	18
Dividend (Net)(GBp)	3.1	11.75	9.8	6.5	
Revenue	1,409m	2,914m	2,703m	2,309m	1,874m
Operating Costs	–	2,273m	2,152m	1,848m	1,494m
~ Depreciation	–	283m	250m	221m	204m

Here is a typical sector comparison page.

Use the drop-down menus to select P/E, EPS etc

Safeway PLC	LSE GBp	374	+1/2	O 373 ¾	H 373 ¾	L 372 ¾	C 373	SC

Sort by... Ascending Descending   FTA Retailers, Food

Name	EPS FY	PE	Div Yld %	DPS FY	ROE
	GBp			GBp	
FTSE All Share Retailers Food In		18.47	2.940%		
Safeway PLC	27.3	13.66	4.725%	17.625	15.39%
1 ASDA Group PLC	8.95	22.07	1.994%	3.9375	16.58%
2 Availeon PLC	(0.38)	–	–	–	–
3 Brake Bros PLC	29.2	23.80	1.888%	13.125	18.88%
4 Budgens PLC	4.67	14.45	2.685%	1.8125	10.12%
5 Cullens Holdings	(1.87)	–	–	–	6.93%
6 Farepak PLC	13.93	13.50	3.408%	6.4063	265.73%
7 Greggs PLC	103.3	19.85	2.073%	42.5	24.56%
8 Iceland Group	9.53	12.59	5.625%	6.75	13.06%
9 J Sainsbury PLC	22.99	21.81	3.128%	15.688	11.19%
10 John Lusty	0.47805	17.78	–	–	356.79%
11 Kwik Save Group	27.75	10.99	8.197%	25	11.13%
12 Morrison Supermk	11.45	22.79	0.850%	2.2188	14.73%
13 Park Food	4.1	11.10	8.187%	3.725	232.69%
14 Regina PLC	(0.42)	–	–	–	–

Using the following information calculate the EPS and P/E ratios for Tesco and Safeway.

Year to July 1997	Tesco	Safeway
Net attributable profits	£520m	£294.4
Issued ordinary shares	2,162m	1,100m
EPS	24.05p	26.76p
Share price	532p	373p
P/E ratio	22.12	13.94

Within the equity markets, fund managers base their investment decisions on analyses carried out by market players offering equity research. These analysts may be part of a fund manager's organisation or they may be a specialist external organisation. From this wide range of analytical research **consensus estimates** are calculated and published by specialists such as *Extel* and *BARRA* and appear on services such as Reuters. Before moving, look at the below consensus estimates page showing consensus values for EPS, P/E and dividend yield for Reuters shares.

Reuters	LSE	GBp	685	+4 1/2	O 676	H 690	L 676	C 676	CE
Source EFP			Est Year	Est Year					
Date of Estimates: 19Dec97			31Dec97	31Dec98		○ FY 1	○ FY 2		

	Est Year 31Dec97	Est Year 31Dec98
EPS Median Estimate - GBp	29.5	32.2
EPS High Estimate - GBp	34.6	34
EPS Low Estimate - GBp	28.3	29.9
EPS Growth on Previous Year	-3.50%	9.20%
EPS Std Deviation	0.51	1.04
Coefficient of Variation	1.73%	3.23%
Number of Estimates	23	22
Number of Estimates Up/Dn (w)	0 ↓0	0 ↓0
1 Mth Change in EPS Median	0.00%	-0.62%
3 Mth Change in EPS Median	-1.67%	-3.01%
PE	22.92	20.99
PE FTSE All Share Index	19.95	15.76
PE FTSE All Share Media Index	27.09	-
DPS - GBp	13.30	15.00
DPS Growth on Previous Year	13.20%	12.80%
Div Yld	1.967%	2.219%
Div Yld FTSE All Share Index	3.150%	2.990%
Div Yld FTSE All Share Media Index	2.410%	-
Pretax Profit - GBP	690m	752.5m
Pretax Profit High - GBP	821.4m	799.1m
Pretax Profit Low - GBP	664m	720m
Pretax Profit Growth	-1.60%	9.10%
Net Asset Value - GBp	-	-
Net Asset Value Growth	-	-

Estimate History For 31Dec97

Estimate Quality
Shape of Distribution: Uniform   Outliers Excluded: Yes
Sample Size: More than five analysts
Sample Size Quality: Good

The consensus EPS value can be calculated from the current EPS value and the consensus EPS growth rate.

Description		
MSCI sector: Business & Public Services		
FTA sector: Media		
BVPS: 74.38	Price/Book:	9.09
Market Cap: GBP	11,453m	
	1st Half	Full Year
Preliminary	30Jun97 GBP	31Dec96 GBP
EPS GBp	-	30.4
Pretax Profit/Loss	333m	599m
Revenue	1,409m	2,703m

Current EPS

Consensus EPS

EPS Median Estimate - GBp	29.5	32.2
EPS High Estimate - GBp	34.6	34
EPS Low Estimate - GBp	28.3	29.9
EPS Growth on Previous Year	-3.50%	9.20%
EPS Std Deviation	0.51	1.04
Coefficient of Variation	1.73%	3.23%

Growth rate

Examples
Tesco's consensus or prospective EPS can be calculated from its current value, 24.05, multiplied by the consensus EPS growth rate of 6.7%. Current share price is 532p.

Consensus EPS = 24.05 × 1.067   = 25.66
Prospective P/E ratio = 532/25.66 = 20.73
(Previous calculation   = 22.12)

Safeway's consensus or prospective EPS can be calculated from its current value, 26.76, multiplied by the consensus EPS growth rate of −1.3%. Current share price is 373p.

Consensus EPS = 26.76 × 0.987   = 26.41
Prospective P/E ratio = 373/27.11 = 13.76
(Previous calculation   = 13.94)

On the prospective P/E ratio basis, Tesco's shares still look overpriced but the difference between the Tesco and Safeway ratios is not as great as before. Estimated growth, EPS and P/E ratios for an organisation and its market sector rivals are displayed below on a Reuters screen.

Tesco PLC	LSE	GBp	532 ½	-5	O 535	H 537	L 531	C 536	SC

Sort by...
○ Ascending ○ Descending   FTA   Retailers, Food

Name	Est Grth FY1	EPS Grth Yr	Est EPS FY1	EPS FY	Est PE FY1
			GBP	GBp	-
FTSE All Share Retailers Food In					
Tesco PLC	+6.70%	+3.36%	0.257	24.7	20.86
6 Farepak PLC	+11.50%	+11.96%	0.14	13.93	13.43
7 Greggs PLC	+15.20%	+21.09%	1.11	103.3	18.47
8 Iceland Group	+4.90%	+2.63%	0.138	9.53	8.70
9 J Sainsbury PLC	+11.50%	-3.05%	0.26	22.99	19.29
10 John Lusty	+73.60%	-	0.009	0.47805	9.44
11 Kwik Save Group	-3.80%	-10.46%	0.267	27.75	11.42
12 Morrison Supermk	+7.60%	+10.83%	0.118	11.45	22.12
13 Park Food	-11.50%	+7.44%	0.036	4.1	12.64
14 Regina PLC	-	-	-	(0.42)	-
15 Safeway PLC	-1.30%	+2.06%	0.27	27.3	13.81
16 Somerfield PLC	-1.30%	-	0.29	32.3	8.74
17 Tesco PLC	+6.70%	+3.36%	0.257	24.7	20.86
18 Thorntons PLC	+6.70%	+6.11%	0.133	13.32	21.54
19 Watson & Philip	+25.40%	+9.28%	0.425	33.9	12.98

So how do investors use P/E ratios? Look at the Reuters page below:

- A high historic P/E ratio relative to the sector suggests that the organisation is a leader in its industry group or that the share is overvalued.

For Tesco the P/E ratio is high

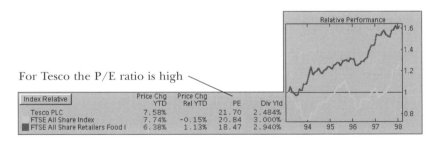

Index Relative	Price Chg YTD	Price Chg Rel YTD	PE	Div Yld
Tesco PLC	7.58%		21.70	2.484%
FTSE All Share Index	7.74%	-0.15%	20.84	3.000%
■ FTSE All Share Retailers Food I	6.38%	1.13%	18.47	2.940%

- A low historic P/E ratio relative to the sector suggests poor organisation performance or that the share is undervalued.

For Safeway the P/E ratio is low

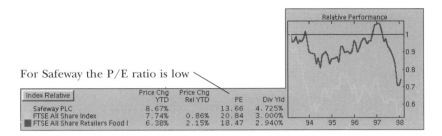

Index Relative	Price Chg YTD	Price Chg Rel YTD	PE	Div Yld
Safeway PLC	8.67%		13.66	4.725%
FTSE All Share Index	7.74%	0.86%	20.84	3.000%
■ FTSE All Share Retailers Food I	6.38%	2.15%	18.47	2.940%

- Check the Relative Performance chart for the share over the last 5 years.

  Relative Performance is a measure of how well an individual share is performing relative to the market or market sector as a whole over a specified period (Relative strength is a measure of how well an individual share is performing relative to a market index).

- Investors concentrate on the prospective P/E ratio to see how cheap/expensive the organisation becomes if there is a large change. A rise/fall in EPS or an acquisition may trigger an action to buy or sell.

It is important to remember that P/E ratio comparisons are usually only reliable for organisations in the same market sector, for example, FT All Share Retailers Food Industry. Investors would be unwise to compare organisations across market sectors or across different countries without a great deal of careful analysis.

One final measure involving the P/E ratio is that of **earnings yield**. This is the percentage reciprocal value of P/E.

$$\text{Earnings yield \%} = \frac{100}{\text{P/E ratio}}$$

Earnings yield is used by investors and analysts to compare different organisations in much the same way as P/E ratios are used.

Dividend Cover

This ratio gives an indication of how many times the organisation could afford to pay out a dividend without using profits from previous years or, how much profits could fall before the dividend payment is jeopardized.

$$\text{Dividend cover} = \frac{\text{Earnings per share}}{\text{Dividend per share}}$$

Example

For 1996, Reuters dividend cover was 30.4/11.75 = 2.58

This means that Reuters can afford to pay its last dividend 2.58 times over.

The consensus dividend cover estimate for 1997 is 29.50/13.40 = 2.20.

Payout Ratio

This is the reciprocal of dividend cover. The size of the dividend payout, relative to the earnings of the organisation, is at the discretion of the board of directors. The payout ratio is therefore a useful number for tracking the historical policy of an organisation in this respect and for forecasting future dividend payments if the earnings forecast is known.

$$\text{Payout ratio} = \frac{\text{Dividend per share}}{\text{Earnings per share}}$$

 Using the following information calculate the payout ratio for Reuters shares 1992–1996. Also calculate the consensus payout ratio for 1997 if the estimated EPS is 29.50 and the estimated dividend is 13.40p.

P & L/Income Statement	Full Year 31Dec96 GBP	Full Year 31Dec95 GBP	Full Year 31Dec94 GBP	Full Year 31Dec93 GBP	Full Year 31Dec32 GBP
EPS(Net pre ext)(GBp)	30.40	25.80	21.70	18.00	15.45
Dividend (Net)(GBp)	11.75	9.80	8.00	6.50	5.30
Revenue	2,914m	2,703m	2,309m	1,874m	1,567.6m

1992 =

1993 =

1994 =

1995 =

1996 =

1997 =

You can check your answer on the next page.

REUTERS

Using the following information calculate the payout ratio for Reuters shares 1992–1996. Also calculate the consensus payout ratio for 1997 if the estimated EPS is 29.50 and the estimated dividend is 13.40p.

$$1992 = \mathbf{0.343}$$
$$1993 = \mathbf{0.361}$$
$$1994 = \mathbf{0.368}$$
$$1995 = \mathbf{0.380}$$
$$1996 = \mathbf{0.387}$$
$$1997 = \mathbf{0.454}$$

The Wall Street Journal *New York Stock Exchange Transactions*

| 52 week | | | | | Yld | |
High	Low	Stock	Div	%	PE	Close
38	29	FordMotor	1.54	4.7	10	33
28	26	FordMotor pf	2.06	7.5	27	

This example shows the difference in ordinary and preferred shares.

Financial and Technical Information

Electronic information such as that supplied by Reuters is not the only source of information for investors. Many still rely on financial newspapers or sections within national daily newspapers, for example, the *Financial Times* and *The Wall Street Journal*. Each newspaper publishes security prices daily but each has a slightly different way of presenting the information! Here are a few examples:

Financial Times *Media section*

	Price	1997/1998 + or −	high/low		Yld Grs	P/E
Reuters	632	−9	665	507	2.7	22.4

Current mid-share price — Gain + Loss − — Range of share prices — Annual return on £100 of stock

Charts

The information in newspapers or from a quote screen is limited if an historical view of prices and trends is required. Many analysts and investors use historical patterns of share price movements such as those provided by an electronic information service such as Reuters.

The charts displayed here have been produced using Reuters 3000. The colours of the screens shown here have been changed so that they can be seen more readily on the printed page.

A weekly bar chart of Reuters share Open/High/Low/Close prices, January 1993 to January 1998.

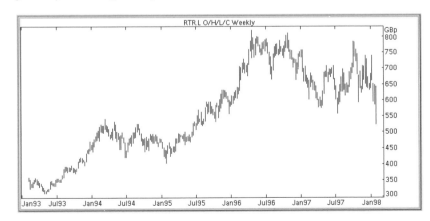

A daily bar chart of Reuters share Open/High/Low/Close prices, January 1997 to January 1998.

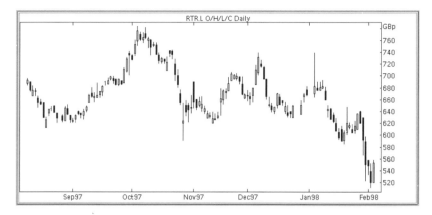

A daily candlestick chart of Reuters share Open/High/Low/Close prices, September 1997 to January 1998.

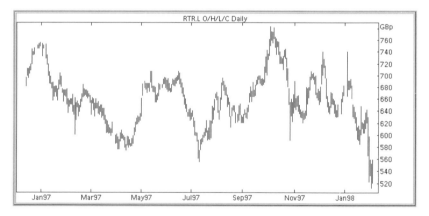

If you need to know more about Technical Analysis and charts, then you may find it useful to refer to the *Introduction to Technical Analysis*, ISBN 0 471 83127 1 book in this series.

Total Return on Equities

So far you have seen how a variety of ratios are used to value equities. All these techniques are based on **fundamental analysis** using historic data.

The growth in global financial markets over the last few decades has necessitated the development of analytical tools which are based on quantitative methods to value equities and predict the future prices of shares.

Rate of Return

Within the financial markets the **time value of money** is important. This means that the **Present Value (PV)** of money is worth **more** than its **Future Value (FV)**. For example, if you have savings of $1000 today – the present time – you have the opportunity to invest your savings and earn interest. But, if you are promised and receive a $1000 at a future date, that is all you will have.

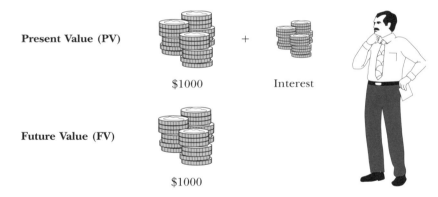

Present Value (PV)   +

$1000   Interest

Future Value (FV)

$1000

Obviously investors are interested in the future value of their investments and need some kind of indication to guide their investment decisions. The simplest guide is **return**. In effect, the return on an investment is the difference between the cost of buying and selling any financial instrument. An investor hopes that the selling price will be greater than the buying price but there is always an element of risk!

$$\text{Return} = (\text{Selling price} - \text{Buying price})$$

... Equation 1a

In the case of a fixed income instrument such as a bond, valuation techniques are relatively straightforward as future cash flows are known with some degree of certainty.

But equities instruments are irredeemable and dividend flows from ordinary shares are not necessarily guaranteed. In these circumstances the **Total return** on equities is used.

$$\text{Total return} = (\text{Selling price} - \text{Buying price} + \text{Dividends} + \text{Reinvestment income} - \text{Dealing expenses} - \text{taxes})$$

... Equation 1b

Total return takes into account how the dividends may be reinvested to generate income. There are two basic ways in which dividends may be reinvested:

- Using the money markets

- Dividends reinvested in the same stock

Any calculation of return or total return using Equations 1a and 1b gives no indication of performance. In other words, how well is a particular equity performing compared with other equities? How attractive an investment is the equity?

To help overcome this difficulty the total return can be expressed as a holding period return which is a function of the buying price expressed as a percentage as shown in Equation 2.

$$\text{Holding period return \%} = \frac{\text{Total return}}{\text{Buying price}} \times 100$$

... Equation 2

The rate of return provides some guide for the investor if returns are compared for **similar** maturity periods. But what if the maturity periods are different? For example, is a 10% rate of return over one month a better deal than an 8% rate over one year?

This problem is resolved using **annualised** rates of return which express any rate of return as a percentage for a **one year period** – as defined in Equation 3.

$$\begin{aligned}\text{Annualised rate} & \\ \text{of return as \%} & \\ & = 100 \times \left[\left(\frac{\text{Holding period return}}{100} \right)^{\frac{1}{\text{yrs}}} \right] - 1\end{aligned}$$

... Equation 3

The interest payment for a bond is stated as an annualised rate of return or coupon rate for the maturity of the bond. This means that the bond's future value can be calculated.

The greater the annualised rate of return and maturity period, the greater the Future Value and therefore the greater the return on the investment.

Simple and Compound Interest

In its most basic form an annualised rate of return can be expressed as a **simple interest rate** where the interest is paid at the end of the investment period regardless of its length. The Future Value (FV) of an investment with simple interest for a known Present Value (PV), Return rate (R) as a decimal can be calculated using Equation 4.

$$FV = PV \times [1 + R]$$

... Equation 4

In practice, of course, interest is reinvested and interest may be earned on interest – in other words **compounded**.

In such circumstances the Future Value for compound interest is given by Equation 5.

$$FV = PV \times [1 + R]^n$$

n = number of years

... Equation 5

Equation 5 can be rewritten on terms of Present Value to produce Equation 6.

$$PV = \frac{FV}{[1 + R]^n}$$

... Equation 6

You may be asking yourself where this is leading. The importance of Equation 6 is that if a FV is known or required, then it is possible to calculate the PV of this FV and the process is known as **discounting a future cash flow**. R is now the required return or yield on the instrument.

The process of calculating the PV for a stream of cash flows is the same as for the single case, except the PV calculation is required for **each** cash flow.

In general for a fixed income instruments such as a bond the Total PV is given by Equation 7.

$$PV_{Total} = \frac{C_1}{(1 + R)} + \frac{C_2}{(1 + R)^2} + ... + \frac{C_n + P}{(1 + R)^n}$$

... Equation 7

P = Principal
C = Coupon rate as a %
R = Rate of return as a decimal
n = Number of years

Before moving on look at the below Reuters screen displaying total return and returns on dividends information.

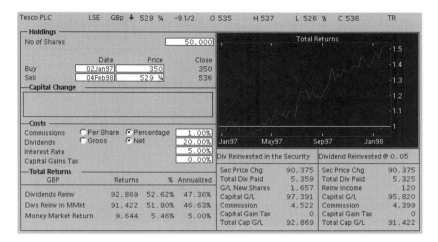

The development of these equations has been necessary in order to consider two well known quantitative methods of valuing equities which are now described briefly.

- Dividend Discount Model (DDM)

- Beta valuation techniques

Dividend Discount Model (DDM)

This model values common stock as the sum of the discounted PVs of its estimated future cash flows.

The model uses Equation 7 and estimates all future cash flows arising during the holding period. The model treats the calculation of PV as if the equity was a fixed income instrument and the equation now looks like this:

$$\text{Share price (PV)} = \frac{D_1}{(1+R)} + \frac{D_2}{(1+R)^2} + \ldots + \frac{D_n + P}{(1+R)^n}$$

... Equation 8

P_n = Future sale price of share
D = Expected dividend per share
R = Required rate of return as a decimal
n = Number of years stock is held – holding period

Since the future cash flows are uncertain, the required return rate on the equity reflects two factors:

1. The yield on a risk-free money market investment, plus

2. A risk premium to compensate for uncertainty in cash flows – the market risk on a stock

The DDM is obviously very sensitive to the value of R. A low value increases the share price (PV) of the equity whereas a high R value depresses the market value.

Beta Valuation Techniques

One of the problems with the DDM is the value of R which should be used when discounting uncertain cash flows. What is the required rate on an equity? What risk premium should be added? Beta valuation techniques which include the **Capital Asset Pricing Model (CAPM)** are complex and are only discussed here briefly.

Beta

Beta is defined as follows:

 It is a measure of the variability of return on a stock for a 1% change in the return on the whole market.

The higher the beta value of a stock, the greater its required return. In other words, it is a riskier investment than the equity market as a whole. Beta is a sensitivity measure and is estimated statistically on the historic returns on the stock against the returns on the whole market over a sample period – usually five years.

Another way of looking at the beta for a stock is as the stock's contribution to the volatility of the total market portfolio.

Capital Asset Pricing Model (CAPM)

In essence the CAPM uses the premise that in an **efficient market** the required rate of return on a particular stock is proportional to the risk on that stock and can be calculated using Equation 9.

$$R = R_f + ß \times (R_m - R_f)$$

... Equation 9

R = Expected rate of return
R_f = Return available on risk free fixed income investment over holding period
R_m = Estimated return on a market portfolio of stocks
ß = Stock's beta value

An efficient market means that all information about the stock is available to investors. The market portfolio is a microcosm of the composition of the market as a whole. In practice, the stocks comprising Stock Indices such as the FTSE 100 Index and the S&P 500 Index approximate closely enough a market portfolio.

Example
XYZ stock has an estimated ß of 0.4 and analysts predict a Total return for this stock of 11.0% over the next year. The Equity Market is expected to produce a return of 7.7% and the risk free interest rate is 5.0% over the same period.

Calculate the expected return on the XYZ shares. Using Equation 9:

$$R = 5.0 + 0.4 \times (7.7 - 5.0)$$
$$= 5.0 + 1.08$$
$$= 6.08\%$$

The CAPM calculation suggests a much lower rate than that predicted by the analysts. This means that the stock promises above average returns for the risk involved and therefore may be attractive to investors in index-tracking funds.

So how successful are these total return quantitative models? In practice, both the DDM and CAPM have proved to be limited in their use. However, the CAPM is useful in that it helps investors identify the balance between risk and return on individual stocks within their portfolios. Many of the most successful investors pick stocks based on fundamental analysis, sometimes with help from technical analysis. None of the most successful individual investors currently use quantitative analysis!

Summary

You have now finished the fourth section of this book and you should have clear understanding of the basics of equity valuation, including:

- how to calculate important ratios to evaluate a stock's value
- sources of financial and technical information
- how to determine rate of return and present and future value

As a check on your understanding you should try the Quick Quiz Questions on the next page. You may also find the Overview Section to be a helpful learning tool.

Your notes

Quick Quiz Questions

1. XYZ shares are quoted at 228p and the organisation announces a dividend of 5.00p and an EPS of 12.2. What is the dividend cover?
   - ☐ a) 0.41
   - ☐ b) 2.19
   - ☐ c) 2.44
   - ☐ d) 18.69

2. XYZ shares are quoted at 228p and the organisation announces a dividend of 5.00p and an EPS of 12.2. What is the dividend yield?
   - ☐ a) 0.41
   - ☐ b) 2.19
   - ☐ c) 2.44
   - ☐ d) 18.69

3. ABC is a UK organisation and decides to issue scrip shares on a two-for-five basis. If an investor decides to take up the offer how many shares does he hold after issue?
   - ☐ a) 2
   - ☐ b) 5
   - ☐ c) 7

4. XYZ is a UK organisation which decides to offer its investors a one-for-two rights issue at 140p. The current shares are worth 200p. If all the rights shares are taken up what will the ex-rights price be?
   - ☐ a) 200p
   - ☐ b) 180p
   - ☐ c) 160p
   - ☐ d) 140p

5. An organisation has a P/E ratio of 22.5 and an EPS of 10.4. What is the market share price?
   - ☐ a) 234p
   - ☐ b) 230p
   - ☐ c) 134p
   - ☐ d) 104p

6. XYZ share price is 220p and the EPS is 15.6. What is XYZ's earnings yield?
   - ☐ a) 7.02%
   - ☐ b) 7.09%
   - ☐ c) 7.56%
   - ☐ d) 8.00%

7. Which of the following does the Dividend Discount Model value a security as?
   - ☐ a) Its net asset value per share
   - ☐ b) The sum of all future dividends plus the expected capital gain
   - ☐ c) The sum of the PVs of all future dividends, discounted by the risk-free rate
   - ☐ d) The sum of the PVs of all future dividends, discounted by the required rate of return on the class of share

8. What is the ß of the following portfolio of shares?

	ß	% of portfolio
XYZ	1.40	15
AYZ	0.66	32
BYZ	1.14	53

   - ☐ a) 1.025
   - ☐ b) 1.067
   - ☐ c) 1.089
   - ☐ d) 1.141

You can check your answers on page 172.

Overview

Equity valuation is a method for determining a stock's value.

Equity Valuation

Return on Equities
- Dividends
- Capital Gain/ Loss

Valuation Ratios and Techniques

Price/Book Value and Book Value Per Share (BVPS)

$$\text{Price/Book ratio} = \frac{\text{Market capitalisation}}{\text{Shareholder's fund}}$$

$$\text{Book value per share} = \frac{\text{Shareolder's fund}}{\text{Number of shares issued}}$$

$$\text{Price/Book ratio} = \frac{\text{Market share price}}{\text{BVPS}}$$

Dividend Yield

$$\text{Dividend yield} = \frac{\text{Gross dividend per share} \times 100}{\text{Share price}}$$

Earnings Per Share

$$\text{EPS} = \frac{\text{Total profits after taxes and interest have been paid}}{\text{Number of shares issued}}$$

Price/Earnings Ratio

$$\text{P/E} = \frac{\text{Market price per share}}{\text{Earnings per share}}$$

Dividend Cover

$$\text{Dividend cover} = \frac{\text{Earnings per share}}{\text{Dividend per share}}$$

Payout Ratio

$$\text{Payout ratio} = \frac{\text{Dividend per share}}{\text{Earnings per share}}$$

Financial and Technical Information
- Print media
- Electronic media

Total Return on Equities

- Rate of Return

$$\text{Return} = (\text{Selling price} - \text{Buying price})$$
$$\dots \textit{Equation 1a}$$

$$\text{Total return} = (\text{Selling price} - \text{Buying price} + \text{Dividends} + \text{Reinvestment income} - \text{Dealing expenses} - \text{taxes})$$
$$\dots \textit{Equation 1b}$$

$$\text{Holding period return} \% = \frac{\text{Total return}}{\text{Buying price}} \times 100$$

$$\text{Annualised rate of return as} \% = \frac{\text{Rate of return as} \%}{\text{Investment period in years}}$$

$$= 100 \times \left[\left(\frac{\text{Holding period return}}{100} \right)^{\frac{1}{\text{yrs}}} - 1 \right]$$
$$\dots \textit{Equation 3}$$

- Simple and Compound Interest

$$FV = PV \times [1 + R]$$
$$\dots \textit{Equation 4}$$

$$FV = PV \times [1 + R]^n$$
$$n = \text{number of years}$$
$$\dots \textit{Equation 5}$$

$$PV = \frac{FV}{[1 + R]^n}$$
$$\dots \textit{Equation 6}$$

$$PV_{\text{Total}} = \frac{C_1}{(1 + R)} + \frac{C_2}{(1 + R)^2} + \dots + \frac{C_n + P}{(1 + R)^n}$$
$$\dots \textit{Equation 7}$$

- Dividend Discount Model

$$\text{Share price (PV)} = \frac{D_1}{(1 + R)} + \frac{D_2}{(1 + R)^2} + \dots + \frac{D_n + P}{(1 + R)^n}$$

- Beta Valuation Techniques
Beta is a measure of the variability of return on a stock for a 1% change in the return on the whole market.
- Capital Asset Pricing Model)

Quick Quiz Answers

	✓ or ✗
1. c)	☐
2. b)	☐
3. c)	☐
4. b)	☐
5. a)	☐
6. b)	☐
7. d)	☐
8. a)	☐

How well did you score? You should have managed to get most of these questions correct.

Further Resources

Books

Getting Started in Security Analysis
Peter J. Klein, John Wiley & Sons, Inc., 1998
ISBN   0 471 25487 8

Investments: Analysis and Management
Charles P. Jones, John Wiley & Sons, Inc., 6th Edition 1997
ISBN   0 471 16959 5

The Mathematics of Investing: A Complete Reference
Michael C. Thomsett, John Wiley & Sons, Inc., 1989
ISBN   0 471 50664 8

Pricing Convertible Bonds
Kevin B. Connolly, John Wiley & Sons, Inc., 1998
ISBN   0 471 97872 8

Quantitative Financial Economics: Stocks, Bonds and Foreign Exchange
Keith Cuthbertson, John Wiley & Sons, Inc., 1996
ISBN   0 471 95360 1

Relative Dividend Yield: Common Stock Investing for Income and Appreciation
Anthony E. Spare, John Wiley & Sons, Inc., 2nd Edition 1999
ISBN   0 471 32705 0

Internet

RFT Web Site
• **http://www.wiley.rft.reuters.com**
This is the series' companion web site where additional quiz questions, updated screens and other information may be found.

Exchanges

Refer to the back of this book for a listing of worldwide stock exchange web sites.

This section of the book should take about sixty minutes of study time. You may not take as long as this or you may take a little longer – remember your learning is individual to you.

If you see a broker jump out of the window, jump after him – there is sure to be money in it.

Voltaire (1694–1778)

Introduction

By now you should be aware that equities, equity-linked securities such as ADRs, and derivatives are either traded on a regulated exchange or OTC. The trading methods used on the LSE, NYSE and TSE have been described briefly in *Section 2: How Do the Equity Markets Work?* You should also understand the differences between quote- and order-driven systems for trading equities which were explained in the same section.

This section is concerned with the following:

- Important intermediaries and the financial institutions in which they operate

- Important groups of investors

- Regulation of the markets

Before moving on it may be useful if you try the activity opposite. No specific answer is given as you can check with the appropriate materials in *Section 2: How Do the Equity Markets Work?*

What are the basic differences between quote- and order-driven trading systems for equities? Illustrate your answer with reference to the way particular stock exchanges operate.

Market Makers

These are individuals or firms who are registered with a stock exchange and are prepared to make a market in particular security. In other words, they quote two-way buy (bid) and sell (ask) prices for shares issued by an organisation listed on the stock exchange. The difference between the prices is called the **spread** and represents the market makers' profit.

Bid	Ask or Offer
The price prepared to **buy**	The price prepared to **sell**
Lower price	**Higher** price

On the LSE, depending on the particular equity, market makers quote two-way prices for the Normal Market Size (NMS). Market makers may be asked to quote for transactions larger than the NMS. In these circumstances the market maker will often quote a different price than that displayed on the exchange information system.

Historically on the LSE, market makers are the modern counterpart of the stockjobbers. For the quote-driven SEAQ system, market makers are obliged to quote two-way prices which are constantly revised depending on supply and demand.

In return for accepting the obligations of acting as a market maker these market players gain the following privileges:

- Only market makers are allowed to input prices into SEAQ

- Market makers are exempt stamp duty (a type of tax) on purchases

- Market makers occasionally need to borrow securities to cover short positions which are caused by a sale or excess of sales over purchases in anticipation of a fall in prices. The borrowing is arranged through the stock exchange money brokers.

- Access to an InterDealer Broker network which allows market makers to buy and sell large volumes of securities anonymously

The introduction of the electronic order-driven SETS system on the LSE has changed the trading method for the equities comprising the FTSE 100 Index. Now market makers and brokers enter their orders into the order book which are then processed automatically. The order book entries are anonymous and counterparties to a match are only informed of each other's identity after the trade has taken place. Shares of organisations outside those comprising the FTSE 100 Index are still quoted using the SEAQ system.

```
AIR.L                                              08:48
SEAQ GBp  AIRTOURS PLC         Cls   1295-1310     REUTER
NMS 10     PL 60                               GMT 08:48
                           Net 0      H 1308     L 1296
Vol 2.3                                        News  :
Last  ↑1308      1296                               5/5

 SBCW  HOAE  MLSB       1295-1310     BZWE  MLSB  HOAE
BZWE  1290-1310    10x10  08:14  NWSL  1295-1315  10x10  08:27
HOAE  1295-1310    10x10  08:24  SBCW  1295-1310  10x10  08:25
MLSB  1295-1310    10x10  08:24  UBS.  1295-1310  10x10  08:26
```

Brokers

There are three main types of broker you will encounter on worldwide markets. Their titles and their roles may vary, but in general terms the three main types of broker are:

- **Broker Dealers**
  These market players combine the roles of market makers and broker to transact business with other market makers. These brokers act as agents for clients for which they charge a negotiable commission or brokerage. Brokers of this type can trade on their account. A broker dealer has a duty to execute trades to a client's **'best advantage'**. This means selling for the highest price possible and buying at the lowest price possible – seen from the client's point of view.

- **Agency or Client Brokers**
  Brokers of this type act on behalf of their institutional and individual clients and charge a negotiable commission for their services. These brokers cannot take positions on their own account. Some brokers of this type provide an execution-only service – in the US these are known as Discount brokers. In other cases Agency or Client brokers provide a discretionary management and research service for which clients pay a fee.

- **InterDealer Brokers (IDBs)**
  These brokers act as intermediaries exclusively to market makers or broker dealers who wish to trade anonymously. IDBs help market makers execute large trades by matching the other side of the trade with one or more counterparties.

There are a number of reasons why buyers and sellers of equities may not want to deal directly and prefer to use brokers. These reasons include the following:

- Market makers in some quote-driven systems can only deal with other market makers and not with the clients directly. Clients can only trade using the services of a client or agency broker.

- Obtaining the best price for a trade in different financial centres may be both time consuming and expensive for an individual.

- Buyers and sellers may wish to remain anonymous while negotiating a price.

Securities Houses

Securities houses have undergone great changes in recent years, in that many of the large houses have merged to combine resources. Securities houses carry out many roles including:

- **Securities dealings.** They may be market makers and/or broker dealers.

- **Corporate finance**. This relates to issuing securities, take-overs and mergers, defence against take-over, underwriting and employee share schemes.

- **Asset management**. This includes the management of funds for pensions, corporations, nonprofit organisations and wealthy individuals. It may also include management of their own unit and investment trusts.

- **Investment research**. This ranges from long-term future market analysis to real-time price analysis.

- **Derivatives**. This area deals with instruments derived from existing instruments such as futures, options and warrants.

- **Brokerage services**. This usually involves sales teams fulfilling client orders and managing client money and securities.

- **Risk management**. In cases where the security house uses its own capital to facilitate transactions, the risk involved has to be assessed, for example, in the underwriting of new share issues. Risk management is a middle-office function overseeing the activities of the front office – the trading environment – and the back office where transactions are settled.

Offering such a wide range of services within the same organisation is not without problems. Although some services complement one another and information can be freely exchanged, shared knowledge between corporate finance and asset management services for example are likely to result in a conflict of interests.

The sharing of information is strictly controlled, or forbidden in some instances, between the various functions within a security house. The term "Chinese Wall" refers to the imaginary wall that a security house imposes to prevent or minimise conflicts of interest.

Data Requirements and Analysis

Access to market prices, trading volumes, current news, etc are all vital requirements for market players in the equity markets. Market analysts need access to up-to-date information on macro-economic indicators and statistics such as Gross National Product (GNP), together with historic data on individual organisations covering company reports, balance sheets etc. Electronic information services

such as Reuters provide this type of local-time information. See the sample screens below.

Market players use all of this information to calculate various ratios to measure the performance of equities, portfolios of securities, etc against a variety of benchmarks and/or indices. The process described here is known as ratio analysis and is the most common type of **fundamental analysis** which is carried out in assessing the suitability of equities as investments. It has been suggested that over 80% of UK and US analysts use fundamental analysis as the basis for their recommendations.

Technical analysis (called Charting historically) is a method of predicting price movements and future market trends by studying charts of past market action. These charts take into account the price of instruments, volumes of trading and, where applicable, open-interest in the instruments.

The following table broadly summarises the differences between fundamental and technical analyses.

Fundamental Analysis	Technical Analysis
Focuses on what **ought** to happen in a market	Focuses on what **actually** happens in a market
Factors involved in price analysis include: • Supply and demand • Seasonal cycles • Weather • Government policy	Charts are based on market action involving: • Price • Volume – all markets • Open interest – futures only Seasonality in commodities

In practice many market players use technical analysis in conjunction with fundamental analysis to determine their trading strategy.

Quantitative Analysis

This type of analysis uses mathematical models such as the **Dividend Discount Model (DDM)** and the **Capital Asset Pricing Model (CAPM)** to value equities in order to assess the risk/return characteristics of an equity investment portfolio. These models are discussed more fully in the following sections.

Electronic information systems, such as Reuters, supply much of the historical data, prices and analytical tools required by equity markets market players. Look at the samples on this page.

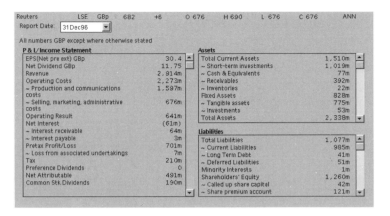

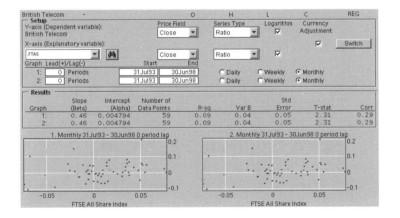

The Trading Environment

To give you a flavour of how the players in these markets operate, look at the diagram below and on the following pages describing a typical day's events. The flow of research information and dealings is indicated by arrows. The following pages show a sample Reuters screen for each player and the reasons why each element of the screen is used.

Some screens may look complicated, but you will learn how to refer to them as you go through the rest of the book.

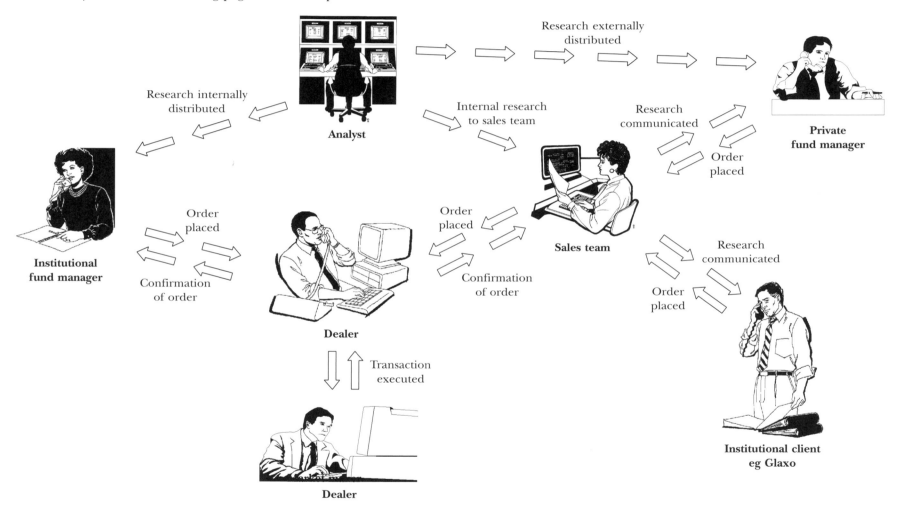

Research externally distributed

Research internally distributed

Analyst

Internal research to sales team

Research communicated

Private fund manager

Order placed

Institutional fund manager

Order placed

Confirmation of order

Dealer

Order placed

Confirmation of order

Sales team

Research communicated

Order placed

Transaction executed

Dealer

Institutional client eg Glaxo

Market player	Examples of screens that could be used
 **Analyst**	Analysts usually have a specialist area and so may research a sector or market area. They also compare similar markets/ sectors in different countries. In this example the analyst is interested in chemicals – particularly in the German markets. The analyst's screens would look something like this: **1** German Chemical sector chain **2** Quote list of recently recommended stocks **3** German DAX Index – the main stock index **4** Tic graph of the DAX index **5** German chemical sector news **6** Background information on a particular company 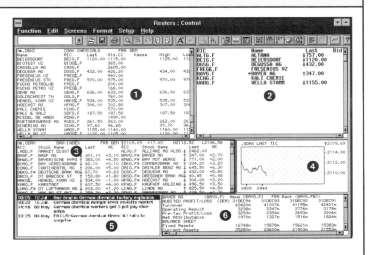
 **Sales team**	The sales team screens might include a quotes list of stocks they have recommended to their target clients, market commentaries from different countries, time and sales for a particular stock and market stock rankings. **1** Quotes list of stocks of interest **2** Time and sales for a specific stock – to get a closer look at performance/trade history **3** Top ten stocks by volume, for example, the French market **4** Top ten stocks by volume, for example, the German market **5 6 7** Market reports for Germany, UK and France 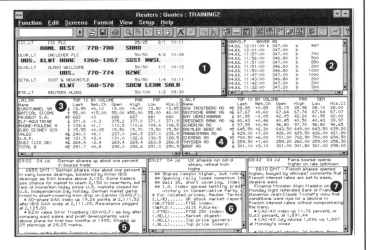

Market player	Examples of screens that could be used
  **Institutional fund manager** **Private fund manager**	Institutional and private fund managers will have a quotes list of the stocks in their portfolios. They will also use spreadsheet software to calculate their positions on bought and sold stocks. They would normally use an electronic information service for historic analysis. **1** Quotes list of stocks in the portfolio **2** Market Index Chain **3** DAX Index – the main German stock index **4** CAC 40 Index – the main French stock index **5** Equity News could be on the stocks in their portfolio (quotes list) **6** Alerts 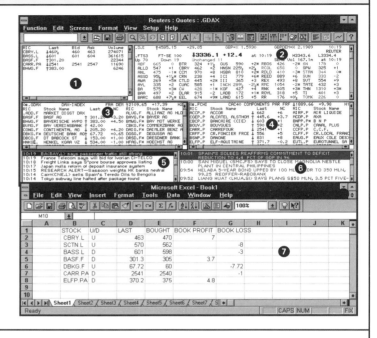
 **Institutional client, eg, a corporation**	In this case the corporate client will be interested in his own company as well as displaying a quotes list of the stocks he is investigating. **1** Best bid/ask prices for stocks of interest **2** Own company 'touch' price **3** Company news **4** German chemical sector news **5** Quotes list of stocks of interest **6** Market report on London 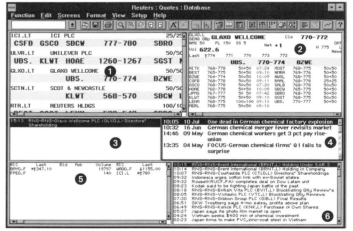

REUTERS

Market player	Examples of screens that could be used
Dealer	Dealers will display the prices of the stocks in which they are making trades. They may also display time and sales for particular stocks and a ticker to show all market trades. Alerts will be displayed to keep them up-to-date with the latest news affecting the markets. **❶** German DAX Index **❷** Time and sales for a specific stock **❸** Ticker of trades on the DAX **❹** Tic graph of DAX Index **❺** Alerts

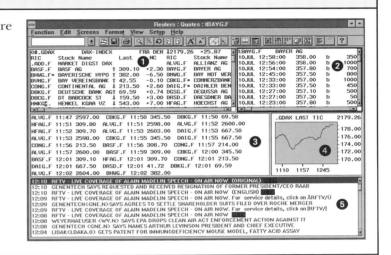

Market player	Examples of screens that could be used
Dealer	Market makers screens are very similar to those of the dealers. In addition to sector and index information they may display top ten volume information. **❶** German Chemical sector **❷** Time and Sales for a specific stock **❸** German DAX Index **❹** Top ten stocks by volume in German market **❺** Alerts

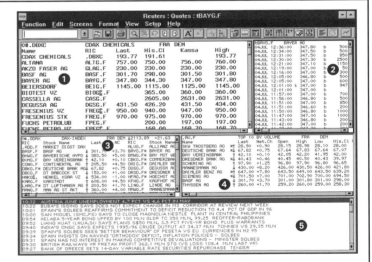

Investors

There are two basic types of investor:

- Individuals

- Institutions

Individuals have always invested in the equity markets but globally the total number of shares owned by individuals has fallen dramatically as a result of the increasing growth of investments on behalf of pension funds, unit trusts, investment trusts, etc. For example, on the LSE over 60% of shares were owned by individuals in 1950 whereas the figure for 1996 was only approximately 20%. During the same period on the NYSE, individual ownership of shares has dropped from over 90% to about 48%. Even though the percentage of equity held by individuals is declining with respect to the total invested on stock exchanges, it would still appear that individuals prefer investing in equity rather than debt instruments. The chart below shows the relative ratio in the US for 1996 was 4:1 in favour of equity investment.

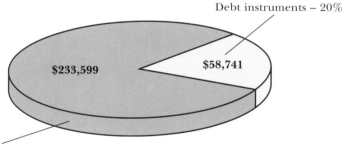

Debt instruments – 20%

$58,741

$233,599

Equity instruments – 80%

Source: Investment Company Institute

Individual ownership of equity has declined at the expense of institutional investors. On the NYSE in 1996 institutional ownership of the total equity held was 45.6% whilst on the LSE the figure was approximately 80%. But who are these institutional investors?

Before moving on try the activity below...

List as many types of institutional investor as you can think of. Which do you imagine is the most important in terms of equity holdings?

You can check your answer on the next page.

The most important of the institutional investors include the following:

- Investment banks

- Banks

- Corporations

- Government agencies

- Insurance companies

- Pension funds

- Investment funds – investment trusts and unit trusts

- Fund managers

Merchant Banks

Merchant banks who did not buy stock exchange firms still have £billions under fund management and therefore still invest in equities. Merchant banks advise foreign governments, companies and organisations on mergers and acquisitions.

Corporations

Corporate finance departments not only look after the organisation's own funds but also invest spare funds in the capital markets.

Government Agencies

Although governments are generally borrowers of funds in the capital markets, some government agencies are actively involved in managing investments, for example, for public sector pension funds.

Insurance Companies

General insurance companies may run a variety of funds for life, pensions, general insurance, endowments, etc. The success of these funds is measured on a competitive basis in tables against indices such as the FTSE 100 Index. Insurance companies are a major influence on the equities markets by withholding funds as well as investing. Some insurance companies have their own investment management subsidiaries.

Life Assurance Companies

Life assurance companies sell a variety of long-term investment products such as personal pension plans. These plans often provide a lump sum after a number of years' contributions and also include an insurance policy against the death of the insured.

The holder of the pension plan has some control over the contributions made and how the funds are to be allocated. However, the investment portfolios held by life assurance companies are broadly the same as those held by pension funds and represent long-term investments.

Pension Funds

These funds form the largest single group of investors on a global scale. In 1995, global pension assets amounted to $8,176 billion. The chart below indicates some of the largest sources of pension fund assets by country – the US amount accounts for over 50% of the global total.

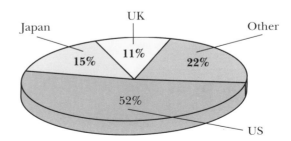

	$ bn
US	4,258
Japan	1,263
UK	879
Other	1,776
Total	**8,176**

Source: InterSec Research Corp.

Some of the largest pension funds belong to the largest organisations issuing equity. Look below at the top 10 pension fund assets for UK pension funds in 1995. How many belong to large organisations issuing equity?

Pension fund	£ billion
CMT Pensions Trustee Services	16.8
British Telecommunications	16.4
Electricity Supply	12.5
Post Office	10.9
Railways Pension Fund	10.5
Universities Superannuation Scheme	9.8
British Gas	8.1
Barclays Bank	6.9
BP	7.6
National Westminster Bank	6.5

Source: HSBC James Capel

Pension fund managers are looking for the best long-term return on their investments. In general, returns on equity out-perform those on debt instruments which is reflected in the proportion of assets invested in equity. In the UK a total of 81% of pension fund assets is involved in equity in 1996–57% domestic and 24% international. In the US the total investment in equities for state and government funds was 51% in 1996.

It is important to recognise that not all pension funds are self-managed by their parent organisations. Many smaller funds are managed by other independent financial institutions or fund managers.

The table below indicates the top 10 fund management organisations for 1995.

Fund manager		£ billion
Prudential Portfolio Mgrs	Insurance Co.	82.1
Mercury Asset Management	Independent	75.6
Schroder Investment Mgt.	Investment Bank	74.0
Commercial Union Inv. Mgt.	Insurance Co.	66.0
Morgan Grenfell Ass. Mgt	Investment Bank	60.9
Fleming Inv. Mgt.	Investment Bank	55.6
PDFM Ltd	Investment Bank	52.1
Standard Life	Insurance Co.	43.7
INVESCO	Independent	41.7
Norwich Union	Insurance Co.	41.0

Source: HSBC James Capel

Investment Funds

Many small investors can take part in the equity markets without actually own shares in individual organisations through the use of two types of **collective funds**:

- Investment Trusts (UK)/Closed-end publicly quoted funds (US)

- Unit Trusts (UK)/Open-end mutual funds (US)

Investment Trusts

These are organisations quoted on a stock exchange with a fixed amount of authorised share capital. In this case the shareholder's money is invested in the shares of other listed organisations. Hence in the US these trusts are referred to as closed-end publicly quoted funds. The trust managers are responsible for investing the trust's capital in the best way to produce the highest profit which is then paid as a dividend to the shareholders in the normal way.

REUTERS

New shares in the trust cannot be created on demand, rather, new shares can be issued if the listing exchange authorises the trust to do so. Trading in trust shares is carried out in exactly the same way as for trading shares in other organisations.

Investment trusts can spread their investment risk over many shares, either on the domestic market or overseas. They may also specialise in certain types of investment. An investment trust is also allowed to borrow capital for further investment.

The idea of investment trusts is over a hundred years old – The Foreign and Colonial Government Trust was quoted on the LSE in the 1870s. However the spreading of risk was not always entirely successful as is the case today! In 1890 some investors lost heavily in the so-called Baring Crisis.

Baring Crisis of 1890

In the late 1880s, Baring Brothers' merchant bank undertook loans and guarantees for large capital sums in the Argentine Republic. The Republic continually defaulted on repayments and by 1890 Barings' heavy obligations precipitated a general financial crisis with liabilities amounting to £21 million. The Bank of England in conjunction with other UK banks stepped in and took over the liabilities. Later Baring Brothers was reorganised as a limited company with capital of £1 million.

Unit Trusts

Open-end funds such as these do not have a fixed amount of shares – the equity fund is variable depending on the number of units or shares in existence at any one time. Investors in unit trusts receive **units** proportional to their investment which can be sold back to the organisation at any time. The investor's capital is pooled in a trust fund which is then invested in securities according to the requirements of the trust deed. The units represent equal shares in the trust's investment portfolio. Investors receive no share of any profits directly but they can raise capital by selling their units.

Unit trusts were introduced into the UK in the early 1930s based on the **mutual funds** operating in the US. Many types of unit trusts are now available specialising in different financial markets, geographical areas and risk profiles. They can also be used as an alternative way of funding benefits on pensions, mortgages and life assurance policies.

The total global assets of mutual funds as of the third quarter 1998 was $7,631 billion. Although a huge amount it was not as large as the global assets of pension funds mentioned previously – $8,176 billion. The greatest amount of mutual funds was in the US which accounted for nearly two-thirds of the total global assets. The chart below indicates the top five countries in terms of mutual fund assets as of the third quarter of 1998.

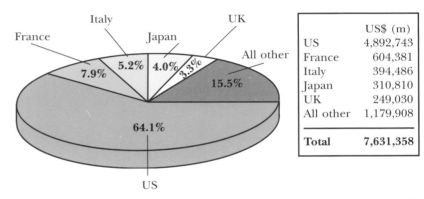

	US$ (m)
US	4,892,743
France	604,381
Italy	394,486
Japan	310,810
UK	249,030
All other	1,179,908
Total	**7,631,358**

Source: Investment Company Institute – International Mutual Funds Survey, Q3, 1998

Fund Managers

Another way of considering the way in which capital is invested on behalf of organisations is as a **fund management** process. In essence fund managers operating in insurance companies, investment banks, independent firms, pension funds etc invest funds on behalf of their institutions and other clients. The role of the fund manager is to invest cash flows from pension contributions, insurance premiums, personal savings to meet the investment objectives of the particular fund.

The activities of fund management therefore covers both those of front, middle and back office including the following:

- Investment strategy, asset allocation and risk management

- Research and analysis

- Equity trading using brokers

- Trading in the money markets, debt markets and foreign exchange

- Compliance, settlement and administration of transactions

The chart below summarises the various fund management activities.

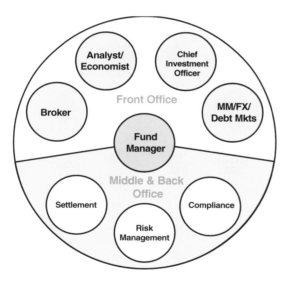

Fund management comprises many specialised organisations and investments. See the examples below:

Type of –	Examples
Institution	Insurance Co. Investment Bank Pension fund Independent firm
Fund	Insurance policies Pension funds Unit Trusts Investment Trusts
Client	Individuals – domestic and overseas Institutions – domestic and overseas
Asset	Equities Long-term Debt instruments Short-term Money Market/FX instruments Property

The table below shows a breakdown of the investment holdings of some funds for 1995.

A = Merill Lynch

B = Lehman Brothers

C = Nikko Securities

D = Daiwa Europe

E = UBS International Investment

Holdings by instrument, %	A	B	C	D	E
Equities	50	60	65	60	37
Bonds	45	35	30	40	55
Cash	5	5	5	0	8
	100	100	100	100	100

Equity holdings by area, %	A	B	C	D	E
Americas					
US	39	44	35	31	28
Other	4	2	2	5	0
Europe					
UK	8	9	9	11	14
Germany	4	4	7	6	5
France	3	6	3	4	13
Others	9	12	2	11	13
Asia					
Japan	22	9	32	21	17
Others	11	14	10	11	10
	100	100	100	100	100

Bond holdings by currency, %	A	B	C	D	E
USD	25	53	45	44	53
JPY	24	0	18	20	9
GBP	5	9	7	5	5
DEM	6	13	15	20	16
FRF	8	13	10	6	7
Others	32	12	5	5	10
	100	100	100	100	100

Source: The Economist

The Role of An Investment Fund Manager

Depending on the enthusiasm of the chief investment officer, morning meetings start at 8.15 am or 8.30 am. The meeting reviews briefly the day's financial news and company results relating to stocks held in clients' portfolios, changes on house buy/sell lists, instructions on marketing reports, meetings and administration matters etc which need immediate attention. Investment fund managers have to present themselves at the meeting fully briefed on their respective areas of specialisation on all these matters.

Investment fund managers either put on their own trades or write dealing tickets which they pass on to the UK or overseas dealer. The dealer has more time to seek out the best price or accumulate the desired size of holding over a period of days.

Investment fund managers are only happy when at their desks reviewing and managing their portfolios. They talk to brokers about the market, about new ideas on what to buy or sell and how the day's events may affect their holdings.

They review the piles of brokers' stock recommendations that arrive daily on their desks. They carry out their own analyses of balance sheets and profit and loss accounts, often preparing written valuations or 'front sheets' of the key points and financial ratios to support a recommendation to 'buy, sell or hold' a share. They also review price changes on the stocks in their portfolios daily, as well as changes in the size of holdings, and in sector or geographical allocations arising through price movements or stock trades.

Investment fund managers have to write regular internal and external reports on the progress of their portfolios or on their areas of specialisation. Written reports often have to be prepared for weekly or monthly 'in house' investment meetings as well as half-yearly reports to clients – pension funds, Unit and Investment Trusts and individuals. Managers responsible for foreign markets may go on fact finding trips to the US, Asia and Europe and they are usually required to write reports on their company visits.

Meetings are the bane of the investment fund manager's life. There are weekly meetings to review portfolio changes and monthly meetings to review strategy, asset allocation and performance. There are marketing meetings to talk to clients and there are 'beauty parades' for new business. Investment fund managers live on broker's lunches and adrenalin! You can see specialist financial information and recommendations from organisations such as S&P Marketscope, CDA Spectrum etc using electronic information systems such as Reuters as seen on the sample screens below.

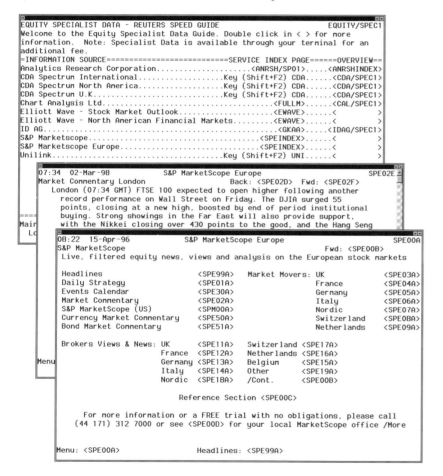

Regulation of the Markets

Many stock exchanges originally operated from public meeting places such as coffee houses as no formal exchange building existed. In such circumstances there were few rules and the activities of the market players often involved overspeculation, fraud and deception. Some of the worst financial scandals happened in these early markets – The South Sea Bubble scandal is probably one of the most famous.

South Seas Bubble Scandal of 1720

In 1711 the South Seas Company was founded to trade with Spanish America – mainly in slaves. The lists were opened and the issue was subscribed to quickly. By 1720 there was an incredible boom in the stocks as a result of the Company's proposal to take over the national debt, which Parliament had accepted. In one day alone £1.5 million was subscribed. The shares had risen from 128.5 in January 1720 to over 1000 by that August. At the time the value of the prices at which shares were changing hands was about £500 million – five times the value of all the cash in Europe. Inevitably the bubble burst and by December many investors who had borrowed heavily to buy stock were ruined.

Gradually exchanges became more formalised and were located in permanent, purpose built premises. The exchanges also introduced their own rules and regulations which were administered on a self-regulatory basis. More recently many world wide government agencies and international bodies have been created to oversee the activities and regulate the different financial markets.

The purpose of regulation is to ensure the financial security of participants and counterparties and ensure standardisation of procedures. In particular, market regulation aims to:

- Protect investors – especially individual investors

- Allow markets to function smoothly and efficiently

- Minimise the impact of adverse market movements on the economy at large

- Foster competitive practices

- Prevent unfair practices

Most regulatory bodies share these broad aims. Two areas which most often cause concern are those of disclosure of financial information and **insider trading**. Insider trading is where a market player has access to market sensitive information, for example, knowledge of plans for a corporate take-over bid, which is not publicly known and uses the information to profit in the markets.

Domestic Regulatory Bodies

In most countries the government has a range of bodies to regulate the markets. Central banks such as the Fed and the Bank of England have certain direct responsibilities for regulating the primary market whereas regulations governing secondary market activities are the responsibility of a variety of government agencies.

In the US, the **Securities and Exchange Commission (SEC)** is the principal regulatory authority. However SEC operates with the following organisations to ensure the markets are fair and run smoothly:

- The **Federal Reserve** which sets margin requirements on equity and equity options trading

- The **Commodity Futures Trading Commission (CFTC)** which regulates trading in futures and options

- **NASD**, a self-regulatory organisation that oversees Nasdaq

- The exchanges such as NYSE who are self-regulating

In the UK, the **Securities and Investment Board (SIB)** exercises regulation of the financial markets on behalf of HM Treasury. In 1997 SIB formerly changed its name to the **Financial Services Authority (FSA)** and over a staged period its powers will be extended. The FSA will acquire regulatory and registration functions currently operated by a number of bodies including the **Securities and Futures Authority (SFA)**. This is a **Self-Regulatory Organisation (SRO)** which is responsible for markets in securities, futures and options, commodities and currencies together with the activities of brokers and dealers.

FSA (SIB) also operates with **Recognised Investment Exchanges (RIEs)** such as the LSE. The current regulatory structure in the UK is illustrated in the chart below.

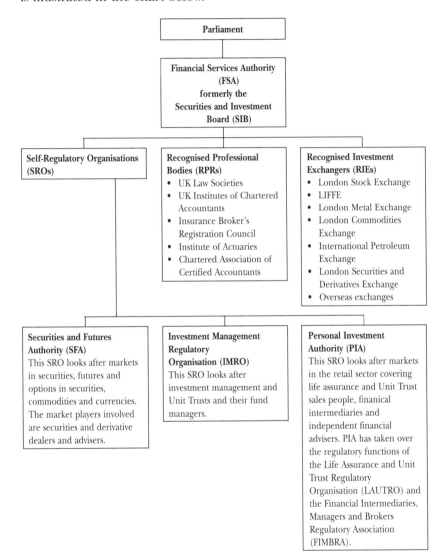

International Regulatory Bodies

Although most of the rules of these organisations cannot be legally enforced these self-regulatory bodies provide recommendations to ensure ethical and standardised trading practices in the international capital markets. The main organisations are briefly described here.

Bank for International Settlement (BIS)

This is an association of central banks which is concerned with safeguarding the stability of the international financial markets.

International Securities Markets Association (ISMA)

A self-regulating body whose members are the major banks engaged in the Eurobond markets. ISMA operates the **Transaction Exchange System (TRAX)** which is a real-time on-line facility for the comparison and confirmation of transactions between dealers.

International Swaps and Derivatives Association (ISDA)

A self-regulating body which is primarily concerned with the OTC Swaps and derivatives markets.

Summary

You have now finished the last section of the book and you should have a clear understanding of the trading in the equity markets including:

- Important intermediaries and the financial institutions in which they operate

- Important groups of investors

- Regulation of the markets

As a check on your understanding you should try the Quick Quiz Questions on the next page. You may also find the Overview Section to be a helpful learning tool.

Quick Quiz Questions

1. What is the name of the modern counter-part of a stock jobber?
   - ☐ a) Agency broker
   - ☐ b) Broker dealer
   - ☐ c) IDB
   - ☐ d) Market maker

2. Of which of the following self regulating organisations would a UK broker dealer typically be a member?
   - ☐ a) SFA
   - ☐ b) PIA
   - ☐ c) IMRO
   - ☐ d) NASD

3. Which of the following are privileges of a market maker trading on the LSE?
   - ☐ a) Access to the IDB network
   - ☐ b) Exemption of stamp duty on the purchase of securities
   - ☐ c) Allowed to borrow stock via approved money brokers
   - ☐ d) Allowed to deal anonymously with broker dealers

4. Which of the following is true concerning the value of a unit in a unit trust?
   - ☐ a) It is the same as the price paid for it
   - ☐ b) It is determined by an independent valuer
   - ☐ c) It is directly linked to the underlying value of assets
   - ☐ d) It is reset corresponding to LIBOR periods

5. In which of the following ways do broker dealers operate when acting as agents?
   - ☐ a) On their own account
   - ☐ b) On behalf of their clients
   - ☐ c) On an inter agency basis
   - ☐ d) As an intermediary for a trade between market makers

6. List at least four roles undertaken by a typical securities house.

You can check your answers on page 195.

Overview

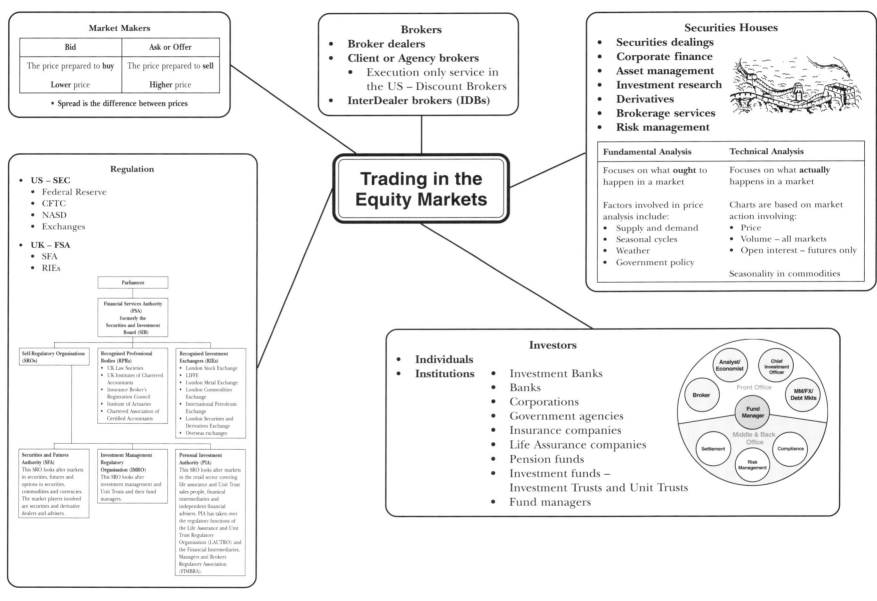

Market Makers

Bid	Ask or Offer
The price prepared to **buy**	The price prepared to **sell**
Lower price	**Higher** price

- Spread is the difference between prices

Brokers
- **Broker dealers**
- **Client or Agency brokers**
  - Execution only service in the US – Discount Brokers
- **InterDealer brokers (IDBs)**

Securities Houses
- **Securities dealings**
- **Corporate finance**
- **Asset management**
- **Investment research**
- **Derivatives**
- **Brokerage services**
- **Risk management**

Fundamental Analysis	Technical Analysis
Focuses on what **ought** to happen in a market	Focuses on what **actually** happens in a market
Factors involved in price analysis include: • Supply and demand • Seasonal cycles • Weather • Government policy	Charts are based on market action involving: • Price • Volume – all markets • Open interest – futures only Seasonality in commodities

Regulation
- **US – SEC**
  - Federal Reserve
  - CFTC
  - NASD
  - Exchanges
- **UK – FSA**
  - SFA
  - RIEs

Parliament

Financial Services Authority (FSA) formerly the Securities and Investment Board (SIB)

Self-Regulatory Organisations (SROs)

Recognised Professional Bodies (RPRs)
- UK Law Societies
- UK Institutes of Chartered Accountants
- Insurance Broker's Registration Council
- Institute of Actuaries
- Chartered Association of Certified Accountants

Recognised Investment Exchangers (RIEs)
- London Stock Exchange
- LIFFE
- London Metal Exchange
- London Commodities Exchange
- International Petroleum Exchange
- London Securities and Derivatives Exchange
- Overseas exchanges

Securities and Futures Authority (SFA)
This SRO looks after markets in securities, futures and options in securities, commodities and currencies. The market players involved are securities and derivative dealers and advisers.

Investment Management Regulatory Organisation (IMRO)
This SRO looks after investment management and Unit Trusts and their fund managers.

Personal Investment Authority (PIA)
This SRO looks after markets in the retail sector covering life assurance and Unit Trust sales people, finanical intermediaries and independent financial advisers. PIA has taken over the regulatory functions of the Life Assurance and Unit Trust Regulatory Organisation (LAUTRO) and the Financial Intermediaries, Managers and Brokers Regulatory Association (FIMBRA).

Investors
- **Individuals**
- **Institutions**
  - Investment Banks
  - Banks
  - Corporations
  - Government agencies
  - Insurance companies
  - Life Assurance companies
  - Pension funds
  - Investment funds – Investment Trusts and Unit Trusts
  - Fund managers

Trading in the Equity Markets

Quick Quiz Answers

		✓ or ✗
1	d)	☐
2.	a)	☐
3.	a), b) and c)	☐
4.	c)	☐
5.	b)	☐
6.	Securities dealings	☐
	Corporate finance	☐
	Asset management	☐
	Investment research	☐
	Derivatives trading	☐
	Brokerage services	☐
	Risk management	☐

How well did you score? You should have scored at least 5. If you didn't, you may need to review the materials again.

Further Resources

Books

The Alchemy of Finance
George Soros, J. Wiley & Sons, 1994
ISBN   0 4710 4206 4

A Short History of Financial Euphoria
John K. Galbraith, Penguin Books, 1990
ISBN   0 14 023856 5

Investments: Analysis and Management
Charles P. Jones, John Wiley & Sons, Inc., 6th Edition 1998
ISBN   0 471 16959 5

Risk and Regulation in Global Securities Markets
Richard Dale, John Wiley & Sons, Inc., 1996
ISBN   0 471 95781 X

The Stock Market
Richard J. Teweles and Edward S. Bradley, John Wiley & Sons, Inc., 7th Edition 1998
ISBN   0 471 19134 5

Publications

British Invisibles
• Fund Management – City Business Series – 1997
• Banking – City Business Series – 1997

National Association of Securities Dealers
• Securities Regulation in the US

Financial Services Authority
• Financial Services Authority: An Outline

Further Resources (continued)

Internet

RFT Web Site
- **http://www.wiley.rft.reuters.com**

This is the series' companion web site where additional quiz questions, updated screens and other information may be found.

Investment Company Institute
- **http://www.ici.org**

Exchanges

Refer to the back of this book for a listing of worldwide stock exchange contact information and web sites.

Your notes

REUTERS

Glossary of Equity Related Terms

compiled from Professor Campbell R. Harvey's Hypertextual
Finance Glossary

Entries in this glossary are compiled from Professor Campbell R.
Harvey's Hypertextual Finance Glossary. The full version can be
found on the internet at the URL address, http://www.duke.edu/
~charvey. The Publisher will not be responsible for any inaccuracies
found in the glossary below. Queries and reproduction requests
should be addressed to Professor Harvey at charvey@mail.duke.edu.

A

Adjusted Present Value (A.P.V.)
The net present value analysis of an asset if financed solely by equity
(present value of un- levered cash flows), plus the present value of
any financing decisions (levered cash flows). In other words, the
various tax shields provided by the deductibility of interest and the
benefits of other investment tax credits are calculated separately.
This analysis is often used for highly leveraged transactions such as a
leveraged buy-out.

All Or None Order (A.O.N.)
Used in context of general equities. A limited price order which is
to be executed in its entirety or not at all (no partial transaction),
and thus is testing the strength/conviction of the counterparty.
Unlike an F.O.K. order, an A.O.N. order is not to be treated as
cancelled if not executed as soon as it is represented in the trading
crowd, but instead remains alive until executed or cancelled. The
making of "all or none" bids or offers in stocks is prohibited and the
making of "all or none" bids or offers in bonds is subject to the
restrictions of Rule 61. A.O.N. orders are not shown on the
specialist's book because they can not be traded in pieces. Antithesis
of any-part-of order. See: F.O.K. order.

All-Or-None Underwriting
An arrangement whereby a security issue is canceled if the
underwriter is unable to re-sell the entire issue.

Alpha
Measure of risk adjusted performance. An alpha is usually generated
by regressing the security or mutual fund's excess return on the S&P
500 excess return. The beta adjusts for the risk (the slope
coefficient). The alpha is the intercept. Example: Suppose the
mutual fund has a return of 23% and the short-term interest rate is
5% (excess return is 20%). During the same time the market excess
return is 9%. Suppose the beta of the mutual fund is 2.0 (twice as
risky as the S&P 500). The expected return given the risk is
2 3 9% 5 18%. The actual excess return is 20%. Hence, the alpha is
2% or 200 basis points. Alpha is also known as Jensen Index.
Related: Risk adjusted return.

Alternative Order
Used in context of general equities. Order giving a broker a choice
between two courses of action either to buy or sell, never both.
Execution of one course automatically eliminates the other. An
example is a combination buy limit/buy stop order, wherein the buy
limit is below the current market and the buy stop is above. If the
order is for one unit of trading when one part of the order is
executed on the occurrence of one alternative, the order on the
other alternative is to be treated as cancelled. If the order is for an
amount larger than one unit of trading, the number of units
executed determine the amount of the alternative order to be
treated as cancelled. Either-or order.

American Depository Receipts (A.D.R.s)
Certificates issued by a U.S. depositary bank, representing foreign
shares held by the bank, usually by a branch or correspondent in
the country of issue. One A.D.R. may represent a portion of a
foreign share, one share or a bundle of shares of a foreign
corporation. If the A.D.R.'s are "sponsored," the corporation
provides financial information and other assistance to the bank and
may subsidize the administration of the A.D.R.s. "Unsponsored"
A.D.R.s do not receive such assistance. A.D.R.s carry the same
currency, political and economic risks as the underlying foreign
share. Arbitrage keeps the prices of A.D.R.s and underlying foreign
shares, adjusted for the SDR/ordinary ration essentially equal.
American depository shares(A.D.S.s) are a similar form of
certification.

Glossary of Equity Related Terms

A.D.R. Fees
Fees associated with the creating or releasing of A.D.R.s from ordinary shares, charged by the commercial banks with correspondent banks in the international sites.

A.D.R. Ratio
The number of ordinary shares into which an A.D.R. can be converted.

American Depository Share (A.D.S.)
Foreign stock issued in the U.S. and registered in the A.D.R. system.

American Option
An option that may be exercised at any time up to and including the expiration date. Related: European option

American Shares
Securities certificates issued in the U.S. by a transfer agent acting on behalf of the foreign issuer. The certificates represent claims to foreign equities.

American Stock Exchange (A.M.E.X.)
Stock exchange with the third largest volume of trading in the U.S. Located at 86 Trinity Place in downtown Manhattan. The bulk of trading on A.M.E.X. consists of index options (computer technology index, institutional index, major market index) and shares of small to medium-size companies is predominant. Recently merged with N.A.S.D.A.Q.

American-Style Option
An option contract that can be exercised at any time between the date of purchase and the expiration date. Most exchange-traded options are American style.

Amsterdam Exchanges (A.E.X.)
Exchange that comprises the A.E.X.-Effectenbeurs, the A.E.X.-Optiebeurs (formerly the European Options Exchange or E.O.E.) and the A.E.X.-Agrarische Termijnmarkt. A.E.X.-Data Services is the operating company responsible for the dissemination of data from the Amsterdam Exchanges via its integrated Mercury 2000 system.

Analyst
Employee of a brokerage or fund management house who studies companies and makes buy-and-sell recommendations on stocks of these companies. Most specialize in a specific industry.

Annual Fund Operating Expenses
For investment companies, the management fee and "other expenses," including the expenses for maintaining shareholder records, providing shareholders with financial statements, and providing custodial and accounting services. For 12b-1 funds, selling and marketing costs are also included.

Annual Percentage Rate (A.P.R.)
The periodic rate times the number of periods in a year. For example, a 5% quarterly return has an A.P.R. of 20%.

Annual Percentage Yield (A.P.Y.)
The effective, or true, annual rate of return. The A.P.Y. is the rate actually earned or paid in one year, taking into account the affect of compounding. The A.P.Y. is calculated by taking one plus the periodic rate and raising it to the number of periods in a year. For example, a 1% per month rate has an A.P.Y. of 12.68% (1.01^{12} -1).

Annual Rate Of Return
There are many ways of calculating the annual rate of return. If the rate of return is calculated on a monthly basis, we sometimes multiply this by 12 to express an annual rate of return. This is often called the annual percentage rate (A.P.R.). The annual percentage yield annual percentage yield (A.P.Y.), described above, is used to include the affect of compounding interest.

Annual Report
Yearly record of a publicly held company's financial condition. It includes a description of the firm's operations, as well as balance sheet, income statement and cash flow statement information. S.E.C. rules require that it be distributed to all shareholders. A more detailed version is called a 10-K.

REUTERS

Annualized Gain

If stock X appreciates 1.5% in one month, the annualized gain for that stock over a twelve month period is 12*1.5% 5 18%. Compounded over the twelve month period, the gain is $(1.015)^{12} - 1 = 19.6\%$.

Annualized Holding Period Return

The annual rate of return that when compounded t times, generates the same t-period holding return as actually occurred from period 1 to period t.

Any-Or-All Bid

Often used in risk arbitrage. Takeover bid where the acquirer offers to pay a set price for all outstanding shares of the target company, or any part thereof; contrasts with two tier bid.

Any-Part-Of Order

Used in context of general equities. Order to buy or sell a quantity of stock in pieces if necessary. Antithesis of an all-or-none order (A.O.N.).

Arbitrage

The simultaneous buying and selling of a security at two different prices in two different markets, resulting in profits without risk. Perfectly efficient markets present no arbitrage opportunities. Perfectly efficient markets seldom exist. However, arbitrage opportunities are often precluded because of transactions costs.

Arbitrage Pricing Theory (A.P.T.)

An alternative model to the capital asset pricing model developed by Stephen Ross and based purely on arbitrage arguments. The A.P.T. implies that there are multiple risk factors that need to be taken into account when calculating risk adjusted performance or alpha.

Arbitrageur

Often used in risk arbitrage. One who profits from the differences in price when the same, or extremely similar, security, currency, or commodity is traded on two or more markets. He does so by simultaneously purchasing and selling these securities to take advantage of pricing differentials (spreads) created by market conditions. See: risk arbitrage, convertible arbitrage, index arbitrage, and international arbitrage.

Asian Option

Option based on the average price of the underlying assets during the life of the option.

Ask

This is the quoted ask, or the lowest price an investor will accept to sell a stock. Practically speaking, this is the quoted offer at which an investor can buy shares of stock; also called the offer price.

Asset Allocation Decision

The decision regarding how an institution's funds should be distributed among the major classes of assets in which it may invest.

Asset Classes

Categories of assets, such as stocks, bonds, real estate and foreign securities.

Asset/Equity Ratio

The ratio of total assets to stockholder equity.

Asset Pricing Model

A model for determining the required or expected rate of return on an asset. Related: Capital asset pricing model and arbitrage pricing theory.

At-The-Money

An option is at-the-money if the strike price of the option is equal to the market price of the underlying security. For example, if xyz stock is trading at 54, then the xyz 54 option is at-the-money.

Auction Markets

Markets in which the prevailing price is determined through the free interaction of prospective buyers and sellers, as on the floor of the stock exchange.

Auction Rate Preferred Stock (A.R.P.S.)

Floating rate preferred stock, the dividend on which is adjusted every seven weeks through a Dutch auction.

Australian Stock Exchange (A.S.X.)
Established in 1987 following the amalgamation of the six independent stock exchanges operating in the Australian State capitals. The A.S.X. is the tenth largest stock exchange in the world on the basis of domestic capitalization.

Autex
Used in context of general equities. Video communication network through which brokerage houses alert institutional investors of their desire to transact block business (a purchase or sale) in a given security. Indications transmit small, medium, and large sizes only, with occasional limits mentioned. Supers are messages with specific size and price included. Both "indications" and "supers" can only be seen by customers (institutional subscribers to Autex). Trade recaps, advertised block trades entered by the dealer/subscribers, are also displayed, but can be seen by both institutions and dealers. See: expunge, size.

Authorized Shares
Number of shares authorized for issuance by a firm's corporate charter.

Automated Clearing House (A.C.H.)
A collection of 32 regional electronic interbank networks used to process transactions electronically with a guaranteed one-day bank collection float.

Automated Order System (A.O.S.)
Investment banks computerized order-entry system which sends single order entries to D.O.T. (Odd-Lot) or to investment banks floor brokers on the exchange. (Round lot, G.T.C. orders)

Automated Pit Trading (A.P.T.)
Introduced in 1989, A.P.T. is the L.I.F.F.E. screen-based trading system that replicates the open outcry method of trading on screen. A.P.T. is used to extend the trading day for the major futures contracts as well as to provide a daytime trading environment for non-floor trading products.

Average
An arithmetic mean return of selected stocks intended to represent the behavior of the market or some component of it. One good example is the widely quoted Dow Jones Industrial Average, which adds the current prices of the 30 DJIA's stocks, and divides the results by a predetermined number, the divisor.

Average Rate Of Return (A.R.R.)
The ratio of the average cash inflow to the amount invested.

B

Balance Sheet
Also called the statement of financial condition, it is a summary of a company's assets, liabilities, and owners' equity.

Bank for International Settlements (B.I.S.)
An international bank headquartered in Basel, Switzerland, which serves as a forum for monetary cooperation among several European central banks, the Bank of Japan, and the U.S. Federal Reserve System. Founded in 1930 to handle the German payment of World War I reparations, it now monitors and collects data on international banking activity and promulgates rules concerning international bank regulation.

Basis
Regarding a futures contract, the difference between the cash price and the futures price observed in the market. Also, it is the price an investor pays for a security plus any out-of-pocket expenses. It is used to determine capital gains or losses for tax purposes when the stock is sold.

Basis Price
Price expressed in terms of yield to maturity or annual rate of return.

Bear
An investor who believes a stock or the overall market will decline. A bear market is a prolonged period of falling stock prices, usually by 20% or more. Related: bull.

Bearer Share
Mainly applies to international equities. Security not registered on the books of the issuing corporation and thus payable to whoever possesses the shares. Negotiable without endorsement and transferred by delivery, thus avoiding some of the administrative hassles associated with ordinary shares. Dividends are payable upon presentation of dividend coupons, which are dated or numbered.

Bear Market
Any market in which prices are in a declining trend. For a prolonged period, usually falling by 20% or more.

Benchmark
The performance of a predetermined set of securities, used for comparison purposes. Such sets may be based on published indexes or may be customized to suit an investment strategy.

Best-Efforts Sale
A method of securities distribution/underwriting in which the securities firm agrees to sell as much of the offering as possible and return any unsold shares to the issuer. As opposed to a guaranteed or fixed price sale, where the underwriter agrees to sell a specific number of shares (with the securities firm holding any unsold shares in its own account if necessary).

Beta
The measure of a fund's or stocks risk in relation to the market, or an alternative benchmark. A beta of 1.5 means that a stock's excess return is expected to move 1.5 times the market excess returns. E.g. if market excess return is 10% then we expect, on average, the stock return to be 15%. Beta is referred to as an index of the systematic risk due to general market conditions that cannot be diversified away.

Beta Equation
The beta of a fund is determined as follows: Regress excess returns of stock y on excess returns of the market. The slope coefficient is beta. Define n as number of observation numbers. Beta = [(n)(sum of (xy))] − [(sum of x)(sum of y)]/[(n)(sum of (xx))] − [(sum of x)(sum of x)] where:
n = # of observations (36 months)
x = rate of return for the S&P 500 Index
y = rate of return for the fund
Related: Alpha.

Bid Price
This is the quoted bid, or the highest price an investor is willing to pay to buy a security. Practically speaking, this is the available price at which an investor can sell shares of stock. Related: Ask , offer.

Bid-Asked Spread
The difference between the bid and asked prices.

Big Bang
The term applied to the liberalization in 1986 of the London Stock Exchange (L.S.E.) in which trading was automated with the use of computers.

Big Board
A nickname for the New York Stock Exchange (N.Y.S.E.). Also known as The Exchange. More than 2,000 common and preferred stocks are traded. Founded in 1792, the N.Y.S.E. is the oldest exchange in the United States, and the largest. It is located on Wall Street in New York City.

Block Trade
A large trading order, defined on the New York Stock Exchange as an order that consists of 10,000 shares of a given stock or a total market-value of $200,000 or more.

Block Trader
A dealer who will take a position in the block transactions to accommodate customer buyers and sellers of blocks. See dealer, market maker, principal.

Blue-Chip Company
Used in the context of general equities. Large and creditworthy company. Company renowned for the quality and wide acceptance of its products or services, and for its ability to make money and pay dividends. Gilt-edged security.

Blue-Sky Laws
State laws covering the issue and trading of securities.

Boilerplate
Standard terms and conditions.

Book Value
A company's book value is its total assets minus intangible assets and liabilities, such as debt. A company's book value might be more or less than its market value.

Book Value Per Share (B.V.P.S.)
The ratio of stockholder equity to the average number of common shares. Book value per share should not be thought of as an indicator of economic worth, since it reflects accounting valuation (and not necessarily market valuation).

Bottom-Up Equity Management Style
A management style that de-emphasizes the significance of economic and market cycles, focusing instead on the analysis of individual stocks.

Bought Deal
Security issue where one or two underwriters buy the entire issue.

Breadth Of The Market
Used in the context of general equities. Percentage of stocks participating in a particular market move. Technical analysts say there was significant 'breadth' if 2/3 of the stocks listed on an exchange moved in the same direction during a trading session.

Break Price
Used in the context of general equities. Change one's offering or bid prices to move to a more realistic, tight level where execution is more feasible. Often done to trim one's position, thus "breaking price" from where the trades occurred (if long, "break price" downward 1/8 a point or more).

Broker
An individual who is paid a commission for executing customer orders. Either a floor broker who executes orders on the floor of the exchange, or an upstairs broker who handles retail customers and their orders. Person who acts as an intermediary between a buyer and seller, usually charging a commission. A "broker" who specializes in stocks, bonds, commodities, or options acts as agent and must be registered with the exchange where the securities are traded. Antithesis of dealer.

Brokered Market
A market where an intermediary offers search services to buyers and sellers.

Bubble Theory
Security prices sometimes move wildly above their true values until the "bubble bursts".

Bull
An investor who thinks the market will rise. Related: bear.

Bull Market
Any market in which prices are in an upward trend.

Bullish, Bearish
Words used to describe investor attitudes. Bullish refers to an optimistic outlook while bearish means a pessimistic outlook.

Buy
To purchase an asset; taking a long position.

Buy-And-Hold Strategy
A passive investment strategy with no active buying and selling of stocks from the time the portfolio is created until the end of the investment horizon.

Buying The Index
Purchasing the stocks in the S&P 500 in the same proportion as the index to achieve the same return.

Buy On Close
To buy at the end of the trading session at a price within the closing range.

Buy On Margin
A transaction in which an investor borrows to buy additional shares, using the shares themselves as collateral.

Buy-Side Analyst
A financial analyst employed by a non-brokerage firm, typically one of the larger money management firms that purchase securities on their own accounts.

C

Call
An option that gives the right to buy the underlying futures contract.

Callable
Mainly applies to convertible securities. Redeemable by the issuer before the scheduled maturity under specific conditions and at a stated price, which usually begins at a premium to par and declines annually. Bonds are usually "called" when interest rates fall so significantly that the issuer can save money by floating new bonds at lower rates.

Call An Option
To exercise a call option.

Call Date
A date before maturity, specified at issuance, when the issuer of a bond may retire part of the bond for a specified call price.

Call Option
An option contract that gives its holder the right (but not the obligation) to purchase a specified number of shares of the underlying stock at the given strike price, on or before the expiration date of the contract.

Call Premium
Premium in price above the par value of a bond or share of preferred stock that must be paid to holders to redeem the bond or share of preferred stock before its scheduled maturity date.

Call Price
The price, specified at issuance, at which the issuer of a bond may retire part of the bond at a specified call date.

Call Protection
A feature of some callable bonds that establishes an initial period when the bonds may not be called.

Call Provision
An embedded option granting a bond issuer the right to buy back all or part of the issue prior to maturity.

Call Risk
The combination of cash flow uncertainty and reinvestment risk introduced by a call provision.

Canadian Dealing Network (C.D.N.)
The organized O.T.C. market of Canada. Formerly known as the Canadian Over-the counter Automated Trading System (COATS), the C.D.N. became a subsidiary of the Toronto Stock Exchange in 1991.

Canadian Exchange Group (C.E.G.)
The C.E.G. is an association between the Toronto Stock Exchange, the Montreal Exchange, the Vancouver Stock Exchange, the Alberta Stock Exchange and the Winnipeg Stock Exchange for the purpose of providing Canadian market data to customers outside Canada.

Glossary of Equity Related Terms

"Can Get $xxx"
Refers to over-the-counter trading. "I have a buyer who will pay $xxx for the stock"; usually a standard markdown (1/8) from $xxx is applied to this price in bidding the seller for his stock. Antithesis of "cost me".

"Cannot Compete"
Used in the context of general equities. Cannot accommodate customers (i.e., compete with other market-makers) at that price level, often due to not having a natural opposite side of the trade.

Capital
Money invested in a firm.

Capital Allocation Decision
Allocation of invested funds between risk-free assets and the risky portfolio.

Capital Asset Pricing Model (C.A.P.M.)
An economic theory that describes the relationship between risk and expected return, and serves as a model for the pricing of risky securities. The C.A.P.M. asserts that the only risk that is priced by rational investors is systematic risk, because that risk cannot be eliminated by diversification. The C.A.P.M. says that the expected return of a security or a portfolio is equal to the rate on a risk-free security plus a risk premium.

Capital Market
The market for trading long-term debt instruments (those that mature in more than one year).

Capital Stock
Stock authorized by a firm's charter and having par value, stated value, or no par value. The number and value of issued shares are usually shown, together with the number of shares authorized, in the capital accounts section of the balance sheet. See: Common stock.

Capital Structure
The makeup of the liabilities and stockholders' equity side of the balance sheet, especially the ratio of debt to equity and the mixture of short and long maturities.

Capital Surplus
Amounts of directly contributed equity capital in excess of the par value.

Capitalization
The debt and/or equity mix that funds a firm's assets.

Capitalization Ratios
Also called financial leverage ratios, these ratios compare debt to total capitalization and thus reflect the extent to which a corporation is trading on its equity. Capitalization ratios can be interpreted only in the context of the stability of industry and company earnings and cash flow.

Carrying Costs
Costs that increase with increases in the level of investment in current assets.

Carrying Value
Book value.

Cash
The value of assets that can be converted into cash immediately, as reported by a company. Usually includes bank accounts and marketable securities, such as government bonds and Banker's Acceptances. Cash equivalents on balance sheets include securities (e.g., notes) that mature within 90 days.

Cash Equivalent
A short-term security that is sufficiently liquid that it may be considered the financial equivalent of cash.

Cash Flow Per Common Share
Cash flow from operations minus preferred stock dividends, divided by the number of common shares outstanding.

Cash Markets
Also called spot markets, these are markets that involve the immediate delivery of a security or instrument. Related: Derivative markets.

Cash Offer
Often used in risk arbitrage. Proposal, either hostile or friendly, to acquire a target company through the payment of cash for the stock of the target. Compare to exchange offer.

Cash Price
Applies to derivative products. See: Spot price.

Cash Sale/Settlement
Used in the context of general equities. Transaction in which the contract is settled on the same day as the trade date, or next day if the trade is after 2:30 p.m. E.S.T. And the parties agree to this procedure. Often settled in this way because a party is strapped for cash and cannot wait until the regular, five business day, settlement. See: Settlement date.

Cash Settlement Contracts
Futures contracts, such as stock index futures, that settle for cash, not involving the delivery of the underlying.

Cash Transaction
A transaction where exchange is immediate, as contrasted to a forward contract, which calls for future delivery of an asset at an agreed-upon price.

Chartists
Related: technical analysts.

Chicago Board Options Exchange (C.B.O.E.)
A securities exchange created in the early 1970s for the public trading of standardized option contracts. Locale where the trading of stock options, foreign currency options, and index options (S&P 100, 500, and O.T.C. 250 index) is predominant.

Chicago Mercantile Exchange (C.M.E.)
A not-for-profit corporation owned by its members. Its primary functions are to provide a location for trading futures and options, collect and disseminate market information, maintain a clearing mechanism and enforce trading rules. Applies to derivative products. A locale where the trading of futures (O.T.C. 250 industrial stock price index, S& P 100 and 500 index) and futures options (S&P 500 stock index) is predominant.

Chinese Wall
Communication barrier between financiers (investment bankers) and traders. This barrier is erected to prevent the sharing of inside information that bankers are likely to have.

Class
Applies to derivative products. Options of the same type — put or call — with the same underlying security.

Clear
A trade is settled out by the seller delivering securities and the buyer delivering funds in proper form. A trade that does not clear is said to fail. Comparison of the details of a transaction between broker/dealers prior to settlement; final exchange of securities for cash on delivery.

Clear A Position
To eliminate a long or short position, leaving no ownership or obligation.

Clearinghouse
An adjunct to a futures exchange through which transactions executed on its floor are settled by a process of matching purchases and sales. A clearing organization is also charged with the proper conduct of delivery procedures and the adequate financing of the entire operation.

Close A Position
Used in the context of general equities. Eliminate an investment from one's portfolio, by either selling a long position or covering a short position.

Close, The
The period at the end of the trading session. Sometimes used to refer to closing price. Related: Opening, the.

Closed-End Fund
An investment company that sells shares like any other corporation and usually does not redeem its shares. A publicly traded fund sold on stock exchanges or over the counter that may trade above or below its net asset value. Related: Open-end fund.

Closely Held Company
A company who has a small group of controling shareholders. In contrast, a widely-held firm has many shareholders. It is difficult or impossible to wage a proxy battle for any closely-held firm.

Closing Transaction
Applies to derivative products. Buy or sell transaction that eliminates an existing position (selling a long option or buying back a short option). Antithesis of opening transaction.

Cluster Analysis
A statistical technique that identifies clusters of stocks whose returns are highly correlated within each cluster and relatively uncorrelated between clusters. Cluster analysis has identified groupings such as growth, cyclical, stable and energy stocks.

Come Out Of The Trade
Used in the context of general equities. Trader's resulting position in a security from executing a trade (or the expectations thereof). Antithesis of going into the trade.

Commission
The fee paid to a broker to execute a trade, based on number of shares, bonds, options, and/or their dollar value. In 1975, deregulation led to the creation of discount brokers, who charge lower commissions than full service brokers. Full service brokers offer advice and usually have a full staff of analysts who follow specific industries. Discount brokers simply execute a client's order — and usually do not offer an opinion on a stock. Also known as a round-turn.

Commission Broker
A broker on the floor of an exchange who acts as agent for a particular brokerage house and buys and sells stocks for the brokerage house on a commission basis.

Commission House
A firm which buys and sells futures contracts for customer accounts. Related: futures commission merchant, omnibus account.

Commitment
A trader is said to have a commitment when he assumes the obligation to accept or make delivery on a futures contract. Related: Open interest.

Commitment Fee
A fee paid to a commercial bank in return for its legal commitment to lend funds that have not yet been advanced. Often used in risk arbitrage. Payment to institutional investors in the U.K. (pension funds and life insurance companies) by the lead underwriter of a takeover that takes place when the underwriter provides the target company's shareholders with a cash alternative for a target company's shares in exchange for the bidding companies' shares. The payment is typically 0.5% for the first 30 days, 1.25% for each week thereafter and a final 0.75% acceptance payment when the takeover is completed.

Committee on Uniform Securities Identification Procedures (C.U.S.I.P.)
Committee that assigns identifying numbers and codes for all securities. These "C.U.S.I.P." numbers and symbols are used when recording all buy or sell orders.

Commodities Exchange Center (C.E.C.)
The location of five New York futures exchanges: Commodity Exchange, Inc. (COMEX), the New York Mercantile Exchange (NYMEX), the New York Cotton Exchange, the Coffee, Sugar and Cocoa Exchange (CSC), and the New York futures Exchange (NYFE).

Commodity
A commodity is food, metal, or another physical substance that investors buy or sell, usually via futures contracts.

Commodity Futures Trading Commission (C.F.T.C.)
Applies to derivative products. Commodity futures trading commission is an agency created by Congress in 1974 to regulate exchange trading in futures.

Common Shares
In general, there are two types of shares, common and preferred stock. The common shares usually entitle the shareholders to vote at shareholders meetings. The common shares have a discretionary dividend.

Common Stock
These are securities that represent equity ownership in a company. Common shares let an investor vote on such matters as the election of directors. They also give the holder a share in a company's profits via dividend payments or the capital appreciation of the security. Used in the context of general equities.) units of ownership of a public corporation with junior status to the claims of secured/ unsecured creditors, bond and preferred shareholders in the event of liquidation.

Common Stock/Other Equity
Value of outstanding common shares at par, plus accumulated retained earnings. Also called shareholders' equity.

Common Stock Equivalent
A convertible security that is traded like an equity issue because the optioned common stock is trading high.

Common Stock Market
The market for trading equities, not including preferred stock.

Common Stock Ratios
Ratios that are designed to measure the relative claims of stockholders to earnings (cash flow per share), and equity (book value per share) of a firm.

Competitive Bidding
A securities offering process in which securities firms submit competing bids to the issuer for the securities the issuer wishes to sell.

Conditional Call
Mainly applies to convertible securities. Circumstances under which a company can effect an earlier call, usually stated as percentage of a stock's trading price during a particular period, such as 140% of the exercise price during a 40-day trading span.

Confirmation
The written statement that follows any "trade" in the securities markets. Confirmation is issued immediately after a trade is executed. It spells out settlement date, terms, commission, etc.

Consolidated Tape
Used for listed equity securities. Combined ticker tapes of the N.Y.S.E. and the curb. Network A covers the N.Y.S.E.-listed securities and is used to identify the originating market. Network B does the same for AMEX-listed securities and also reports on securities listed on regional stock exchanges. See tape.

Conversion Value
Also called parity value, the value of a convertible security if it is converted immediately.

Convertible Exchangeable Preferred Stock
Convertible preferred stock that may be exchanged, at the issuer's option, into convertible bonds that have the same conversion features as the convertible preferred stock.

"Cost Me"
Refers to over-the-counter trading. "The price I must pay to obtain the securities you wish to buy is [$]" usually, a standard markup (1/8) is then applied for resale to this buyer. Antithesis of "can get".

Counterparties
The parties to an interest rate swap.

Country Economic Risk
Developments in a national economy that can affect the outcome of an international financial transaction.

Country Risk
General level of political, financial and economic uncertainty in a country affecting the value of loans or investments in that country.

Covered Call
A short call option position in which the writer owns the number of shares of the underlying stock represented by the option contracts. Covered calls generally limit the risk the writer takes because the stock does not have to be bought at the market price, if the holder of that option decides to exercise it.

Covered Put

A put option position in which the option writer also is short the corresponding stock or has deposited, in a cash account, cash or cash equivalents equal to the exercise of the option. This limits the option writer's risk because money or stock is already set aside. In the event that the holder of the put option decides to exercise the option, the writer's risk is more limited than it would be on an uncovered or naked put option.

Cross

Used for listed equity securities. Securities transaction in which the same broker acts as agent for both sides of the trade; a legal practice only if the broker first offers the securities publicly at a price higher than the bid.

CREST

CREST is CrestCo's real-time settlement system for UK and Irish shares and other corporate securities. From 1999, CrestCo will also take ownership of government bond and money markets settlement in the UK.

"Customer Picking Prices"

Used in the context of general equities.
General: Customer is firm on price and has set the price(s) at which he wishes to transact the security. Thus, the trader is not attempting to "properly" price the trade or get one side a better price.
Missing a print: "Customer has asked us to" print to satisfy "because he has missed a print."
O.T.C.: "Stock is trading away due to a customer asking for better prices."
Swap: "Customer has selected the prices to be used in executing a swap."

D

Daily Price Limit

The maximum that many commodities, futures and options markets are allowed to rise or fall in a day. Exchanges usually impose a daily price limit on each contract.

Date Of Payment

Date dividend checks are mailed.

Date Of Record

Date on which holders of record in a firm's stock ledger are designated as the recipients of either dividends or stock rights.

Day Order

Used in the context of general equities. Request from a customer to either buy or sell stock, which, if not cancelled or executed the day it is placed, automatically expires. All orders are day orders unless otherwise specified. Traders often make calls before the opening to check for renewals.

Day Trading

Refers to establishing and liquidating the same position or positions within one day's trading.

Dealer

An entity that stands ready and willing to buy a security for its own account (at its bid price) or sell from its own account (at its ask price). Used in the context of general equities. Individual or firm acting as a principal in a securities transaction. Principals are market makers in securities, and thus trade for their own account and risk. Antithesis of broker.

Debt/Equity Ratio

Indicator of financial leverage. Compares assets provided by creditors to assets provided by shareholders. Determined by dividing long-term debt by common stockholder equity.

Debt Instrument

An asset requiring fixed dollar payments, such as a government or corporate bond.

Debt Swap

A set of transactions (also called a debt-equity swap) in which a firm buys a country's dollar bank debt at a discount and swaps this debt with the central bank for local currency that it can use to acquire local equity.

Dedicated Capital
Total par value (number of shares issued, multiplied by the par value of each share). Also called dedicated value.

Deferred Equity
A common term for convertible bonds because of their equity component and the expectation that the bond will ultimately be converted into shares of common stock.

Delayed Opening
Used for listed equity securities. Postponement of the start of trading in a stock until a gross imbalance in buy and sell orders is corrected. Such an imbalance is likely to follow on the heels of a significant event such as a takeover offer. See: suspended trading.

Delayed Settlement/Delivery
Used in the context of general equities. Transaction in which the contract is settled in excess of five full business days. Seller's option. See: dividend play, settlement.

Delivery
The tender and receipt of an actual commodity or financial instrument in settlement of a futures contract.

Delta
Also called the hedge ratio, the ratio of the change in price of a call option to the change in price of the underlying stock. Applies to derivative products. Measure of the relationship between an option price and the underlying futures contract or stock price. For a call option, a delta of 0.50 means a half-point rise in premium for every dollar that the stock goes up. As options near expiration, in-the-money call option contracts approach a delta of 1.0, while in the money put options approach a delta of -1.

Derivative Instruments
Contracts such as options and futures whose price is derived from the price of the underlying financial asset.

Dilution Protection
Mainly applies to convertible securities. Standard provision whereby the conversion ratio is changed accordingly in the case of a stock dividend or extraordinary distribution to avoid dilution of a convertible bondholder's potential equity position. Adjustment usually requires a split or stock dividend in excess of 5% or issuance of stock below book value.

Direct Placement
Selling a new issue not by offering it for sale publicly, but by placing it with one of several institutional investors.

Discount
Used in the context of general equities.
Convertible: difference between gross parity and a given convertible price. Most often invoked when a redemption is expected before the next coupon payment, making it liable for accrued interest for which he may never be compensated. Antithesis of premium.
General: information that has already been taken into account and is built into a stock or market.

Dividend Payout Ratio
Percentage of earnings paid out as dividends. Straight equity: price lower than that of the last sale or inside market.

Dividend Rate
The fixed or floating rate paid on preferred stock based on par value.

Dividend Reinvestment Plan (D.R.P.)
Automatic reinvestment of shareholder dividends in more shares of a company's stock, often without commissions. Some plans provide for the purchase of additional shares at a discount to market price. Dividend reinvestment plans allow shareholders to accumulate stock over the long term using dollar cost averaging. The D.R.P. is usually administered by the company without charges to the holder.

Dividend Rights
A shareholders' rights to receive per-share dividends identical to those other shareholders receive.

Dividends Per Share
Dividend paid for the past 12 months divided by the number of common shares outstanding, as reported by a company. The number of shares often is determined by a weighted average of shares outstanding over the reporting term.

Dividend Yield (Funds)
Indicated yield represents return on a share of a mutual fund held over the past 12 months. Assumes fund was purchased 1 year ago. Reflects effect of sales charges (at current rates), but not redemption charges.

Dividend Yield (Stocks)
Indicated yield represents annual dividends divided by current stock price.

Dow Jones Industrial Average
This is the best known U.S. index of stocks. It contains 30 stocks that trade on the New York Stock Exchange. The Dow, as it is called, is a barometer of how shares of the largest U.S. companies are performing. There are hundreds of investment indexes around the world for stocks, bonds, currencies and commodities. The Dow is a price-weighted average of 30 actively traded blue chip stocks, primarily industrials.

Dow Theory
Used in the context of general equities. Technical theory that a major trend in the stock market must be confirmed by simultaneous movement of the Dow Jones Industrial Average and the Dow Jones Transportation Average to new highs or lows.

Dual Listing
Used for listed equity securities. Listing of a security on more than one exchange, thus increasing the competition for bid and offer prices, the liquidity of the securities, and the number of hours when the stock can be traded (if listed both on the east and west coasts.) See: listed security.

Duration
A common gauge of the price sensitivity of a fixed income asset or portfolio to a change in interest rates.

E

Earnings Per Share (E.P.S.)
E.P.S., as it is called, is a company's profit divided by its number of outstanding shares. If a company earned $2 million in one year had 2 million shares of stock outstanding, its EPS would be $1 per share. In calculating E.P.S., the company often uses a weighted average of shares outstanding over the reporting term.

EDGAR
The Securities & Exchange Commission uses Electronic Data Gathering and Retrieval to transmit company documents such as 10-Ks, 10-Qs, quarterly reports, and other S.E.C. filings, to investors.

Effective Annual Yield
Annualized interest rate on a security computed using compound interest techniques.

Effective Call Price
The strike price in an market redemption provision plus the accrued interest to the redemption date.such as 10-Ks, 10-Qs, quarterly reports, and other S.E.C. filings, to investors.

Efficient Frontier
The combinations of securities portfolios that maximize expected return for any level of expected risk, or that minimizes expected risk for any level of expected return. Pioneered by Harry Markowitz.

Efficient Market Hypothesis
In general the hypothesis states that all relevant information is fully and immediately reflected in a security's market price thereby assuming that an investor will obtain an equilibrium rate of return. In other words, an investor should not expect to earn an abnormal return (above the market return) through either technical analysis or fundamental analysis. Three forms of efficient market hypothesis exist: weak form (stock prices reflect all information of past prices), semi-strong form (stock prices reflect all publicly available information) and strong form (stock prices reflect all relevant information including insider information).

Efficient Portfolio
A portfolio that provides the greatest expected return for a given level of risk (i.e. standard deviation), or equivalently, the lowest risk for a given expected return.

Either-Or Order
Used in the context of general equities. See: Alternative order.

Emerging Markets
The financial markets of developing economies.

Equal Dollar Swap
Used in the context of general equities. Selling common stock/convertibles in one company and reinvesting the proceeds in as many shares of 1) another type of security issued by the company, or 2) another security of the same type but of another company — as can be bought with the proceeds of the sale. See: equal shares swap.

Equal Shares Swap
Mainly applies to convertible securities. Selling the underlying common and reinvesting the proceeds in as much convertible as could be converted into the number of shares of common just sold. See equal dollar swap.

Equity
Represents ownership interest in a firm. Also the residual dollar value of a futures trading account, assuming its liquidation occurs at the going trade price.

Equity Cap
An agreement in which one party, for an upfront premium, agrees to compensate the other at specific time periods if a designated stock market benchmark is greater than a predetermined level.

Equity Options
Securities that give the holder the right (but not the obligation) to buy or sell a specified number of shares of stock, at a specified price for a certain (limited) time period. Typically one option equals 100 shares of stock.

Equity Swap
A swap in which the cash flows exchanged are based on the total return on some stock market index and an interest rate (either a fixed rate or floating rate). Related: interest rate swap.

Eurobond
A bond that is (1) underwritten by an international syndicate, (2) issued simultaneously to investors in a number of countries, and (3) issued outside the jurisdiction of any single country.

Eurocurrency
Euro just means outside your country. So a Eurodollar is a certificate of deposit in U.S. dollars in some other country (though mainly traded in London). A Euroyen is a CD in yen outside of Japan.

Euroequity issues
Securities sold in the Euromarket. That is, securities initially sold to investors simultaneously in several national markets by an international syndicate. Euromarket. Related: external market

European Association of Securities Dealers Automated Quotation (E.A.S.D.A.Q.)
European Association of Securities Dealers Automated Quotation system. European equivalent of N.A.S.D.A.Q.

European, Australian, and Far East index (E.A.F.E. index)
Stock index, computed by Morgan Stanley Capital International.

European Currency Unit (E.C.U.)
An index of foreign exchange consisting of about 10 European currencies, originally devised in 1979. See: Euro

European Monetary System (E.M.S.)
An exchange arrangement formed in 1979 that involves the currencies of European Union member countries.

European Option
Option that may be exercised only at the expiration date. Related: American option.

European Options Exchange (E.O.E.)
Now AEX-Optiebeurs. See: Amsterdam Exchanges (AEX).

Glossary of Equity Related Terms

European Union (E.U.)
An economic association of European countries founded by the Treaty of Rome in 1957 as a common market for six nations. It was known as the European Community before 1993 and is currently comprised of 15 European countries. Its goals are a single market for goods and services without any economic barriers and a common currency with one monetary authority. The E.U. was known as the European Community until January 1, 1994.

E.U.R.E.X.
The European derivatives exchange formed in 1998 following the merger of the Deutsche Terminbörse (DTB) and the Swiss Options and Financial Futures Exchange (SOFFEX).

Exchange
The marketplace in which shares, options and futures on stocks, bonds, commodities and indices are traded. Principal US stock exchanges are: New York Stock Exchange (N.Y.S.E.), American Stock Exchange (A.M.E.X.) and the National Association of Securities Dealers Automatic Quotation System (N.A.S.D.A.Q.).

Exchange, The
A nickname for the New York Stock Exchange. Also known as the Big Board. More than 2,000 common and preferred stocks are traded. The exchange is the oldest in the United States, founded in 1792, and the largest. It is located on Wall Street in New York City.

Exchangeable
Mainly applies to convertible securities. Right of an issuer, if so stated, to exchange a convertible debenture for an existing convertible preferred with identical terms. Most often used if a corporation has an immediate need for equity capital and has a currently low tax rate, and thus expects either or both conditions to change. This would make the debenture less attractive due to the interest tax deductibility being lost.

Exchangeable Instrument
Mainly applies to convertible securities. Bond or preferred stock, exchangeable into the common stock of a different public corporation (i.e., Spin off).

Exchange Controls
Governmental restrictions on the purchase of foreign currencies by domestic citizens or on the purchase of the local domestic currency by foreigners.

Exchange Of Stock
Acquisition of another company by purchase of its stock in exchange for cash or shares.

Exchange Offer
An offer by the firm to give one security, such as a bond or preferred stock, in exchange for another security, such as shares of common stock.

Ex-Dividend
This literally means "without dividend." The buyer of shares when they are quoted ex-dividend is not entitled to receive a declared dividend. Used in the context of general equities. It is the interval between the record date and the payment date during which the stock trades without its dividend — the buyer of a stock selling ex-dividend does not receive the recently declared dividend. Antithesis of cum dividend.

Execution
The process of completing an order to buy or sell securities. Once a trade is executed, it is reported by a Confirmation Report; settlement (payment and transfer of ownership) occurs in the U.S. between 1 (mutual funds) and 5 (stocks) days after an order is executed. Settlement times for exchange listed stocks are in the process of being reduced to three days in the U. S. The time greatly varies across countries. For example, in France, settlements are only once per month.

Exercise
To implement the right of the holder of an option to buy (in the case of a call) or sell (in the case of a put) the underlying security.

Expected Return
The expected return on a risky asset based on a probability distribution for the possible rates of return. Expected return equals some risk free rate (generally the prevailing U.S. Treasury note or bond rate) plus a risk premium (the difference between the historic market return, based upon a well diversified index such as the S&P 500 and the historic U.S. Treasury bond) multiplied by the assets beta. The conditional expected return varies through time as a function of current market information.

Expense Ratio
The percentage of the assets that were spent to run a mutual fund (as of the last annual statement). This includes expenses such as management and advisory fees, overhead costs and 12b-1 (distribution and advertising) fees. The expense ratio does not include brokerage costs for trading the portfolio, although these are reported as a percentage of assets to the S.E.C. by the funds in a Statement of Additional Information (SAI). The SAI is available to shareholders on request. Neither the expense ratio or the SAI includes the transaction costs of spreads, normally incurred in unlisted securities and foreign stocks. These two costs can add significantly to the reported expenses of a fund. The expense ratio is often termed an Operating Expense Ratio (O.E.R.).

Ex-Rights
In connection with a rights offering, shares of stock that are trading without the rights attached.

External Market
Also referred to as the international market, the offshore market, or, more popularly, the Euromarket, the mechanism for trading securities that (1) at issuance are offered simultaneously to investors in a number of countries and (2) are issued outside the jurisdiction of any single country. Related: internal market.

F

Fast Market
Used in the context of general equities. Excessively rapid trading in a specific security that causes a delay in the electronic updating of its last sale and market conditions, particularly in options.

Fill
The price at which an order is executed.

Fill Or Kill Order (F.O.K.)
A trading order that is canceled unless executed within a designated time period. Used in the context of general equities. A market or limited price order which is to be executed in its entirety as soon as it is represented in the trading crowd, and, if not so executed, is to be treated as cancelled. For purposes of this definition, a stop is considered an execution. Equivalent to A.O.N. and I.O.C. simultaneously.

Financial Analysts
Also called securities analysts and investment analysts, professionals who analyze financial statements, interview corporate executives, and attend trade shows, in order to write reports recommending either purchasing, selling, or holding various stocks.

Financial Engineering
Combining or dividing existing instruments to create new financial products.

Financial Future
A contract entered into now that provides for the delivery of a specified asset in exchange for the selling price at some specified future date.

Financial Intermediaries
Institutions that provide the market function of matching borrowers and lenders or traders.

Financial Leverage
Use of debt to increase the expected return on equity. Financial leverage is measured by the ratio of debt to debt plus equity.

Glossary of Equity Related Terms

Financial Market
An organized institutional structure or mechanism for creating and exchanging financial assets.

Financial Risk
The risk that the cash flow of an issuer will not be adequate to meet its financial obligations. Also referred to as the additional risk that a firm's stockholder bears when the firm utilizes debt and equity.

Financial Times (F-T)-Actuaries Indices
Used for listed equity securities. Share price indices for U.K. companies together with earnings yield, price earnings ratio, and dividend yield. The denominator in the index formula is the market capitalization at the base date, adjusted for all capital changes affecting the particular index since the base date. See: footsie.

Fixed-Income Instruments
Assets that pay a fixed-dollar amount, such as bonds and preferred stock.

Floor Broker
Used for listed equity securities. Member of an exchange who is an employee of a member firm and executes orders, as agent, on the floor of the exchange for clients.

Footsie
Mainly applies to international equities. Financial times (f-t)-actuaries 100 index: "Dow average" of London.

Forced Conversion
Mainly applies to convertible securities. Occurs when a convertible security is called in by the issuer, usually when the underlying stock is selling well above the conversion price. Thus, they assure the bonds will be retired without requiring any cash payment. Upon conversion into common, the carrying value of the bonds becomes part of a corporation's equity, thus strengthening the balance sheet and enhancing future debt issuing capability.

Foreign Equity Market
That portion of the domestic equity market that represents issues floated by foreign companies.

Forward Contract
A cash market transaction in which delivery of the commodity is deferred until after the contract has been made. It is not standardized and is not traded on organized exchanges. Although the delivery is made in the future, the price is determined at the initial trade date.

Fourth Market
Direct trading of large in exchange-listed securities between investors without the use of a broker.

Fundamental Analysis
Security analysis that seeks to detect misvalued securities through an analysis of the firm's business prospects. Research analysis often focuses on earnings, dividend prospects, expectations for future interest rates, and risk evaluation of the firm. Used in the context of general equities. Antithesis of technical analysis. In macroeconomic analysis, information such as interest rates, G.N.P., inflation, unemployment, and inventories are used to predict the direction of the economy, and henceforth the Stock market. In microeconomic analysis, information such as balance sheet, income statement, products, management and other market items are used to forecast a company's imminent success or failure, and hence the future price action of the stock.

Future
A term used to designate all contracts covering the sale of financial instruments or physical commodities for future delivery on a commodity exchange.

REUTERS

Futures Contract
Agreement to buy or sell a set number of shares of a specific stock in a designated future month at a price agreed upon today by the buyer and seller. The contracts themselves are often traded on the futures market. A futures contract differs from an option because an option is the right to buy or sell, whereas a futures contract is the promise to actually make a transaction. A future is part of a class of securities called derivatives, so named because such securities derive their value from the worth of an underlying investment.

G

Gap Opening
Used in the context of general equities. Opening price that is substantially higher or lower than the previous day's closing price, usually because of some extraordinarily positive or negative news.

Gearing
Financial leverage.

Get Hit
Go lower in price, due to bids in the stock or market being hit, causing those bids to vanish and be replaced by lower ones. Come in. Antithesis of on the take.

Glass-Steagall Act
A 1933 act in which Congress forbade commercial banks to own, underwrite, or deal in corporate stock and corporate bonds.

Globalization
Tendency toward a worldwide investment environment, and the integration of national capital markets.

Going-Private Transactions
Publicly owned stock in a firm is replaced with complete equity ownership by a private group. The shares are delisted from stock exchanges and can no longer be purchased in the open markets.

Good Through/Until Date Order
Used in the context of general equities. Market or limited price order which is to be represented in the trading crowd for a stated period of time unless cancelled, executed, or changed, after which such order or the portion thereof not executed is to be treated as cancelled.

Good 'Til Cancelled Order (G.T.C.)
It means an order to buy or sell stock that is good until you execute or cancel it. Brokerages usually set a limit of 30–60 days, at which the G.T.C. order expires if not restated. (In contrast to a day order.)

Goodwill
Excess of the purchase price over the fair market value of the net assets acquired under the purchase method of accounting.

Gray Market
Purchases and sales of Eurobonds that occur before the issue price is finally set.

Graveyard Market
Used in the context of general equities. Bear market wherein investors who sell are faced with substantial losses, while potential investors prefer to stay liquid; that is, to keep their money in cash or cash equivalents until market conditions improve.

Growth Manager
A money manager who seeks to buy stocks that are typically selling at relatively high P/E ratios due to high earnings growth, with the expectation of continued high or higher earnings growth.

Growth Stock
Common stock of a company that has an opportunity to invest money and earn more than the opportunity cost of capital.

H

Hedge
A transaction that reduces the risk of an investment.

Hedged Portfolio
A portfolio consisting of the long position in the stock and the long position in the put option, so as to be riskless and produce a return that equals the risk-free interest rate.

Held At The Opening
Used for listed equity securities. Not open for trading due to specialist or regulators disallowing trading to occur until imbalances dissipate or news is allowed to disseminate.

Held Order
Used for listed equity securities. Order which must be executed without hesitation (market held — Hit the bid or take the offer in line) or if the stock can be bought or sold at that price (held limit order) in sufficient quantity.

High Flyer
Used in the context of general equities. High-priced and highly speculative stock that moves up and down sharply over a short period. Generally glamorous in nature due to the capital gains potential associated with them; also used to describe any high-priced stock. Antithesis of sleeper.

High Price
The highest (intraday) price of a stock over the past 52 weeks, adjusted for any stock splits.

Hit The Bid
A dealer who agrees to sell at the bid price quoted by another dealer is said to "hit" that bid. Antithesis of take the offer.

Holding Period
Length of time that an individual holds a security.

Hong Kong Futures Exchange (H.K.F.E.)
Established in 1976, the Hong Kong Futures Exchange (H.K.F.E.) operates futures and options markets in index, stock, interest rate and foreign exchange products.

Horizontal Spread
The simultaneous purchase and sale of two options that differ only in their exercise date.

Hot
Used in the context of general equities. Active, usually with positive price implications.

"How Are You Making XXX?"
"What is your market in a particular stock?" See: quotation.

Hybrid Security
A convertible security whose optioned common stock is trading in a middle range, causing the convertible security to trade with the characteristics of both a fixed-income security and a common stock instrument.

I

Idiosyncratic Risk
Unsystematic risk or risk that is uncorrelated to the overall market risk. In other words, the risk that is firm specific and can be diversified through holding a portfolio of stocks.

Imbalance Of Orders
Used for listed equity securities. Too many market orders of one kind — to buy or to sell or limit orders to buy up or sell down, without matching orders of the opposite kind. An imbalance usually follows a dramatic event such a takeover, research recommendation, death of a key executive, or a government ruling that will significantly affect the company's business. If it occurs before the stock exchange opens, trading in the stock is delayed. If it occurs during the trading day, the specialist halts and then suspends trading (with floor governor's approval) until enough matching orders can be found to make an orderly market.

Immediate Or Cancelled Order (I.O.C. Order)
Used in the context of general equities. Market or limited price order which is to be executed in whole or in part as soon as such order is represented in the trading crowd. The portion not executed is to be treated as cancelled. A stop is considered an execution in this context. See: A.O.N. order, F.O.K. order.

Immediate Settlement
Delivery and settlement of securities within five business days.

Implied Volatility
The expected volatility in a stock's return derived from its option price, maturity date, exercise price, and riskless rate of return, using an option-pricing model such as Black/Scholes.

In & Out
Refers to over-the-counter trading. Trade in which the trader has both the buyers and sellers lined up for a clean trade. See: cross.

In Between
Used in the context of general equities. Priced higher than the bid price but lower than the offer price. See: in the middle.

Income Stock
Common stock with a high dividend yield and few profitable investment opportunities.

Index
Often applies to derivative products. Statistical composite that measures changes in the economy or in financial markets, often expressed in percentage changes from a base year or from the previous month. Most relevantly, indices measure the ups and downs of stock, bond , and some commodities markets, reflecting market prices and weighing of the companies on the index.

Index Arbitrage
An investment/trading strategy that exploits divergences between actual and theoretical futures prices. For example, the simultaneous buying (selling) of stock index futures (i.e., S&P 500) while selling (buying) the underlying stocks of that index, capturing as profit the temporarily-inflated basis between these two baskets. Often, the point where profitability exists is expressed at the block call as a number of points the future must be over or under the underlying basket for an arbitrage opportunity to exist. See: program trading.

Index Fund
Investment fund designed to match the returns on a stock market index. Mutual fund whose portfolio matches that of a broad-based index such as the S&P 500 and whose performance therefore mirrors the market as represented by that index.

Indexing
A passive instrument strategy consisting of the construction of a portfolio of stocks designed to track the total return performance of an index of stocks.

Index Model
A model of stock returns using a market index such as the S&P 500 to represent common or systematic risk factors.

Inflation Risk
Also called purchasing-power risk, the risk that changes in the real return the investor will realize after adjusting for inflation will be negative.

Informationless Trades
Trades that are the result of either a reallocation of wealth or an implementation of an investment strategy that only utilizes existing information.

In-House
Used in the context of general equities. Keeping an activity within the firm. For example, rather than go to the marketplace and sell a security for a client to anyone, an attempt is made to find a buyer to complete the transaction with the firm. Although a listed trade must be brought to the floor of the stock exchange, matching supply with demand within the confines of the firm results in greater commissions for the firm.

Initial Margin
Used in the context of general equities. 1) Amount of money deposited by both buyers and sellers of futures contracts to ensure performance of the terms of the contract; 2) amount of cash or eligible securities required to be deposited with a broker before engaging in margin transactions.

Initial Public Offering (I.P.O.)
A company's first sale of stock to the public. Securities offered in an I.P.O. are often, but not always, those of young, small companies seeking outside equity capital and a public market for their stock. Investors purchasing stock in I.P.O.s generally must be prepared to accept very large risks for the possibility of large gains. I.P.O.'s by investment companies (closed-end funds) usually contain underwriting fees which represent a load to buyers.

In Play
Often used in risk arbitrage. Company that has become the target of a takeover, and whose stock has now become a speculative issue.

Insider Information
Material information about a company that has not yet been made public. It is illegal for holders of this information to make trades based on it, however received.

Instinet (Institutional Networks Corporation)
Computerized subscriber service that serves as a vehicle for the fourth market. "Instinet" is registered with the S.E.C. As a stock exchange if numbers among its subscribers a large number of mutual funds and other institutional investors linked to each other by computer terminals. The system permits subscribers to display bids and offers (which are exposed system-wide for whatever length of time the initiating party specifies) and to consummate trades electronically. Instinet is largely used by market-makers, but, as mentioned, non-market-makers and customers have equal access.

Institutional Investors
Organizations that invest, including insurance companies, depository institutions, pension funds, investment companies, mutual funds, and endowment funds.

Instruments
Financial securities, such as money market instruments or capital market instruments.

Intermarket Trading System (I.T.S.)
Electronic communications network linking the trading floors of seven registered exchanges to permit trading among them in stocks listed on either the N.Y.S.E. or A.M.E.X. and one or more regional exchanges. Through I.T.S., any broker or market-maker on the floor of any participating exchange can reach out to other participants for an execution whenever the nationwide quote shows a better price available. A floor broker on the exchange can enter an I.T.S. order to assure that he will get all of an offering or bid, instead of splitting it up with competing brokers.

Interest Rate Risk
The risk that a security's value changes due to a change in interest rates. For example, a bond's price drops as interest rates rise. For a depository institution, also called funding risk, the risk that spread income will suffer because of a change in interest rates.

Intermediation
Investment through a financial institution. Related: disintermediation.

Internal Market
The mechanisms for issuing and trading securities within a nation, including its domestic market and foreign market. Compare: external market.

International Arbitrage
Simultaneous buying and selling of foreign securities and A.D.R.s to capture the profit potential created by time, currency, and settlement inconsistencies that vary across international borders.

International Depository Receipt (I.D.R.)
A receipt issued by a bank as evidence of ownership of one or more shares of the underlying stock of a foreign corporation that the bank holds in trust. The advantage of the I.D.R. structure is that the corporation does not have to comply with all the regulatory issuing requirements of the foreign country where the stock is to be traded. The U.S. version of the I.D.R. is the American Depository Receipt (A.D.R.).

International Finance Corporation (I.F.C.)
A corporation owned by the World Bank that produces a number of well known stock indexes for emerging markets.

International Security Market Association (I.S.M.A.)
Swiss law association located in Zurich that regroups all the participants on the Eurobond primary and secondary markets. Establishes uniform trading procedures in the international bond markets.

International Swap Dealers Association (I.S.D.A.)
Formed in 1985 to promote uniform practices in the writing, trading, and settlement of swaps and other derivatives.

In-The-Money
A put option that has a strike price higher than the underlying futures price, or a call option with a strike price lower than the underlying futures price. For example, if the March COMEX silver futures contract is trading at $6 an ounce, a March call with a strike price of $5.50 would be considered in-the-money by $0.50 an ounce. Related: put. Antithesis of Out of the money.

Intrinsic Value Of An Option
The amount by which an option is in-the-money. An option which is not in-the-money has no intrinsic value.

Investment Bank
Financial intermediaries who perform a variety of services, including aiding in the sale of securities, facilitating mergers and other corporate reorganizations, acting as brokers to both individual and institutional clients, and trading for their own accounts. See: Underwriters.

Investment Management
Also called portfolio management and money management, the process of managing money.

Investment Trust
A closed-end fund regulated by the Investment Company Act of 1940. These funds have a fixed number of shares which are traded on the secondary markets similarly to corporate stocks. The market price may exceed the net asset value per share, in which case it is considered at a "premium." When the market price falls below the (N.A.V.)/share, it is at a "discount." Many closed-end funds are of a specialized nature, with the portfolio representing a particular industry, country, etc. These funds are usually listed on US and foreign exchanges.

Investor
The owner of a financial asset.

Investor's Equity
The balance of a margin account. Related: buying on margin, initial margin requirement.

J

Japanese Association of Securities Dealers Automated Quotation System (J.A.S.D.A.Q.)
Japanese equivalent of N.A.S.D.A.Q..

Johannesburg Stock Exchange (J.S.E.)
Established in 1886, the Johannesburg Stock Exchange (J.S.E.) is the only stock exchange in South Africa. Gold and mining stocks form the majority of shares listed.

Joint Account
An agreement between two or more firms to share risk and financing responsibility in purchasing or underwriting securities.

"Just Me Asking"
Used in the context of general equities. "Not a customer request for information."

Glossary of Equity Related Terms

K

Kansas City Board of Trade (K.C.B.T.)
The US-based futures and options exchange for No. 2 red wheat futures and options, Value Line Index futures and Mini Value Line futures and options.

Kappa
The ratio of the dollar price change in the price of an option to a 1% change in the expected price volatility.

"Kick It Out"
Used in the context of general equities. "Liquidate (sell a long/cover a short) a position without regard for price."

Kuala Lumpur Commodities Exchange (K.L.C.E.)
The Malaysian commodity exchange for trading futures in crude palm oil, crude palm kernel oil, tin, rubber and cocoa.

Kuala Lumpur Options and Financial Futures Exchange (K.L.O.F.F.E.)
Established in 1995, the Kuala Lumpur Options and Financial Futures Exchange (K.L.O.F.F.E.) offers equity derivative products based on underlying instruments traded on the Kuala Lumpur Stock Exchange (K.L.S.E.).

Kuala Lumpur Stock Exchange (K.L.S.E.)
Established in 1973, the Kuala Lumpur Stock Exchange (KLSE) is the only stock exchange in Malaysia.

L

Last Trading Day
The final day under an exchange's rules during which trading may take place in a particular futures or options contract. Contracts outstanding at the end of the last trading day must be settled by delivery of underlying physical commodities or financial instruments, or by agreement for monetary settlement depending upon futures contract specifications.

Lead Manager
The commercial or investment bank with the primary responsibility for organizing syndicated bank credit or bond issued. The lead manager recruits additional lending or underwriting banks, negotiates terms of the issue with the issuer, and assesses market conditions.

Lead Underwriter
The head of a syndicate of financial firms that are sponsoring an initial public offering of securities or a seconday offering of securities. Could also apply to bond issues.

Leading The Market
Used in the context of general equities. Stock or group of stocks moving with the market as a whole, but moving in advance of the general market.

LEAPS
Long-term equity anticipation securities. Long-term options.

Less Developed Countries (L.D.C.s)
Also known as emerging markets. Per capita G.D.P. is below a World Bank determined level.

Letter Stock
Privately placed common stock, so-called because the S.E.C. requires a letter from the purchaser stating that the stock is not intended for resale.

Leverage
Used in the context of general equities. For corporations, property of rising or falling at a proportionally greater amount than comparable investments. For example, an option is said to have high leverage relative to the underlying stock because a price change in the stock may result in a relatively large increase or decrease in the value of the option. The use of debt financing.

REUTERS

Leveraged Buyout (L.B.O.)

A transaction used for taking a public corporation private financed through the use of debt funds: bank loans and bonds. Because of the large amount of debt relative to equity in the new corporation, the bonds are typically rated below investment grade, properly referred to as high-yield bonds or junk bonds. Investors can participate in an L.B.O. through either the purchase of the debt (i.e., purchase of the bonds or participation in the bank loan) or the purchase of equity through an L.B.O. fund that specializes in such investments.

Leveraged Equity

Stock in a firm that relies on financial leverage. Holders of leveraged equity face the benefits and costs of using debt.

Leveraged Recapitalization

Often used in risk arbitrage. Popular form of shark repellant whereby a public company takes on significant additional debt with the purpose of either paying an extraordinary dividend or repurchasing shares, leaving the public shareholders with a continuing interest in a more financially-leveraged company.

Liability Swap

An interest rate swap used to alter the cash flow characteristics of an institution's liabilities so as to provide a better match with its assets.

Limit Order

An order to buy a stock at or below a specified price or to sell a stock at or above a specified price. For instance, you could tell a broker "buy me 100 shares of XYZ Corp at $8 or less" or to "sell 100 shares of XYZ at $10 or better." The customer specifies a price and the order can be executed only if the market reaches or betters that price. A conditional trading order designed to avoid the danger of adverse unexpected price changes.

Limit Order Book

A record of unexecuted limit orders that is maintained by the specialist. These orders are treated equally with other orders in terms of priority of execution.

Limited-Liability Instrument

A security, such as a call option, in which the owner can only lose his initial investment.

Liquidation

When a firm's business is terminated, assets are sold, proceeds pay creditors and any leftovers are distributed to shareholders. Any transaction that offsets or closes out a long or short position. Related: buy in, evening up, offset liquidity.

Liquidity

A market is liquid when it has a high level of trading activity, allowing buying and selling with minimum price disturbance. Also a market characterized by the ability to buy and sell with relative ease. Antithesis of illiquid.

Listed Security

Used for listed equity securities. Stock or bond that has been accepted for trading by one of the organized and registered securities exchanges in the United States. Generally, the advantages of being "listed" are that exchanges provide: a) an orderly marketplace; b) liquidity; c) fair price determination; d) accurate and continuous reporting on sales and quotations; e) information on listed companies; and f) strict regulation for the protection of securityholders. Antithesis of O.T.C. Security.

Load Fund

A mutual fund with shares sold at a price including a large sales charge — typically 4% to 8% of the net amount indicated. Some "no-load" funds have distribution fees permitted by article 12b-1 of the Investment Company Act; these are typically 0. 25%. A "true no-load" fund has neither a sales charge nor Freddie Mac (Federal Home Loan Mortgage Corporation) program, the aggregation that the fund purchaser receives some investment advice or other service worthy of the charge.

The London Interbank Offered Rate (L.I.B.O.R.)

The rate of interest that major international banks in London charge each other for borrowings. Many variable interest rates in the U.S. are based on spreads off of L.I.B.O.R. There are many different L.I.B.O.R. tenors.

London International Financial Futures Exchange (L.I.F.F.E.)
A London exchange where Eurodollar futures as well as futures-style options are traded. By contrast with the bid rate L.I.B.I.D. quoted by banks seeking such deposits.

Long Hedge
The purchase of a futures contract(s) in anticipation of actual purchases in the cash market. Used by processors or exporters as protection against an advance in the cash price. Related: hedge, short hedge.

Long Position
An options position where a person has executed one or more option trades where the net result is that they are an "owner" or holder of options (i. e. the number of contracts bought exceeds the number of contracts sold). For equities, it occurs when an individual owns securities. An owner of 1,000 shares of stock is said to be "Long the stock." Related: Short position.

Long-Term Debt/Capitalization
Indicator of financial leverage. Shows long-term debt as a proportion of the capital available. Determined by dividing long-term debt by the sum of long-term debt, preferred stock and common stockholder equity.

M

Make A Market
A dealer is said to make a market when he quotes bid and offered prices at which he stands ready to buy and sell.

Making Delivery
Refers to the seller's actually turning over to the buyer the assets agreed upon in a forward contract.

Management Buyout (M.B.O.)
Leveraged buyout whereby the acquiring group is led by the firm's management.

Margin
This allows investors to buy securities by borrowing money from a broker. The margin is the difference between the market value of a stock and the loan a broker makes. Related: security deposit (initial).

Margin Account (Stocks)
A leverageable account in which stocks can be purchased for a combination of cash and a loan. The loan in the margin account is collateralized by the stock and, if the value of the stock drops sufficiently, the owner will be asked to either put in more cash, or sell a portion of the stock. Margin rules are federally regulated, but margin requirements and interest may vary among broker/dealers.

Margin Call
A demand for additional funds because of adverse price movement. Maintenance margin requirement, security deposit maintenance.

Mark-To-Market
The process whereby the book value or collateral value of a security is adjusted to reflect current market value.

Marketability
A negotiable security is said to have good marketability if there is an active secondary market in which it can easily be resold.

Market Conversion Price
Also called conversion parity price, the price that an investor effectively pays for common stock by purchasing a convertible security and then exercising the conversion option. This price is equal to the market price of the convertible security divided by the conversion ratio.

Market Cycle
The period between the 2 latest highs or lows of the S&P 500, showing net performance of a fund through both an up and a down market. A market cycle is complete when the S&P is 15% below the highest point or 15% above the lowest point (ending a down market).

Market-If-Touched (M.I.T.)
A price order, below market if a buy or above market if a sell, that automatically becomes a market order if the specified price is reached.

Market Maker
Used in the context of general equities. One who maintains firm bid and offer prices in a given security by standing ready to buy or sell round lots at publicly quoted prices. See: agent, dealer, specialist.

Market Model
This relationship is sometimes called the single-index model. The market model says that the return on a security depends on the return on the market portfolio and the extent of the security's responsiveness as measured, by beta. In addition, the return will also depend on conditions that are unique to the firm. Graphically, the market model can be depicted as a line fitted to a plot of asset returns against returns on the market portfolio.

Market Overhang
The theory that in certain situations, institutions wish to sell their shares but postpone the share sales because large orders under current market conditions would drive down the share price and that the consequent threat of securities sales will tend to retard the rate of share price appreciation. Support for this theory is largely anecdotal.

Marketplace Price Efficiency
The degree to which the prices of assets reflect the available marketplace information. Marketplace price efficiency is sometimes estimated as the difficulty faced by active management of earning a greater return than passive management would, after adjusting for the risk associated with a strategy and the transactions costs associated with implementing a strategy.

Market Portfolio
A portfolio consisting of all assets available to investors, with each asset held in proportion to its market value relative to the total market value of all assets.

Market Prices
The amount of money that a willing buyer pays to acquire something from a willing seller, when a buyer and seller are independent and when such an exchange is motivated by only commercial consideration.

Market Timing
Asset allocation in which the investment in the equity market is increased if one forecasts that the equity market will outperform T-bills and decrease when market is anticipated to underpreform.

Matched Orders
Used for listed equity securities. Participate in equal amounts of a trade at a certain price, particularly when two parties have the same level of priority on the exchange floor (this requires standing in the trading crowd).

Member Firm
Used for listed equity securities. Brokerage firm that has at least one membership on a major stock exchange even though, by exchange rules, the membership in the name of an employee and not of the firm itself.

Menu
Used in the context of general equities. Hierarchy of choices concerning price and volume of bids or offers proposed to a customer (e.g. Menu of offerings to a customer buyer - a) 10m @ 24 1/4; b) 25m @ 24 1/2; or c) 50m @ 24 3/4).

Merc, The
Chicago Mercantile Exchange.

Merchant Bank
A British term for a bank that specializes not in lending out its own funds, but in providing various financial services such as accepting bills arising out of trade, underwriting new issues, and providing advice on acquisitions, mergers, foreign exchange, portfolio management, etc.

Modern Portfolio Theory
Principals underlying the analysis and evaluation of rational portfolio choices based on risk-return trade-offs and efficient diversification.

Money Market Fund
A mutual fund that invests only in short term securities, such as bankers' acceptances, commercial paper, repurchase agreements and government bills. The net asset value per share is maintained at $1.00. Such funds are not federally insured, although the portfolio may consist of guaranteed securities and/or the fund may have private insurance protection.

Mutual Fund
Mutual funds are pools of money that are managed by an investment company. They offer investors a variety of goals, depending on the fund and its investment charter. Some funds, for example, seek to generate income on a regular basis. Others seek to preserve an investor's money. Still others seek to invest in companies that are growing at a rapid pace. Funds can impose a sales charge, or load, on investors when they buy or sell shares. Many funds these days are no load and impose no sales charge. Mutual funds are investment companies regulated by the Investment Company Act of 1940. Related: open-end fund, closed-end fund.

Mutual Offset
A system, such as the arrangement between the Chicago Mercantile Exchange (C.M.E.) and Singapore International Monetary Exchange (S.I.M.E.X.), which allows trading positions established on one exchange to be offset or transferred on another exchange.

N

National Association Of Securities Dealers (N.A.S.D.)
Refers to over-the-counter trading. Nonprofit organization formed under the joint sponsorship of the investment bankers' conference and the S.E.C. to comply with the Maloney Act, which provided for the regulation of the O.T.C. market.

National Association Of Securities Dealers Automatic Quotation System (N.A.S.D.A.Q.)
An electronic quotation system that provides price quotations to market participants about the more actively traded common stock issues in the O.T.C. market. About 4,000 common stock issues are included in the N.A.S.D.A.Q. system.

National Futures Association (N.F.A.)
The futures industry self regulatory organization established in 1982.

National Market System (N.M.S.)
Refers to over-the-counter trading. System of trading O.T.C. stocks under the sponsorship of the N.A.S.D.. Must meet certain criteria for size, profitability and trading activity. More comprehensive information is available for N.M.S. stocks than for non-N.M.S. stocks traded O.T.C. (high, low, and last-sale prices, cumulative volume figures, and bid and ask quotations throughout the day), due to the fact that market-makers must report the actual price and number of shares comprising each transaction within 90 seconds vs. non-real-time reporting for non-N.M.S. stocks (thus, last sale prices and minute-to-minute volume updates are not possible).

"Need The Tick"
Used for listed equity securities. "Need the stock to trade up/down at least one tick (1/8) in order to comply with such regulations as those governing short sales/corporate repurchases."

Negotiated Offering
An offering of securities for which the terms, including underwriters' compensation, have been negotiated between the issuer and the underwriters.

Net Adjusted Present Value
The adjusted present value minus the initial cost of an investment.

Net Asset Value (N.A.V.)
The value of a fund's investments. For a mutual fund, the net asset value per share usually represents the fund's market price, subject to a possible sales or redemption charge. For a closed end fund, the market price may vary significantly from the net asset value.

Net Book Value
The current book value of an asset or liability; that is, its original book value net of any accounting adjustments such as depreciation.

Net Change
This is the difference between a day's last trade and the previous day's last trade.

Net Position
The value of the position subtracting out the initial cost of setting up the position. For example, if 100 options where purchased for $1 each and the option is currently trading for $9 then the value of the net position is $900 - $100 = $800.

Net Present Value (N.P.V.)
The present value of the expected future cash flows minus the cost.

New-Issues Market
The market in which a new issue of securities is first sold to investors.

New York Stock Exchange (N.Y.S.E.)
Also known as the Big Board or The Exchange. N.Y.S.E. composite index. Composite index covering price movements of all new world common stocks listed on the New York Stock Exchange. It is based on the close of the market on December 31, 1965 at a level of 50.00, and is weighted according to the number of shares listed for each issue. Print changes in the index are converted to dollars and cents so as to provide a meaningful measure of changes in the average price of listed stocks. The composite index is supplemented by separate indices for four industry groups: industrial, transportation, utility, and finance.

Nikkei Stock Average
Mainly applies to international equities. Price-weighted average of 225 stocks of the first section of the Tokyo Stock Exchange started on May 16, 1949. Japanese equivalent of the U.S.'s Dow.

No Book
Used for listed equity securities. Not much, if any, stock is being bid for or offered at the present time by customers nor the specialist.

Noise
Price and volume fluctuations that can confuse interpretation of market direction. Used in the context of general equities. Stock market activity caused by program trades, dividend rolls, and other phenomena not reflective of general sentiment. Antithesis of real.

Nominal Quotation
Used in the context of general equities. Bid and offer prices given by a market-maker for the purpose of valuation, not as an invitation to trade; must be specifically identified as such by prefixing the quotes F.Y.I. (for your information) or F.V.O. (for valuation only).

Nonmember Firm
Used for listed equity securities. Brokerage firm that is not a member of an organized exchange (N.Y.S.E.). Such firms execute their trades either through member firms, on regional exchanges where they are members, or in the third market.

Nonsystematic Risk
Nonmarket or firm-specific risk factors that can be eliminated by diversification. Also called unique risk or diversifiable risk. Systematic risk refers to risk factors common to the entire economy.

Not A Name With Us
Refers to over-the-counter trading. Not a registered market-maker in the security, especially in O.T.C. and convertibles, or having nothing real to do.

Not Held Order (N.H. Order)
Mainly applies to international equities. Market or limit order in which the customer does not desire to transact automatically at the inside market (market held) but instead has given the trader or floor broker (listed stock) time and price discretion in executing on a best efforts basis and will not hold the broker responsible if he misses the print within his limits (limit not held) or obtains a worse price (market not held). The order is marked "not held, disregard tape/D.R.T., take time" or bears any such qualifying notation, excluding "or better". See: held order.

Notification Date
The day the option is either exercised or expires.

O

Odd Lot
A trading order for less than 100 shares of stock. Compare round lot.

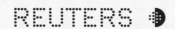

Off-Board
Used for listed equity securities. Transacted away from a national securities exchange even though the stock itself is listed, such as on the N.Y.S.E., and instead of on the O.T.C. market, a regional exchange, or in the third or fourth markets (between customers directly). After 9:30 a.m., if the stock has not opened due to the exchange's discretion, trading can occur elsewhere, but the trader must assume the role of a quasi-specialist in the process.

Offer
Indicates a willingness to sell at a given price. Related: bid

Offer Price
See: offer.

Offerings
Often refers to initial public offerings. When a firm goes public and makes an offering of stock to the market.

Off-Floor Order
Used for listed equity securities. 1) Order to buy or sell a security that originates off the floor of an exchange; customer orders originating with brokers, as distinguished from orders placed by floor members trading for their own accounts. Exchange rules require that an off-floor order be executed before orders initiated on the floor. Upstairs order. Antithesis of on-floor order; 2) order not handled on the floor but instead upstairs.

On The Money
Used in the context of general equities. In-line, or at the same price, as the last sale.

On The Take
Used in the context of general equities. Price moving upward, due to an increased level of buyers taking offerings, causing those offerings to vanish and be replaced by higher ones. Antithesis of come in, get hit.

Open
Used in the context of general equities. Having either buy or sell interest at the indicated price level and side of a preceding trade. "Open on the buy/sell side," means open to customer buyers/sellers, not that he/she wants to buy/sell but rather that he wants to find buyers/sellers (meaning that he/she is a seller/buyer). Antithesis of clean.

Open Contracts
Contracts which have been bought or sold without the transaction having been completed by subsequent sale or purchase, or completed by making or taking actual delivery of the financial instrument or physical commodity.

Open-End Fund
Used in the context of general equities. Mutual fund that continually creates new shares on demand. Mutual fund shareholders buy the funds at net asset value and may redeem them at any time at the prevailing market prices. Antithesis of closed-end fund.

Open Interest
The total number of derivative contracts traded that have not yet been liquidated either by an offsetting derivative transaction or by delivery. Related: liquidation.

Open (Good-Til-Cancelled) Order
An individual investor can place an order to buy or sell a security. This open order stays active until it is completed or the investor cancels it. Used in the context of general equities. G.T.C. order.

Open Position
A net long or short position whose value will change with a change in prices.

Open-Outcry
The method of trading used at futures exchanges, typically involving calling out the specific details of a buy or sell order, so that the information is available to all traders.

Opening
The period at the beginning of the trading session officially designated by the exchange, during which all transactions are considered made "at the opening". Related: Close

Opening Price
The range of prices at which the first bids and offers were made or first transactions were completed.

Optimal Portfolio
An efficient portfolio most preferred by an investor because its risk/reward characteristics approximate the investor's utility function. A portfolio that maximizes an investor's preferences with respect to return and risk.

Option
Gives the buyer the right, but not the obligation, to buy or sell an asset at a set price on or before a given date. Investors, not companies, issue options. Investors who purchase call options bet the stock will be worth more than the price set by the option (the strike price), plus the price they paid for the option itself. Buyers of put options bet the stock's price will go down below the price set by the option. An option is part of a class of securities called derivatives, so named because these securities derive their value from the worth of an underlying investment.

Options Contract
A contract that, in exchange for the option price, gives the option buyer the right, but not the obligation, to buy (or sell) a financial asset at the exercise price from (or to) the option seller within a specified time period, or on a specified date (expiration date).

Options Clearing Corporation (O.C.C.)
Applies to derivative products. Financial institution that is the actual issuer and guarantor of all listed option contracts.

Or Better
Used in the context of general equities. Indication on the order ticket of a limit order to buy or sell securities at a price better than the specified limit price if a better price can be obtained; does not imply a not-held order, but rather puts more emphasis on executing at the limit if available.

Order
Instruction to a broker/dealer to buy, sell, deliver, or receive securities or commodities which commits the issuer of the "order" to the terms specified. See: indication, inquiry, bid wanted, offer wanted.

Ordinary Shares
Mainly applies to international equities. Shares of non-U.S. companies traded in their individual home markets. Usually cannot be delivered in the U.S. See: A.D.R.

Organized Exchange
A securities marketplace wherein purchasers and sellers regularly gather to trade securities according to the formal rules adopted by the exchange.

Out-Of-The-Money Option
A call option is out-of-the-money if the strike price is greater than the market price of the underlying security. i.e. you have the right to purchase a security at a price greater than the market price, which is not valuable. A put option is out-of-the-money if the strike price is less than the market price of the underlying security.

Out There
Used in the context of general equities. Indication that buyer(s) and/or (more often) seller(s) exist in the market due to trading and inquiry activity, and should be found to get their order. "Feels like IBM is 'out there'."

Overhang
Used in the context of general equities. Sizable block of securities or commodities contracts that, if released on the market, would put

downward pressure on prices; prohibits buying activity that would otherwise translate into upward price movement. Examples include shares held in a dealer's inventory, a large institutional holding, a secondary distribution still in registration, and a large commodity position about to be liquidated.

Oversold
Used in the context of general equities. Technically too low in price, and hence a technical correction is expected. Antithesis of overbought.

Oversubscribed Issue
Investors are not able to buy all of the shares or bonds they want, so underwriters must allocate the shares or bonds among investors. This occurs when a new issue is underpriced or in great demand because of growth prospects.

Over-The-Counter (O.T.C.)
A decentralized market (as opposed to an exchange market) where geographically dispersed dealers are linked together by telephones and computer screens. The market is for securities not listed on a stock or bond exchange. The N.A.S.D.A.Q. market is an O.T.C. market for U.S. stocks. Antithesis of listed.

P

P&L
Profit and loss statement for a trader.

P/E
See: Price/Earnings ratio.

P/E Effect
That portfolios with low P/E stocks have exhibited higher average risk-adjusted returns than high P/E stocks. Related: value manager.

P/E Ratio
Assume XYZ Co. sells for $25.50 per share and has earned $2.55 per share this year; $25. 50 = 10 times $2. 55 XYZ stock sells for 10 times earnings. P/E = Current stock price divided by trailing annual earnings per share or expected annual earnings per share.

Pacific Stock Exchange
Used for listed equity securities. Regional exchange located in Los Angeles and San Francisco; only U.S. listed exchange open between 4:00 and 4:30.

Par
Equal to the nominal or face value of a security. A bond selling at "par," for instance, is worth an amount equivalent to its original issue value or its value upon redemption at maturity — typically $1000/bond. See: discount, premium.

Paper Gain (Loss)
Unrealized capital gain (loss) on securities held in a portfolio, based on a comparison of current market price to original cost.

Participating Buyer/Seller
Used for listed equity securities. (1)Customer willing to buy/sell in-line with market. (2)Buyer/seller who goes along with another buyer/seller in a percentage order.

Participation Certificates
Used in the context of general equities. Certificate representing an interest in a pool of funds or in other instruments, such as foreign securities, that allow participation in the rise or fall of a security or group of securities.

Payout Ratio
Generally, the proportion of earnings paid out to the common stockholders as cash dividends. More specifically, the firm's cash dividend divided by the firm's earnings in the same reporting period.

Perfect Capital Market
A market in which there are never any arbitrage opportunities.

Perfect Hedge
A financial result in which the profit and loss from the underlying asset and the hedge position are equal.

Performance Evaluation
The evaluation of a manager's performance which involves, first, determining whether the money manager added value by outperforming the established benchmark (performance measurement) and, second, determining how the money manager achieved the calculated return (performance attribution analysis).

Performance Shares
Shares of stock given to managers on the basis of performance as measured by earnings per share and similar criteria. A control device used by shareholders to tie management to the self-interest of shareholders.

Perpetual Warrants
Warrants that have no expiration date.

Philadelphia Stock Exchange (P.H.L.X.)
A securities exchange where American and European foreign currency options on spot exchange rates are traded.

Pink Sheets
Refers to over-the-counter trading. Daily publication of the national quotation bureau that details the bid and ask prices of thousands of O.T.C. stocks, as well as market-makers who trade each stock.

Pit
A specific area of the trading floor that is designed for the trading of commodities, individual futures, or option contracts.

Plain Vanilla
A term that refers to a relatively simple derivative financial instrument, usually a swap or other derivative that is issued with standard features.

Portfolio Beta
Used in the context of general equities. The beta of the portfolio is the weighted sum of the individual asset betas. The weights are simply the investment weights in the portfolio. E.g. if 50% of money in stock A with a beta of 2.00 and 50% of money in stock B with a beta of 1.00; the portfolio beta is 1.50. Relative volatility of an individual securities portfolio, taken as a whole, as measured by the individual stock betas of the securities making it up. A beta of 1.05 relative to the S&P 500 implies that if the S&P's excess return increases by 10% the portfolio is expected to increase by 10.5%.

Position
A market commitment; the number of contracts bought or sold for which no offsetting transaction has been entered into. The buyer of a commodity is said to have a long position and the seller of a commodity is said to have a short position. Related: open contracts.

Preference
Refers to over-the-counter trading. Select a dealer to handle a trade despite his market not being the best available. Often the "preferenced dealer" will then move his market in-line.

Preference Stock
A security that ranks junior to preferred stock but senior to common stock in the right to receive payments from the firm; essentially junior preferred stock.

Preferred Equity Redemption Stock (PERC)
Preferred stock that converts automatically into equity at a stated date. A limit is placed on the value of the shares the investor receives.

Preferred Shares
Preferred shares give investors a fixed dividend from the company's earnings. And more importantly: preferred shareholders get paid before common shareholders. See: preferred stock.

Preferred Stock

A security that shows ownership in a corporation and gives the holder a claim, prior to the claim of common stockholders, on earnings and also generally on assets in the event of liquidation. Most preferred stock pays a fixed dividend that is paid prior to the common stock dividend, stated in a dollar amount or as a percentage of par value. This stock does not usually carry voting rights. The stock shares characteristics of both common stock and debt.

Premium

(1) for a bond above the par value. (2) The price of an option contract; also, in futures trading, the amount the futures price exceeds the price of the spot commodity. For convertibles, amount by which the price of a convertible exceeds parity, and is usually expressed as a percentage. If a stock is trading at $45 and the bond convertible at $50 is trading at 105, the premium is $15, or 16.66% (15/90). If the premium is high, the bond trades like any fixed income bond, if low, like a stock. See: gross parity, net parity. For futures, excess of fair value of future over the spot index, which in theory will equal the Treasury bill yield for the period to expiration minus the expected dividend yield until the future's expiration. For options, price of an option in the open market (sometimes refers to the portion of the price that exceeds parity). For straight equity, price higher than that of the last sale or inside market. Related: inverted market premium payback period. Also called break-even time, the time it takes to recover the premium per share of a convertible security.

Present Value

The amount of cash today that is equivalent in value to a payment, or to a stream of payments, to be received in the future. To determine the present value, each future cash flow is multiplied by a present value factor. For example, if the opportunity cost of funds is 10%, the present value of $100 to be received in one year is $100 \times (1/1 + .10) = \$91$.

Price/Book Ratio

Compares a stock's market value to the value of total assets less total liabilities (book value). Determined by dividing current stock price by common stockholder equity per share (book value), adjusted for stock splits. Also called Market-to-Book.

Price Risk

The risk that the value of a security (or a portfolio) will decline in the future. Or, a type of mortgage-pipeline risk created in the production segment when loan terms are set for the borrower in advance of terms being set for secondary market sale. If the general level of rates rises during the production cycle, the lender may have to sell his originated loans at a discount.

Price/Sales Ratio

Determined by dividing current stock price by revenue per share (adjusted for stock splits). Revenue per share for the P/S ratio is determined by dividing revenue for past 12 months by number of shares outstanding.

Primary Market

The first buyer of a newly issued security buys that security in the primary market. All subsequent trading of those securities is done in the secondary market.

Private Placement

The sale of a bond or other security directly to a limited number of investors. Used in the context of general equities. For example, sale of stocks, bonds, or other investments directly to an institutional investor like an insurance company, avoiding the need for S.E.C. registration if the securities are purchased for investment as opposed to resale. Antithesis of public offering.

Profit Taking

Used in the context of general equities. Action by short-term securities traders to cash-in on gains created by a sharp market rise, which pushes Down prices temporarily but implies an upward market trend. See: ring the [cash] register.

Program Trading

Trades based on signals from computer programs, usually entered directly from the trader's computer to the market's computer system and executed automatically. Applies to derivative products. This process of electronic execution of trading of a basket of stocks simultaneously, for index arbitrage, portfolio restructuring, or outright buy/sell interests.

Prospectus
Formal written document to sell securities that describes the plan for a proposed business enterprise, or the facts concerning an existing one, that an investor needs to make an informed decision. Prospectuses are used by mutual funds to describe the fund objectives, risks and other essential information.

Provisional Call Feature
A feature in a convertible issue that allows the issuer to call the issue during the non-call period if the price of the stock reaches a certain level. Mainly applies to convertible securities. right of an issuer to accelerate the first redemption date if the underlying common should trade at or above a certain level for a sustained period. Most typical terms are 150% of conversion price for 20 consecutive days. Note that under these circumstances the security has appreciated, at a minimum, 50% since being issued.

Public Offering
Used in the context of general equities. Offering to the investment public, after registration requirements of the S.E.C. have been complied with, usually by an investment banker or a syndicate made up of several investment bankers, at a public offering price agreed upon between the issuer and the investment bankers. Antithesis of private placement. See primary distribution and secondary distribution.

Put Option
This security gives investors the right to sell (or put) a fixed number of shares at a fixed price within a given time frame. An investor, for example, might wish to have the right to sell shares of a stock at a certain price by a certain time in order to protect, or hedge, an existing investment.

Put Price
The price at which the asset will be sold if a put option is exercised. Also called the strike or exercise price of a put option.

Q

Quality Option
Also called the swap option, the seller has choice of deliverables in Treasury Bond and Treasury note futures contract. Related: cheapest to deliver issue.

Quick Ratio
Indicator of a company's financial strength (or weakness). Calculated by taking current assets less inventories, divided by current liabilities. This ratio provides information regarding the firm's liquidity and ability to meet its obligations. Also called the Acid Test ratio.

Quotation
Used in the context of general equities. Highest bid and lowest offer (asked) price currently available on a security or a commodity. Insider market.

R

Random Walk
Theory that stock price changes from day to day are at random; the changes are independent of each other and have the same probability distribution. Many believers of the random walk theory believe that it is impossible to outperform the market consistently without taking additional risk.

Reading The Tape
Used in the context of general equities. Judging the performance of stocks by monitoring changes in price as they are displayed on the ticker tape.

Real Time
A real time stock or bond quote is one that states a security's most recent offer to sell or bid (buy). A delayed quote shows the same bid and ask prices 15 minutes and sometimes 20 minutes after a trade takes place.

Rebalancing
Realigning the proportions of assets in a portfolio as needed.

Recapitalization Proposal
Often used in risk arbitrage. Plan by a target company to restructure the firm's capitalization (debt and equity) in a way to ward off a hostile or potential suitor.

Record Date
(1) Date by which a shareholder must officially own shares in order to be entitled to a dividend. For example, a firm might declare a dividend on Nov 1, payable Dec 1 to holders of record Nov 15. Once a trade is executed an investor becomes the "owner of record" on settlement, which currently takes 5 business days for securities, and one business day for mutual funds. Stocks trade ex-dividend the fourth day before the record date, since the seller will still be the owner of record and is thus entitled to the dividend. (2) The date that determines who is entitled to payment of principal and interest due to be paid on a security. The record date for most M.B.S.s is the last day of the month, however the last day on which they may be presented for the transfer is the last business day of the month. The record date for C.M.O.s and asset-backed securities vary with each issue.

Red Herring
A preliminary prospectus containing information required by the S.E.C.. It excludes the offering price and the coupon of the new issue.

Reference Rate
A benchmark interest rate (such as LIBOR), used to specify conditions of an interest rate swap or an interest rate agreement.

Regional Stock Exchanges
Used for listed equity securities. Organized national securities exchanges located outside of New York city and registered with the S.E.C. They include: Boston, Cincinnati, Intermountain (Salt Lake City - dormant, owned by COMEX), Midwest (Chicago), Pacific (Los Angeles and San Francisco), Philadelphia (Philadelphia and Miami), and Spokane (local mining & Canadian issues, non-reporting trades) stock exchanges.

Registered Representative
A person registered with the C.F.T.C. who is employed by, and soliciting business for, a commission house or futures commission merchant.

Registered Trader
A member of the exchange who executes frequent trades for his or her own account.

Registration
Used in the context of general equities. Process set up the Securities Exchange Acts of 1933 and 1934 whereby securities that are to be sold to the public are reviewed by the S.E.C.

Registration Statement
A legal document that is filed with the S.E.C. to register securities for public offering. Used in the context of general equities. This document details the purpose of a proposed public offering of securities. The statement outlines financial details, a history of the company's operations and management, and other facts of importance to potential buyers. See: registration.

Regular Settlement
Used in the context of general equities. Transaction in which the stock contract is settled and delivered on the fifth full business day following the date of the transaction (trade date). In Japan, regular settlement occurs three business days following the trade date, and in London, two weeks following the trade date (at times, three weeks). In France, once per month.

Relative Strength
A stock's price movement over the past year as compared to a market index (like the S&P 500). Value below 1.0 means the stock shows relative weakness in price movement (underperformed the market); a value above 1.0 means the stock shows relative strength over the 1-year period. Equation for Relative Strength: [current stock price/year-ago stock price] divided by [current S&P 500/year-ago S&P 500]. Note this is a potentially misleading indicator of performance because it does not take risk into account.

Resistance Level
A price level above which it is supposedly difficult for a security or market to rise. Used in the context of general equities. Price ceiling at which technical analysts note persistent selling of a commodity or security. Antithesis of support level.

Restricted
Used in the context of general equities. Placement on a list which dictates that the trader may not maintain positions, solicit business, or provide indications in a stock, but may serve as broker in agency trades after being properly cleared. Placement on a restricted list is due to Investment bank involvement with the company on non-public activity (i.e., mergers and acquisitions defense), affiliate ownership, or underwriting activities; signified on the Quotron by a flashing "R." A restricted list and the stocks on it should never be conveyed to anyone outside of the trading areas, much less outside of the firm.

Return On Assets (R.O.A.)
Indicator of profitability. Determined by dividing net income for the past 12 months by total average assets. Result is shown as a percentage. R.O.A. can be decomposed into return on sales (net income/sales) multiplied by asset utilization (sales/assets).

Return On Equity (ROE)
Indicator of profitability. Determined by dividing net income for the past 12 months by common stockholder equity (adjusted for stock splits). Result is shown as a percentage. Investors use R.O.E. as a measure of how a company is using its money. R.O.E. may be decomposed into return on assets (R.O.A.) multiplied by financial leverage (total assets/total equity).

Return On Investment (ROI)
Generally, book income as a proportion of net book value.

Reversal
Used in the context of general equities. Turn, Unwind. For convertible reversal, selling a convertible and buying the underlying common, usually done by an arbitrageur. For market reversal, change in direction in the stock or commodity futures markets, as charted by technical analysts in trading ranges. For options reversal, closing the positions of each aspect of an options spread or combination strategy.

Right
Privilege granted to existing shareholders of a corporation to subscribe to shares of a new issue of common stock before it is offered to the public. Such a right, which normally has a life of two to four weeks, is freely transferable and entitles the holder to buy the new common stock below the public offering price. See: warrant.

Rights Offering
Issuance of "rights" to current shareholders allowing them to purchase additional shares, usually at a discount to market price. Shareholders who do not exercise these rights are usually diluted by the offering. Rights are often transferable, allowing the holder to sell them on the open market to others who may wish to exercise them. Rights offerings are particularly common to closed end funds, which cannot otherwise issue additional common stock.

Risk
Often defined as the standard deviation of the return on total investment. Degree of uncertainty of return on an asset. In context of asset pricing theory. See: Systematic risk

Risk Arbitrage
Traditionally, the simultaneous purchase of stock in a company being acquired and sale of stock of the acquirer. Modern "risk arbitrage" focuses on capturing the spreads between the market value of an announced takeover target and the eventual price at which the acquirer will buy the target's shares.

Risk Management
The process of identifying and evaluating risks and selecting and managing techniques to adapt to risk exposures.

Round Lot
A trading order typically of 100 shares of a stock or some multiple of 100. Related: odd lot.

Run
A run consists of a series of bid and offer quotes for different securities or maturities. Dealers give to and ask for runs from each other.

Runoff
Used for listed equity securities. Series of trades printed on the ticker tape that occur on the N.Y.S.E. before 4:00 p.m., but are not reported until afterwards due to heavy trading and hence the late tape.

S

Scalp
To trade for small gains. It normally involves establishing and liquidating a position quickly, usually within the same day.

Seasoned
For seasoned equity, having gained a reputation for quality with the investing public and enjoying liquidity in the secondary market; when applied to convertibles, having traded for at least 90 days after issued in Europe, and is thus available for sale legally to U.S. investors.

Secondary Distribution/Offering
Used in the context of general equities. Public sale of previously issued securities held by large investors, usually corporations, or institutions as distinguished from a primary distribution, where the seller is the issuing corporation. The sale is handled off the N.Y.S.E., by a securities firm or a group of firms and the shares are usually offered at a fixed price related to the current market price of the stock.

Secondary Market
The market where securities are traded after they are initially offered in the primary market. Most trading is done in the secondary market. The New York Stock Exchange, as well as all other stock exchanges, the bond markets, etc., are secondary markets. Seasoned securities are traded in the secondary market.

Securities & Exchange Commission (S.E.C.)
The S.E.C. is a federal agency that regulates the U.S. financial markets. This federal agency also oversees the securities industry and promotes full disclosure and protection of the investing public against malpractice in the securities markets.

Securitization
The process of creating a pass-through, such as the mortgage pass-through security, by which the pooled assets become standard securities backed by those assets. Also, refers to the replacement of nonmarketable loans and/or cash flows provided by financial intermediaries with negotiable securities issued in the public capital markets.

Security
Piece of paper that proves ownership of stocks, bonds and other investments.

Selling Short
If an investor thinks the price of a stock is going down, the investor could borrow the stock from a broker and sell it. Eventually, the investor must buy the stock back on the open market. For instance, you borrow 1000 shares of XYZ on July 1 and sell it for $8 per share. Then, on Aug 1, you purchase 1000 shares of XYZ at $7 per share. You've made $1000 (less commissions and other fees) by selling short.

Sell Limit Order
Conditional trading order that indicates that a security may be sold at the designated price or higher. Related: buy limit order.

Sell-Side Analyst
Also called a Wall Street analyst, a financial analyst who works for a brokerage firm and whose recommendations are passed on to the brokerage firm's customers.

Settlement Date
The date on which payment is made to settle a trade. For stocks traded on US exchanges, settlement is currently 3 business days after the trade. For mutual funds, settlement usually occurs in the U.S.the day following the trade. In some regional markets, foreign shares may require months to settle.

Settlement Price
A figure determined by the closing range which is used to calculate gains and losses in futures market accounts. Settlement prices are used to determine gains, losses, margin calls, and invoice prices for deliveries. Related: closing range.

Shadow Stock

First, a public company may create a stock that strips out the market wide movements for the purpose of rewarding managers. That is, the management might have done a great job - but the traded stock plummets because the market as a whole plummets. A second interpretation of shadow stock is a phantom stock that is created by a private company (i.e. that does not have stock traded either on exchange or over the counter) again for the purpose of performance evaluation and rewards.

Shareholders

Person or entity that owns share in a corporation.

Shareholders' Equity

This is a company's total assets minus total liabilities. A company's net worth is the same thing.

Shares

Certificates or book entries representing ownership in a corporation or similar entity.

Shelf Registration

A procedure that allows firms to file one registration statement covering several issues of the same security. It is the term used for S.E.C. Rule 415 adopted in the 1980's, which allows a corporation to comply with registration requirements up to two years prior to a public offering of securities. With the registration "on the shelf," the corporation, by simply updating regularly filed annual, quarterly, and related reports to the S.E.C., can go to the market as conditions become favorable with a minimum of administrative preparation and expense.

Short Hedge

The sale of a futures contract(s) to eliminate or lessen the possible decline in value of an approximately equal amount of the actual financial instrument or physical commodity. Related: Long hedge.

Short Position

Occurs when a person sells stocks he or she does not yet own. Shares must be borrowed, before the sale, to make "good delivery" to the buyer. Eventually, the shares must be brought back to close out the transaction. This technique is used when an investor believes stock price will go down.

Short Sale

Selling a security that the seller does not own but is committed to repurchasing eventually. It is used to capitalize on an expected decline in the security's price.

Short Squeeze

A situation in which a lack of supply tends to force prices upward. In particular, a situation when prices of a stock or commodity futures contracts start to move up sharply and many traders with short positions are forced to buy stocks or commodities in order to cover their positions and prevent (limit) losses. This sudden surge of buying leads to even higher prices, further aggravating the losses of short sellers who have not covered their positions.

Show Me Buyer/Seller

Used in the context of general equities. Customer who has not placed a firm order to buy stock but has requested that the salesman show him/her available stock for sale or purchase, along with the asking/bid price, due to his/her interest in buying/selling the stock. See: bidding buyer.

Shut Out The Book

Used for listed equity securities. Exclude a public bid or offer from participation in a print.

Size

Large in size, as in the size of an offering, the size of an order, or the size of a trade. Size is relative from market to market and security to security. Context: "I can buy size at 102-22," means that a trader can buy a significant amount at 102-22. Small is >10,000 shares. Medium is 15,000 - 25,000 shares. Good is 50,000 shares. Size is 100,000 shares. Good six figure size is 200,000 - 300,000 shares. Multiple six figure size is >300,000 shares of the market is actual number of shares represented in one's market, or bid and offering; unless specified, assumed to be at least 500 to 1000 shares, depending on the stock.

Sleeper

Used in the context of general equities. Stock in which there is little investor interest but which has significant potential to gain in price once its attractions are recognized. Antithesis of high flyer.

SPRDs
SPRDS (Spiders) are designed to track the value of the Standard & Poors 500 Composite Price Index. They are known as Spiders which is short for Standard&Poor's Depositary Receipt. They trade on the American Stock Exchange under the symbol SPY. They are similar to closed-end funds but are formally known as, UIT, a unit investment trust. One SPDR unit is valued at approximately one tenth (1/10) of the value of the S&P 500. Dividends are disbursed quarterly, and are based on the accumulated stock dividends held in trust, less any expenses of the trust. See: Mid-cap SPRD.

Special Dividend
Also referred to as an extra dividend. Dividend that is unlikely to be repeated.

Specialist
On an exchange, the member firm that is designated as the market maker (or dealer for a listed common stock). Only one specialist can be designated for a given stock, but dealers may be specialists for several stocks. In contrast, there can be multiple market makers in the O.T.C. market. This member of a stock exchange who maintains a "fair and orderly market" in one or more securities. Major functions include executing limit orders on behalf of other exchange members for a portion of the floor broker's commission, and buying or selling for his own account to counteract temporary imbalances in supply and demand and thus prevent wide swings in stock prices.

Speculator
One, who attempts to anticipate price changes and, through buying and selling contracts, aims to make profits. A speculator does not use the market in connection with the production, processing, marketing or handling of a product. See: trader.

Split
Sometimes, companies split their outstanding shares into a larger number of shares. If a company with 1 million shares did a two-for-one split, the company would have 2 million shares. An investor with 100 shares before the split would hold 200 shares after the split. The investor's percentage of equity in the company remains the same, and the price of the stock he owns is one-half the price of the stock on the day prior to the split.

Split Stock
Used in the context of general equities. (1) Purchases or sales shared with others. (2) Division of the outstanding shares of a corporation into a large number of shares. Ordinarily, splits must be noted by directors and approved by shareholders.

Spot Price
The current market price of the actual physical commodity. Also called cash price. Current delivery price of a commodity traded in the spot market, in which goods are sold for cash and delivered immediately. Cash price. Antithesis of futures price.

Spot Secondary
Used in the context of general equities. Secondary distribution which may not require an S.E.C. registration statement and may be attempted without delay, an underwriting discount is normally contained in these offerings.

Spread
(1) The gap between bid and ask prices of a stock or other security. (2) The simultaneous purchase and sale of separate futures or options contracts for the same commodity for delivery in different months. Also known as a straddle. (3) Difference between the price at which an underwriter buys an issue from a firm and the price at which the underwriter sells it to the public. (4) The price an issuer pays above a benchmark fixed-income yield to borrow money.

SPX
Applies to derivative products. Symbol for the S&P 500 index.

Stated conversion price
At the time of issuance of a convertible security, the price the issuer effectively grants the security holder to purchase the common stock, equal to the par value of the convertible security divided by the conversion ratio.

Stock
Ownership of a corporation which is represented by shares which represent a piece of the corporation's assets and earnings.

Stock Dividend
Payment of a corporate dividend in the form of stock rather than cash. The stock dividend may be additional shares in the company, or it may be shares in a subsidiary being spun off to shareholders. Stock dividends are often used to conserve cash needed to operate the business. Unlike a cash dividend, stock dividends are not taxed until sold.

Stock Exchanges
Formal organizations, approved and regulated by the Securities and Exchange Commission (S.E.C.), that are made up of members that use the facilities to exchange certain common stocks. The two major national stock exchanges are the New York Stock Exchange (N.Y.S.E.) and the American Stock Exchange (A.S.E. or A.M.E.X.). Five regional stock exchanges include the Midwest, Pacific, Philadelphia, Boston, and Cincinnati. The Arizona Stock Exchange is an after hours electronic marketplace where anonymous participants trade stocks via personal computers.

Stock Exchange Automated Quotation System (S.E.A.Q.)
London's N.A.S.D.A.Q. system.

Stock Exchange of Hong Kong (S.E.H.K.)
The Stock Exchange of Hong Kong (S.E.H.K.) is the only stock exchange in Hong Kong.

Stockholder's Equity
The residual claims that stockholders have against a firm's assets, calculated by subtracting total liabilities from total assets.

Stockholder Equity
Balance sheet item that includes the book value of ownership in the corporation. It includes capital stock, paid in surplus, and retained earnings.

Stock Index Option
An option in which the underlying is a common stock index.

Stock Option
An option in which the underlying asset is the common stock of a corporation.

Stock Repurchase
A firm's repurchase of outstanding shares of its common stock.

Stock Split
Occurs when a firm issues new shares of stock but in turn lowers the current market price of its stock to a level that is proportionate to pre-split prices. For example, if IBM trades at $100 before a 2-for-1 split, after the split it will trade at $50 and holders of the stock will have twice as many shares as they had before the split. See: split.

Stop-Limit Order
A stop order that designates a price limit. In contrast to the stop order, which becomes a market order once the stop is reached, the stop-limit order becomes a limit order.

Stop Order (Or Stop)
An order to buy or sell at the market when a definite price is reached, either above (on a buy) or below (on a sell) the price that prevailed when the order was given.

Street
Brokers, dealers, underwriters, and other knowledgeable members of the financial community; from Wall Street financial community.

Street Name
Describes securities assets held by a broker on behalf of a client but registered in the name of the Wall Street firm.

Support Level
A price level below which it is supposedly difficult for a security or market to fall. That is, the price level at which a security tends to stop falling because there is more demand than supply; can be identified on a technical basis by seeing where the stock has bottomed in the past.

Suspended Trading
Used in the context of general equities. Temporary halt in trading in a particular security, in advance of a major news announcement or to correct an imbalance of orders to buy and sell.

Swap
An arrangement whereby two companies lend to each other on different terms, e.g. in different currencies, and/or at different interest rates, fixed or floating.

Swaption
Options on interest rate swaps. The buyer of a swaption has the right to enter into an interest rate swap agreement by some specified date in the future. The swaption agreement will specify whether the buyer of the swaption will be a fixed-rate receiver or a fixed-rate payer. The writer of the swaption becomes the counterparty to the swap if the buyer exercises.

Symbol
Used in the context of general equities. Letters used to identify companies used on the consolidated tape and other locations.

Synthetics
Customized hybrid instruments created by blending an underlying price on a cash instrument with the price of a derivative instrument. It is a combination of security holdings which mimics the price movement of another, single security (i.e., synthetic call: long position in a stock combined with a put on that position; a protected long sale; synthetic put: short position in a stock combined with a call on that position; a protected short sale).

T

Take A Position
To buy or sell short; that is, to have some amount that is owned or owed on an asset or derivative security.

Take The Offer
Used in the context of general equities. Buy stock by accepting a floor broker's (listed) or dealer's (O.T.C.) offer at an agreed-upon volume. Antithesis of hit the bid.

Tax Selling
Used in the context of general equities. Unloading of long positions in stock for tax purposes, usually to use these capital losses to offset previously earned profit. See: wash sale.

Technical Rally
Used in the context of general equities. Short rise in securities or commodities futures prices within a general declining trend. Such a rally may result because investors are bargain hunting or because analysts have noticed a particular support level at which securities usually bounce up. Antithesis of correction.

Tender Offer
General offer made publicly and directly to a firm's shareholders to buy their stock at a price well above the current market price.

10-K
Annual report required by the S.E.C. each year. Provides a comprehensive overview of a company's state of business. Must be filed within 90 days after fiscal year end. A 10-Q report is filed quarterly.

10-Q
Quarterly report required by the S.E.C. each quarter. Provides a comprehensive overview of a company's state of business.

Thin Market
A market in which trading volume is low and in which consequently bid and asked quotes are wide and the liquidity of the instrument traded is low. Condition of very little stock to buy or sell. Illiquid.

Three-Phase DDM
A version of the dividend discount model which applies a different expected dividend rate depending on a company's life-cycle phase, growth phase, transition phase, or maturity phase.

Tick
Refers to the minimum change in price a security can have, either up or down. Related: point.

Ticker Tape
Used in the context of general equities. Computerized device that relays to investors around the world the stock symbol and the latest price and volume on securities as they are traded.

Tick-Test Rules

S.E.C.-imposed restrictions on when a short sale may be executed, intended to prevent investors from destabilizing the price of a stock when the market price is falling. A short sale can be made only when either (1) the sale price of the particular stock is higher than the last trade price (referred to as an uptick trade) or (2) if there is no change in the last trade price of the particular stock, the previous trade price must be higher than the trade price that preceded it (referred to as a zero uptick).

Time Premium

Also called time value, the amount by which the option price exceeds its intrinsic value. The value of an option beyond its current exercise value representing the optionholder's control until expiration, the risk of the underlying asset, and the riskless return.

T.S.E. 100 (Toronto Stock Exchange 100 Index)

Canadian form of a Dow Jones Industrial index.

Total Return

In performance measurement, the actual rate of return realized over some evaluation period. In fixed income analysis, the potential return that considers all three sources of return (coupon interest, interest on coupon interest, and any capital gain/loss) over some investment horizon.

Trade

A verbal (or electronic) transaction involving one party buying a security from another party. Once a trade is consummated, it is considered "done" or final. Settlement occurs 1-5 business days later.

Trade Date

In an interest rate swap, the date that the counterparties commit to the swap. Also, the date on which a trade occurs. Trades generally settle (are paid for) 1-5 business days after a trade date. With stocks, settlement is generally 3 business days after the trade. For equities, the day on which a security or a commodity future trade actually takes place. The settlement date usually follows the trade date by five business days, but varies depending on the transaction and method of delivery used.

Traders

Persons who take positions in securities and their derivatives with the objective of making profits. Traders can make markets by trading the flow. When they do that, their objective is to earn the bid/ask spread. Traders can also be of the sort who take proprietary positions whereby they seek to profit from the directional movement of prices or spread positions.

Trading Costs

Costs of buying and selling marketable securities and borrowing. Trading costs include commissions, slippage, and the bid/ask spread. See: transaction costs.

U

Uncovered Call

A short call option position in which the writer does not own shares of underlying stock represented by his option contracts. Also called a "naked" asset, it is much riskier for the writer than a covered call, where the writer owns the underlying stock. If the buyer of a call exercises the option to call, the writer would be forced to buy the asset at current market price.

Uncovered Put

A short put option position in which the writer does not have a corresponding short stock position or has not deposited, in a cash account, cash or cash equivalents equal to the exercise value of the put. Also called "naked" puts, the writer has pledged to buy the asset at a certain price if the buyer of the options chooses to exercise it. The nature of uncovered call options means the writer's risk is unlimited. With uncovered put options, the risk is limited to the value of the stock (adjusted for premium received.)

Underlying

The "something" that the parties agree to exchange in a derivative contract.

Underlying Security
For options, the security subject to being purchased or sold upon exercise of an option contract. For example, IBM stock is the underlying security to IBM options. For Depository receipts, the class, series and number of the foreign shares represented by the depository receipt.

Underperform
When a security is expected to, or does appreciate at a slower rate than the overall market.

Underwriter
A party that guarantees the proceeds to the firm from a security sale, thereby in effect taking ownership of the securities. Or, stated differently, a firm, usually an investment bank, that buys an issue of securities from a company and resells it to investors.

Underwriting Fee
The portion of the gross underwriting spread that compensates the securities firms that underwrite a public offering for their underwriting risk.

Unit
Used in the context of general equities. More than one class of securities traded together (i.e., one common share and three subscription warrants).

Unit Investment Trust
Money invested in a portfolio whose composition is fixed for the life of the fund. Shares in a unit trust are called redeemable trust certificates, and they are sold at a premium to net asset value.

Unsystematic Risk
Also called the diversifiable risk or residual risk. The risk that is unique to a company such as a strike, the outcome of unfavorable litigation, or a natural catastrophe that can be eliminated through diversification. Related: Systematic risk.

Upstairs Market
A network of trading desks for the major brokerage firms and institutional investors that communicate with each other by means of electronic display systems and telephones to facilitate block trades and program trades.

Up Tick
Used in the context of general equities. Plus tick.

Utility Function
A mathematical expression that assigns a value to all possible choices. In portfolio theory, the utility function expresses the preferences of economic entities with respect to perceived risk and expected return.

V

Value Manager
A manager who seeks to buy stocks that are at a discount to their "fair value" and sell them at or in excess of that value. Often a value stock is one with a low price to book value ratio. Opposite to growth stock.

Volatility
A measure of risk based on the standard deviation of the asset return. Also, volatility is a variable that appears in option pricing formulas. In the option pricing formula, it denotes the volatility of the underlying asset return from now to the expiration of the option. Some have created volatility indices. Here is an example, scale is 1–9; higher rating indirectly higher risk:

Std Deviation	Rating	Std Deviation	Rating
up to 7. 99	1	20. 00–22. 99	6
8. 00–10. 99	2	23. 00–25. 99	7
11. 00–13. 99	3	26. 00–28. 99	8
14. 00–16. 99	4	29. 00 and up	9
17. 00–19. 99	5		

Volume
This is the daily number of shares of a security that change hands between a buyer and a seller.

Voting Rights
The right to vote on matters that are put to a vote of security holders. For example the right to vote for directors.

W

Waiting Period
Time during which the Securities and Exchange Commission (S.E.C.) studies a firm's registration statement. During this time the firm may distribute a preliminary prospectus.

Wall Street
Generic term for firms that buy, sell, and underwrite securities.

Wall Street Analyst
Related: Sell-side analyst.

Warrant
A security entitling the holder to buy a proportionate amount of stock at some specified future date at a specified price, usually one higher than current market. This "warrant" is then traded as a security, the price of which reflects the value of the underlying stock. Warrants are issued by corporations and often used as a "sweetener" bundled with another class of security to enhance the marketability of the latter. Warrants are like call options, but with much longer time spans — sometimes years. In addition, warrants are offered by corporations whereas exchange traded call options are not issued by firms.

Wash Sale
Used in the context of general equities. Purchase and sale of a security either simultaneously or within a short period of time, often done with the intention of recognizing a tax loss without altering one's position. See: tax selling.

Watch List
A list of securities selected for special surveillance by a brokerage, exchange or regulatory organization; firms on the list are often takeover targets, companies planning to issue new securities or stocks showing unusual activity.

Weekend Effect
The common recurrent low or negative average return from Friday to Monday in the stock market.

Well Diversified Portfolio
A portfolio spread out over many securities in such a way that the weight of any security is small. The risk of a well-diversified portfolio closely approximates the systemic risk of the overall market, the unsystematic risk of each security having been diversified out of the portfolio.

When Issued (W.I.)
Used in the context of general equities. When, as if issued: refers to a transaction made conditionally because a security, although authorized, has not yet been issued. Treasury securities, new issues of stocks and bonds, stocks that have split, and in-merger situations after the time the proxy has become effective but before completion, are all traded on a when issued basis. With ice.

White Knight
A friendly potential acquirer sought out by a target firm that is threatened by a less welcome suitor.

White Squire
Often used in risk arbitrage. White knight who buys less than a majority interest.

Window Dressing
Used in the context of general equities. Trading activity near the end of a quarter or fiscal year that is designed to dress up a portfolio to be presented to clients or shareholders. For example, a portfolio manager may sell losing positions in his portfolio so he can display only positions that have gained in value.

Working Order
Used in the context of general equities. Order that exists in the marketplace, whereby a broker is bidding or offering to fill the order in a series of lots at opportune times in hope of obtaining the best price.

World Equity Benchmark Series (W.E.B.S.)
The World Equity Benchmark Series are similar to SPDRs. W.E.B.S. trade on the AMEX, and track the Morgan Stanley Capital International (MSCI) country indexes. W.E.B.S. are available for these countries: Australia, Austria, Belgium, Canada, France, Germany, Hong Kong, Italy, Japan, Malaysia Free, Mexico, Netherlands, Singapore, Spain, Sweden, Switzerland, and United Kingdom.

Writer
The seller of an option, usually an individual, bank, or company, that issues the option and consequently has the obligation to sell the asset (if a call) or to buy the asset (if a put) on which the option is written if the option buyer exercises the option.

X

XMI
Applies to derivative products. Quotron symbol for the Major Market Index (MMI).

Y

Z

Zabara
Mainly applies to international equities. Japanese securities transactions conducted on the principal of auction, i.e., (1) price priority in that the selling (buying) order with the lowest (highest) price takes precedence over other orders, and (2) time priority in that an earlier order takes precedence over other orders at the same price.

Zero-Minus Tick
Used in the context of general equities. Sale that takes place at the same price as the previous sale, but at a lower price than the last different price. Antithesis of zero-plus tick.

Zero-Plus Tick
Used for listed equity securities. Transaction at the same price as the preceding trade, but higher than the preceding trade at a different price. Antithesis of zero-minus tick. See: short sale.

Directory of Futures & Options Exchanges

courtesy of Numa Financial Systems Ltd

The following directory is taken from the Numa Directory of Futures & Options Exchanges which can be found on the internet at the URL address, http://www.numa.com/ref/exchange.htm. The Publisher will not be responsible for any inaccuracies found in the listing below. Kindly address any queries Numa Financial Systems Ltd via their home page at http//www.numa.com.

Argentina

Buenos Aires Stock Exchange
(Bolsa de Comercio de Buenos Aires)
Sarmiento 299, Buenos Aires
Tel: +54 1 313 3334
Fax: +54 1 312 9332
Email: cau@sba.com.ar
URL: http://www.merval.sba.com.ar

Merfox
(Mercados de Futuros y Opciones SA)
Samiento 299, 4/460, Buenos Aires
Tel: +54 1 313 4522
Fax: +54 1 313 4472

Buenos Aires Cereal Exchange
(Bolsa de Cereales de Buenos Aires)
Avenida Corrientes 127, Buenos Aires
Tel: +54 1 311 9540
Fax: +54 1 311 9540
Email: bolcerc@datamarkets.com.ar

Buenos Aires Futures Market
(Mercado a Termino de Buenos Aires SA)
Bouchard 454, 5to Piso, Buenos Aires
Tel: +54 1 311 47 16
Fax: +54 1 312 47 16

Rosario Futures Exchange
(Mercado a Termino de Rosario)
Cordoba 1402, Pcia Santa Fe, Rosario
Tel: +54 41 21 50 93
Fax: +54 41 21 50 97
Email: termino@bcr.com.ar

Rosario Stock Exchange
(Mercado de Valores de Rosario SA)
Cordoba Esquina Corrientes, Pcia Santa Fe, Rosario
Tel: +54 41 21 34 70
Fax: +54 41 24 10 19
Email: titulos@bcr.com.ar

Rosario Board of Trade
(Bolsa de Comercio de Rosario)
Cordoba 1402, Pcia Santa Fe, Rosario
Tel: +54 41 21 50 93
Fax: +54 41 21 50 97
Email: titulos@bcr.com.ar

La Plata Stock Exchange
(Bolsa de Comercio de La Plata)
Calle 48, No. 515, 1900 La Plata, Buenos Aires
Tel: +54 21 21 47 73
Fax: +54 21 25 50 33

Mendoza Stock Exchange
(Bolsa de Comercio de Mendoza)
Paseo Sarmiento 199, Mendoza
Tel: +54 61 20 23 59
Fax: +54 61 20 40 50

Cordoba Stock Exchange
(Bolsa de Comercio de Cordoba)
Rosario de Santa Fe 231, 1 Piso, Cordoba
Tel: +54 51 22 4230
Fax: +54 51 22 6550
Email: bolsacba@nt.com.ar

Mercado Abierto Electronico SA
(Mercado Abierto Electronico SA)
25 de Mayo 565, 4 Piso, Buenos Aires
Tel: +54 1 312 8060
Fax: +54 1 313 1445

Armenia

Yerevan Stock Exchange
22 Sarian Street, Yerevan Centre
Tel: +374 2 525 801
Fax: +374 2 151 548

Australia

Australian Stock Exchange
Exchange Centre, 20 Bond Street, Sydney
Tel: +61 29 227 0000
Fax: +61 29 235 0056
Email: info@asx.com.au
URL: http://www.asx.com.au

Sydney Futures Exchange
SFE
30-32 Grosvenor Street, Sydney
Tel: +61 29 256 0555
Fax: +61 29 256 0666
Email: sfe@hutch.com.au
URL: http://www.sfe.com.au

Austria

Austrian Futures & Options Exchange
(Osterreichische Termin Und Optionenborse)
OTOB
Strauchgasse 1-3, PO Box 192, Vienna
Tel: +43 1 531 65 0
Fax: +43 1 532 97 40
Email: contactperson@otob.ada.at
URL: http://www.wtab.at

Vienna Stock Exchange
(Wiener Borse)
Wipplingerstrasse 34, Vienna
Tel: +43 1 53 499
Fax: +43 1 535 68 57
Email: communications@vienna-stock-exchange.at
URL: http://www.wtab.at

Bahrain

Bahrain Stock Exchange
P.O. Box 3203, Manama
Tel: +973 261260
Fax: +973 256362
Email: bse@bahrainstock.com
URL: http://www.bahrainstock.com

Bangladesh

Dhaka Stock Exchange
Stock Exchange Building, 9E & 9F, Motijheel C/A, Dhaka
Tel: +880 2 956 4601
Fax: +880 2 956 4727
Email: info@dse.bdnet.net

Barbados

Securities Exchange of Barbados
5th Floor, Central Bank Building, Church Village, St Michael
Tel: +1809/1246 246 436 9871
Fax: +1809/1246 246 429 8942
Email: sebd@caribf.com

Belgium

Brussels Stock Exchange
(Societe de la Bourse de Valeurs Mobilieres de Bruxelles)
Palais de la Bourse, Brussels
Tel: +32 2 509 12 11
Fax: +32 2 509 12 12
Email: dan.maerten@pophost.eunet.be
URL: http://www.stockexchange.be

European Association of Securities Dealers Automated Quotation
EASDAQ
Rue des Colonies, 56 box 15, 1000 Brussels
Tel: +32 2 227 6520
Fax: +32 2 227 6567
Email: easdaq@tornado.be
URL: http://www.easdaq.be/

Belgian Futures & Options Exchange
BELFOX
Palais de la Bourse, Rue Henri Mausstraat, 2, Brussels
Tel: +32 2 512 80 40
Fax: +32 2 513 83 42
Email: marketing@belfox.be
URL: http://www.belfox.be

Antwerp Stock Exchange
(Effectenbeurs van Antwerpen)
Korte Klarenstraat 1, Antwerp
Tel: +32 3 233 80 16
Fax: +32 3 232 57 37

Bermuda

Bermuda Stock Exchange
BSE
Email: info@bse.com
URL: http://www.bsx.com

Bolivia

Bolivian Stock Exchange
(Bolsa Boliviana de Valores SA)
Av. 16 de Julio No 1525, Edif Mutual La Paz, 3er Piso, Casillia 12521, La Paz
Tel: +591 2 39 29 11
Fax: +591 2 35 23 08
Email: bbvsalp@wara.bolnet.bo
URL: http://bolsa-valores-bolivia.com

Botswana

Botswana Stock Exchange
5th Floor, Barclays House, Khama Crescent, Gaborone
Tel: +267 357900
Fax: +267 357901
Email: bse@info.bw

Brazil

Far-South Stock Exchange
(Bolsa de Valores do Extremo Sul)
Rua dos Andradas, 1234-8 Andar, Porte Alegre
Tel: +55 51 224 3600
Fax: +55 51 227 4359

Santos Stock Exchange
(Bolsa de Valores de Santos)
Rua XV de Novembro, 111, Santos
Tel: +55 132 191 5119
Fax: +55 132 19 1800

Regional Stock Exchange
(Bolsa de Valores regional)
Avenida Dom Manuel, 1020, Fortaleza
Tel: +55 85 231 6466
Fax: +55 85 231 6888

Parana Stock Exchange
(Bolsa de Valores do Parana)
Rua Marechal Deodoro, 344-6 Andar, Curitiba
Tel: +55 41 222 5191
Fax: +55 41 223 6203

Minas, Espirito Santo, Brasilia Stock Exchange
(Blsa de Valores Minas, Espirito Santo, Brasilia)
Rua dos Carijos, 126-3 Andar, Belo Horizonte
Tel: +55 31 219 9000
Fax: +55 21 273 1202

Rio de Janeiro Stock Exchange
(Bolsa de Valores de Rio de Janeiro)
Praca XV de Novembro No 20, Rio de Janeiro
Tel: +55 21 271 1001
Fax: +55 21 221 2151
Email: info@bvrj.com.br
URL: http://www.bvrj.com.br

Sao Paolo Stock Exchange
(Bolsa de Valores de Sao Paolo)
Rua XV de Novembro 275, Sao Paolo
Tel: +55 11 233 2000
Fax: +55 11 233 2099
Email: bovespa@bovespa.com.br
URL: http://www.bovespa.com.br

Bahia, Sergipe, Alagoas Stock Exchange
(Bolsa de Valores Bahia, Sergipe, Alagoas)
Rua Conselheiro Dantas, 29-Comercio, Salvador
Tel: +55 71 242 3844
Fax: +55 71 242 5753

Brazilian Futures Exchange
(Bolsa Brasileira de Futuros)
Praca XV de Novembro, 20, 5th Floor, Rio de Janeiro
Tel: +55 21 271 1086
Fax: +55 21 224 5718
Email: bbf@bbf.com.br

The Commodities & Futures Exchange
(Bolsa de Mercadoris & Futuros)
BM&F
Praca Antonio Prado, 48, Sao Paulo
Tel: +55 11 232 5454
Fax: +55 11 239 3531
Email: webmaster@bmf.com.br
URL: http://www.bmf.com.br

Pernambuco and Paraiba Stock Exchange
(Bolsa de Valores de Pernambuco e Paraiba)
Avenida Alfredo Lisboa, 505, Recife
Tel: +55 81 224 8277
Fax: +55 81 224 8412

Bulgaria

Bulgarian Stock Exchange
1 Macedonia Square, Sofia
Tel: +359 2 81 57 11
Fax: +359 2 87 55 66
Email: bse@bg400.bg
URL: http://www.online.bg/bse

Canada

Montreal Exchange
(Bourse de Montreal)
ME
The Stock Exchange Tower, 800 Square Victoria, C.P. 61, Montreal
Tel: +1 514 871 2424
Fax: +1 514 871 3531
Email: info@me.org
URL: http://www.me.org

Vancouver Stock Exchange
VSE
Stock Exchange Tower, 609 Granville Street, Vancouver
Tel: +1 604 689 3334
Fax: +1 604 688 6051
Email: information@vse.ca
URL: http://www.vse.ca

Winnipeg Stock Exchange
620 - One Lombard Place, Winnipeg
Tel: +1 204 987 7070
Fax: +1 204 987 7079
Email: vcatalan@io.uwinnipef.ca

Alberta Stock Exchange
21st Floor, 300 Fifth Avenue SW, Calgary
Tel: +1 403 974 7400
Fax: +1 403 237 0450

Toronto Stock Exchange
TSE
The Exchange Tower, 2 First Canadian Place, Toronto
Tel: +1 416 947 4700
Fax: +1 416 947 4662
Email: skee@tse.com
URL: http://www.tse.com

Winnipeg Commodity Exchange
WCE
500 Commodity Exchange Tower, 360 Main St., Winnipeg
Tel: +1 204 925 5000
Fax: +1 204 943 5448
Email: wce@wce.mb.ca
URL: http://www.wce.mb.ca

Toronto Futures Exchange
TFE
The Exchange Tower, 2 First Canadian Place, Toronto
Tel: +1 416 947 4487
Fax: +1 416 947 4272

Cayman Islands

Cayman Islands Stock Exchange
CSX
4th Floor, Elizabethan Square, P.O Box 2408 G.T., Grand Cayman
Tel: +1345 945 6060
Fax: +1345 945 6061
Email: CSX@CSX.COM.KY
URL: http://www.csx.com.ky/

Chile

Santiago Stock Exchange
(Bolsa de Comercio de Santiago)
La Bolsa 64, Casilla 123-D, Santiago
Tel: +56 2 698 2001
Fax: +56 2 672 8046
Email: ahucke@comercio.bolsantiago.cl
URL: http://www.bolsantiago.cl

Bolsa Electronica de Chile
Huerfanos 770, Piso 14, Santiago
Tel: +56 2 639 4699
Fax: +56 2 639 9015
Email: info@bolchile.cl
URL: http://www.bolchile.cl

China

Wuhan Securities Exchange Centre
WSEC
2nd Floor, Jianghchen Hotel, Wuhan
Tel: +86 27 588 4115
Fax: +86 27 588 6038

China Zhengzhou Commodity Exchange
CZCE
20 Huanyuan Road, Zhengzhou
Tel: +86 371 594 44 54
Fax: +86 371 554 54 24

Shanghai Cereals and Oils Exchange
199 Shangcheng Road, Pudong New District, Shanghai
Tel: +86 21 5831 1111
Fax: +86 21 5831 9308
Email: liangzhu@public.sta.net.cn

China -Commodity Futures Exchange, Inc of Hainan
CCFE
Huaneng Building, 36 Datong Road, Haikou, Hainan Province
Tel: +86 898 670 01 07
Fax: +86 898 670 00 99
Email: ccfehn@public.hk.hq.cn

Guandong United Futures Exchange
JingXing Hotel, 91 LinHe West Road, Guangzhou
Tel: +86 20 8755 2109
Fax: +86 20 8755 1654

Shenzhen Mercantile Exchange
1/F Bock B, Zhongjian Overseas Decoration , Hua Fu Road, Shenzhen
Tel: +86 755 3343 502
Fax: +86 755 3343 505

Shanghai Stock Exchange
15 Huang Pu Road, Shanghai
Tel: +86 216 306 8888
Fax: +86 216 306 3076

Beijing Commodity Exchange
BCE
311 Chenyun Building, No. 8 Beichen East Road, Chaoyang District, Beijing
Tel: +86 1 492 4956
Fax: +86 1 499 3365
Email: sunli@intra.cnfm.co.cn

Shenzhen Stock Exchange
203 Shangbu Industrial Area, Shenzhen
Tel: +86 755 320 3431
Fax: +86 755 320 3505

Colombia

Bogota Stock Exchange
BSE
Carrera 8, No. 13-82 Pisos 4-9, Apartado Aereo 3584, Santafe de Bogota
Tel: +57 243 6501
Fax: +57 281 3170
Email: bolbogot@bolsabogota.com.co
URL: http://www.bolsabogota.com.co

Medellin Stock Exchange
(Bolsa de Medellin SA)
Apartado Aereo 3535, Medellin
Tel: +57 4 260 3000
Fax: +57 4 251 1981
Email: 104551.1310@compuserve.com

Occidente Stock Exchange
(Bolsa de Occidente SA)
Calle 10, No. 4-40 Piso 13, Cali
Tel: +57 28 817 022
Fax: +57 28 816 720
Email: bolsaocc@cali.cetcol.net.co
URL: http://www.bolsadeoccidente.com.co

Costa Rica

National Stock Exchange
(Bolsa Nacional de Valores, SA)
BNV
Calle Central, Avenida 1, San Jose
Tel: +506 256 1180
Fax: +506 255 0131

Cote D'Ivoire (Ivory Coast)

Abidjan Stock Exchange
(Bourse des Valeurs d'Abidjan)
Avenue Marchand, BP 1878 01, Abidjan 01
Tel: +225 21 57 83
Fax: +225 22 16 57

Croatia (Hrvatska)

Zagreb Stock Exchange
(Zagrebacka Burza)
Ksaver 208, Zagreb
Tel: +385 1 428 455
Fax: +385 1 420 293
Email: zeljko.kardum@zse.hr
URL: http://www.zse.hr

Cyprus

Cyprus Stock Exchange
CSE
54 Griva Dhigeni Avenue, Silvex House, Nicosia
Tel: +357 2 368 782
Fax: +357 2 368 790
Email: cyse@zenon.logos.cy.net

Czech Republic

Prague Stock Exchange
PSE
Rybna 14, Prague 1
Tel: +42 2 2183 2116
Fax: +42 2 2183 3040
Email: marketing@pse.vol.cz
URL: http://www.pse.cz

Denmark

Copenhagen Stock Exchange & FUTOP
(Kobenhavns Fondsbors)
Nikolaj Plads 6, PO Box 1040, Copenhagen K
Tel: +45 33 93 33 66
Fax: +45 33 12 86 13
Email: kfpost@xcse.dk
URL: http://www.xcse.dk

Ecuador

Quito Stock Exchange
(Bolsa de Valores de Quito CC)
Av Amazonas 540 y Carrion, 8vo Piso
Tel: +593 2 526 805
Fax: +593 2 500 942
Email: bovalqui@ecnet.ec
URL: http://www.ccbvq.com

Guayaquil Stock Exchange
(Bolsa de Valores de Guayaquil, CC)
Av. 9 de Octubre, 110 y Pinchina, Guayaquil
Tel: +593 4 561 519
Fax: +593 4 561 871
Email: bvg@bvg.fin.ec
URL: http://www.bvg.fin.ec

Egypt

Alexandria Stock Exchange
11 Talaat Harp Street, Alexandria
Tel: +20 3 483 7966
Fax: +20 3 482 3039

Cairo Stock Exchange
4(A) El Cherifeen Street, Cairo
Tel: +20 2 392 1402
Fax: +20 2 392 8526

El Salvador

El Salvador Stock Exchange
(Mercado de Valores de El Salvador, SA de CV)
6 Piso, Edificio La Centroamericana, Alameda Roosevelt No 3107,
San Salvador
Tel: +503 298 4244
Fax: +503 223 2898
Email: ggbolsa@gbm.net

Estonia

Tallinn Stock Exchange
Ravala 6, Tallinn
Tel: +372 64 08 840
Fax: +372 64 08 801
Email : tse@depo.ee
URL: http://www.tse.ee

Finland

Helsinki Stock Exchange
HSE
Fabianinkatu 14, Helsinki
Tel: +358 9 173 301
Fax: +358 9 173 30399
Email : mika.bjorklund@hex.fi
URL: http://www.hse.fi

Finnish Options Exchange
(Suomen Optioporssi Oy)
FOEX
Erottajankatu 11, Helsinki
Tel: +358 9 680 3410
Fax: +358 9 604 442
Email : info@foex.fi
URL: http://www.foex.fi

Finnish Options Market
SOM
Keskuskatu 7, Helsinki
Tel: +358 9 13 1211
Fax: +358 9 13 121211
Email : webmaster@hex.fi
URL: http://www.som.fi

France

Paris Stock Exchange
(Bourse de Paris)
39 rue Cambon, Paris
Tel: +33 1 49 27 10 00
Fax: +33 1 49 27 13 71
Email: 100432.201@compuserve.com

MONEP
(Marche des Options Negociables de Paris)
MONEP
39, rue Cambon, Paris
Tel: +33 1 49 27 18 00
Fax: +33 1 9 27 18 23
URL: http://www.monep.fr

MATIF
(Marche a Terme International de France)
MATIF
176 rue Montmartre, Paris
Tel: +33 33 1 40 28 82 82
Fax: +33 33 1 40 28 80 01
Email : larrede@matif.fr
URL: http://www.matif.fr

Germany

Stuttgart Stock Exchange
(Baden-Wurttembergische Wertpapierborse zu Stuttgart)
Konigstrasse 28, Stuttgart
Tel: +49 7 11 29 01 83
Fax: +49 7 11 22 68 11 9

Hanover Stock Exchange
(Niedersachsische Borse zu Hanover)
Rathenaustrasse 2, Hanover
Tel: +49 5 11 32 76 61
Fax: +49 5 11 32 49 15

Dusseldorf Stock Exchange
(Rheinisch-Westfalische Borse zu Dusseldorf)
Ernst-Schneider-Platz 1, Dusseldorf
Tel: +49 2 11 13 89 0
Fax: +49 2 11 13 32 87

Berlin Stock Exchange
(Berliner Wertpapierborse)
Fasanenstrasse 85, Berlin
Tel: +49 30 31 10 91 0
Fax: +49 30 31 10 91 79

German Stock Exchange
(Deutsche Borse AG)
FWB
Borsenplatz 4, Frankfurt-am-Main
Tel: +49 69 21 01 0
Fax: +49 69 21 01 2005
URL: http://www.exchange.de

Hamburg Stock Exchange
(Hanseatische Wertpapierborse Hamburg)
Schauenburgerstrasse 49, Hamburg
Tel: +49 40 36 13 02 0
Fax: +49 40 36 13 02 23
Email: wertpapierboerse.hamburg@t-online.de

Deutsche Terminborse
DTB
Boersenplatz 4, Frankfurt-am-Main
Tel: +49 69 21 01 0
Fax: +49 69 21 01 2005
URL: http://www.exchange.de

Bavarian Stock Exchange
(Bayerische Borse)
Lenbachplatz 2(A), Munich
Tel: +49 89 54 90 45 0
Fax: +49 89 54 90 45 32
Email: bayboerse@t-online.de
URL: http://www.bayerischeboerse.de

Bremen Stock Exchange
(Bremer Wertpapierborse)
Obernstrasse 2-12, Bremen
Tel: +49 4 21 32 12 82
Fax: +49 4 21 32 31 23

Ghana

Ghana Stock Exchange
5th Floor, Cedi House, Liberia Road, PO Box 1849, Accra
Tel: +233 21 669 908
Fax: +233 21 669 913
Email : stockex@ncs.com.gh
URL: http://ourworld.compuserve.com/homepages/khaganu/
stockex.htm

Greece

Athens Stock Exchange
ASE
10 Sophocleous Street, Athens
Tel: +30 1 32 10 424
Fax: +30 1 32 13 938
Email: mailto:aik@hol.gr
URL: http://www.ase.gr

Honduras

Honduran Stock Exchange
(Bolsa Hondurena de Valores, SA)
1er Piso Edificio Martinez Val, 3a Ave 2a Calle SO, San Pedro Sula
Tel: +504 53 44 10
Fax: +504 53 44 80
Email: bhvsps@simon.intertel.hn

Hong Kong

Hong Kong Futures Exchange Ltd
HKFE
5/F, Asia Pacific Finance Tower, Citibank Plaza, 3 Garden Road
Tel: +852 2842 9333
Fax: +852 2810 5089
Email: prm@hfke.com
URL: http://www.hkfe.com

Hong Kong Stock Exchange
SEHK
1st Floor, One and Two Exchange Square, Central
Tel: +852 2522 1122
Fax: +852 2810 4475
Email: info@sehk.com.hk
URL: http://www.sehk.com.hk

Chinese Gold and Silver Exchange Society
Gold and Silver Commercial Bui, 12-18 Mercer Street
Tel: +852 544 1945
Fax: +852 854 0869

Hungary

Budapest Stock Exchange
Deak Ferenc utca 5, Budapest
Tel: +36 1 117 5226
Fax: +36 1 118 1737
URL: http://www.fornax.hu/fmon

Budapest Commodity Exchange
BCE
POB 495, Budapest
Tel: +36 1 269 8571
Fax: +36 1 269 8575
Email: bce@bce-bat.com
URL: http://www.bce-bat.com

Iceland

Iceland Stock Exchange
Kalkofnsvegur 1, Reykjavik
Tel: +354 569 9775
Fax: +354 569 9777
Email: gw@vi.is

India

Cochin Stock Exchange
38/1431 Kaloor Road Extension, PO Box 3529, Emakulam, Cochin
Tel: +91 484 369 020
Fax: +91 484 370 471

Bangalore Stock Exchange
Stock Exchange Towers, 51, 1st Cross, JC Road, Bangalore
Tel: +91 80 299 5234
Fax: +91 80 22 55 48

The OTC Exchange of India
OTCEI
92 Maker Towers F, Cuffe Parade, Bombay
Tel: +91 22 21 88 164
Fax: +91 22 21 88 012
Email: otc.otcindia@gems.vsnl.net.in

Jaipur Stock Exchange
Rajasthan Chamber Bhawan, MI Road, Jaipur
Tel: +91 141 56 49 62
Fax: +91 141 56 35 17

The Stock Exchange ñ Ahmedabad
Kamdhenu Complex, Ambawadi, Ahmedabad
Tel: +91 79 644 67 33
Fax: +91 79 21 40 117
Email: supvsr@08asxe

Delhi Stock Exchange
3&4/4B Asaf Ali Road, New Delhi
Tel: +91 11 327 90 00
Fax: +91 11 327 13 02

Madhya Pradesh Stock Exchange
3rd Floor, Rajani Bhawan, Opp High Court, MG Road, Indore
Tel: +91 731 432 841
Fax: +91 731 432 849

Magadh Stock Exchange
Industry House, Suinha Library Road,
Patna
Tel: +91 612 223 644

Pune Stock Exchange
Shivleela Chambers, 752 Sadashiv Peth, Kumethekar Road, Pune
Tel: +91 212 441 679

The Stock Exchange, Mumbai
Phiroze Jeejeebhoy Towers, Dalal Street, Bombay
Tel: +91 22 265 5860
Fax: +91 22 265 8121
URL: http://www.nseindia.com

Uttar Pradesh Stock Exchange
Padam Towers, 14/113 Civil Lines, Kanpur
Tel: +91 512 293 115
Fax: +91 512 293 175

Bhubaneswar Stock Exchange Association
A-22 Falcon House, Jharapara, Cuttack Road, Bhubaneswar
Tel: +91 674 482 340
Fax: +91 674 482 283

Calcutta Stock Exchange
7 Lyons Range, Calcutta
Tel: +91 33 209 366

Coimbatore Stock Exchange
Chamber Towers, 8/732 Avanashi Road, Coimbatore
Tel: +91 422 215 100
Fax: +91 422 213 947

Madras Stock Exchange
Exchange Building, PO Box 183, 11 Second Line Beach, Madras
Tel: +91 44 510 845
Fax: +91 44 524 4897

Ludhiana Stock Exchange
Lajpat Rai Market, Near Clock Tower, Ludhiana
Tel: +91 161 39318

Kanara Stock Exchange
4th Floor, Ranbhavan Complex, Koialbail, Mangalore
Tel: +91 824 32606

Hyderabad Stock Exchange
3-6-275 Himayatnagar, Hyderabad
Tel: +91 842 23 1985

Gauhati Stock Exchange
Saraf Building, Annex, AT Road, Gauhati
Tel: +91 361 336 67
Fax: +91 361 543 272

Indonesia

Jakarta Stock Exchange
(PT Bursa Efek Jakarta)
Jakarta Stock Exchange Building, 13th Floor, JI Jenderal Sudiman,
Kav 52-53, Jakarta
Tel: +62 21 515 0515
Fax: +62 21 515 0330
Email: webmaster@jsx.co.id
URL: http://www.jsx.co.id

Surabaya Stock Exchange
(PT Bursa Efek Surabaya)
5th Floor, Gedung Madan Pemuda, 27-31 Jalan Pemuda, Surabaya
Tel: +62 21 526 6210
Fax: +62 21 526 6219
Email: heslpdesk@bes.co.id
URL: http://www.bes.co.id

Indonesian Commodity Exchange Board
(Badan Pelaksana Bursa Komoditi)
Gedung Bursa, Jalan Medan Merdeka Selatan 14, 4th Floor, Jakarta
Pusat
Tel: +62 21 344 1921
Fax: +62 21 3480 4426

Capital Market Supervisory Agency
(Baden Pelaksana Pasar Modal)
BAPEPAM
Jakarta Stock Exchange Building, 13th Floor, JI Jenderal Sudiman,
Kav 52-53, Jakarta
Tel: +62 21 515 1288
Fax: +62 21 515 1283
Email: bapepam@indoexchange.com
URL: http://www.indoexchange.com/bapepam

Iran

Tehran Stock Exchange
228 Hafez Avenue, Tehran
Tel: +98 21 670 309
Fax: +98 21 672 524
Email: stock@neda.net
URL: http://www.neda.net/tse

Ireland

Irish Stock Exchange
28 Anglesea Street, Dublin 2
Tel: +353 1 677 8808
Fax: +353 1 677 6045

Irish Futures & Options Exchange
IFOX
Segrave House, Earlsfort Terrace, Dublin 2
Tel: +353 1 676 7413
Fax: +353 1 661 4645

Israel

Tel Aviv Stock Exchange Ltd
TASE
54 Ahad Haam Street, Tel Aviv
Tel: +972 3 567 7411
Fax: +972 3 510 5379
Email: etti@tase.co.il
URL: http://www.tase.co.il

Italy

Italian Financial Futures Market
(Mercato Italiano Futures)
MIF
Piazza del Gesu' 49, Rome
Tel: +39 6 676 7514
Fax: +39 6 676 7250

Italian Stock Exchange
(Consiglio de Borsa)
Piazza degli Affari, 6, Milan
Tel: +39 2 724 261
Fax: +39 2 864 64 323
Email: postoffice@borsaitalia.it
URL: http://www.borsaitalia.it

Italian Derivatives Market
IDEM
Piazza Affari 6, Milan
Tel: +39 2 72 42 61
Fax: +39 2 72 00 43 33
Email: postoffice@borsaitalia.it
URL: http://www.borsaitalia.it

Jamaica

Jamaica Stock Exchange
40 Harbour Street, PO Box 1084, Kingston
Tel: +1809 809 922 0806
Fax: +1809 809 922 6966
Email: jse@infochan.com
URL: http://www.jamstockex.com

Japan

Tokyo Commodity Exchange
(Tokyo Kogyoin Torihikijo)
TOCOM
10-8 Nihonbashi, Horidome-cho, Chuo-ku, 1-chome, Tokyo
Tel: +81 3 3661 9191
Fax: +81 3 3661 7568

Japan Securities Dealing Association
(Nihon Shokengyo Kyokai)
Tojyo Shoken Building, 5-8 Kayaba-cho, 1-chome, Nihonbashi, Tokyo
Tel: +81 3 3667 8451
Fax: +81 3 3666 8009

Osaka Textile Exchange
(Osaka Seni Torihikijo)
2-5-28 Kyutaro-machi, Chuo-ku, Osaka
Tel: +81 6 253 0031
Fax: +81 6 253 0034

Tokyo Stock Exchange
(Tokyo Shoken Torihikijo)
TSE
2-1 Nihombashi-Kabuto-Cho, Chuo-ku, Tokyo
Tel: +81 3 3666 0141
Fax: +81 3 3663 0625
URL: http://www.tse.or.jp

Latvia

Riga Stock Exchange
Doma Iaukums 6, Riga
Tel: +7 212 431
Fax: +7 229 411
Email: rfb@mail.bkc.lv
URL: http://www.rfb.lv

Lithuania

National Stock Exchange of Lithuania
Ukmerges St 41, Vilnius
Tel: +370 2 72 14 07
Fax: +370 2 742 894
Email: office@nse.lt
URL: http://www.nse.lt

Luxembourg

Luxembourg Stock Exchange
(Societe Anonyme de la Bourse de Luxembourg)
11 Avenue de la Porte-Neuve
Tel: +352 47 79 36-1
Fax: +352 47 32 98
Email: info@bourse.lu
URL: http://www.bourse.lu

Macedonia

Macedonia Stock Exchange
MSE
Tel: +389 91 122 055
Fax: +389 91 122 069
Email: mse@unet.com.mk
URL: http://www.mse.org.mk

Malaysia

Kuala Lumpur Commodity Exchange
KLCE
4th Floor, Citypoint, Komplex Dayabumi, Jalan Sulta Hishamuddin,
Kuala Lumpur
Tel: +60 3 293 6822
Fax: +60 3 274 2215
Email: klce@po.jaring.my
URL: http://www.klce.com.my

Kuala Lumpur Stock Exchange
KLSE
4th Floor, Exchange Square, Off Jalan Semantan, Damansara
Heights, Kuala Lumpur
Tel: +60 3 254 64 33
Fax: +60 3 255 74 63
Email: webmaster@klse.com.my
URL: http://www.klse.com.my

The Kuala Lumpur Options & Financial Futures Exchange
KLOFFE
10th Floor, Wisma Chase Perdana, Damansara Heights, Jalan
Semantan, Kuala Lumpur
Tel: +60 3 253 8199
Fax: +60 3 255 3207
Email: kloffe@kloffe.com.my
URL: http://www.kloffe.com.my

Malaysia Monetary Exchange BHD
4th Floor, City Point, PO Box 11260, Dayabumi Complex, Jalan
Sultan Hishmuddin, Kuala Lumpur
Email: mme@po.jaring.my
URL: http://www.jaring.my/mme

Malta

Malta Stock Exchange
27 Pietro Floriani Street, Floriana, Valletta 14
Tel: +356 244 0515
Fax: +356 244 071
Email: borza@maltanet.omnes.net

Mauritius

Mauritius Stock Exchange
Stock Exchange Commission, 9th Floor, SICOM Building, Sir
Celicourt Anselme Street, Port Louis
Tel: +230 208 8735
Fax: +230 208 8676
Email: svtradha@intnet.mu
URL: http://lynx.intnet.mu/sem/

Mexico

Mexican Stock Exchange
(Bolsa Mexicana de Valores, SA de CV)
Paseo de la Reforma 255, Colonia Cuauhtemoc, Mexico DF
Tel: +52 5 726 66 00
Fax: +52 5 705 47 98
Email: cinform@bmv.com.mx
URL: http://www.bmv.com.mx

Morocco

Casablanca Stock Exchange
(Societe de la Bourse des Valeurs de Casablanca)
98 Boulevard Mohammed V, Casablanca
Tel: +212 2 27 93 54
Fax: +212 2 20 03 65

Namibia

Namibian Stock Exchange
Kaiserkrone Centre 11, O Box 2401, Windhoek
Tel: +264 61 227 647
Fax: +264 61 248 531
Email: tminney@nse.com.na
URL: http://www.nse.com.na

Netherlands

Financiele Termijnmarkt Amsterdam NV
FTA
Nes 49, Amsterdam
Tel: +31 20 550 4555
Fax: +31 20 624 54l6

AEX-Stock Exchange
AEX
Beursplein 5, PO Box 19163, Amsterdam
Tel: +31 20 550 4444
Fax: +31 20 550 4950
URL: http://www.aex.nl/

AEX-Agricultural Futures Exchange
Beursplein 5, PO Box 19163, Amsterdam
Tel: +31 20 550 4444
Fax: +31 20 623 9949

AEX-Options Exchange
AEX
Beursplein 5, PO Box 19163, Amsterdam
Tel: +31 20 550 4444
Fax: +31 20 550 4950
URL: http://www.aex-optiebeurs.ase.nl

New Zealand

New Zealand Futures & Options Exchange Ltd
NZFOE
10th Level, Stock Exchange Cen, 191 Queen Street, Auckland 1
Tel: +64 9 309 8308
Fax: +64 9 309 8817
Email: info@nzfoe.co.nz
URL: http://www.nzfoe.co.nz

New Zealand Stock Exchange
NZSE
8th Floor Caltex Tower, 286-292 Lambton Quay, Wellington
Tel: +64 4 4727 599
Fax: +64 4 4731 470
Email: info@nzse.org.nz
URL: http://www.nzse.co.nz

Nicaragua

Nicaraguan Stock Exchange
(BOLSA DE VALORES DE NICARAGUA, S.A.)
Centro Financiero Banic, 1er Piso, Km. 5 1/2 Carretera Masaya
Email: info@bolsanic.com
URL: http://bolsanic.com/

Nigeria

Nigerian Stock Exchange
Stock Exchange House, 8th & 9th Floors, 2/4 Customs Street, Lagos
Tel: +234 1 266 0287
Fax: +234 1 266 8724
Email: alile@nse.ngra.com

Norway

Oslo Stock Exchange
(Oslo Bors)
OSLO
P.O. Box 460, Sentrum, Oslo
Tel: +47 22 34 17 00
Fax: +47 22 41 65 90
Email: informasjonsavdelingen@ose.telemax.no
URL: http://www.ose.no

Oman

Muscat Securities Market
Po Box 3265, Ruwi
Tel: +968 702 665
Fax: +968 702 691

Pakistan

Islamabad Stock Exchange
Stock Exchange Building, 101-E Fazal-ul-Haq Road, Blue Area, Islamabad
Tel: +92 51 27 50 45
Fax: +92 51 27 50 44
Email: ise@paknet1.ptc.pk

Karachi Stock Exchange
Stock Exchange Building, Stock Exchange Road, Karachi
Tel: +92 21 2425502
Fax: +92 21 241 0825
URL: http://www.kse.org

Lahore Stock Exchange Po Box 1315, 19 Khayaban e Aiwan e Iqbal, Lahore
Tel: +92 42 636 8000
Fax: +92 42 636 8484

Panama

Panama Stock Exchange
(Bolsa de Valores de Panama, SA)
Calle Elvira Mendex y Calle 52, Edif Valarino, Planta Baja
Tel: +507 2 69 1966
Fax: +507 2 69 2457
URL: http://www.urraca.com/bvp/

Paraguay

Ascuncon Stock Exchange
(Bolsa de Valores y Productos de Ascuncion)
Estrella 540, Ascuncion
Tel: +595 21 442 445
Fax: +595 21 442 446
Email: bolsapya@pla.net.py
URL: http://www.pla.net.py/bvpasa

Peru

Lima Stock Exchange
(La Bolsa de Valores de Lima)
Pasaje Acuna 191, Lima
Tel: +51 1 426 79 39
Fax: +51 1 426 76 50
Email: web_team@bvl.com.pe
URL: http://www.bvl.com.pe

Philippines

Philippine Stock Exchange
Philippine Stock Exchange Cent, Tektite Road, Ortigas Centre, Pasig
Tel: +63 2 636 01 22
Fax: +63 2 634 51 13
Email: pse@mnl.sequel.net
URL: http://www.pse.com.ph

Manila International Futures Exchange
MIFE
7/F Producer's Bank Centre, Paseo de Roxas, Makati
Tel: +63 2 818 5496
Fax: +63 2 818 5529

Poland

Warsaw Stock Exchange
Gielda papierow, Wartosciowych w Warszawie SA, Ul Nowy Swiat 6/12, Warsaw
Tel: +48 22 628 32 32
Fax: +48 22 628 17 54
Email: gielda@kp.atm.com.pl

Portugal

Oporto Derivatives Exchange
(Bolsa de Derivados do Oporto)
BDP
Av. da Boavista 3433, Oporto
Tel: +351 2 618 58 58
Fax: +351 2 618 56 66

Lisbon Stock Exchange
(Bolsa de Valores de Lisboa)
BVL
Edificio da Bolsa, Rua Soeiro Pereira Gomes, Lisbon
Tel: +351 1 790 99 04
Fax: +351 1 795 20 21
Email: webmaster@bvl.pt
URL: http://www.bvl.pt

Romania

Bucharest Stock Exchange
BSE
Doamnei no. 8, Bucharest
Email: bse@delos.ro
URL: http://www.delos.ro/bse/

Romanian Commodities Exchange
(Bursa Romana de Marfuri SA)
Piata Presei nr 1, Sector 1, Bucharest
Tel: +40 223 21 69
Fax: +40 223 21 67

Russian Federation

Moscow Interbank Currency Exchange
MICEX
21/1, Sadovaya-Spasskay, Moscow
Tel: +7 095 705 9627
Fax: +7 095 705 9622
Email: inmicex@micex.com
URL: http://www.micex.com/

Russian Exchange
RCRME
Myasnitskaya ul 26, Moscow
Tel: +7 095 262 06 53
Fax: +7 095 262 57 57
Email: assa@vc-rtsb.msk.ru
URL: http://www.re.ru

Moscow Commodity Exchange
Pavilion No. 4, Russian Exhibition Centre, Moscow
Tel: +7 095 187 83 07
Fax: +7 095 187 9982

St Petersburg Futures Exchange
SPBFE
274 Ligovski av., St Petersburg
Tel: +7 812 294 15 12
Fax: +7 812 327 93 88
Email: seva@spbfe.futures.ru

Siberian Stock Exchange
PO box 233, Frunze St 5, Novosibirsk
Tel: +7 38 32 21 06 90
Fax: +7 38 32 21 06 90
Email: sibex@sse.nsk.su

Moscow Central Stock Exchange
9(B) Bolshaya Maryinskaya Stre, Moscow
Tel: +7 095 229 88 82
Fax: +7 0995 202 06 67

Moscow International Stock Exchange
MISE
Slavyanskaya Pl 4, Bld 2, Moscow
Tel: +7 095 923 33 39
Fax: +7 095 923 33 39

National Association of Securities Market Participants
(NAUF)
Floor 2, Building 5, Chayanova Street 15, Moscow
Tel: +7 095 705 90
Fax: +7 095 976 42 36
Email: naufor@rtsnet.ru
URL: http://www.rtsnet.ru

Vladivostock Stock Exchange
VSE
21 Zhertv Revolyutsii Str, Vladivostock
Tel: +7 4232 22 78 87
Fax: +7 4232 22 80 09

St Petersburg Stock Exchange
SPSE
274 Ligovsky pr, St Petersburg
Tel: +7 812 296 10 80
Fax: +7 812 296 10 80
Email: root@lse.spb.su

Saudi Arabia

Saudi Arabian Monetary Authority
SAMA
PO Box 2992, Riyadh
Tel: +966 1 466 2300
Fax: +966 1 466 3223

Singapore

Singapore Commodity Exchange Ltd
SICOM
111 North Bridge Road, #23-04/, Peninsula Plaza
Tel: +65 338 5600
Fax: +65 338 9116
Email: sicom@pacific.net.sg

Stock Exchange of Singapore
No. 26-01/08, 20 Cecil Street, The Exchange
Tel: +65 535 3788
Fax: +65 535 6994
Email: webmaster@ses.com.sg
URL: http://www.ses.com.sg

Singapore International Monetary Exchange Ltd
SIMEX
1 Raffles Place, No. 07-00, OUB Centre
Tel: +65 535 7382
Fax: +65 535 7282
Email: simex@pacific.net.sg
URL: http://www.simex.com.sg

Slovak Republic

Bratislava Stock Exchange
(Burza cenny ch papierov v Bratislave)
BSSE
Vysoka 17, Bratislava
Tel: +42 7 5036 102
Fax: +42 7 5036 103
Email: kunikova@bsse.sk
URL: http://www.bsse.sk

Slovenia

Commodity Exchange of Ljubljana
Smartinskal 52, PO Box 85, Ljubljana
Tel: +386 61 18 55 100
Fax: +386 61 18 55 101
Email: infos@bb-lj.si
URL: http://www.eunet.si/commercial/bbl/bbl-ein.html

Ljubljana Stock Exchange, Inc
LJSE
Sovenska cesta 56, Lbujljana
Tel: +386 61 171 02 11
Fax: +386 61 171 02 13
Email: info@jse.si
URL: http://www.ljse.si

South Africa

Johannesburg Stock Exchange
JSE
17 Diagonal Street, Johannesburg
Tel: +27 11 377 2200
Fax: +27 11 834 3937
Email: r&d@jse.co.za
URL: http://www.jse.co.za

South African Futures Exchange
SAFEX
105 Central Street, Houghton Estate 2198, Johannesburg
Tel: +27 11 728 5960
Fax: +27 11 728 5970
Email: jani@icon.co.za
URL: http://www.safex.co.za

Spain

Citrus Fruit and Commodity Market of Valencia
(Futuros de Citricos y Mercaderias de Valencia)
2, 4 Libreros, Valencia
Tel: +34 6 387 01 88
Fax: +34 6 394 36 30
Email: futuros@super.medusa.es

Spanish Options Exchange
(MEFF Renta Variable)
MEFF RV
Torre Picasso, Planta 26, Madrid
Tel: +34 1 585 0800
Fax: +34 1 571 9542
Email: mefrv@meffrv.es
URL: http://www.meffrv.es

Spanish Financial Futures Market
(MEFF Renta Fija)
MEFF RF
Via Laietana, 58, Barcelona
Tel: +34 3 412 1128
Fax: +34 3 268 4769
Email: marketing@meff.es
URL: http://www.meff.es

Madrid Stock Exchange
(Bolsa de Madrid)
Plaza de la Lealtad 1, Madrid
Tel: +34 1 589 26 00
Fax: +34 1 531 22 90
Email: internacional@bolsamadrid.es
URL: http://www.bolsamadrid.es

Barcelona Stock Exchange
Paseo Isabel II No 1, Barcelona
Tel: +34 3 401 35 55
Fax: +34 3 401 38 59
Email: agiralt@borsabcn.es
URL: http://www.borsabcn.es

Bilbao Stock Exchange
(Sociedad Rectora de la Bolsa de Valoes de Bilbao)
Jose Maria Olabarri 1, Bilbao
Tel: +34 4 423 74 00
Fax: +34 4 424 46 20
Email: bolsabilbao@sarenet.es
URL: http://www.bolsabilbao.es

Valencia Stock Exchange
(Sociedad Rectora de la Bolsa de Valoes de Valencia)
Libreros 2 y 4, Valencia
Tel: +34 6 387 01 00
Fax: +34 6 387 01 14

Sri Lanka

Colombo Stock Exchange
CSE
04-01 West Bloc, World Trade Centre, Echelon Square, Colombo 1
Tel: +94 1 44 65 81
Fax: +94 1 44 52 79
Email: cse@sri.lanka.net
URL: http://www.lanka.net/cse/

Swaziland

Swaziland Stock Market
Swaziland Stockbrokers Ltd, 2nd Floor Dlan'ubeka House, Walker St, Mbabane
Tel: +268 46163
Fax: +268 44132
URL: http://mbendi.co.za/exsw.htm

Sweden

The Swedish Futures and Options Market
(OM Stockholm AB)
OMS
Box 16305, Brunkebergstorg 2, Stockholm
Tel: +46 8 700 0600
Fax: +46 8 723 1092
URL: http://www.omgroup.com

Stockholm Stock Exchange Ltd
(Stockholm Fondbors AB)
Kallargrand 2, Stockholm
Tel: +46 8 613 88 00
Fax: +46 8 10 81 10
Email: info@xsse.se
URL: http://www.xsse.se

Switzerland

Swiss Options & Financial Futures Exchange AG
SOFFEX
Selnaustrasse 32, Zurich
Tel: +41 1 229 2111
Fax: +41 1 229 2233
Email: webmaster@swx.ch
URL: http://www.bourse.ch

Swiss Exchange
SWX
Selnaustrasse 32, Zurich
Tel: +41 1 229 21 11
Fax: +41 1 229 22 33
URL: http://www.bourse.ch

Taiwan

Taiwan Stock Exchange
Floors 2-10, City Building, 85 Yen Ping Road South, Taipei
Tel: +886 2 311 4020
Fax: +886 2 375 3669
Email: intl-aff@tse.com.tw
URL: http://www.tse.com.tw

Thailand

The Stock Exchange of Thailand
SET
2nd Floor, Tower 1, 132 Sindhorn Building, Wireless Road, Bangkok
Tel: +66 2 254 0960
Fax: +66 2 263 2746
Email: webmaster@set.or.th
URL: http://www.set.or.th

Trinidad and Tobago

Trinidad and Tobago Stock Exchange
65 Independence Street, Port of Spain
Tel: +1809 809 625 5108
Fax: +1809 809 623 0089

Tunisia

Tunis Stock Exchange
(Bourse des Valeurs Mobilieres de Tunis)
Centre Babel - Bloc E, Rue Jean-Jacques Rousseau, Montplaisir,
Tunis
Tel: +216 1 780 288
Fax: +216 1 789 189

Turkey

Istanbul Stock Exchange
(Istanbul Menkul Kiymetler Borasi)
ISE
Istinye, Istanbul
Tel: +90 212 298 21 00
Fax: +90 212 298 25 00
Email: info@ise.org
URL: http://www.ise.org

United Kingdom

The London Securities and Derivatives Exchange
OMLX
107 Cannon Street, London
Tel: +44 171 283 0678
Fax: +44 171 815 8508
Email: petter.made@omgroup.com
URL: http://www.omgroup.com/

International Petroleum Exchange of London Ltd
IPE
International House, 1 St. Katharine's Way, London
Tel: +44 171 481 0643
Fax: +44 l71 481 8485
Email: busdev@ipe.uk.com
URL: http://www.ipe.uk.com

London International Futures & Options Exchange
LIFFE
Cannon Bridge, London
Tel: +44 171 623 0444
Fax: +44 171 588 3624
Email: exchange@liffe.com
URL: http://www.liffe.com

London Metal Exchange
LME
56 Leadenhall Street, London
Tel: +44 171 264 5555
Fax: +44 171 680 0505
Email: lsnow@lmetal.netkonect.co.uk
URL: http://www.lme.co.uk

The Baltic Exchange
Tel: +44 171 623 5501
Fax: +44 171 369 1622
Email: enquiries@balticexchange.co.uk
URL:http://www.balticexchange.co.uk

London Stock Exchange
LSE
Old Broad Street, London
Tel: +44 171 797 1000
Fax: +44 171 374 0504

Tradepoint Investment Exchange
35 King Street, London
Tel: +44 171 240 8000
Fax: +44 171 240 1900
Email: g171@dial.pipex.com
URL: http://www.tradepoint.co.uk

London Commodity Exchange
LCE
1 Commodity Quay, St. Katharine Docks, London
Tel: +44 171 481 2080
Fax: +44 171 702 9923
URL: http://www.liffe.com

United States

New York Stock Exchange
NYSE
11 Wall Street, New York
Tel: +1 212 656 3000
Fax: +1 212 656 5557
URL: http://www.nyse.com

Minneapolis Grain Exchange
MGE
400 S. Fourth St., Minneapolis
Tel: +1 612 338 6216
Fax: +1 612 339 1155
Email: mgex@ix.netcom.com
URL: http://www.mgex.com

Philadelphia Stock Exchange
PHLX
1900 Market Street, Philadelphia
Tel: +1 215 496 5000
Fax: +1 215 496 5653
URL: http://www.phlx.com

Kansas City Board of Trade
KCBT
4800 Main St., Suite 303, Kansas City
Tel: +1 816 753 7500
Fax: +1 816 753 3944
Email: kcbt@kcbt.com
URL: http://www.kcbt.com

Chicago Board Options Exchange
CBOE
400 S. LaSalle Street, Chicago
Tel: +1 312 786 5600
Fax: +1 312 786 7409
Email: investor_services@cboe.com
URL: http://www.cboe.com

Chicago Board of Trade
CBOT
141 West Jackson Boulevard, Chicago
Tel: +1 312 435 3500
Fax: +1 312 341 3306
Email: comments@cbot.com
URL: http://www.cbt.com

New York Mercantile Exchange
NYMEX
4 World Trade Center, New York
Tel: +1 212 938 222
Fax: +1 212 938 2985
Email: marketing@nymex.com
URL: http://www.nymex.com

Chicago Stock Exchange
CHX
One Financial Place, 440 S. LaSalle St, Chicago
Tel: +1 312 663 222
Fax: +1 312 773 2396
Email: marketing@chiacgostockex.com
URL: http://www.chicagostockex.com

MidAmerica Commodity Exchange
MIDAM
141 W. Jackson Boulevard, Chicago
Tel: +1 313 341 3000
Fax: +1 312 341 3027
Email: comments@cbot.com
URL: http://www.midam.com

Philadelphia Board of Trade
1900 Market Street, Philadelphia
Tel: +1 215 496 5357
Fax: +1 215 496 5653

The Cincinnati Stock Exchange
400 South LaSalle Street, Chicago
Tel: +1 312 786 8803
Fax: +1 312 939 7239

Boston Stock Exchange, Inc
BSE
38th Floor, One Boston Place, Boston
Tel: +1 617 723 9500
Fax: +1 617 523 6603
URL: http://www.bostonstock.com

Nasdaq Stock Market
1735 K Street NW, Washington DC
Tel: +1 202 728 8000
Fax: +1 202 293 6260
Email: fedback@nasdaq.com
URL: http://www.nasdaq.com

American Stock Exchange
AMEX
86 Trinity Place, New York
Tel: +1 212 306 1000
Fax: +1 212 306 1802
Email: jstephan@amex.com
URL: http://www.amex.com

New York Cotton Exchange
NYCE
4 World Trade Center, New York
Tel: +1 212 938 2702
Fax: +1 212 488 8135
URL: http://www.nyce.com

Pacific Stock Exchange, Inc
PSE
301 Pine Street, San Francisco
Tel: +1 415 393 4000
Fax: +1 415 393 4202
URL: http://www.pacificex.com

Chicago Mercantile Exchange
CME
30 S. Wacker Drive, Chicago
Tel: +1 312 930 1000
Fax: +1 312 930 3439
Email: info@cme.com
URL: http://www.cme.com

Coffee, Sugar & Cocoa Exchange Inc.
CSCE
4 World Trade Center, New York
Tel: +1 212 938 2800
Fax: +1 212 524 9863
Email: csce@ix.netcom.com
URL: http://www.csce.com

Venezuela

Maracaibo Stock Exchange
(Bolsa de Valores de Maracaibo)
Calle 96, Esq Con Avda 5, Edificio
Banco Central de Vene, Piso 9, Maracaibo
Tel: +58 61 225 482
Fax: +58 61 227 663

Venezuela Electronic Stock Exchange
(de Venezuela)
C·mara de Comercio de Valencia, Edif. C·mara de Comercio, Av.
BolÌvar, Valencia, Edo. Carabobo, Apartado 151
Tel: +58 57.5109
Fax: +58 57.5147
Email: set@venezuelastock.com
URL: http://www.venezuelastock.com

Caracas Stock Exchange
(Bolsa de Valores de Caracas)
Edificio Atrium, Piso 1 Calle Sorocaima, Urbanizacion, El Rosal,
Caracas
Tel: +58 2 905 5511
Fax: +58 2 905 5814
Email: anafin@true.net
URL: http://www.caracasstock.com

Yugoslavia

Belgrade Stock Exchange
(Beogradska Berza)
Omladinskih 1, 3rd Floor, PO Box 214, Belgrade
Tel: +381 11 19 84 77
Fax: +381 11 13 82 42
Email: beyu@eunet.yu

Zimbabwe

Zimbabwe Stock Exchange
5th Floor, Southampton House, Union Avenue, Harare
Tel: +263 4 736 861
Fax: +263 4 791 045

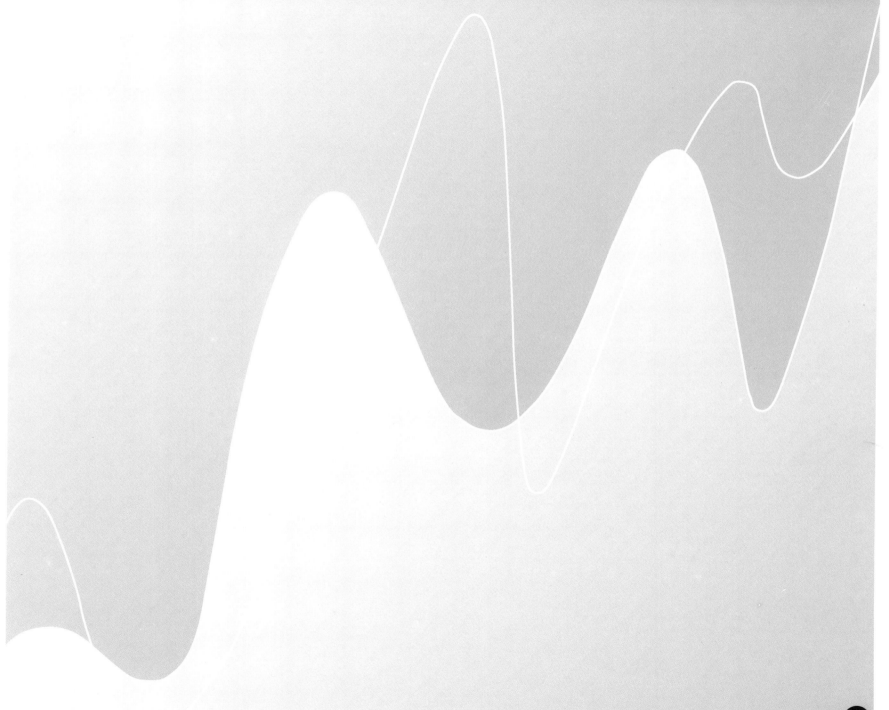